Peggy

Peggy

The Life of Margaret Ramsay
Play Agent

COLIN CHAMBERS

Let every eye negotiate for itself
And trust no agent

Much Ado About Nothing

London
NICK HERN BOOKS

A Nick Hern Book

Peggy first published in 1997 in Great Britain by
Nick Hern Books Limited, 14 Larden Road, London W3 7ST

Copyright © 1997 by Colin Chambers

Colin Chambers has asserted his right to be identified as
the author of this work

Peggy Ramsay's letters and the business documents of
Margaret Ramsay Ltd. are quoted by permission of the
Peggy Ramsay Foundation, a charity for writers and new writing

Lines from *Absurd Person Singular* by Alan Ayckbourn
are quoted with permission of the author

Extracts from Joe Orton's writings are quoted with permission
of Leonie Barnett for the Orton Estate

British Library cataloguing data for this book is available
from the British Library

ISBN 1 85459 119 3

Typeset by Country Setting, Woodchurch, Kent TN26 3TB
Printed in Great Britain by Mackays of Chatham, plc

To Jane

Contents

Foreword

The origins of this book about Peggy Ramsay go back to 1981 when I had recently published my first book, *Other Spaces: New Theatre and the RSC*, and, by coincidence, had just been appointed the RSC's literary manager. I was keen to write another book, and, in my new post, was conscious of the role played in the theatre by people operating 'in the wings'. Adding in my interest in contemporary playwrights, I approached Nick Hern, then the drama editor at Methuen and the person responsible for *Other Spaces*. I suggested a book about the famous play agent Peggy Ramsay, who represented many of my favourite writers.

'No chance,' came Hern's reply. 'I have just tried to get her to write her autobiography, and her refusal was as adamant as it was charming. She would never agree to anyone writing a book about her.'

I accepted his wisdom and let the matter rest. My own subsequent dealings with Peggy Ramsay through my work at the RSC fully confirmed Nick Hern's judgement, although she was always friendly and generous towards me. I remember in particular a small thing; I was writing a book about the Unity Theatre and out of the blue she sent me a postcard, giving me the address of someone she thought I should contact for my research. I had never mentioned my book to Peggy, and it was only a postcard, but that gesture of unsolicited help stayed with me.

In 1989, to my amazement, I discovered that several writers with whom I was working were being interviewed for a BBC-TV documentary on Peggy that was to be broadcast the following March; I knew the producer, and she confirmed that Peggy had, indeed, agreed to allow such a programme to be made. I contacted both Nick Hern, now running his own firm, and Peggy's assistant, Tom Erhardt, whose advice we readily accepted. 'Let her get over the TV programme and, when she returns from her holiday in Tunisia, why don't you just take her out for lunch and ask her,' he said. 'But don't tell her beforehand why you want to meet.'

A table was booked at Sheekeys, a fish restaurant not far from Peggy's office and one of her favourite haunts. It was late May. Nick and I fussed nervously over the seating arrangements, and I decided to wait alone at the table while he and Tom Erhardt would escort Peggy from the office. Sheekeys had been refurbished but it retained its atmosphere of a theatrical parlour, decorated with a clutter of showbiz portraits. I notice I'm sitting under the gaze of the young Paul Scofield, pre Sir Thomas More. I am the only customer in this part of the restaurant, tucked well away from the door and the street. Every time a waiter crosses the floorboards, I look up anxiously and take another sip of my dry martini. At last, they come; she arrives like royalty and slips off her cardigan to reveal a North African tan. 'I don't sunbathe, of course, dear. It's my only holiday. There are few English people and lots of Germans. It's strange not to hear your mother tongue spoken.' We chat about holidays, the Barbican – 'Terry Hands needs a knighthood to help push the RSC along' - and the TV programme. 'I don't remember a thing about it, except I know I received a lot of unwanted scripts afterwards. Some nice woman took me out to lunch and somehow I ended up agreeing.'

Cue for Nick Hern to introduce our idea. 'Oh, no, a book about me would be terribly boring, wouldn't it?' I jumped in: 'But it would be about the writers, Peggy.' 'Ah, the writers. Well, if it's about the writers, then of course there's no problem.' And that was it.

Peggy allowed me access to all her papers and spent a great deal of time talking to me about her life and work. I went to her office in Goodwin's Court in early June to begin what turned out to be eleven months of wading through her files, ledgers, scrap books and script log books. During that period the offices were set on fire. This inevitably disrupted my own work as well as the firm's, though for my purposes very little was lost. A few months later Peggy died, and I was left to continue without her help. I finished this part of my research just as the agency completed its merger with a new firm and moved out of Goodwin's Court. Peggy's papers were gathered together in an archive and held by the Peggy Ramsay Foundation, which had been set up by her executors.

I had also begun interviewing many of her clients and associates. Over a couple of years I spoke to around 60 of her writers and about 150 people who had known her or had worked with her at some time in her life. Overwhelmingly they were generous with their time. (Out of the more than 200 people I contacted, only three former clients did not reply and one director she had worked with in the 1950s refused to talk.)

A fair amount of detective work was involved in piecing together her life before she became an agent. For her years after that, while reference books yielded many facts, I still had to rely on the personal accounts of participants in order to reveal her story. There was much checking and cross-checking as memories differed, and I have tried to be as accurate as possible in recounting what information was made available to me. My sources are listed at the end of the book in the notes to each chapter.

I want to thank all those who helped me make this book possible and, in particular, I would like to offer special thanks to Mary Burnett, Simon Callow, Michael Codron, Tom Erhardt, Laurence Harbottle, David Hare, Ben Jancovich, Rob Marx, Richard Nelson, Sarah Nicholls and Rosemary Wilton.

When I began working on the book I did not know Peggy very well. By the time I had completed the first draft, she had become my familiar; it seemed as if she was impishly thwarting my attempts to embrace new technology (my word processor blew up and the floppy drive on its replacement soon crashed) and was hovering over my shoulder to challenge my every word. At times I came to loathe her and was glad that she had not been my agent, but, as I came to write the final chapter of the final draft, I felt a loss as I recorded her death and the end of her agency. I had laid Peggy's ghost to rest; I only hope that I have done her justice.

COLIN CHAMBERS
London, March 1997

Peggy

Chapter One

Under African Skies

*'When we are saying that one does not recognise
the many selves one has been, this doesn't include childhood
because, curiously enough, that remains with you,
and does not change.'*

Peggy to an English friend

PEGGY RAMSAY was extraordinary. Out of the happenstance of her existence she fashioned a startling phenomenon – the most potent and influential play agency the theatrical world has ever seen. Peggy was this agency and the agency was Peggy. Through her magnetic allure and her blazing, forthright personality, she transformed herself into a legendary figure, a towering landmark of her time.

Peggy belonged to a world of sacred monsters where the only authority was the authority of a spirit that lies beyond passion, a rapture bred of intense sensibility and intelligent discrimination. Creative ability and the character to exploit it were the currency of value, rather than money or success. She turned would-be writers into professional playwrights by holding them in thrall to this universe while marshalling in the most practical and hard-nosed way the many forces – managers, directors, designers, actors – that were necessary to make such a desire become a reality.

As an agent, her private and her professional lives were kept distinct and apart. She was as severely protective of the former as she was unguardedly open about the latter. Most of her clients knew very little of the background that had shaped the woman to whom they had entrusted their careers. Some who knew her well, or thought they did, were surprised after her death to discover important aspects of her life of which they had been completely unaware.

Peggy

She repeatedly declined without hesitation to write her autobiography, because, she said – as if merely stating the obvious – that she could never tell the truth, thereby consciously contradicting the very characteristic of fearless and unfiltered candour that was her hallmark. She resisted personal publicity until very late in her life and only then agreed to interviews with reluctance at a time when she knew, though would not wish openly to acknowledge, that her powers were seriously in decline.

Memory defines its owner and its owner's place in history yet is frequently unreliable, even if significant. Peggy's memory, which was particularly errant, she used sometimes mischievously, sometimes quixotically, and sometimes simply out of her own firm sense of propriety or self-defence, to control the flow of biographical information. She also used her memory selectively to keep herself young. The few early experiences to which she did refer, while frequently differing in detail – often drastically – do, nevertheless, retain a strong emotional coherence. While she may have remembered incidents that did not occur, or may not have occurred, for Peggy each of them certainly did happen, if only because, in the act of telling, they assumed a palpable existence. Like the characters in any creation, they also took on lives of their own, often contradictory and independent of their creator.

Throughout her life Peggy had many selves. Mostly, she kept them separate and separated; a new time, a new place, a new self. However, she did not change her personalities like she changed her hats. This was not a display of serial schizophrenia, more a refined sense of the proportions of human existence, an assertion of individual will in the face of what she saw as a cosmic serendipity governing life.

She played many different parts, and the most famous, that of agent, which occupied the last 35 years of her life, itself required different facets of her personality to be brought into play, depending on client, need, and context – worldly-wise philosopher, protective guardian or reprimanding termagant; strict nanny one moment, knowing coquette the next. She was at once honing, revising and endlessly performing her own unfolding story in the service of her god, the unforgiving tyrant she called talent. Her anecdotes were told in a way that turned them into fables, and they always held an allegorical purpose, whether it was immediately clear or not. Like a priestess with a driven, dauntless spirit, she had a lesson for every client in every situation.

Working and being with playwrights indulged her own interest in fiction. She strove to create, though not on paper but in life. All the world was a stage to Peggy; to really *be* was to create, so her life was constantly vivid. Life was an art form, a text itself, and living it was an act of creation. 'We are all everything,' she would say, 'and we must be *available* for life.'

Peggy lived life on the hoof, taking it as it came, with no regard to record or posterity. It seems entirely appropriate, therefore, that her death certificate should carry a different date of birth to that recorded on her birth certificate, albeit by only one day, and that her obituaries should not only contain very little information about her life before she became an agent but should reproduce this difference in her official biography, as if she were mocking humdrum reality from the beyond.

Her age was a taboo subject, but she could turn this conventional weapon in the armoury of female self-protection into a defiant signal both of self-identity and disregard for the merely factual. She once claimed that when she applied for a passport and did not have her birth certificate with her she gave her age as seven years younger than she was. She was certainly pleased when people habitually put her a good five to ten years younger than she turned out to be; it was a tribute to her vivacity and a pleasing snub to mortality.

*

'I'm not easy to deal with'

Both Peggy's parents were born in England, but they came from quite different backgrounds. Annie Rhoda Adams, known as Nance or Nancy, came from Tutbury in the Potteries. (She acquired a double-barrelled surname when her mother re-married. This token of refinement seems to have suited the image Peggy's mother had of herself.) By way of contrast, her father – John (Jack) Charles Venniker – came from an émigré Jewish family. His father, Abraham Phineas Velenski, had travelled to South Africa from central Europe, having been driven out of his homeland in the disputed territory where Lithuania and Poland have historically overlapped. The Velenski family dates back to nobles of the 17th century and bears the crest of the Farensbach arms, named after a general who was elevated during an important siege and who took the name Felinski. The Velenskis were related to the Welensky family, one of whose sons was Sir Roy, the last Prime Minister of the Federation of Rhodesia and Nyasaland.

In the early 1900s Phineas Velenski was involved in deals that brought him at least three pieces of farm land, known as Wilge River, Broadlands and Seekoeigat; the latter, roughly translated, means Hippopotamus Hole. They were situated on the River Olifants in the basin of the Little Karoo, a few miles outside Oudtshoorn, a town which, at the time, was the centre of both South African and world ostrich farming. Phineas Velenski took up this thriving business and established his own company. His first wife Fanny died in 1903 and he remarried in 1907. He died in Germany in 1911, bequeathing to his son Jack – Peggy's father – the family farm.

Fanny Velenski was in London when Jack was born. He qualified in medicine and surgery at Durham Medical School, Newcastle upon Tyne. He was wounded at Caledon River in the second of the Boer Wars whilst serving as a civil surgeon/medical officer to the Highland Light Infantry and was decorated. Back in Britain, he collected a row of further medical qualifications and became a Fellow of the Royal College of Surgeons in Edinburgh. He also followed the 'pioneer' trail, trekking through what is now southern Zimbabwe, and later crossed Canada and the USA too.

In a foretaste of Peggy's own less than secure relationship to historical accuracy, official documents relating to his life in both medicine and the military offer contradictory facts (for instance, he is recorded as studying in different places at the same time), and he has two dates of birth that differ by four years.

After his mother died, he converted from Judaism to Christianity and changed his surname from Velenski to Venniker. The reasons lying behind this transformation are not clear; for Peggy, however, it made a lasting impression. It was not a religious issue for her – she was brought up a Christian but not in a very strict way. For her it was a matter of identity. She felt the conversion smacked of a pretence perpetrated in order to gain acceptance and success. Peggy used to say bitterly that it was because her mother, who was a snob, did not want to be known to be married to a Jew.

The Velenski family was a prominent one in Oudtshoorn, which had a large and prospering Jewish community – so much so that it was known as 'The New Jerusalem'. Orthodox members of the Velenski family would have rejected Jack following his conversion but he was not disinherited. He was not alone in the area in marrying a non-Jewish wife, and changing surnames was not uncommon then. He might have felt an obligation to his family to change his name once he had changed his religion. His sister Sadie also changed her name at the same time and went on to become a Christian missionary. It is also possible he changed his name because of anti-semitism, in order to help his career in South Africa, particularly as it lay within the military; the name Venniker, however, has no obvious South African connections and sounds only slightly as if it might be Afrikaans. Another theory was that Jack did not mind being Jewish but preferred not to be recognised as a Lithuanian/Polish Jew.

The change of name remained a great family mystery. The first wife of Peggy's brother Tony did not learn of it until ten years after their marriage, and his son recalls it being a subject that touched an exposed nerve even 90 years after it happened.

Whatever the circumstances were, it is clear that Jack Venniker was restless. He and Nancy went to South Africa, were married in Oudtshoorn in October 1905 and set off on a grand honeymoon tour around the world. They arrived in Australia, and in October 1907 he was registered to practise medicine in New South Wales. They went to a little town in that state called Molong – Aboriginal for 'place of many rocks' – which lies in the stony outcrops just beyond the Blue Mountains 200 miles by rail to the north-west of Sydney. It was situated in sheep country, known for its wheat, orchards and vineyards as well as its wool. Molong is described in a gazetteer as being beautiful with pink blossoms adorning the streets. Its population then was 1254, many of them small landowners. Were the Vennikers visiting relatives or friends? Or were they travelling inland – further north-west beyond Wellington was a noted ostrich farm – and decided to stop in Molong when they discovered that Nancy was pregnant?

Jack Venniker is recorded as being an Hon. medical officer at the Molong Hospital in 1908, the year that his daughter Margaret Francesca was born. The date of 27 May is given on the birth certificate and the place as Bank Street, Molong. There is no record of an address or house number in Bank Street. Peggy, as she was always known, may have been born in one of Molong's private hospitals, which usually took maternity cases and were run by midwives. Two are known to have operated then. The birth was registered in July. By 1909 Jack Venniker was no longer on the books of the Molong Hospital.

Obituarists not only mistook the date of Peggy's birth but also the location, citing Molong variously as having become absorbed into Sydney or being an outlying suburb. They may have taken their cue from Peggy who, in her eighties, said it had lain just beyond Sydney and no longer existed. Presumably to Peggy, it never had.

It is not known how long the Vennikers stayed in Australia nor their itinerary thereafter. They appear to have been on a tour that lasted anything from two to six years. Either on this or subsequent trips their visits took in Europe (and probably England, to see family), islands in the Pacific, and the Near and the Far East. Peggy gave different lengths of time for being abroad, which is not surprising given that she was a child. She did remember quite distinctly living in Japan at the age of about four or five. She recalled with fervour the Japanese theatre and the cherry blossom ('something I can never forget – it filled the universe'). She also remembered the farm at Oudtshoorn boasting wall hangings and other decorative pieces brought back from their foreign journeys.

From such early experiences sprang a great deal of Peggy's approach to life and theatre, as well as her love of the grace and spareness of Oriental art. She later collected Japanese prints, especially erotic ones: 'they're having such a wonderful time, dear'. Two of her Japanese theatre prints were considered by experts to be of great historical value. She also took an interest in eastern philosophy, which suffused her own ideas. She corresponded with the poet James Kirkup about Japanese literature and in particular the charismatic writer Mishima, who committed suicide in 1970 and whose plays she would have liked to represent. She recommended to Richard Eyre, artistic director of the National Theatre, the work of an earlier Japanese playwright, Chikamitsu Monzaemon, and five years after her death an adaptation of his 18th-century drama, *Fair Ladies at a Game of Poem Cards*, appeared at the NT.

These exotic travels with her family opened up new worlds to Peggy but they also contributed to her own sense of rootlessness; life in a series of hotels in different countries may have been exciting but none was home; she felt treated like a trunk and had sharp memories of having to wait for luggage to arrive and then it being sent on. Possessions as well as people were always on the move.

War put a stop to the family's peregrinations. Jack Venniker was called away to serve with the Royal Army Medical Corps at Ypres in 1914 and returned to join the South African Medical Corps in 1916, serving in east Africa where he contracted malaria. The family moved five times between 1917-1926 as Jack Venniker received various postings, to a laboratory at Potchefstrom treating tropical diseases, to the Tempe Military Hospital, Bloemfontein, and – three times – to Roberts Heights, the largest military base in South Africa, just west of Pretoria.

In 1926 the by now Lt.-Col. Venniker retired from the army and settled at the family farm in Oudtshoorn, which boasted some 10,000 ostriches. Unfortunately for him, this move coincided with the end of the boa boom, and he faced financial disaster. He had not diversified, for example, into sheep farming, and his reliance on the ostrich had left the farm vulnerable to changes in fashion. Venniker decided to emigrate but that proved more difficult than expected because he could not dispose of the farm very easily. His father's firm had used the land in mortgage deals and loans, and now Venniker faced considerable litigation concerning its subdivision and sale. The legal procedures left him poorer both in health and in pocket, and left Peggy with an abiding distrust of lawyers and the courts. Jack and Nancy Venniker eventually moved to the Channel Islands and then to England. They both died in Brighton, he in 1958 and she in 1963, leaving Peggy £3,000 with which she bought a house there. Friends and colleagues recall that Peggy showed no emotion at the news of their deaths.

Nancy Venniker was the controlling force at home to whom everyone deferred – Jack, her elder by some ten years, included. To Peggy her mother was attractive but cool; she enjoyed the social round but she felt she was living in a cultural desert, a view that Peggy came to hold, although from a completely different vantage point. Mrs Venniker imported furniture and fittings from the home country in order to establish an English sitting room in the midst of the harsh Karoo landscape, a dissonance with a touch of the absurd that Peggy was to relish. Her mother further attempted to nurture a semblance of salon civilisation by arranging musical recitals. It is likely that at such gatherings Peggy first came across musicians and began her love of music. Peggy met among others the composer/violinist Jan Kubelik, when he was touring South Africa with his accompanist Francesco Ticciati. No doubt Mrs Venniker considered this kind of social mixing preferable to that of associating with a film company, which once visited the town to much clamour and which Peggy remembered as an exciting interruption in the usual local routine.

Peggy's loathing of her mother was profound. Peggy had once even tried to kill her, but the hot iron she had launched at her missed. Half a century later, Peggy still felt the same rage with herself as she had done at the time – for failing so miserably in her attempted matricide. Peggy said that her father knew of these impulses of hers and accepted them casually.

When her mother died, among her effects was a bundle of letters that her mother had kept. After reading a few, it became clear to Peggy that, extraordinarily, they were correspondence between her mother and a lover. Peggy read no further and burnt them.

While Peggy hated both her parents, her mother without qualification, she did grant her father an unsentimental recognition of at least a few points in his favour, mostly his sense of adventure and his sexual magnetism. The other side of this coin, however, was the betrayal that it entailed. She recalled him accompanying her on school seaside trips and choosing the pretty female teachers for companionship. Later he would turn up at college with his mistresses, whom he appeared to assume Peggy would not recognise as such. Nevertheless, when remembering the life of the military camps, she would say that, despite herself, she did find the dashing colonel type very attractive.

9

Peggy

When Peggy was almost 13, Tony, her only sibling, was born. He was to share his father's looks, athleticism and profession, yet to Peggy he was anathema. According to Tony's family, Nancy, who knew she had lost the love of her husband, doted on Tony and kept him and Peggy apart, reinforcing the natural separation that stemmed from the difference in years and the fact that Peggy was at boarding school while Tony was at home. Tony adored his elder sister but she was never close to him, not even when the opportunity arose in England. He arrived two years after her for his secondary education and stayed to attend medical school. He returned to South Africa after the war with his first wife, Wendy, whose family had taken him in as an evacuee. She remembers Peggy meeting them a couple of times before they left England and Peggy being 'irritable, cold, and bored with the bother of having to see us'.

Tony had a good voice and once contemplated becoming an actor until Peggy dissuaded him. His voice came into its own, however, when he became a popular radio doctor in South Africa, and he won an enormous audience when he described over the airwaves his own death from cancer. Tony would visit Peggy on his trips to England, but they usually ended up arguing. Peggy never forgave him for living with apartheid, although she did send money when she heard of his illness, from which he died in 1989. As with the death of her parents, it was an event that left her cold.

Peggy maintained that she took little sustenance from her childhood, save in her imagination. It certainly did not give her any lasting sense of family. She would recommend in later years as essential reading Lévi-Strauss' autobiographical travel book *Tristes Tropiques* (*A World on the Wane*), in which the renowned anthropologist views life as becoming unbearably overcrowded the very moment that even just one brother or sister is born.

The lack of sibling companionship and the constant moving meant a lonely upbringing for Peggy. On the occasions when she was living at Oudtshoorn, which was mainly during the holidays, she did have a little contact with a couple of cousins, but mostly she was alone there as a child. This isolation compelled her to reflect more intensively on her surroundings, which made a lasting impression on her. She created her own world and developed an appreciation of solitude.

From her childhood, Peggy treasured random memories of eating prickly pears, which had to be boiled first, of the river running through the farm, which was often dry, and of an island in the river with mulberry trees in its midst. The farm itself was reached by horse-drawn carriage down a narrow path that was engulfed in exotic foliage. It provided a fantasy setting that was inhabited more by ostriches than by human beings. Peggy could describe an ostrich vividly; six foot six tall, small head with outrageous eyelashes, a snake of a neck, short wings, long legs that kicked, and double-toed feet with a dinosaur spur. They were fast and dangerous, but she learned how to catch and ride them. Their leg meat made raw biltong, which was spiced and wind-dried and eaten as a snack. Peggy hated it, as she did their eggs, which were eaten scrambled, although she did like a Cape corn speciality, mealie meal.

During the ostrich boom, the farmers could make money fairly easily and quickly. They built their own expansive homes that were dubbed ostrich palaces, complete with grandiose pillars and idiosyncratic extravagances such as sunken baths and neo-Gothic turrets. Along with the ostriches themselves, they added to Peggy's sense of the surreal.

Yet, for her, the grandeur of the locality came not so much from the architecture as from the whole setting – the shapes, colours, smells, sounds, and atmosphere. She was gripped by the memory of immense skies and vast semi-desert land stretching one way to the Swartberg, a mountain range that divided the Little from the Great Karoo, and the other way towards the coast and the Outeniqua Mountains. She remembered the intense heat of the summer and the cool nights in winter coming after a hot day, the windswept passes, the insects and the colours made brilliant by the sun but weird as the light changed toward dusk: the sandstone ochres, the greens of grasses, shrubs and aloes, and the purple of the alfalfa that was planted as feed for the ostriches.

'I . . . have a vice,' she wrote to an English friend years later. 'It's being unable to pass pictures of the Great Karoo, where I was brought up . . . You can have no idea of the dry heat and the colour, or the sound or perfume of the place. While you are doing your cricket matches I am projecting myself back to hot days under mulberry trees, or swimming in brackish water, or picking grapes in the vineyards, or eating water-melons on the stoep under African skies.'

Like Alan Paton and others who have written about this landscape, Peggy found it 'stunningly, memorably beautiful', but she also saw as a child that with this beauty came a starkness and a desolation. She believed that her own wildness of character stemmed from having been brought up in these wide vistas, cruel colours and brutal winds with 'the whole indifference of nature set before my eyes'.

She enjoyed walking and communing with nature, but she also read a great deal and communed even more actively with literature. Her reading may have been a flight from, yet also into, loneliness, but it was not an escape into a make-believe world of fairy stories. Her reading was drawn from an adult selection of books, ranging from Tennyson to Proust, the most memorable and influential of her adolescent literary discoveries. She had to lock herself away to read, otherwise she would have been distracted by the delights of her surroundings. Although Afrikaans literature was good, she could well understand why the people were not cultured. 'With that climate and that landscape, why would you be?'

Peggy was clear about the peculiar power of her memories of childhood. She once deflated the overweeningly proud father of a ten-year-old boy who had just had a play produced at a prestigious London studio theatre by telling him that she herself had reached her peak at seven: 'After that it has all been downhill.' She also knew that childhood memories were stronger and more abundant than ever the reality was. The important point was that for her the images of childhood remained bright and, along with her burgeoning literary taste and discrimination, fed into her views on art and life, which were defiantly both unsentimental and romantic at the same time.

Formal education seems hardly to have impinged, except in the opportunities that it afforded her to read, and she spoke much less about her schooling than about Japan and the South African landscape. She told Robert Bolt that she attended a nunnery in France when she was of primary school age and was left there all alone, even through the holidays. Her only contact with the family, she said, was receiving postcards from her mother. This story fits in with her mother's ambition, her father's wanderings and Peggy's later love of French culture but was not repeated by Peggy to any others who were close to her.

Peggy seems to have been taught by several French and/or German governesses before attending as a boarder the Collegiate School, Port Elizabeth, when she was ten years old. This was a school for the daughters of wealthy sheep farmers and of the professional middle classes, designed to prepare its charges for marriage to suitably eligible gentlemen. Peggy later went briefly to Girton in Johannesburg, which may have been a private finishing school or crammer. She remembered truanting on Saturday mornings to visit a local cinema/café where one could see a different film each weekend and eat a snack at the same time, a combination of pleasures that Peggy recalled with childlike joy. It was much more to her taste than the bad theatre she saw in town.

It is not clear to which school she was referring when she recalled feeling conscious of being Jewish. She said that no one would talk to a Jew – the 'yids' they were called; they were considered beyond the pale because they did not believe in Christ and, indeed, had been responsible for his murder. Even though she was only half-Jewish, from the father's and not the mother's side of the family, this awareness of anti-semitism and of being an outsider, of being different, stayed with her into adulthood. In discussions on Nazism, she would remind people of the persecution of the Jews in South Africa long before Hitler came to power in Germany. She would also muse on her sense of Jewishness and what it may have contributed to her character; maybe her enjoyment of good talking and good food, her liking for diamonds and pearls, or her sensuality and appetite for life and literature in which high ideals were always tempered with the coarseness of reality?

When she was 18 she went to Rhodes University in Grahamstown, nicknamed 'Grimstown.' She was studying zoology, botany, English and psychology for a three-year BSC course but took no exams and left without qualifications at the end of her first academic year – out of boredom, she claimed.

College records do not bear out her occasional and no doubt consciously outlandish claims to considerable early prowess at tennis that ranged from being ladies' champion of Natal to representing South Africa, an ambition foisted upon her by her mother. It was commonplace for the white population in South Africa to be sporting and athletic, and Peggy, who as a child swam and rode horses on the farm as well as ostriches, might well have played tennis to quite a high standard. Later in life, when she lost hopelessly to a client, she said she had forgotten how to play. 'I wasn't *that* good,' she said. She had given up the game, she added, when she discovered that her mother was encouraging her to play in the hope of her finding an acceptable husband. Peggy followed tennis – she particularly was drawn to the destructive talent of 'bad boy' John McEnroe and had a huge poster of him in the office during his 'superbrat' phase. She judged the English to be no good at the game. When she first played in England she said she played left rather than right-handed in order to compensate for the deficiencies in the skills of her opponents. To her astonishment, she found that this gave her extraordinary dreams. As an agent she advised some of her clients to become ambidextrous in order to reap similar benefits.

Her college does have a record, however, of her prowess at a more obviously pertinent activity; she appeared to much local acclaim in *Lady Windermere's Fan* at Rhodes University in the role of the beguiling and beautiful Mrs Erlynne, powerful, independent, witty but socially outcast, a woman 'with a past' who spends much of the play protecting her secret.

Peggy

The university magazine praised Miss Venniker's interpretation, which was 'remarkable for its insight into character; she acted with fine restraint throughout, and showed capabilities as an emotional actress which one hopes will be given further scope.' Little could the author of those words have guessed at quite what proportions Peggy's 'further scope' would attain.

A university contemporary of hers recalls Peggy as being strikingly pretty, bright, intelligent, cultured and well read, combining the best elements of introversion and extroversion. This colleague also remembers an outstanding and popular lecturer, good looking and slim, much in demand among the female students, who was called Norman Ramsay and who, he thought, had been asked by Peggy's father to be her guardian at the university. Instead, Ramsay swept Peggy off her feet and married her.

Sixteen years her elder, Ramsay came from a well-connected Scottish family and had seen military service in France, Palestine and Japan. He had worked for the Indian government in Kashmir before becoming a teacher of English at the largest boys' school in Rhodesia. From there he joined Rhodes University in 1925, packed the first Mrs Ramsay off back to England, and was appointed Senior Lecturer in charge of the newly formed Department of Psychology.

Ramsay and his psychology student, Peggy, became constant companions. 'He ate me alive,' said Peggy. 'He was determined to have me.' She left the university, moved in with him, and became engaged to be married. The result was a disaster. He started to come home drunk, and it gradually became clear that he was a liar. The sexual side of the relationship turned into a nightmare. Peggy began to think that she did not like sex until she realised that the problem was him not her. She said that Ramsay raped her. She had serious second thoughts, but her parents insisted on the marriage going ahead; Ramsay had a good military record and was about to become a professor.

The service took place on 29 September 1928, nine months after she had left university. The church was situated hundreds of miles from where they lived, in Port Elizabeth, where Peggy had attended school. Her brother did not come to the wedding, but Mrs Anderson, head of the local collegiate school who adored her former pupil, did. Peggy recounted that as she walked up the aisle her only thought was 'What on earth am I doing here dressed up like this?'

Peggy was very disturbed by her sexual experiences with Ramsay. She said that the relationship was consummated before the marriage but never after. She was to make light of this in later years when she told different versions of her 'fainting virgin' anecdote. She had told Ramsay rather flirtatiously that she was frigid because she thought that this would make her an inviting and interesting case study. After the horrors of her time with him, she then employed this alleged frigidity to avoid having sex on her wedding night. In another version, Peggy explained both her nuptial abstinence and the question that she had asked herself at the altar by the simple fact that she had already fallen in love with somebody else. Her new lover had been in the congregation, and she had kept him fixed in her mind's eye throughout the ceremony and into the night.

Not only was the marriage a mistake, Ramsay's career prospects soon crumbled. His elevation to a professorship was blocked as he became embroiled in several disputes within the university – an unpaid account, missing library books, exam scripts not returned, queries over his qualifications, and, the most damaging as it turned out, concerns over his work outside of the university.

He was the director of a company that made gramophone needles out of prickly pear thorns; they were said to produce a softer sound than other available needles, which was true for one or two playings but not thereafter. There is a suggestion that some of the university establishment, who were outraged at this recent divorcee leading one of his students away from her studies and into marriage, used the possible conflict bet-ween Ramsay's academic career and his business interests as a cover to punish him. Whatever the motives, he was ordered to stop his work at the local gramophone needle factory, which counted Peggy among its six book-keepers. He resisted and, in the ensuing rumpus, was forced to resign from the university.

Regarded by many at Rhodes as a scoundrel, Ramsay was, never-theless, accepted by several colleagues as an amusing, even charismatic, eccentric who had not undertaken anything illegal within the university.

This may not have been the case, however, as far as his company was concerned. At a time before the advent of domestic radio when there was great demand for gramophone needles, Ramsay persuaded a number of local people to invest in the business in the hope of earning a quick and easy return. Peggy said that he kept conning people out of money in order to keep the company going, but it finally crashed in the middle of 1929 – a little before Wall Street – and Ramsay had to make his escape.

England offered a new future to both of them, although for quite different reasons. He and Peggy boarded a ship for Southampton. It was the last time she ever saw South Africa.

Chapter Two

*If It's Tuesday
It Must Be Macbeth*

*'There was one red dress in the company
and we used to circulate it. If you got the red dress
you had the big scene in the third act
and the round of applause that went with it.'*

Peggy on touring *Smilin' Through* in the war

PEGGY arrived in England both extremely pleased to have escaped what she saw as the prison of provincial South African life, with the thrilling prospect of a new world ahead, and highly conscious of a different kind of imprisonment from which she had not yet escaped, that of her dreadful marriage to Norman Ramsay.

She already held romantic notions about life and love which had been severely tested by the painful experience of the marriage. Whatever sexual relationships she had had remained a secret, but she did tell stories of youthful obsessions. Her favourite featured a pilot lover in the mould of the adventurer Denys Finch Hatton. Peggy's airman was said to be famous but, as was the custom with her stories, the other people in them were not named. There was an airfield near the family farm, and she would describe how the unnamed pilot would fly low over the house and bombard her with love letters from the sky. On one occasion he crash-landed and was rushed to hospital. Forbidden to see him, she escaped from her house through a window and made her way to his bedside. One version of this story has her visit him in gaol; in another she is sent away from the farm in order to cure her of the infatuation.

An airman lover also figures in other romantic stories she told. An amalgam of details drawn from different versions reveals this airman to be a poet whom she called Roley, which was short for Rowland. He went

17

missing, presumed dead, in World War II, maybe during or not long after the Battle of Britain. He was said to have left her all his worldly goods. No trace has been found of him, however, and several close friends never heard her mention him, yet one of her secretaries said she kept a photograph of him by her bed. She did tell some friends of an unspecified incident in wartime concerning a lover who was killed, and said that the incident had devastated her emotionally. Although to one colleague she described the lost lover as her brother, it seems more likely that she was referring to the pilot, who emerges as possibly the only true love of her life, against the loss of whom she measured all subsequent relationships. She said that just after the war she used to see the dead airman in the street as if he were still alive.

Peggy talked about other lovers who were musicians. She told Robert Bolt that she fell in love with one, the violin virtuoso Jascha Heifetz, when she was aged 17. He was five or six years older and was touring South Africa. As a musician, he was known for his command of technique, his concentration, the boldness in his playing, but also for a certain hauteur. He was cold and unsmiling, and in recording studios he would keep his distance from the other musicians. He had a reputation for being an extremely private man, which, along with his immense talent, would have attracted Peggy, as might his fondness for fast cars, firearms, tennis and cards. (She liked cards and gambling; she played bridge – with Omar Sharif among others – and it was said she broke the bank at Ostend for a young man on her first visit to a casino in her early 20s. It was even rumoured that before she became an agent she enjoyed a spell as a professional gambler at the tables. She enjoyed a flutter on the horses, particularly on Desert Orchid, as well as on the stock exchange.)

Peggy told various Heifetz stories, while being careful not to mention his name. In many of them, it was Heifetz who fell in love with her, and not the other way around. The maestro became so besotted with her that he demanded she attend each concert he played; without her presence in the audience, he would be unable to perform. She soon became bored with traipsing around after him and with hearing the same pieces played over and over again. Enjoying the innuendo, she would complain of how small his repertoire was – an anecdote reworked by her client David Hare in his play *The Bay at Nice*. Her boredom with the affair, however, no doubt masked many other emotions, as the outcomes of subsequent relationships were to suggest.

With such instincts it is easy to see why Peggy wanted to forge a new life. She made no secret of her hatred for Ramsay, who had surrounded himself in London with what Peggy called 'pseudo-gents and bores'. Although she felt she should take responsibility for the break-up of the marriage, she never felt any guilt. She loathed being called Mrs Ramsay but kept the 'borrowed' surname after she left him, and she wore her wedding ring until she died.

Stories of the final separation form one of the great Peggy legends; like an eager dramatist she relished the telling of the story, and the delivery was as important as the detail. Whilst this frequently differed – from taking one day to three months – her versions were consistent on the awfulness of the marriage yet its usefulness as an escape route from South Africa and from her parents. In one version Peggy walks off the ship at Southampton and, as if liberated by the merest touch of English soil, leaves Ramsay there and then without hesitation; in another, they arrive in London in a taxi and, as it pulls up at a set of traffic lights, she suddenly opens the door and just flees; in yet another, Ramsay locks her in a hotel room in London and she wriggles free through a window (shades of her South African pilot story). There was a variant of the latter version, in which it was she who locked the door in order to barricade herself in and then escaped through the window while he tried to beat the door down. The account she gave 50 years later when she finally divorced Ramsay has them moving into a flat in Hanover Court in West London. After a few months and many rows she decides to leave. He follows her to a hotel near Euston, where she has gone to stay before travelling to a friend's in the country, and he takes back her luggage. She abandons the suitcases and with them all her belongings. She has no passport, no birth or marriage certificates, no spare clothes, but she has her freedom. And she never sees Ramsay again.

Peggy said that she had £10 when she left Ramsay and it seems probable that she did have to start from scratch in this new country, an independent but unaccommodated woman. She had to fall back upon her own resources, which in the early 1930s for a young woman was no small order. This tough start gave her a long-standing admiration for the virtues of self-reliance and an antipathy to any who expected 'something for nothing'.

She last heard of Ramsay in 1932 when the husband of a friend of Peggy's reported that by chance he had come across him in a prison in the south of France. For many years afterwards Peggy had a fear of bumping into him again and would even go to the point of hiding in doorways to avoid the possibility.

Before she left Ramsay, Peggy had been looking for ways of passing her time. She was spurred on to take singing lessons because she remembered that a fortune-teller had told her mother during pregnancy that she would give birth to a daughter who would be a wonderful singer. (A variant has the fortune teller talking direct to a young Peggy.) After leaving Ramsay, she told her teacher, Hubert Oliver of Hampstead, that she would have to stop the lessons because she could no longer afford them. She had seen an advertisement placed by the Carl Rosa Opera Company, which announced forthcoming auditions for its chorus at the Lyceum Theatre. Oliver taught her Elizabeth's greeting from *Tannhäuser* as an audition piece. The leading touring opera company of its day, the Carl Rosa had popularised Wagner in the 1890s and had retained his work in the repertoire. During the 1930s and '40s, the company performed most of the opera that was heard in Britain outside of London, although by this time it was way past its best.

Peggy was now living in digs in St. John's Wood. Staying in the same house as Peggy was a young music student, Barbara Wright, who was to become a noted translator of French writers and a client of Peggy's. Although Peggy was not that much older than Wright, the gap was large enough to make both a difference and a strong impression. Wright remembers Peggy as 'very attractive and magnetic; she was like a countess to me. She could command the interest of anyone she wanted, with the lifting of a little finger.'

One day, she and Wright were travelling on the top of a bus to visit a gallery, and they had a row over who should pay the fare, each insisting that she and not the other should do so. Peggy eventually won but, not to be outfaced, Wright threw her own coins out of the bus window. Peggy really liked her for that.

So, with no particular ambition and no evident means to support herself, Peggy auditioned for the Carl Rosa company. She knew nothing of opera and, despite her mother's salon recitals and her own experiences with famous musicians, she was not particularly musical herself.

'I shrieked that dreadful, frightful aria,' she recalled caustically. 'I belted it out. I had to – I was the only thin singer, the others were all voluminous.' Skinny or not, she was taken on, and thus began a life on the road which she followed on and off for the next two decades. There is no evidence of her using an agent, and neither the actors' union Equity nor the casting directory Spotlight has any record of her. Biographies in theatre programmes, press cuttings and colleagues' memories are the only means of tracing Peggy's existence as a performing artist. To complicate matters, Peggy may have appeared under another surname when she started out in the chorus; she wrote to an acquaintance in the early 1960s that this had been her practice. When she became an actress, however, records show that she used the name of her discarded husband.

It appears that she took a break from the Carl Rosa in the mid-1930s and rejoined it during 1935, in time to enjoy what for her was the high point of her operatic career – an appearance at the historic Lyceum Theatre, London, in *Die Fledermaus*. The following year, Peggy switched from singing to acting. With the Carl Rosa, she had proven herself to be adept at speaking on stage, and she was offered the opportunity to appear in musical theatre, in a touring production of the Ivor Novello hit *Glamorous Night*. She claimed that she played the lead role that had been made famous in the original production by Mary Ellis, although the touring production in fact featured Muriel Barron in the part. It seems that Peggy understudied the role and may, therefore, have played it on occasion. It is possible that she thought she should have played it, or that when she did, she believed that she gave a better performance than Muriel Barron. Peggy, despite her habitual self-deprecation, did hold on to self-belief, and harboured a desire, however circumscribed, to be remembered as a star. She used to tell of a backstage meeting with Noël Coward, who came to see her after a show, when the Master predicted that this indeed would be her fate. Prince Littler, the manager who produced the tour of *Glamorous Night*, obviously agreed, but Peggy declined his offer of a contract to sing in a series of shows, preferring instead to stick with her acting.

Characteristically, Peggy assessed her acting to be only a mite better than her singing, although not by a huge margin. Colleagues remember her as pretty and petite with good, clear diction, but her poor eyesight – she normally wore bifocals – often gave her a glazed appearance on stage. Oddly enough, she looked fairly ordinary in costume, in contrast to how remarkable she looked in her own clothes. In performance she tended to fall back on what she had done in rehearsal, even if asked to produce something different, and what she had done in rehearsal was to play herself but not as exceptionally or forcefully as she actually was off stage; she played the mask, not the real thing.

Joseph O'Conor, with whom she acted at the Q Theatre in west London and in a couple of television productions, and who, as a playwright, became an early client, says her acting style was lucid and downright; she spoke with 'a murderous but somehow distracted clarity, as though she would much rather be uttering her own words than someone else's.'

She was remembered for individual traits; a slightly magisterial, stately walk, bending at the knees, her long strides exaggerated by girlish shoes, a loquacious, sharp tongue, and a maniacal, pealing laugh.

She found enjoyment in the theatrical adventure, with all its traditional accoutrements – the affairs with young actors, the grind, the modest income, the landladies, the breakfasts, the warmth of the people she encountered or their derision, and, above all, the uncertainty and transience of the life.

Yet Peggy was not the stereotypical touring thespian. She did not act the life and soul of the green room and was more likely to be discussing a Flaubert novel or Jung's psychoanalysis than the latest theatrical gossip. Whatever else, she was never a shy or silent member of a company.

On one tour, of a play about juvenile delinquency by Elsa Shelley called *Pick-Up Girl*, Peggy joined late to replace an actress who had fallen out with the director. A young Peter Wyngarde was in the cast. One day he missed a matinée performance because he had mixed up the days and had gone to the cinema instead. Peggy decided to help and covered up for him. When he returned to the theatre for the evening performance, he found a note from Peggy. 'I've told them you had gone to a matinée of the pre-London tour of the Old Vic with both Olivier and Richardson in the same production. And that *I* thought you'd learn more there than at *our* matinée. Back me up. Peggy.' The fact that the Old Vic was not expected in town for another two weeks seemed to have escaped her and landed Wyngarde in even deeper trouble. 'I was severely reprimanded for making up such a poor excuse,' says Wyngarde. Peggy simply roared with laughter.

During the tour of *Glamorous Night*, Peggy had a row with another chorine, 'a particularly sly and insinuating blonde', Peggy recalled. Peggy was 'goaded beyond reason' by the 'small bitchiness of small people' and threw herself physically upon this woman. A fight ensued, said Peggy, 'such as Zola described in *L'Assommoir* – torn clothes, blood flowing from cheeks, hair ripped out by the roots.' The stage manager finally separated them. According to Peggy, 'the blonde never goaded again.'

Singing and acting were not important to Peggy, they were just haphazard steps on an unsought road to somewhere and something else which at that time she could not see or define and yet which she later believed to have been in some modest sense predestined. She acted to earn money, she said, and was contemptuous of most of the theatre in which she was involved. This ranged from touring shows, reps such as Leeds, and pantomime to *Peter Pan* and, if Peggy is to be believed, a Max Reinhardt production of *A Midsummer Night's Dream*.

She remembered appearing with Trevor Howard at Harrogate ('a pocket of the south, the only flabby town in Yorkshire'). She and Howard visited the local gaol where she seriously believed she would not be let out because she 'played a criminal lunatic so effectively that the jail doctor believed I'd been inside.'

Although the stage was not a career for her, her time on the road, along with the contacts that she made, turned out to be a valuable practical apprenticeship for her life to come as an agent. It gave her a first-hand knowledge of the bread-and-butter side of the profession, whether it was how managements operated or which shows worked in front of which audiences in different parts of the land.

In 1938, another advertisement, another move, this time to Ireland with Carl F. Clopet's rep company in his first season at the Cork Opera House. The company was based in England and went to Ireland for four weeks but stayed fourteen. It returned the following year on a visit that took in Dublin and Belfast as well as Cork and played more than a dozen productions in its repertoire. Peggy's acting was hailed by a local newspaper critic, and she became something of a minor celebrity, singing for the local operatic society that helped out with Clopet's shows. Clopet, a grandee of the casting couch, offered her the pick of the roles, including St. Joan and Camille, if she would become his lover. Her reply was to depart for England. Peggy led an active sex life but on her own terms. Unsurprisingly, she said that the actress who did surrender to Clopet's advances was a disaster.

Peggy's time in Ireland, during which she met Micheál MacLíammoír, fostered in her a fondness for the Irish but a dislike of a kind of swaggering 'boyo' acting, which, to her taste, was too crude and provincial.

On her return to England she undertook her most demanding role. Just as war was breaking out, she played Lady Macbeth for the Festival Repertory Company in Cambridge as it came briefly under the leadership of two actors, Arthur Young and William Devlin. The venue had been made famous by Terence Gray, who had left in the early 1930s. The company of which Peggy was a member turned out to be the last company to play at the Georgian playhouse which Gray had redesigned before it was turned into a workshop and costume store. Peggy's season also included appearances in an ancient Indian drama called *Sakantula*, Clifford Bax's *The Rose Without a Thorn* and Denis Johnston's *The Golden Cuckoo* (months before the London production by Devlin's friend Hugh Hunt, which Hunt always believed, mistakenly, to be the British première).

Devlin, a leading Shakespearean actor with the Old Vic, played the Thane to Peggy's Lady Macbeth, and was said by the reviewer of the principal university arts magazine to be the best Macbeth he had seen in what was one of the worst productions he had ever witnessed. Peggy was judged to have given a 'professional' performance and to have been 'sensitive' though 'not first rate'. Peggy was having an affair with Devlin, and this no doubt had affected his choice of role for her. They even rehearsed in the bedroom. Her own memory of this pinnacle in her life treading the boards was characteristically unsentimental: 'I think he thought I was a better actress than I was. I wasn't very good, but I found the mad scene easy.'

Peggy was very close to Devlin. She said that she even considered having children with him but he was already married (into a famous theatrical family, the Cassons). War interrupted, although it did not end, their relationship. It took Devlin to the horsed Cavalry and then the army, and it took Peggy on tour again. She was a couple of years too old for the female call-up but did talk of having driven an ambulance with an actress friend (an unlikely occurrence unless it was a private ambulance. She did not pass her driving test until the 1960s and on the evidence of her road skills then any ambulance that she drove would have curtailed life rather than saved it).

While Devlin was away, Peggy met the man with whom she was to live on and off for the rest of her life. She was appearing in a tour of *Smilin' Through* by Allan Langdon Martin that lasted more than a year, and in the cast was the matinée idol William Roderick. They were born in the same year – Peggy was five months younger – and her father and Bill's had attended medical college together. Roderick was due to become a doctor too but decided on an acting career instead, as did his twin brother, John.

Despite Peggy's long association with Bill, the Roderick family never got to know Peggy well: Bill's mother called her 'the sweet little singer'. Bill's other brother, Michael, remembers the first time he saw Peggy, when the tour of *Smilin' Through* visited Darlington where he was stationed. They were all to meet in the market place; when he arrived he saw her scattering pound notes in the wind. He did not remember why she was doing this, if he ever knew, but the striking image remained.

Bill Roderick enjoyed a long run in 1945 in Edward Percy's *The Shop at Sly Corner* and was a regular actor in leading rep companies, particularly under William Armstrong at Liverpool. He played Archbishop Cranmer and understudied Paul Scofield as Sir Thomas More in the first production of *A Man for All Seasons*, the most successful play that Peggy was ever to represent, and then played the part of More on tour in the US to great acclaim. But, for reasons unknown, he withdrew from the profession not long afterwards to live permanently with Peggy.

Roderick was a handsome actor, if something of an introvert, and was said to be much sought after by other actresses. Maybe this was part of his attraction? (Peggy was rumoured to have 'stolen' him from Dorothy Reynolds, the actress who became known as the co-author of *Salad Days*.) Peggy's affairs with other men caused rifts between her and Roderick, but, according to friends and colleagues, she in turn had to cope with his hard drinking, of which she cured him, and his regular use of prostitutes, whom he visited because he did not like 'nice' women.

They lived together after the war, but Peggy was alone for long periods, both because of Roderick's acting commitments and because of the fluctuating state of their relationship, which reached a low point at the time when Peggy set up the agency. Roderick resurfaced more significantly in the early 1960s (the period of *A Man for All Seasons*) when Peggy had become established. Peggy wanted to be in the driving seat in any relationship and was terrified of being loved. She was bored by Roderick's adulation, and said that it was he who suggested they come to a permanent arrangement. This, he said, could be agreed on any terms she liked as long as it included them living together. Peggy would never have proposed such an idea herself, even if she had desired it, and yet, regardless of her fears, she replied, 'Well, if you *insist*, dear.' At work, the subject of her partnership with Roderick, like reference to her age, was taboo.

Bill Roderick was devoted to Peggy. He looked after all the domestic arrangements and stage managed that side of her life. They hardly socialised, and he rarely came to see her at the office or accompanied her to the theatre. Friends said that, although he was a good actor who was none too keen on acting (a trait shared by Bill Devlin), it was unlike him to retire so completely from social as well as theatrical life. Peggy did not acknowledge his indispensable support during the last thirty years of her life; often it seemed as if Roderick did not exist. He had an ear problem, for example, and would sometimes fall down, yet Peggy would tell others there was nothing wrong with him. She took him for granted, assuming he would always be there; it was only after he died that she fully realised how much he had meant to her.

After *Smilin' Through* came a four-month tour of a light comedy, *Bachelor Father*. This was followed in 1944 by a five-month tour of Rose Franken's *Claudia*, in which Peggy played a Russian opera singer and was directed by William Armstrong, a former leading actor and illustrious figure in the repertory movement. He had just finished running the Liverpool Playhouse after 22 years and was branching out at the age of 62. Peggy, who was well read, says he gave her a book by Kafka because he wanted it explained to him. He also gave her some play scripts, which had been sent to him by managers who hoped he might agree to direct them. This proved to be fortuitous. Not only did Peggy unravel the mysteries of Kafka for Armstrong, she discussed the scripts with him and discovered that she was quite a good judge of a text; 'I knew what it was like to say the lines,' she said modestly. More importantly, she found out that she enjoyed reading them. She read more and soon became a freelance reader for different managements. In the process, she also began to meet and help some of the authors, earning herself a minor reputation as a play doctor.

In May 1945, Peggy made her only West End appearance, in Edward Lipscomb's *The Gay Pavilion*, starring Frederick Valk, Mary Ellis and Frank Allenby. Billed as the first production of the European peace, it was presented by a new management run by Peter Daubeny, who had worked at Liverpool under Armstrong, the director of the play. Just as she had finally arrived in the West End, Armstrong inadvertently altered the path of Peggy's life by commending her play-reading skills to Daubeny, who, not being a keen reader himself, took her out of the show and installed her in his office instead. Here she not only read scripts that had been sent in to Daubeny but began to learn about management and in particular the economics of producing plays. She also met several people who were to play an important part in her future, such as Frith Banbury, who was appearing in the Daubeny show, *Jacobowsky and the Colonel*, and her future patron Edward Sutro, who was one of Daubeny's backers.

Sutro, by profession a farmer, was a well-known figure in theatrical circles. An ardent first-nighter, he wore a scarlet-lined cape, carried a cane, and was known as the 'milk train millionaire' because he travelled cheaply despite his considerable wealth. He took Peggy to first nights, which was a boon to her because, although she did not like the occasions, it helped her keep up with what was happening in the theatre.

He generally encouraged Peggy and gave her plays to read as well. One, called *Grand National Night*, was written by a wife and husband team, Dorothy and Campbell Christie, who had had two plays produced in 1935 but none since. Sutro had rescued it from Daubeny's office, where it had lain unread before Peggy's arrival. She recommended the play, and Sutro passed it on to H.M. Tennent, the most powerful management in the West End. They opened *Grand National Night* in June 1946 at the Apollo Theatre and it ran for more than 250 performances. It is understandable that the Christies came to regard Peggy as a fine reader too, as well as a good omen, and they, along with Sutro, were to provide the main impetus behind the establishment of Peggy's agency.

Peggy's useful experience with Daubeny was deepened by her next theatrical adventure, which, although brief and in parts stormy, proved decisive in pointing her away from acting toward what was still as yet an undefined future role behind the scenes. In the first flush of government funding for the arts, which continued from wartime into peacetime, the Bristol Old Vic Company was set up at Britain's oldest working theatre under the leadership of the director Hugh Hunt. He asked his old friend Bill Devlin, who had not long been demobbed, to become the company's main actor.

Hunt was nominated as artistic director in the autumn of 1945 and straightaway went to Bristol to prepare, taking with him Devlin and, at Devlin's suggestion, Peggy, who was to serve as the company's secretary. Peggy put her heart and soul into the project. As is the way in new enterprises, and it must have been especially true just after the war, jobs expand to meet need and are defined by personality more than prescription. Peggy, formally unqualified as she may have been, ended up helping Hunt as his assistant in the choice and casting of the plays, as well as in the setting up of the administration of the company. She was put in charge of publicity and even had to take on responsibility for wigs because the wardrobe mistress did not care for this task. Peggy also played minor roles in *The Beaux' Stratagem* and *Weep for the Cyclops* by Denis Johnston, the first and last productions of the opening, six month-long season, which began in February 1946 and which included three new plays. The motto for this pioneering company was 'Something original, something alive, something adventurous'. It could well have summed up Peggy.

Tanya Moiseiwitch, the gifted stage designer who collaborated often with Hunt and whom he invited to Bristol, remembers that he was keen for her to have a say in the look of the posters and programmes, and asked her to deal with the printers. 'I knew little of this world,' she recounts, and Peggy came to her aid. 'As far as type was concerned I'd heard of only one name – caslon – which seemed suitable for the 18th not the 20th century. Peggy asked me if it had "attention value" – and that's a phrase that's stuck with me. It did, and in the end we used it.'

As a designer, Moiseiwitch had to work with Peggy on the wigs too. One of the hardest tasks is to persuade the actors to wear the wigs in the first place, and often they have to be remade on the actors' heads. 'It has to be handled with due care,' says Moiseiwitch. 'Opening the wig boxes was therefore an event. The first wig to be pulled out was Devlin's, and Peggy just immediately said "Oh Bill, you can't *possibly* wear this, dear." This was the wrong thing to say to an actor, and although he knew her well enough, it still nonplussed him. She was being forceful and unthinking, and she tried my patience to the utmost. It took a lot of repair work to sort it out.'

In *The Beaux' Stratagem* Peggy played a maid. Hunt directed her in one scene to dress Pamela Brown, who was playing Mrs Sullen, on stage. Peggy was too vain to admit to being too short-sighted to be able to see what she was doing. At the dress rehearsal, what was supposed to be a quick change seemed to take an age; the dialogue had to be extended, much to the irritation of the principal actors and the director, as Peggy laboriously tied each lace as if she were reading braille badly.

Peggy only lasted the first season. By the end of it, she and Devlin had parted. He had separated from his first wife, and his future second wife, Meriel Moore, who had been in Clopet's troupe with Peggy, was a member of the Bristol Old Vic company. Peggy and Hugh Hunt agreed to part, too. They were like chalk and cheese. He was scholarly, immoderately shy, and a thoughtful planner. Peggy was the opposite – outspoken, impulsive, with a robust and ribald sense of humour.

The breaking point was a row over actors' pay. In the company there was a strong group of Irish actors who voiced general concern about the level of wages. They found the Welshman Hunt too cold and approached Peggy to talk to Hunt on their behalf. Hunt told Peggy that the actors were not worth any more money, to which she replied that it was all right to starve if you were talented, but there was no point if you were no better than he obviously thought they were.

She carried on working for the Bristol Old Vic for a short while afterwards in London and took with her a new enthusiasm for the whole business of management and the preparation of production. She also took with her more new friendships, in particular that of Noël Willman, whom Hunt believed was the leader of the Irish group that had ganged up with Peggy against him. Willman and Peggy shared a flat over a pub in Bristol, and, in the 1950s, when she was at a very low ebb, he invited her to move into his large flat in Victoria; he occupied the downstairs part of the flat while she and Roderick each had a room upstairs.

Willman was a sharply intelligent gay actor and director. He also had a drink problem which he managed to overcome. He, as director, and Peggy, as agent, collaborated on many productions, including *A Man for All Seasons*. He also introduced Peggy to Katharine Hepburn; the two used to meet whenever they were both in New York at the same time. Like Peggy, Willman was a rather private person and would cut you if he thought you had transgressed against him. On one occasion, she threw a party during his absence without his knowledge, dedicating every room to a different course of the evening meal. On Willman's return, a mutual friend told him how splendid the party had been and how he had especially enjoyed the cheese course in Noël's bedroom. Willman fell out with Peggy after that. When he died in 1989, Peggy, according to Paul Scofield, who visited her shortly afterwards, showed no interest in the fate of her one-time friend.

At Bristol, Peggy had developed a taste for running things and a concomitant desire to expand her horizons accordingly. A chance to indulge the former and go some way towards the latter came at the Q Theatre near Kew Bridge. It was one of the capital's leading little theatres where productions could be tried out before a possible West End transfer. Peggy acted there more than a dozen times between 1948 and 1953. The theatre's owners, Beattie and Jack de Leon, a West End impresario, used to lease the theatre to visiting managements for short periods; in the summer of 1950 an actor called Michael Allinson took the opportunity to try his hand.

Allinson had met Peggy two years earlier when they had both appeared, along with Bill Roderick, in Edward Sheldon's *Romance*, which had played at Watford and Richmond. Allinson had latched on to Peggy, who was ten years his senior, and had moved in to the flat she shared with Roderick in Mornington Crescent. 'She blew me away,' says Allinson. 'I was 29 but green. She knew so much and was so talented.' He had understudied John Clements the following year and was inspired by him to become an actor-manager. With money from his father he decided to pick up the challenge at Q. He knew that he wanted Peggy to be involved in the team as its artistic dynamo.

Peggy had been on tour in a thriller called *Birdcage*, which, luckily as it happened, did not make the hoped for journey into the West End. She had then gone to Brighton to play in rep with Bill Roderick. When she heard of the chance to run Q she returned to London immediately. Peggy and Allinson and a friend of his from the Royal Academy of Dramatic Art called Eric Uttley formed a new management. From July 1950 to January 1951 they presented at Q twenty-six shows, of which just over a fifth were new plays.

Their repertoire included *Red Dragon* by Hugh Hastings, who wrote the West End hit *Seagulls Over Sorrento*, *Harvest Time* by Margaret Luce, who wrote *The Kingmaker* and with whom Peggy subsequently kept in touch, and *Virtuoso* by Cedric Wallis, who also figured in the early days of her agency. Among the directors hired were Jack Minster, with whom she was to work as a reader, and Frank Hauser, then coming to the end of his short time as a BBC Drama Producer. Hauser's production was of a new play by

Howard Clewes called *Quay South*. It was his first venture into the theatre, and Peggy recalls helping Hauser considerably, especially on the technical aspects of the show. Alec Guinness, who had played in a BBC Radio production of Hauser's, came to see *Quay South* after receiving a letter from Hauser, asking if he wanted an assistant. Guinness was impressed by Hauser's production at Q, enough to offer him his first fully professional engagement, co-directing *Hamlet* with Guinness as both his co-director and his star. Hauser subsequently directed Peggy herself at Q, in 1952. They renewed their acquaintance when he took over the Oxford Playhouse, where several of Peggy's clients' plays were performed.

Peggy already knew lots of actors from her own stage work. At Q, she was able to extend her range of contacts; they covered the spectrum from the venerable, like Ronald Adam, and the distinguished, like Freda Jackson, to a rich mix of the established and the up-and-coming, including Joss Ackland, Stanley Baker, Theodore Bikel, Kenneth Griffith, Ferdy Mayne, Anthony Newley, Dandy Nichols, Nicholas Parsons, Patrick Troughton, and Molly Urquhart. One young actor, Laurence Harvey, had to be sacked because he did not know his lines. Later, he was to star in and finish the direction of a film, *A Dandy in Aspic*, written by one of Peggy's clients, Derek Marlowe.

During those six months, Peggy more or less lived at Q. She made sure that she was there at least from 10am to 6pm every day and always stayed on when there was an evening rehearsal or an opening. Finding, casting and producing a new show every week made for frenetic activity. Peggy, for all her impetuousness, had a strangely steadying effect because she concentrated fiercely, held her nerve and stood firmly by her views. The three managers paid themselves £8 a week but ran out of money, lost their investment and had to finish their season earlier than anticipated. Things might have turned out differently if they had not suffered from a combination that autumn of bad fog, a gas strike and a bus strike, and if *Harvest Time* had transferred to the West End as the manager Donald Albery had intended, had he not insisted on changing the leading man.

There was also the figure of Beattie de Leon, the queen of Q, hovering in the background in order to keep a watchful eye on the novices who were running her beloved theatre. Her presence only made Peggy anxious and added to the prudence and caution with which she, Allinson and Uttley ran their season. Peggy felt she could not break new ground, but she did learn an enormous amount about budgeting, casting, managing a theatre, and paying wages, National Insurance stamps and rent, all of which stood her in very good stead when she became an agent. Crucially, she became involved for the first time with agents themselves, the people whom playwrights employ to sell their work and to handle the ensuing contractual arrangements, including the collection, and distribution to the writer, of monies earned.

Peggy plunged headlong at Q into script reading. During breaks in rehearsals or between matinée and evening performances, Peggy would find a spot to bury her head in a play. If it were warm enough, she could be found sitting on the grass of the spare ground next to the theatre, with her back leant against the side of a shed that was the domain of the resident designer, her skirt up over her knees and a text in her hands.

Jack Watling recalls problems rehearsing a revival of Wynyard Browne's *Dark Summer*, when Peggy, who was in the cast, matter-of-factly intervened and simply said, 'This scene won't work unless we cut it here and add something there.' Watling adds, 'Q's resident director Geoffrey Wardell used to say, "If we have Peggy Ramsay in a new play then we can leave the text to her".'

Her interest in new and imaginative work led her to read ever more voraciously. Eager to increase her knowledge, she would spend a great deal of time in the library of the British Drama League (and gave a talk at a BDL weekend school to aspiring dramatists some time before she became a renowned nurturer of playwriting talent). She was teaching herself about art, literature and theatre, reading widely from Aristotle to William Archer, and she would patiently copy into commonplace books page after page of stimulating ideas.

In 1951, she became a director of the First Stage Society, a play reading company, along with the formidable literary agent Suzanne Czech and the actress Selma vaz Dias, whom Peggy knew from having appeared with her at Q. Their collective taste can be seen from their programme, which was much more intellectual fare than Q would allow – work by Gide, de Montherlant, Lorca, Robert Penn Warren, Wolfgang Borchert and new plays such as *Farewell to Faustus* by Leo Lehman and *Alexander the Great* by I.D. Shamah. The Society's first venture, directed by Peggy at the French Institute in London, was a presentation of the chamber opera *Aucassin and Nicolette* by Clifton Parker, with words by Eleanor and Henry Farjeon. In March 1953, Peggy directed a reading of *Sheila* by John Symonds, with whom she was briefly very close and who was the biographer of the satanist, Aleister Crowley. The Society's first full production, staged in 1952 in association with the Institute of Contemporary Arts and the London Theatre Guild, turned out to be an artistic coup. It was *Les Bonnes* by Jean Genet performed in French at the Mercury Theatre, west London – the first time that a play of his had been seen in England.

Oscar Lewenstein, who was running the Royal Court, invited the cast to his theatre where they performed the play first in French and subsequently in English. Selma vaz Dias played Solange and it was directed by Peter Zadek, who was later to win international renown for his innovative productions in Germany. Eduardo Paolozzi, a teacher at the Central School of Art and Design who was to become one of the most celebrated of modern sculptors, was the designer. He had never been near a theatre before, according to Zadek, and turned up to the dress rehearsal with his 'set' which consisted of wallpaper rolls that he thought would stand up with glue but palpably did not. Bunches of flowers were purchased and strewn over the stage instead. Paolozzi recalls that his budget was about £10 for paper, string and cardboard, and that Zadek's behaviour ensured that sculpture, rather than theatre, would be the future beneficiary of Paolozzi's talents.

*

'None of us accepts life as it is, and our silly little heads
are crammed full of romantic dreams and emotions.'

A letter Peggy signed 'Wormwood'

Living in her rundown tenement flat in Mornington Crescent (in what was once the artist Cruickshank's house), overlooking the railway lines going in and out of Euston, Peggy was becoming very knowledgeable about plays but also ever poorer in a rather English, 'genteel' way. She saw life as a stream into which she had been dropped, and she had to bob and duck and ride the eddies as best she could. She was only scraping a living and was emotionally very raw as she let life live her.

Roderick had been upset at her liaison with Allinson, and she in turn was angry with a lover called Charles Fenn because of his involvement with other women. Fenn had met Peggy after he had sent plays to her when she was running Q. But for the fact that she and her management ran out of money, he would have had a production there.

Fenn had been a bell boy on the Cunard, a textile salesman in America, a freelance photographer, and, in World War II, had reputedly recruited Ho Chi Minh in China to work as an American secret agent and had smuggled him into Vietnam. He was also a friend of Ford Madox Ford and eventually became a novelist himself. Fenn recalls that he and Peggy shared a love of the countryside and of flowers. She was particularly fond of paintings and antiques, he says, and she liked to choose visually unusual postcards to send to friends. He remembers Peggy living from hand to mouth but always managing to look stunning on nothing and without apparent effort. She was generous even when hard up, especially with books, which she would unearth in local second-hand shops. She bought him a copy of China's greatest romantic novel, *Dream of the Red Chamber* by Tsao Hsueh-Chin, because of his interest in the Far East, and was then furious with him for not liking it.

Her astuteness and intelligence did not help her accept criticism, and she was quick to take offence. She told Fenn once not to bother to come and see her in a walk-on part at Q, but afterwards, when he had duly missed it, she was deeply hurt and paced the floor of her one-room flat waiting for him to call because she had not expected him to take what she had said at face value. She had too much pride to telephone him herself and gave him hell when they next met.

Fenn recalls both the beginning and the end of their sexual relationship. 'When I asked to make love to her, she was at first reluctant because, as if with a sad memory, it would spoil our otherwise happy friendship. (Alas, how right she was!)' His liaisons with other women made her so unhappy that he knew they must part 'since our relationship was causing her more pain than joy.' He told her 'we could always be friends, she could always count on me – the platitudes a man so often uses to the woman he intends to break away from; but suddenly she threw herself into my arms; and, as soon as we drew apart, began stripping off her clothes and finally threw herself nude on the couch that served as her bed. So of course I made love to her – lovingly I hope and rather believe, because I loved her still – but, alas, not enough to exclude other women!'

Another relationship lasted no more than a single night. She described it as a sudden explosion of desire between her and the man. They swept off to her flat and indulged in a night of the most torrid sexual fireworks. In the morning, she felt nothing for him except that she never wanted to see him again. The man was wounded and uncomprehending, but she was true to her word, and they never did meet again.

She also told a tale of unrequited love – unusual for her – which cast a long shadow; she was in love with a writer in France, whom she did not name. When she went to see him, she discovered that he was in love with, and in turn was loved by, several other women. Crushed, she returned to England. Peggy had never experienced any difficulty in attracting men, but, now in her 40s, she was getting tired of the sexual treadmill and wanted to jump off. 'One night stands,' she once quipped, 'mean touring the country with a manager announcing wearily, "If it's Tuesday, it must be *Macbeth*".'

She felt alone but did not want company; she had rejected her own family yet did not want to make a new one of her own. (Several clients said that Peggy had had at least one abortion, but none could furnish any details. There was also an unsubstantiated rumour that Peggy had in fact given birth and that her child was living somewhere in secret.) Peggy felt drained of life. Social intercourse became trying. She developed a horror of pubs. She even found herself avoiding the cracks in the pavement, fearful that to step on them would mean being swallowed by the earth. She had to hold her breath with great effort and look straight up until the feeling passed. Peggy alluded to having experienced similar symptoms when she apparently suffered some kind of a breakdown, probably in the mid-1930s, which might have been the reason why she left the Carl Rosa Opera Company for a while not long after she had escaped from her husband.

Peggy said that she survived during this period of desolation in the early 1950s by reading Beckett, whose novels presented her with a stoical ideal to which she increasingly aspired.

Her professional as well as her emotional life was also proving highly frustrating. Since the experiences of Bristol and Q she had become more disillusioned with the lot of the actor. 'It's an aimless, idiotic profession,' she commented, although later she thought that it had improved when more intelligent plays were being written, giving actors 'better things to say'. She was in her mid-40s – the 'wrong age' for a stage actress – and was not being offered many parts. Most of what she was offered she did not like. She said that she had earned an unlikely reputation for playing pathetic characters, like the old woman in Noël Coward's *Peace in Our Time*.

For all its shortcomings, however, she did not want to leave the theatre. 'At times in my life,' she wrote, 'emotions have stopped my success in several fields. They get too much and I throw everything away. Theatre is one good sphere for my feelings.' She was not sure where to turn, although years after she became an agent, she admitted that she would have liked to be a director. She said that she had been put off because there were then not enough good plays being written to sustain her interest. At a time before Joan Littlewood had blazed a trail for women as directors, Peggy believed that a woman had to be the assistant; this, nevertheless, was clearly a role that Peggy was not going to fulfil. More tellingly, she once said that she really would like to have been a film director because of the total control they exercised, a glimmer of things to come in Peggy's own life.

She was already reading scripts for, among others, the producing managements H.M. Tennent and Linnit and Dunfee, as well as for the producer Peter Daubeny and for Edward Sutro. She said that she also read for directors whom she knew, such as Murray Macdonald, who directed James Bridie's *Daphne Laureola*, which was presented by Laurence Olivier's production company and which Peggy often talked of having recommended. The eponymous role, played by Edith Evans, is a character with whom Peggy empathised – a bright, intelligent yet lonely woman caged by a 'saviour' millionaire husband and by the expectations of society.

Peggy earned £3 a week from the manager E.P. Clift for reading plays and meeting the authors if required in order to help them rewrite their plays. If the play did not suit Clift but Peggy liked it, she would offer this service to the playwright without being paid. It was during this period that she became critical of, and increasingly angry at, the way in which the agents represented their clients, whether it was the inadequate manner in which the script was first presented to a manager or the poor follow-up She came to know the agents' taste and soon operated her own priority system whereby she put scripts from certain agents at the top of her reading pile and others at the bottom. As she unconsciously began to formulate her ideas about what being a playwrights' agent should mean, she even voiced to Edward Sutro in 1952 the notion that she might become one, although she did nothing to further the thought and, indeed, rejected it as impractical.

The idea took on a reality, however, one weekend a year later at Stockett's Manor, Edward Sutro's 15th-century country house in Surrey where Edward and Joan Sutro held what amounted to a regular salon for theatrical folk. Peggy was a guest on one occasion in 1953 along with Dorothy and Campbell Christie, who, following the success of *Grand National Night*, had always shown their plays to Peggy first. Sutro and the Christies put the idea to her that she should become an agent with their financial backing and with the Christies as her first clients.

Peggy felt that she did not want to invest her energies in the kind of conservative plays the Christies wrote and, without saying this, declined. They pressed her and cited the successes of that year, such as their own *Carrington VC*, *The Bad Samaritan* by William Douglas Home, or *Trial and*

Error by Kenneth Horne, all of which Peggy had recommended but for which she had not been paid any commission. Peggy agreed to think it over. She was modest about her own ability to operate in that world and anxious at the prospect of running an office which would entail responsibility for the livelihoods of other people – both the staff and the clients.

She told Sutro and the Christies that she considered agents to be parasites. When she was running Q, she had been offered a play in which the heroine was an agent. She turned down the play because, in her mind, no heroine could possibly follow such an unattractive profession. Her suitors insisted that she would be different. Finally, aged 45, Peggy changed her mind and agreed to give it a try.

The impulse to take the plunge came at a time when disillusion with her emotional and professional life had coincided at a new low mark. Despite the hesitation and trepidation, taking the decision represented a moment of self-assertion and the triumph of character over circumstance. Becoming an agent was a risk, yet it was a risk worth taking because it offered her a future that she could define and into which she could channel all her energy. She saw it as a way of withdrawing from other people into her own world in which she could be independent and in control. It would allow her to remain in the theatre but on her own terms. It might also earn her a meagre living, but that was of minor importance. More significantly, becoming an agent would allow Peggy, if lucky, to make intimate contact with talent, and that was the prospect that eventually fired her.

Supported by plenty of advice from well wishers like E.P. Clift and Cyril Hogg of Samuel French, the well-known publisher and licensor of plays for the amateur theatre, Peggy set about establishing herself as an agent in the autumn of 1953; while she investigated the business side with Edward Sutro, premises were found by Campbell Christie within what was known in the theatre world as the 'Golden Neighbourhood,' that is in the vicinity of the Garrick Club, the favourite watering hole of the profession's self-proclaimed leaders.

Peggy was to set up her agency in Goodwin's Court, one of the oldest alleyways in the City of Westminster, lying between St. Martin's Lane and Bedfordbury. Goodwin's Court first appeared in the rates book in 1690 as Fishers Alley and many of the buildings dated from then; bomb damage in World War II had led to some refurbishment in period style. Peggy had two small offices situated on the first floor of No. 14, renumbered in the early 1960s as 14a. Below her was a coffee shop, owned by the building's landlords.

What delighted Peggy most was the fact that her office was located in a converted brothel. She shrieked with laughter whenever she recalled being sandwiched between two remaining prostitutes. (She was told in jest by a lively local council officer that should her business not succeed, the building could always revert to its former use.) Peggy not only understood the historic connection between theatre and prostitution – and, as if constantly to remind her, one of the buildings at the end of Goodwin's Court is called Nell Gwynne House – but she also felt at home there because, to her, agents were pimps in any case. She enjoyed playing with the metaphor; she was the strict *madame* indeed, and her clients were the gentlemen callers – and they were overwhelmingly male – who would leave after a satisfying visit with a lighter step and brighter eye. She would sometimes inject a sharp note of reality by telling, without naming names, of a very famous actor who lived nearby and from whose flat emanated the screams of guardsmen being whipped. A few sentences later Peggy would casually mention, *à propos* of nothing, apparently, and without judgement, that among the part-time residents of Goodwin's Court was numbered Michael Redgrave.

Given its location it was not surprising that Goodwin's Court had strong theatrical associations; no 1 was the Masque Book shop and home of the Curtain Press, no 7 was used after the war as workrooms for the Old Vic, and other offices were frequently occupied by theatrical companies, usually managements and agents. These were to include Oscar Lewenstein Plays Ltd., Linnit and Dunfee Ltd., Theatre Projects, Knightsbridge Productions, Bill Freedman Ltd. and Larry Dalzell Associates Ltd. Peggy particularly valued Goodwin's Court later on in her life because it remained quite unlike 'office land' and was free of traffic, being only wide enough for pedestrians – 'a tiny oasis,' she described it, 'rather like an off-shoot of Oxford or Cambridge'.

The lease on the premises was initially held in the name of Campbell Christie, but it turned out that he thought he was only vouching for Peggy's credibility. He was furious when he discovered the real situation, and refused to co-operate any further on securing the future of her office. He insisted the lease was changed after it had run for three months. Luckily the landlords agreed to Peggy taking on the seven-year lease in her own name, even though she had no money in the bank. Technically, as lease-holder, she was now subletting the premises to her agency. If the firm were to close, she would have been personally responsible for the lease. Aptly, it is thought that the cellars to the building once served as a debtors' prison.

Campbell Christie and Edward Sutro asked friends to help with donations of chairs, desks and a typewriter. One piece of furniture that arrived at this time, her chaise longue, was to gain notoriety through her sexual liaison with Eugène Ionesco. She acquired it from Elizabeth Agombar, the resident designer at the Q Theatre who was leaving there and could not take all her belongings with her. Peggy agreed to a price of £2 for the dilapidated but genuine Victorian article but, as far as anyone knows, the money never changed hands.

Peggy began working as a full-time agent on her own behalf a couple of months before Margaret Ramsay Ltd. was officially incorporated on 16 December 1953. Peggy had taken advice from D. Pexton, an income tax expert, on setting up the firm, and on the role of directors, shareholders and herself in relation to the board.

The company records report that the first meeting of the directors and shareholders was held on 4 January 1954 at the Jermyn Street offices of her accountants, Pexton, Goodley & Co. Those present, along with Peggy and D. Pexton, were Campbell Christie, Dorothy Christie, Edward Sutro, Dr. Roderick, Mrs. Roderick (Bill Roderick's parents), and Tomasine Clay, Bill Roderick's aunt and a rich, aspiring playwright who was married to the chairman of the Cambridge University Press. Peggy was appointed managing director and company secretary, and Campbell Christie was made chairman. Dorothy Christie, Edward Sutro, 'Tommie' Clay and, in his absence, Bill Roderick were the four other directors. The share capital was £2,000, which comprised £500 from the Christies via their firm Camdor Plays Ltd, £250 from Sutro, £200 each from Dr. and Mrs. Roderick, £250 from Bill Roderick, and £100 from 'Tommie' Clay, all paid for in cash. Peggy had £500 shares free. She was paid £7 a week plus expenses.

E.P. Clift tried to persuade Cyril Hogg to buy shares. Hogg was sympathetic, and said that he would do his best to send her clients and publish her authors, but he could not become a shareholder because he was already a board member of the largest literary agency, Curtis Brown. Clift wanted to purchase shares but Peggy refused. She told Sutro it would be fatal to have 'a management in with us, as other managements would imagine that Clift got first choice of plays – which he certainly *will not* – and he knows it. He has promised to send us everyone he can.'

In the first year of operation, the agency earned £196 and was left with a balance of only £242. The share capital was raised in January 1955 to £4,000, £3,050 of which was paid up. The original shareholders increased their investment, and a new shareholder, Swedish agent and manager Lars Schmidt, put in £250.

Schmidt, who was soon to marry Ingrid Bergman, was an important figure on the international theatrical scene. His wealthy father had sent him to the United States, where he met influential theatre people like

Rodgers and Hammerstein, as a result of which he became the main representative in Scandinavia of American musicals. He also moved his offices to Paris, which greatly increased the scope of his operation. Peggy had read for Schmidt when Charles Fenn had been his London representative, but she and Schmidt had not previously met. Peggy was to supply many of the English plays that he went on to produce.

Oddly, at the same time as Schmidt bought in his money to the agency, Peggy declined another offer to buy shares, this time from Toby Rowland, who came to her office bearing a cheque already made out to her. Rowland was an American manager whom she came to know well; he had come to England in 1949 and decided he wanted to stay to work in the British theatre. He returned with a work permit and became a permanent resident, eventually obtaining UK citizenship. Peggy helped him on his first London production, of *The Desperate Hours* by Joseph Hayes, which occurred in 1955, the year he tried to buy the shares. Peggy applied the same principle to Rowland as she had done to Clift – no managers as shareholders – whereas Schmidt was deemed acceptable because he was based abroad.

Lars Schmidt joined the board in January 1956 when 'Tommie' Clay left. Clay had shown little interest in the firm after giving initial support and had suggested that the Christies had let her down as a shareholder by not writing the successful play which had been promised to make the agency profitable. (When the would-be commercial hit finally arrived in 1956, a thriller called *The Touch of Fear*, directed by Jack Minster and produced by E.P. Clift at the Aldwych Theatre, it was unable to fulfil the promise and flopped.)

The second year of operation saw the agency's earnings double. Its expenses had risen too, though not by much, and the balance remained stable at £248. Welcome as the increase in income was, it soon became clear, however, that more capital would be needed if the agency were to survive. Peggy was anxious at any increase in the firm's capital, mainly because she did not welcome what she saw as growing pressure on her to be commercially successful, yet she had no option but to find another supporter willing and able to part with some cash. She turned to the composer Clifton Parker, an occasional client of hers who was earning a reasonable living from his many film scores (later to include *Sink the Bismark!*), and whose chamber opera *Aucassin and Nicolette* she had directed in 1951. Parker agreed. He bought £650 worth of shares and joined the board. Peggy always said that without his intervention the firm would have had to close.

At the outset, Peggy knew that she always wanted to be independent. The original investment in the company, however, was not provided in the form of loans but by shareholding, thereby preventing a simple repayment to the original backers, and, on the advice of the accountants, the agency was incorporated in such a way that ultimate control lay with the investors. Peggy had to agree to having a board of share-holding directors simply to obtain the money to launch the agency, but her aim was one day to buy back the shares and be in complete control of the firm.

She had little in common in terms of taste with most of the directors, particularly the Christies. They were not keen on the new intellectual drama to which Peggy was attracted and which implicitly undermined the type of play they wrote and the type of theatre for which they wrote. They were primarily concerned that Peggy did not upset anyone, especially authors whose plays she might reject, and that the agency did not go into debt, despite the fact that Peggy had assured them that in such an eventuality they would be protected as the agency was a limited company. Other than expressing such general worries, the directors – fortunately for Peggy – did not bother her much. She sent them an occasional list of plays that she was dealing with, and they received the annual balance sheet. A couple of times a year in the very beginning of the agency's life Peggy would ask Sutro and the Christies their opinion of a 'well-made' play that she felt she might have judged too harshly.

The first years were difficult. Peggy never expected otherwise. She kept the daily situation from the directors for fear that they would wind the agency up. For instance, in both 1956 and 1959 there were moments when she came very close to the end, with only a couple of hundred pounds between her and ruin. She had to contemplate sacking the staff but told no one, kept going and survived. Earnings improved, and she kept a tight rein on expenditure.

It was only in 1963 that she was able to buy back the shares from the other directors and achieve her ambition of becoming independent. Campbell Christie died a few months later. Some days after the funeral, there was a knock on Peggy's door. It was Dorothy Christie. According to Peggy, she was in shock yet also curiously elated. She told Peggy that in his will Campbell had left £4,000 – a substantial sum then – to a woman whom Dorothy had never met, let alone heard of. Peggy, as it happened, knew that the mystery woman was Campbell's lover. The wronged widow jubilantly announced, however, that she had just come from the churchyard where she had danced on Campbell's grave. 'At last,' thought Peggy, 'a spark of life.'

Chapter Three

Opening Gambit

'When I first became an agent, Margery Vosper
[also an agent] said to me that a play was like a racehorse
and that its chances of success were similar to those
of a punter sticking a pin into a list of runners.
I so disagree with this assessment.
I think that survival depends upon talent.'

MARGARET RAMSAY Play Agent — this was the nomenclature inscribed on the firm's headed notepaper and on a wooden plaque in the office, deliberately distinguishing Peggy from the more commonly used term 'literary agent'. She had picked up the difference while she was a freelance reader. The scripts she liked most, and which were put to the top of her pile, often came from A.D. Peters, who styled himself as a 'play agent', whereas the scripts that she did not like, and which she put to the bottom of her pile, came from those who called themselves 'literary agents'. The description she had chosen was to the point and carried a punch. Peggy needed both qualities herself – and more – as she launched herself upon the theatrical world in what might be regarded as a foolhardy if not reckless manner.

Here was a woman setting up an agency on her own who had no experience of business methods or of selling any commodity, let alone plays. Furthermore, her agency had as yet not one playwright on its books, yet Peggy was striving to survive in what to her taste was a dramatic desert.

The world Peggy found herself in was the world of showbiz, but it was run like a gentleman's club; there was a code of conduct, decency and convention were honoured, and one's word counted. The sovereign of this dominion was the manager Hugh 'Binkie' Beaumont and his firm, H.M.

Tennent, with its star-studded costume drama and glittering first nights, which were society occasions of high fashion reported as news events in themselves. The brief flowering after the war of the poetic drama of Eliot and Fry had faded, and British playwriting, although by no means dead, was in the doldrums; the Royal Court revolution was still two years away.

Although Peggy had a great deal to learn about the agency business, she was determined from the outset to carry on in her own way. This was gradually to set her apart from the other agents, none of whom was the dominating figure that Peggy was to become. More vital to her than business know-how was the ability to appraise talent. The Christies described Peggy in a radio broadcast at the time as 'the best judge in this country of an unperformed play'. Peggy could not understand what the fuss was about. To her, reading an unperformed script was easy; she could not see why so many other people, particularly directors, apparently found it difficult. Spotting talent, she believed, was easy too; the problem lay in its scarcity and whether or not the people who had the talent also had the character to use it properly.

'I can see that the real headache is going to be saying "NO" to so-so plays,' she wrote to Edward Sutro while setting up the agency in late 1953. 'All of ours *must* be salesworthy, so that we can build up a first-class reputation.' She told him that it needed courage to tell an author that a play was bad. Nevertheless, if that were necessary, then that was what she would do. She would strive to send out to managers, who were potential producers of her clients' plays, only scripts that she thought were good. She recognised that there could be a tension between what was good and what was salesworthy, but, as an agent operating in a commercial world, she firmly believed that talent would be rewarded if correctly handled; theatre was not a lottery if talent were put first.

As was common practice in Britain, she decided to represent her clients without their having to sign a contract tying them to her firm. 'One can't create in captivity,' said Peggy. She also refused to act the predator, although clients did come to her from other agencies. She wanted to capture writers by her magnetism rather than by openly luring them to quit their current firm. Agents setting up for the first time or forming a new company would often write around to clients of existing agencies in an attempt to poach them, and it was routine to find agents attending try-outs of plays by new writers ready to snap up the unsuspecting scribes. Peggy did neither and thought both practices despicable. 'I can't tout for work,' she wrote somewhat pompously. 'The author must want to come to us – this isn't arrogance but its opposite – humility.'

She also organised herself differently from other agencies. They tended not to specialise in theatre – it would hardly pay the bills – and to run separate departments each dedicated to the various media, e.g. fiction, film, radio and theatre. Being on her own precluded this possibility but, more importantly, Peggy did not wish to pursue such a route. She wanted to look after all the work produced by her clients, treating them as one whole talent not to be chopped up into different compartments.

Peggy hired a secretary called Diana, who worked mornings only and was the daughter of a general, which Peggy thought would impress the clients. While Diana answered the telephone and typed up Peggy's letters, Peggy cultivated a rudimentary set of business skills as she went along. She believed that 'you can't learn to negotiate – you either have a feel for it or not'. Yet she did seek advice from a few other agents, like Jimmy Wax, Harold Pinter's agent, who helped Peggy on contracts, and from a select group of sympathetic women working in other agencies, like Betty Judkins at Dr Jan van Loewen Ltd., who found Peggy very keen to learn the ropes though quite naive about the 'nuts and bolts' of the business in spite of her theatrical experience and her age. Just as other supporting activities, such as casting and publicity, offered a route into theatre for many women, it was not unusual to find women working as agents, though most of the large companies were run by men. Ironically, one woman who did run her own agency, Margery Vosper, gave Peggy a piece of advice that was exactly the same as Peggy was to give in years to come, 'If you're thinking of becoming an agent – don't'.

At the outset, a huge problem for Peggy was not only finding authors but finding any plays that she could recommend at all. Established writers would have no reason to come to her, and, in any case, she was not interested in merely processing deals for the already successful. She was animated by the prospect of discovering and nurturing untested talent, but where was she to find it?

For a short while after Peggy set up the agency she continued to read scripts for various managers and in this way kept in touch with the plays that were in circulation. She believed advertising one's services to be unseemly, and she could not have afforded to do so on any large scale even if she had wanted to. The best advertisement to her mind would be to have some plays produced and then published; managers and playwrights would see her name and address printed along with the text.

Peggy took on her challenge with extraordinary gusto, drawing firstly on her own contacts. She did not see herself in any sense as trail-blazing. In the context of 1954, she had modest expectations. The scripts that she came across, the managers whom she could approach, the outlets that were available and the taste of the audiences all militated against a radical approach.

It is hard to give accurate details about the number of plays and playwrights that the agency handled in its early days. Comprehensive records do not exist. In the absence of Peggy's requiring a writer to sign a contract with her, an author's name only appears in her ledgers to indicate a business transaction, even if Peggy had been representing the author or the play for some time previously.

From the available data, it seems that in the first two years she managed to get a dozen plays produced on stage, as well as at least five on radio and one on television. She also secured a few options, by which managers paid a sum of money to allow them the opportunity to produce a play within a specified period of time. By the end of the third year, 1956, twenty-two plays had received stage productions, six plays had been broadcast on radio and five on television, and eleven plays were under option.

In several cases, mostly writers living abroad, Peggy did not personally know the authors of the plays; her relationship was simply a business one, and she often represented only one of their titles. There were no more than half a dozen writers at this time with whom she had a relationship that went deeper and further. Either through flattery or forgetfulness, or a mixture of both, she told several of them that they had been her first client.

The very first play that Peggy represented was a one-off for her. It was a children's fairy tale, *The Heartless Princess*, written under the pseudonym of Franklyn Black by an actor friend from her wartime touring days, Frederick Bartman, who became nationally known for his role in the TV soap *Emergency Ward Ten*. Peggy had helped him write *The Heartless Princess* before she became an agent – she had invented some of the plot and a few of the characters. It opened at the Grand Opera House, Harrogate, in December 1953. The agency did not take any commission on the royalties because Margaret Ramsay Ltd. had not been registered yet, and Bartman had made the initial contact with Harrogate himself. Subsequently, Peggy had the play published by Samuel French, to whom she sold half the amateur rights for £50. (This was a method whereby Cyril Hogg at Samuel French helped Peggy in the early days of the agency. The £50 would go to the writer, minus Peggy's commission. Hogg arranged the lettings to amateurs, which Peggy would not normally undertake in any case, and they divided the commission earned on them equally.) *The Heartless Princess* played the following Christmas at the Library Theatre, Manchester, and at this point the agency did take its 10% commission. This was the standard rate that agents took off the gross amount an author earned, which could be a royalty of box office takings or a fee paid for various rights in the exploitation of the play.

The very first playwright whom she personally championed was Leo Lehman, who won the first bursary awarded by the Arts Council to a playwright. Like Bartman, he also knew Peggy from the days before the agency. Lehman had escaped from Poland in 1939 and was interned in Spain before arriving in England with his father. The Polish ministry had given him a grant to attend Southampton University where he began to write. Peggy first met him while she was reading plays for E.P. Clift. One of them was *Home and Continental* in an earlier version called *When in Rome*. She replied direct to Lehman, saying that, although it was not a play for Clift, it was a play that she would like to help promote. It was given a try-out performance at Windsor before being sold to Sheffield. Peggy had also arranged a reading of another of his plays, *Farewell to Faustus*, for the First Stage Society at the Institute of Contemporary Arts. It was directed by Frank Hauser and had Irene Worth in the cast.

As soon as Lehman heard that Peggy had become an agent, he left the agent he was with and joined her. His *Home and Continental*, a semi-autobiographical comedy satirising the English character, was the next of her plays to have a production after *The Heartless Princess*. It opened in Sheffield in April 1954 and was the first play to earn her money at the box office.

Peggy worked hard for Lehman. She introduced him to Peter Zadek, who directed *Who Cares?* at Q, and to Frank Dunlop, who directed *The Innocent Volcano* at Guildford. She sold several of Lehman's plays to television as well as getting him commissions in the medium. He was a playwright of ideas and soon found there was more interest in his writing in German television than in Britain. By the mid-1960s he was concentrating on his work abroad, yet ever thankful to Peggy for her decisive help in getting him established.

The next of Peggy's plays to reach the stage in her first year was another script that she had read before setting up the agency: *The Wooden Dish*, written by the American writer Edmund Morris. Presented by E.P. Clift at the Newcastle Royal, it was directed by Joseph Losey, who was trying to settle in England, having left America in 1952 to avoid appearing before the House UnAmerican Activities Committee. A painful and harsh play set in Texas, *The Wooden Dish* concerns a woman who has to care for her father but who wants a chance to live her own life and has to decide whether or not to put him in a home. Peggy recalled that she bullied

Morris's American agent to allow the play to be seen in England; it was proving difficult to get the play produced in the States and an English production was a lot cheaper. Peggy was not to benefit financially from this advocacy; she had to forego any commission because the play had already been sold to an American management, which, under pressure from her, agreed to lease it to Clift. But she was shrewd enough to realise that, if it were successful, she would earn as much in terms of an enhanced reputation as she would be losing in missed commission.

With a high quality cast led by Wilfrid Lawson and Joan Miller, the production transferred to the Phoenix Theatre in London and marked Peggy's West End début as an agent. Yet, despite being hailed as one of the most exciting plays to be seen in London, it ran for only seven weeks. The capital was sweltering in a heatwave and, at first, there were not many takers for a serious drama. Word of mouth on the production was good, nevertheless, and audience figures began to climb just as Lawson decided to leave the cast in order to earn more money in another show, which H.M. Tennent was to produce at the same theatre. Without Lawson *The Wooden Dish* had no West End future, although Peggy managed to sell it subsequently to twenty reps, for which she did get paid. She also sold the play in several countries abroad as well as to Samuel French, BBC radio, and Australian radio. The money was paid into an American account, ready for any future work that she might have in the US.

American plays were a valuable source of income for Peggy in her first years. Rosemary Casey's *Late Love*, for instance, was a huge success in Liverpool and played more than two dozen reps. Other plays from America that Peggy represented included *Faster, Faster* by William Marchant, *Rashomon* and *Anatol* in versions by Fay and Michael Kanin (brother of Garson), the very English *Come on, Jeeves* by Guy Bolton and P.G. Wodehouse, *Lamp at Midnight* by Barrie Stavis, which was directed by Tyrone Guthrie at Bristol, Madeleine Davidson's *Unfinished Portrait*, *Ulysses in Nighttown* adapted by Marjorie Barkentin, and *A Trip to the Bountiful* by Horton Foote (who won an Oscar for his screenplay of *To Kill a Mockingbird*). As it turned out, Peggy became Foote's producer too. She had to organise a British and Irish tour of *A Trip to the Bountiful*, which included finalising the dates, contracting the actors and arranging the transport of both the cast and the set when the original producer disappeared to Italy.

On these American deals, Peggy took 5% commission, half the normal amount, and in the process made many useful contacts, such as with agents like Miriam Howell, who gave Peggy several plays early on. Lars

Schmidt and Toby Rowland encouraged agents they knew in the States to send plays to Peggy for representation in Britain. There was traffic, too, going in the opposite direction. Peggy used these contacts to build carefully her firm's earnings abroad. When she sold plays to the US, she sold them one by one, using at first a different agent for each play and returning to those she liked later. By not tying herself to a single representative, she retained flexibility and independence. She also came to extend her American network, which included many of the leading American agents of their day, such as Toby Cole, Harold Freedman, Lucy Kroll, Flora Roberts, and Leah Salisbury. Peggy had a particular affinity for the redoubtable Audrey Wood, who was Tennessee Williams' agent. Peggy once said to a client that Audrey Wood 'is the only one I like of the great pantechnicon agents,' to which the client replied, 'not so much a pantechnicon, more a juggernaut.'

Whenever Peggy visited New York, it became the custom for Wood to book her into the Algonquin Hotel, famous as a literary haunt and situated opposite the Royalton where Wood lived. Its elegance suited Peggy, who had a rather snobbish distaste for many things American, although she found her trips to the Big Apple re-charged her batteries. 'Isn't New York wonderful,' she once wrote. 'Walking through those great canyons with skyscrapers towering up on either side by day or by night is marvellous.'

The last of Peggy's plays to be staged in her first year was a comedy by Rex Frost called *The Jolly Fiddler* (subsequently re-titled *Small Hotel*). Frost hailed from Tooting in south London. He had worked as a waiter at the Savoy and at Claridge's, had been a hotel manager with his wife Nancy in Dar-es-Salaam and had run a hotel in Brighton before taking a job in British Rail's Restaurant Car department at Euston in order to write. The play, not surprisingly, is set in a hotel and tells the story of staff resistance to the owners' plans to pension off the head waiter.

Peggy had read the play for a management called ReandcO and had recommended it for production but did not know whether they had actually produced it. On becoming an agent, she wrote to Frost, who had no agent, asking about the fate of the play and offering to send it out to managers 'not as an agent but as an admirer'. He replied that she could be both. The play, directed by Murray Macdonald, whom Peggy knew from her acting days, was seen at the Royal Court, Liverpool, in autumn 1954 at the start of what was hoped would be a pre-London excursion. In October 1955 it did indeed transfer to the West End, playing until the end of January. The *Observer* critic Kenneth Tynan wrote: 'I count this play and

The Pajama Game among the most original I have ever witnessed, in that they both deal with people at work'.

Small Hotel was Peggy's top earner in 1955; excerpts were shown on TV. Peggy believed much of its success was due to its star Gordon Harker, to whom both she and Frost had reason to be thankful. Frost had been having a serious problem with his bank manager, and the agency had been badly in need of cash. If the play had not succeeded as it did, neither Frost nor the agency might have remained solvent. Though the play was revived for a tour in 1977, and Frost was still sending plays to Peggy in the 1980s, he produced nothing else that she promoted.

In the early years, obtaining plays was a random business. Peggy was usually pleased to receive scripts from any source, although the plays that were landed on her by the Christies were sometimes a mixed blessing. There was an increasingly apparent divergence of taste between them and Peggy, and it was embarrassing for her to have to resist their recommendations. She could hardly refuse, however, when they offered her their own first success, a 1935 play called *Someone at the Door*, which she took over from the Curtis Brown agency. It did not succeed this time round, however. Edward Sutro also brought her scripts, by writers like Nigel Balchin and Barbara Bingley, and came back from his trips abroad with foreign plays that he thought might interest Peggy.

In 1955 she asked the Arts Council of Great Britain if it had any new plays it could pass on to her because she was being approached by so many eager managers wishing to produce new plays that she had none left to offer. The reply was negative. She told the Christies and Sutro that she knew she expected too much from writers and that she protected the managers too much, with the result that she could not find enough good scripts to sell them.

'They imagine I'm holding out on them,' she wrote, 'which I am not. Also, I tend to have rows with them, as I am strictly on the side *of the author*, and the managers like you to play *their* game. This is OK when one has authors with really outstanding talent, as the managers HAVE to come crawling, but for the average play they might well try and pay me back. The rows don't last long, but they all think I'm terribly tough, as I WON'T renew their options if they don't bother to cast the play and put it on . . . I still foolishly dream that I shall get half a dozen authors . . . of genius and thus say to hell with the slack managers!'

Radio proved to be a good outlet for Peggy as well as an important source of writers, recommended to her by radio drama staff at the BBC. In her first year as an agent, Peggy represented five plays that were broadcast on the Third Programme, *The Wooden Dish*, *Late Love*, *Judas Iscariot*, a verse play by David Bulwer-Lutyens, and two translations by John Holmstrom, of Büchner's *Danton's Death*, and Pol Quentin's *La Liberté est un dimanche*. In addition, Peggy represented Selma vaz Dias, an actress she had known from the Q Theatre and the First Stage Society, who was commissioned to adapt Jean Rhys' *Good Morning, Midnight*.

The Büchner script was one of the first that Peggy read on becoming an agent. She remembered that she did not sleep at all that night. 'It is the most *wonderful* play,' she said and 'one that I admire extravagantly.' She offered the play to Peter Hall when he was running the Arts Theatre in 1955, and repeatedly pleaded with him over the years to stage it, when he was in charge first of the Royal Shakespeare Company and then the National Theatre. (He finally did, in 1982, when it was presented at the NT's Olivier Theatre in a marvellous production directed by one of Peggy's clients, Peter Gill, in a version written by another, Howard Brenton.) The original radio production, directed by Reggie Smith, had an extraordinary cast, including Selma vaz Dias, Joan Littlewood, Ewan MacColl, Walter Hudd and Donald Wolfit, with whom Peggy struck up a strong relationship 'at long distance' through many extended telephone conversations. She was pleased when later Wolfit took the lead in two plays that she represented, *A Stranger in the Tea* by Lillian and Edward Percy and Bill Naughton's *All in Good Time*.

Her main contact in radio in the mid-50s was the radio drama script editor Barbara Bray, who, along with Donald McWhinnie in the same department, was an innovative force in the medium. Bray recalled Peggy as being the only agent she knew who was 'positively disposed to new things and looking to the future'. They shared an interest in French and other mainland European writers as well as in new home-grown talent. Peggy respected radio and many of the people working in it, such as the producer and writer Alfred Bradley, whom she briefly represented.

Peggy always said radio dramatists did not need an agent; the BBC either does the play or it does not, and if it does, it offers a standard contract that allows little room for manoeuvre. Nevertheless, initial payments could be negotiated, and Peggy did. She had a tussle at first with the BBC over representation of Pol Quentin, whom she had met in London in 1953 when he asked her to act as his agent in England. The BBC, however, said it would only deal with the representative of the official Société des Auteurs, to which all French writers have to belong and to which all their royalties are paid. Peggy argued that French writers were free to choose their own representatives abroad and won the right to act for Quentin.

To Peggy, radio had a value because, where plays were concerned, it was writer-centred. It had offered a platform to much first rate writing talent. 'Pinter,' she said years later, 'is still a radio man whatever else he tries and in some respects so is Beckett, who loves radio above all. Arden, too, is best on radio.' Many of Peggy's clients, most notably Rhys Adrian, John Arden, Caryl Churchill, and David Cregan, wrote major work for radio.

In the newer medium of television, of which Peggy was distrustful, she nonetheless placed several of her clients, such as Leo Lehman, Alwyne Whatsley, who wrote adaptations, Margery Sharp, and Michael Cahill. She also managed to have excerpts from her clients' stage plays broadcast as well as small-screen adaptations of their plays. Much to her surprise, a round-up in 1958 of the year's television highlights mentioned six plays that she represented.

She came to know the TV world quite quickly and disliked the fact that she could not intervene in it as directly and effectively as she could in the theatre. Her feelings for the medium were heavily influenced by the people she found in charge of TV drama production. She was prone to having rows with 'the men in suits', whom she mostly regarded as dim-witted bureaucrats with little feeling for art or talent. She did not think they took writers seriously enough and, in particular, were dangerous for young authors, to whom they offered seductive commissions, tempting them before they had experienced life and thereby destroying their creativity. She recognised that writers, like actors, had to work in several media to earn their living because theatre generally did not pay enough to support them, but this did not diminish her distaste for what she saw as the equivalent of an artistic sausage machine.

Peggy thought television diverted attention from the stage and fed back nothing to her or to her writers. 'My God, how difficult it is to write a good stage play and how comparatively easy it is to write for TV,' she would say. She felt the 'little box' destroyed attention after an hour and could not handle complex things 'in one go'. Television let writers off the hook because they did not need passion to write for it. Theatre was an arena for imaginative discourse allowing for and stimulating a multiplicity of individual responses. Television inherently stifled imaginative debate and its human connections, she believed, thus reducing the possibilities of individual interactions.

Despite her misgivings, Peggy did not entirely scorn TV, especially when it came to certain writers, such as Alan Plater, for whom she saw it as a means to find his voice and identity. She took television seriously enough to phone clients after seeing their plays broadcast so as to offer comments on their work. When she set up the agency she did not own a television set but did, at least, feel the need to buy one in order to learn about how plays worked in the medium. It was only in future years that her authors were to play a leading role in its development, yet even then she remained a sceptical, although influential, figure.

As for film, it was a world that lay even more of a distance away from Peggy's immediate reach. Although she did arrange a film commission in her first year (which came to nothing), it was a few years before she really came to grips with the cinema and, even then, she never really enjoyed it. She only ever felt properly at home in the world of the theatre.

*

'One of the basic problems for playwrights
is to make the ordinary extraordinary,
and the extraordinary ordinary.'

'We have made a lot of progress,' began Peggy's summary to the agency's directors of its first year of operation, 'and certainly a number of admirable contacts. Against this we have had no "luck" of any sort, but in a way I think this is far better that we should begin the really hard way ("hard" is right!).'

None of the directors had an inkling of how hard the beginning of the agency had been for Peggy personally. She did confide, however, in John Holmstrom, who became a close friend and to whom she revealed a different picture to that of the public Peggy, which was all boisterous clamour and bubbly enthusiasm. Such was her state that, after a particularly emotional outburst, she wrote to Holmstrom: 'My noisiness is a kind of despair and is like the ink thrown out by the octopus to defend itself. I am aware of everything, but it's now as if the machine is out of control and the only time I am myself is when I am alone.' She wrote him that at the time when she finally made the decision to become an agent 'it was so painful to see the sun shining that I had to draw the curtains of my room and could only venture out after dark.' She had seen the agency as a way of retreating into her own world and had expected it to be 'a kind of backwater, a quiet oasis. As soon as I began, I realised that it was exactly the opposite – if you only knew how I had to screw myself up each morning to face people, the dread of each step on the stairs for fear they are coming to me, the inward alarm at each telephone ring.

Peggy

'As the day progresses I feel nearer and nearer to hysteria – I *dread* every visitor, and the fact that I can't escape, and am never prepared. Now I've started this thing, I can't stop till I make enough money to hire someone to run the office entirely – then I will simply read the plays and tell the person what to do, and only see people by interview – that is if I survive that long! . . . I adopt a hard, grinding ruthlessness to get me through . . . People are *always* a strain – I never seek them out . . . People . . . to me . . . are a poison or irritant.'

She said she felt like 'a dog, like a female slave' and confessed to a lack of self-confidence. On the plus side, she at least felt that she had conducted herself with a strong sense of honesty and truth. 'I really don't care a damn about what people think of me, as I can live quite alone, and in actual fact do, for I have no one in whom to confide or who cares enough to understand. This isn't asking for sympathy, I don't need it, and I have books and other things which can fill my life completely.' In fact, her main companion at this time seems to have been her cat, which she called Rattigan.

Holmstrom, however, was someone with whom Peggy did like to spend time. She had become a victim of his talent – to use her own words – as soon as she read his translation of *Danton's Death*. He comments that it could not have been his talent alone that interested her. 'We amused each other and had lots of fun. It was a lively, noisy relationship full of laughter.' They went to plays, films and art galleries together, and discussed art and life in the most open, intimate and intense way. In the manner of the English public school system, as friends they referred to each other as 'JH' and Ramsay, not John and Peggy. Holmstrom had left Cambridge University in 1951 and, rather than following his father into his steel manufacturing business in Sheffield, was working as a BBC radio announcer when he first met Peggy.

He recalls himself as being a virginal creature from the North to whom Peggy played the Colette role of older woman of the world, teaching him how to feel. They did not have a sexual relationship, although she encouraged him to talk about his emotional and sexual feelings. He describes himself as being 'a chaste and totally non-genital boy-lover who lived happily in a dream world of his own creation.' Peggy was strongly attracted to his obsession; it fitted her cult of passion, though she was disappointed by his physical abstinence.

'I feel neither friendship nor "sex" for you,' she wrote to Holmstrom, 'but an odd kind of affectionate "passion" which is rather uncomfortable . . . What I cannot bear for you is that you should *miss* anything. You may laugh, and I can't explain it, but I passionately want you to live up to the hilt. This isn't curiosity, I don't really want to be "told" anything, but it would be wonderful to know that you were living, as it were, in affirmation, and not in negation.'

She added a postscript. 'I don't "love" women, but I'm moved by someone's voice, a turn of the head, an expression. I could so easily fall in love with so many women, simply because I *see* them, I allow them to move me. I permit myself to be stirred. This is what you are not doing. You must try and look at everything as if for the first time, you must stretch your feelings out towards them – not asking for anything or wanting anything for yourself, but letting yourself be entangled in their thoughts and moods, for their sakes, as it were, with a sort of benevolent curiosity which has nothing to do with getting anything at all out of it.'

This approach chimed with Peggy's attitude to plays. It was not a yearning for the exotic, which was too obvious to be of genuine interest, but rather a searching for the extraordinary in the ordinary, something magical in the mundane. She thought that good writing revealed this reality behind the facade. By way of example, she quoted to Holmstrom Rattigan's *The Deep Blue Sea* (a play in which Peggy happened to find extraordinary echoes of her own life): trapped in a barren marriage, a woman in her mid-30s is crucified by an intense passion for another, much younger man who is her emotional and intellectual inferior.

'Where Rattigan was so wise was to take an *ordinary woman* – and an Englishwoman at that – and show her clearly under the strain of obsession. And this kind of obsession is far more potent and dangerous than mere drug-taking or the other vices.'

She supported her view with another example, this time taken not from a play but from her own observation of an everyday occurrence. 'Yesterday, in a bus, I saw a man with a pretty and *very* ordinary young woman. And near them I saw a young girl, very plain, the kind of young girl this man would never look at twice. But how extraordinarily foolish of these men to be taken in by these pretty good-time girls, when there were these quiet, plain girls full of extraordinary possibilities of feeling, due to their secret dreams and imaginings. I think someone should write a play on a plain young woman who fulfils herself through dreams. And the astonishment of the young man if he were to allow himself to become entangled with such a nature.'

Holmstrom did write a play, *Quaint Honour*, under the pseudonym Roger Gellert, but it was a play of a different kind. A senior boy at a public school seduces a junior, and they enjoy sex off-stage. The play is humorous and portrays the relationship as happy rather than tragic, which would have been more in keeping with the times. Peggy discussed *Quaint Honour* at length with Holmstrom and was keen to see it performed. As all male homosexual acts were illegal, the play's only chance of production was under club conditions. She knew the owner of the Arts Theatre, Campbell Williams, well and believed that he might be interested. With Peggy's support, he had been trying unsuccessfully to persuade Henri de Montherlant to let the Arts stage *La Ville dont le Prince est un Enfant*, a partly autobiographical play about love of priests for boys in a seminary. (Montherlant did not grant permission for the play to be performed until 1967.) Williams accepted *Quaint Honour*, which was produced at the Arts Theatre Club in May 1958, directed by Frank Dunlop. Kenneth Tynan called it 'the most honest and informative play about homosexuality that has yet been performed in England'. Some reviewers reacted with the expected bile, but there was no great scandal and the play was quickly forgotten. Years later, with the advent of the gay liberation movement, *Quaint Honour* was re-discovered and was published in 1985 in a volume of gay plays. This gave the play its due place in the history of gay drama, though Holmstrom, himself a keen supporter of gay liberation, says that he had no intention of proselytising.

Not long after the first production of *Quaint Honour*, Holmstrom's friendship with Peggy cooled when she found that he was engaged in another platonic relationship, with a female colleague at the BBC. There was even talk of marriage, at which Peggy became abusively jealous. Holmstrom did not marry, and the following year he came to work for Peggy. He subsequently became Peter Hall's script adviser at the newly-formed Royal Shakespeare Company. This was followed by a stint as the *New Statesman*'s drama critic and then as its TV critic. When Holmstrom wanted to escape the confines of journalism, it was Peggy who suggested he set up in business as a boys' outfitter. She invited her clients to make an investment in the firm, alongside her own. After that, Peggy's and Holmstrom's lives took separate paths, although they kept in touch. The shop, Colts, became a surprising success before falling foul of a monetarist influence. Holmstrom returned to the BBC and worked for the rest of his professional life as a Radio 3 presenter. In 1996 he published an encyclopedia on boy actors in the cinema.

Holmstrom remembers a bizarre episode in 1978. 'I was looking through some old papers and chanced on a document in Peggy's writing, dating from 1960, formally presenting me with 10% of her shares in Margaret Ramsay Ltd. I rang Peggy in high good humour, asking her if she had any recollection of this, because I certainly didn't. To my surprise, far from being amused, she reacted with panic, denying that she had ever written such a thing and almost accusing me of forging it. When I sent it to her, she had to agree that she must have written it, but had no idea why, any more than I did. She said it was obviously without legal value, but insisted that I sign a waiver or disclaimer, drawn up by her solicitors, in return for the token sum of £500. Not wishing to quarrel, I agreed. I felt her behaviour had been as ungenerous as her original impulse – whatever it was – had been generous.'

For a while, Holmstrom was the focus for Peggy of an important Cambridge network, which had at its head Holmstrom's best friend Tony White, a charismatic actor who had originally introduced him to Peggy. Following graduation, White enjoyed two successful appearances in the West End before joining the Old Vic company, but then decided to quit the theatre. Peggy's Cambridge connection also embraced four young men who would become distinguished figures in the British theatre; the directors Peter (now Sir Peter) Hall and Peter Wood, and two clients of Peggy's, the designer Tim O'Brien and the director John Barton, whom Peggy represented as an adaptor. The network quickly expanded to take in a subsequent generation that included John Tydeman, future head of BBC Radio Drama, and two more clients, the television playwright Ray Jenkins and the director Richard Cottrell, whom Peggy represented as an adaptor/translator.

Although she was self-taught in things that mattered to her, like the arts, Peggy had a tendency to be impressed by intellectually bright people with a formal education. She craved the injection of such new blood, but, at the same time, she was wary of the academically trained, having abandoned university life herself, believing the ivory towers inhibited proper emotional expression. Her smart young men had to earn their spurs in the harsher world beyond the cloisters.

When Peggy started the agency, Holmstrom helped her out in the office on a loose rota arrangement, as did others, like Tony White. One such helper was another friend of Holmstrom's called Robert Peake, who had worked as an assistant stage manager at Q on a production in which Peggy had appeared. He was running the Cockpit Theatre in Westminster, where he had worked with its founder Ann Jellicoe, who had just left to become a teacher at the Central School of Speech and Drama.

During his time helping out at Goodwin's Court, Peggy asked Peake to read a few plays, including one that Edward Sutro had just brought back from France which was in English. Peggy had read it immediately and was enraptured by it. She told Peake that he should produce it at the Cockpit.

The play was Samuel Beckett's *Waiting for Godot*. Peake declined on the grounds that he would not be able to do it justice.

Peggy did not represent Beckett but she did campaign on his behalf. She sent the play to the Arts Council's drama officer and recalled receiving a rude reply in which the play was described as drivel. An apology did come later. She felt that in some way she owed Beckett her support. In the early 1950s she had read and been spiritually sustained by what fiction of Beckett's she could lay her hands on. There was never a new play that she was as passionate about as *Waiting for Godot*. It shook her to the core and haunted her.

This was not the response elsewhere. Val Gielgud, the head of BBC radio drama, commissioned a report on the play, which was negative, and subsequently rejected *Waiting for Godot* for broadcast. The stage rights had been bought by director Peter Glenville and manager Donald Albery. They intended to produce it together but were having great difficulty with casting. The play had been turned down by leading actors such as Alec Guinness, Michael Hordern and Ralph Richardson, and it seemed possible that a London production might not, after all, be forthcoming. To compli-cate matters further, the Lord Chamberlain's Office, through which all plays to be performed in public had to pass for approval, was objecting to passages in Beckett's script. This ranged from minor emendations that he eventually conceded (the Office wanted 'warts' to replace 'clap', for example) to major changes that he resisted, such as the deletion in the final moments of the play of the stage direction which calls for Estragon's trousers to fall about his ankles.

The play travelled through various hands before it found a home. Albery approached Oscar Lewenstein, who thought of producing it with Ronald Duncan, but they, too, failed to find the cast they believed was necessary for the play to succeed. Glenville then pulled out, leaving Albery without a director.

By chance, events suddenly fell into place very quickly. Albery happened to see a production at the Arts Theatre in March 1955 of a play called *South* by Julien Green, which was directed by the 24-year-old Peter Hall. Albery was impressed by Hall, who, after leaving Cambridge University, had become the director of the Oxford Playhouse before mov-ing to the Arts as an assistant and, in January 1955, its artistic director. Albery approached the theatre's owner Campbell Williams, who sent the play to the producer Toby Rowland for advice. Rowland in turn asked Peggy, who had just helped him choose and cast his first London production. She supported the idea of the Beckett play being presented at the Arts and being directed by Hall. Williams agreed and Albery proceeded.

Once Peter Hall had agreed to direct *Waiting for Godot* Peggy introduced him to Beckett's other writing and helped him find out more about the writer, including getting him to read the novel *Watt*. The delays and uncertainty surrounding the play's future kept Beckett away from London, although Hall managed to talk to him on the phone. Peggy and Hall were anxious that audiences would not know enough about Beckett's intentions to be able to appreciate the play. They were proved partially right, even though the production, which opened at the Arts on 3 August, 1955, turned out to be crucial in gaining Beckett international recognition.

Peggy, by chance, played a crucial part in that too. At the interval on that opening night, she found Harold Hobson, the influential theatre critic of the *Sunday Times* and a noted Francophile, looking depressed. He was not having a good evening. She spent the interval at his side enthusiastically describing the merits of what seemed to him a very peculiar play. She told him she did not want him to give the play a poor review, believing it to be a major work and feeling that Hobson had a reputation to uphold as a fine critic of French drama.

The next day, Hall discussed with Peggy the notices in the daily newspapers. Hall and the cast emerged reasonably well, but she and Hall felt Beckett had been derided. Peggy told Hall of her conversation with Hobson and urged him to send a copy of Beckett's novel *Watt* to Hobson, who, she was sure, would be sympathetic. She telephoned Hobson to discover that he was of a mind to view the play positively, although he had not liked it. Hall remembers that when Campbell Williams told him that *Godot* was to be taken off at the end of the week, he pleaded successfully for a stay of execution at least until after the Sunday notices had appeared. Hall's account may not be entirely accurate, though he stands by his memory; in contrast, Kitty Black, Beckett's London agent at Curtis Brown, said the run was sold out every night.

Hobson's review, nevertheless, proved important. He wrote that Beckett had 'got it all wrong . . . But he had got it wrong in a tremendous way.' Hobson's critical engagement with what he called 'the real McCoy' continued in his column the following week, when he described the play as very funny and referred to *Watt*, a copy of which had been delivered to Hobson via Peggy. The other critical power broker, Kenneth Tynan in the *Observer*, also wrote encouragingly of *Waiting for Godot*. He said that the play made him rethink the rules of drama. He pronounced himself a 'Godotista'. Together, Tynan and Hobson ensured that it was a play that had to be seen.

Peggy

Waiting for Godot duly transferred to the West End where, in spite of the production not finding favour with Beckett, who had finally come over to London, it consolidated the play's celebrity status and helped establish *Waiting for Godot* as one of the key plays of the 20th century.

Peggy, however, knew that Beckett's reputation did not depend on her intervention, nor that of any individual, and she never claimed this. Whenever she recounted her *Waiting for Godot* story it was never in a spirit of self-aggrandisement. Peter Hall acknowledges his debt to her over *Waiting for Godot*, the success of which opened the way for his appointment as the director of the Shakespeare Memorial Theatre and his subsequent creation of the Royal Shakespeare Company.

Peggy met Beckett in London and Paris and remembers attending some Royal Court rehearsals of *Happy Days* when he was present. Mostly her relationship with him was carried out on the telephone. He was the opposite of the excessive 'boyo' Irish character that she had disliked when she was acting in Ireland, and this made her even more fascinated by his background, just as she was conscious of how important her own childhood environment had been in shaping her. When she discovered that one of her clients, Thomas Kilroy, had lived in the same part of Dublin where Beckett had been raised and knew people who knew the Beckett family, she interrogated him about the world in which Beckett grew up.

Peggy revered Beckett and idealised him both as a writer and as a man. She found his writing enormously consoling and, though she did not regard it as optimistic, nor did she believe it to be in the slightest 'anti-life'. It is easy to imagine him being physically and emotionally appealing to her. They were of a similar age – he was two years older than her. She admired his generosity of spirit and his asceticism, and she was drawn to his courage, to his formidable sense of self and to his charismatic, caged passion. He worked hard, was utterly dedicated to his art regardless of personal success and shunned publicity. He was a Nobel prizewinner yet he could talk to a stagehand about ordinary matters like horse racing or cricket. Like her he was an exile and a stoic.

Yet, as if in the belief that wanting something too much would lead to its loss, she did not pursue the relationship as much as she would have liked. And, as if to prove her own resolute independence and lack of sentiment, or possibly as an echo of his own practice, one day in the early '80s, when she happened to come upon his letters to her, she simply threw them all away.

Beckett also provided the link between her and the American director Alan Schneider, who became the chief interpreter of Albee, Pinter and

Beckett in the US. In the mid 1950s, she found Schneider a job and a flat in London, and they remained close. He told her he had read *Waiting for Godot* and wanted to meet the author. Peggy obliged and Schneider saw Hall's London production of the play in the West End with Beckett. Schneider described her as 'my philosophical friend and bubbling, informal agent . . . who knows more about scripts and, perhaps, theatre people than anybody alive.'

Beckett had chosen France as his domicile, and to Peggy France meant culture. There was something of both the snob and the romantic about her love of French style; her favourite French literature – *Madame Bovary*, Maupassant short stories, Zola, Proust, Gide, de Montherlant – all exuded precision and class. She pronounced one of her most beloved words, obsession, in the French manner, with four beats and each 's' hard and sibilant. When she visited Paris with John Holmstrom they stayed at the Hôtel Massena and used to visit a restaurant which she nicknamed The Whores because a special table was kept there for the local prostitutes, complete with their own napkins. Later on, she preferred to book into the Hôtel de Deux Continents in the rue Jacob, where, she believed, Beckett sometimes liked to stay. It was situated in the intellectual Left Bank area and was a neighbour of the bookstore where the Olympia Press of Maurice Girodias had its offices. Girodias had published *Watt* as well as what he called his 'd.b.s' ('dirty books'), such as *The Story of O*. Peggy said that she used to visit the writer William Burroughs, who was also published by Olympia, although she was not a creature of this bohemian milieu even if her taste predisposed her that way.

Peggy would keep in touch with developments in French theatre through clients such as Pol Quentin, Lars Schmidt, one of Peggy's directors, and Eric Kahane, brother to Maurice Girodias, who translated Joe Orton and Harold Pinter into French. Such contacts were especially important in the 1950s when Paris was a vibrant centre of European and international drama; it was host to a spate of influential Brecht productions that heralded his triumphant sweep across the continent; Anouilh and Giraudoux plays were the toast of London; and, above all, it was the home of what became labelled the Theatre of the Absurd, embracing in all their difference the likes of Adamov, Genet and Ionesco as well as Beckett himself.

It was the French who took the lion's share of a decidedly European repertoire in Hall's 18-month reign at the Arts Theatre, during which time he used to discuss with Peggy his choice of play: as well as *Waiting for Godot*, there were plays by Jean Anouilh, André Obey and Eugène Ionesco.

The Lesson was the first work of Ionesco's to be seen in Britain. Hall had been introduced to his plays by John Whiting, after he had directed Whiting's *Saint's Day* at Cambridge University.

Peggy admired Ionesco's ability to make something special out of the everyday and contacted Donald Watson, the translator of *The Lesson*, in order to meet Ionesco while he was visiting London. She was interested in talking to him about what was happening in Paris and about theatre in general. The result of their meeting, however, was that Ionesco asked her to represent him. His current agent in London was the representative of the Société des Auteurs, Dr Jan van Loewen ('the evil doctor', Peggy dubbed him), who was a very dry stick in comparison. Ionesco's contractual arrangements were always complex, partly because his sense of mischief made him want to move for moving's sake, and partly because he suffered from a self-fulfilling paranoia, which meant that he could not trust people for long. Fortunately for Peggy, she had to deal with the obliging Betty Judkins in order to sort out representation for Ionesco's next production. This turned out to be at the Arts Theatre again, a double-bill of *The Bald Prima Donna* and *The New Tenant*. Its success triggered a surge of interest in the playwright who, championed by Peggy, quickly became the latest artistic fashion.

The double-bill also launched the career of its flamboyant director Peter Wood, who was a friend of John Holmstrom's and a regular visitor to Goodwin's Court. Wood had entered the profession after Cambridge by becoming a stage manager on a Binkie Beaumont hit production, *Seagulls over Sorrento*. When Peter Hall went to the Arts, Wood took over from him at the Oxford Playhouse, which then closed through lack of funds, and Wood went to Worthing. Peggy sent him the two Ionesco plays and persuaded Campbell Williams not only to let Wood direct them at the Arts but to appoint him as Hall's successor. During Wood's time there, he also directed *The Iceman Cometh* at Peggy's instigation; later, he was famously to direct John Whiting's *The Devils*, Muriel Spark's *The Prime of Miss Jean Brodie* and Joe Orton's *Loot*, all written by clients of Peggy. 'She was wonderfully encouraging,' says Wood. 'She could see without prejudice and could judge things on their merits. She had a tremendous understanding of people. You were in awe of this because you believed she knew more about you and about others than you did. She had what I call "cognisance in depth", which was wildly impressive. She was dazzling.'

Wood remembers discussing with Ionesco *The Bald Prima Donna*, which was inspired by his idea of English music hall, and Ionesco's belief in the relationship between this tradition and the ideas of Antonin Artaud.

Peggy and Wood took Ionesco to a music hall so that he could judge for himself. When they arrived, the show was not quite what they had expected. A 'naughty' pseudo-French revue, then still just in vogue, was playing, and it contained scenes of nudity, which worried Ionesco because he had brought along his young teenage daughter. The poster outside the theatre had pasted across it the legend 'Ne Le Manquez Pas' (don't miss it). This tickled the absurdist and he agreed to try the show, on the understanding that they would all leave if it became unsuitable for his daughter. Inside, they settled down, recalls Wood, until a voice over the tannoy announced 'and now we proudly present Desirée, a model straight from Paris'. There was much whispering between Ionesco and Peggy. He asked if this was the nude act, and on hearing her reply in the affirmative, he rose from his seat and ushered his daughter into the aisle.

Peggy and Wood dutifully followed toward the exit. During the group's departure, the lights came up on stage to reveal a tableau entitled 'Desirée Goes Shopping'. Desirée at this juncture was not shopping but standing stock still on a mattress like a sculpture, wearing nothing but a hat, a handbag and a pair of shoes. Ionesco, the future Academician, suddenly decided that the tableau was in fact a form of high irony and it was, therefore, perfectly acceptable. The group duly returned to their seats to enjoy the rest of the show, which was noticeably punctuated by the squeals of delight emanating from one of the foremost playwrights in the world.

Peggy threw herself whole-heartedly into Ionesco's cause. In 1957, three of his plays were broadcast on radio, *The Lesson* was seen at Oxford Playhouse, *The Bald Prima Donna* at Nottingham Playhouse, *Amédée* at the Arts Theatre, Cambridge, and *The Chairs* at the Royal Court. Peggy had nagged the theatre's artistic director, George Devine, to stage a play by Ionesco, and he appeared in the production, directed by Tony Richardson, along with the up-and-coming actress Joan Plowright, who was in her 20s yet playing a character who was in her 90s.

In April 1960, Ionesco's reputation reached its peak with a production of *Rhinoceros* at the same theatre, directed by Orson Welles and starring Laurence Olivier. In author, director and star, the production combined three giant egos, and quickly became a talking point beyond literary circles. On the strength of outstanding reviews for Olivier, it transferred to the West End.

Both productions brought Peggy into closer involvement with the Royal Court and Oscar Lewenstein, one of the founders of the English Stage Company who was also starting out as a producer in his own right. He had wanted to stage the world première of *Rhinoceros* but Ionesco had promised this to Jean-Louis Barrault in Paris. Lewenstein, nevertheless, moved quickly to secure the English rights from Peggy and set up the Olivier-Welles partnership. It had been difficult to tell if the production was going to be a success. There had been tension between Olivier and Welles in rehearsal and on the opening night Welles was using a walkie-talkie to issue last-minute orders. As Lewenstein recalls, 'Next day the newspapers were all raves, and we were a tremendous success, packing out the Court for the six weeks we ran there and transferring to the Strand for a further eight weeks, also a sell-out.' Ionesco was furious when *Rhinoceros* came off, due to Olivier's work schedule. It was left to Peggy to explain to Ionesco that Olivier had originally only signed up for the Royal Court run and that without him the show would not survive.

For Ionesco, there followed another double-bill at the Arts Theatre Club, London, of *The Shepherd's Chameleon* and *The Victims of Duty*, and the following year *Jacques* at the Royal Court and *The Killer* at the Bristol Old Vic. Ionesco had become a major figure in British cultural life, and Peggy liked being at the centre of the swirl; his success helped give her the credibility as an agent that she deserved. He duelled with Kenneth Tynan in the columns of the *Observer* after the critic had compared him un-favourably to Brecht. Tynan accused Ionesco of creating plays that had no purchase on social reality, to which Ionesco replied that he had renewed the language of theatre, and therefore of the conception of the world, and was more revolutionary than those who wrote about revolution. The argument was fought out in successive issues of the newspaper until Peggy persuaded Ionesco to call it off, although he had wished to fight on, believing absolutely that he was right. He even ran into trouble with the censor when he wrote a short piece about the Duke and Duchess of Windsor which had been performed privately at the Parisian home of an Argentine millionaire in front of a distinguished audience that included Salvador Dali.

The picture that emerges from Peggy's accounts of Ionesco, a Romanian-born Hitchcock-like figure living, like Peggy, in somebody else's country, is contradictory. His reputation had preceded him and when she met him she became fascinated by his personality; how could this ugly, boring, self-opinionated man create such a marvellous world on stage? He was a terribly sad, wistful, worried figure and yet he released an enormous theatrical force through the depiction of the most ordinary of events. He taught Peggy a great deal, she said, through insight into the minutiae of theatre – 'how to look at a doorknob and make a play out of it' – and he influenced many others to do the same in their own way.

She was fired by his imagination and wanted to know what made him tick. The story has it that she set out to seduce him, as if a sexual liaison could reveal a key that might unlock if not the whole truth then, at the very least, its salient points. She believed that creativity was intimately connected to the deepest recesses of the personality and that sexuality played a defining role in the process.

Ionesco was lonely and so all the more flattered to have her single-minded attention, little realising that he was actually something of a guinea pig. Whilst she bedded Ionesco, four gay friends of hers had gathered at her flat, waiting to discover the outcome and her assessment. Sexually he was very disappointing, she reported; she had not enjoyed the research. Clearly she would rather have been in bed with Beckett, they thought – better sex and more fun.

The affair did not end then, nevertheless, and many stories were generated by ensuing incidents. After the first night of *Rhinoceros* Ionesco was said to have lunged at Peggy in a taxi that was taking him back to his hotel where his wife was waiting for him. As he was about to alight, he asked in fear of betraying himself to his wife, if his eyes were shining too intensely. On another occasion after they had made love, she looked out of the window, saw that it was raining and said 'il pleure' (he weeps) instead of 'il pleut' (it is raining). He was touched because her mispronunciation had transformed what could have remained a merely physical event into a romantic one. Another time, she transformed 'il est mort' (he is dead) into 'il est moru' (he is a cod), and, when congratulating him on having written a superb play, she made the word for play (pièce) sound like the word for 'piss'. He enjoyed her attempts to speak French because verbal errors like this reminded him of his own plays.

Despite saying on camera in a BBC programme about her that she would not go to bed with any of her clients, off camera the Ionesco affair was a part of her life to which she referred openly and, unusually, by name. To the sixteen-year-old Stephen Poliakoff, on his first visit to the office, she pointed to the chaise longue and announced, in a disarmingly straightforward manner as if conducting a tour of a museum, 'that's where Ionesco fucked me.' For such younger clients the affair was to become a hallmark of her status.

Ionesco seems to have been genuinely fond of Peggy even though they both were wilful and would complain about each other to each other and to anyone else who would listen. They both had a propensity for misunderstanding others and a temper with a short fuse. Not surprisingly they were frequently at loggerheads. She called him 'cher maître' but changed this one day after a row to 'cher monstre', a compliment he quickly returned. They bellowed at each other and parted angrily. The next day he returned to her office with a gun and fired it at her. It turned out to be a cigarette lighter, which he then presented to her. She put up her hands in mock horror and screamed with delight, enjoying both the incident itself, which revealed a tantalising touch of cruelty, and the reversal of their normal roles; she generally found him humourless and it was she who by temperament was the more playfully impulsive. This was made clear early on when she welcomed him off the train at Victoria Station in a most extraordinary manner. On her way there she had popped into a shop near Goodwin's Court and had purchased a monkey mask, which she wore to the station. She thought it would amuse him. When she arrived, she put a copy of the *Times* over her face, strode purposefully down the platform, then lowered the newspaper to greet a stony-faced Ionesco, who simply said, 'Hello' as if he had not noticed that she was wearing a mask.

These two incidents, of the lighter and the mask, formed the basis of anecdotes that achieved wide currency as they were passed from client to client and beyond; in some it was Peggy who brought the toy pistol, and in some the monkey mask was turned into a pig or a cat. Whatever the detail, they formed a hilarious and enduring part of the Peggy legend.

Ionesco lived in his own world. The one inhabited by everybody else, from which he thought he was being shielded by his wife, induced in him an unsettling anxiety. Peggy came to the conclusion that much of Ionesco's writing was driven by his perception of his wife's jealousy and her guardian role, which allowed him to remain like a clever, spoilt schoolboy. Ionesco liked whisky but had been forbidden by his doctor to drink it in order to protect his liver. Nevertheless, he continued to drink; whenever his wife was nearby he would derive great satisfaction from taking a furtive nip. While he was having an affair with Peggy behind his wife's back, he in turn suffered fits of jealousy about her. He could not grasp that one of his translators was homosexual, even when told emphatically by the man himself as well as by Peggy, because he was convinced that the translator was chasing his wife. Ionesco was jealous, also, of the success of others; he would check a new book on contemporary theatre to see if his entry were larger than Brecht's. His first question on being told of a new production of a play of his would be to ask the size of the theatre. He was prone to blame collaborators, whether agents, directors, or translators, for his plays not being as successful as he believed they should be. This was another reason for his habit of breaking contracts and changing agents, as well as translators, though often he would return when the next person inevitably fell below the expected standard.

Peggy became bored with Ionesco and with his kind of surrealism. She had been titillated by the sense of fun in the Absurd and was attracted to its darker depths, but philosophically she was more sympathetic to forms of existentialism – life as a series of self-made choices in a hostile world. She was frustrated that Ionesco's sense of humour seemed incapable of reaching beyond frivolity, and she was upset by his vanity and jealousy, which she believed prevented him from developing his talent. By mutual consent, he left to join another agent in 1962, yet, although he would often rail against Peggy – and even claimed he had fired her – they kept in touch; Ionesco could not help but remain fond of his 'cher monstre'.

*

'Though I try and give back to the theatre
a little that it has given me, and try to behave honourably
to everyone I know, there is a priority which transcends everything,
and that is my unswerving loyalty to those authors
who depend upon me to work for them and keep them alive.'

Ionesco was not the only French-speaking writer who was a client of Peggy's. Coming after the Americans in number, the French speakers constituted the largest group of overseas writers whom Peggy represented, mostly for no more than a handful of titles and sometimes for only one. Among others, this group included Arthur Adamov, Fernando Arrabal, Marcel Aymé, Morvan Lebesque, René de Obaldia, Robert Pinget, Armand Salacrou, and Boris Vian. Peggy was particularly keen on Adamov for a while. They shared an interest in Jung, dreams and Büchner. Barbara Bray in the BBC radio script department commissioned a play, *En Fiacre*, and Peggy handled the contract. An exile like Ionesco and like Peggy herself, Adamov was an Azerbaijani who had been educated in Switzerland, Germany and France, where he had decided to stay. He had broken with his friend Ionesco, and they were now sworn enemies. Peggy feared that Adamov and Ionesco might meet in the office, in which case blood was sure to be spilt. In fact, Adamov's visits were more bathetic. Even more than Ionesco, Adamov was a drinker; on one of his visits to London, Peggy had arranged to meet him but he failed to turn up because he was so drunk that he had had no idea where he was or where he was going.

Peggy

In 1958, Peggy went to Paris with John Holmstrom to look for new plays; the French were leading the way in new writing. By the time they went again in 1964, it was evident that French writing was on the wane. Instead, British playwriting had been firmly established in the vanguard, just as Margaret Ramsay Ltd. had itself become renowned as the leading agency for new British playwrights.

The chief reason for this transformation in the agency's fortunes lay in the unprecedented success enjoyed by a client whom she first came across in early 1955, thanks again to Barbara Bray. She took Peggy to dinner to ask if she would help the author of a play that the BBC was soon to broadcast. He had already had a few plays transmitted, but Bray felt he had become stuck as a dramatist. Peggy read the play and found it 'fearfully topical'. *The Last of the Wine* looked critically at a group of people who professed a concern about the nuclear bomb but who did nothing except worry about themselves. Peggy judged the dialogue to have 'a quite exceptional high standard of wit and style'. Most importantly, there was one scene that convinced her that the author, R. O. Bolt, could become a stage playwright.

After the play had been broadcast, Peggy wrote to Bolt, who was then an English teacher living in Somerset. As it happens, another agent had heard the play on the radio and wrote to Bolt as well, promising him fame and fortune. In contrast, Bolt recalled, Peggy's letter, self-typed yet barely decipherable, 'breathed a sort of half-commitment to my plays, which, if they got a great deal better, might be fit to pass on to one of the West End managements.' She told him that he could and should write for the stage, an idea he said he had not thought of until he received her letter. He had only seen a handful of plays and his image of the theatre cast it as 'impossibly glamorous and bohemian.' Peggy said that she would be pleased to act as his agent and wished him good luck.

Bolt was over the moon. At a time before John Osborne 'when one's name was either Rattigan or it was not', as Bolt put it, he was in the enviable position of having not just one but two London agents offering to represent him. He was not sure why – instinct? intuition? – but he chose Peggy and was invited to see her in Goodwin's Court. He scraped the fare to London, made his way from his home in the village of Butleigh to St. Martin's Lane and then turned into the little airless alley where her address was to be found. Feeling absurdly anxious, like a country bumpkin adrift in the big Smoke, he climbed the stairs to the office. As he made the ascent, he was welcomed by the smell of coffee rising from the coffee shop below, a sensation he subsequently always associated with the West End.

The office, according to Bolt, 'was about twelve foot square, the spare furniture was comfortable but not too comfortable. Peggy had a staff of one. This was a secretary enclosed in an even smaller room, about nine feet by five. Peggy was entrancing. The full untrammelled flower of the theatre.' He remembered her as being incisive and tough; she singled out the one good scene and repeated the advice she had given him in the letter. 'Write without ceasing and with enjoyment,' she implored, and sent him away having made him feel tremendous and important, with no clear idea of what had actually happened to him beyond a dream of his name in lights.

Bolt took to his writing with renewed fervour. He was so stimulated by Peggy that he wrote too quickly, and she lashed each one of his efforts. 'She wouldn't even show them to a stage manager let alone to a producing manager,' said Bolt, 'and she was right.' Peggy was also keen to launch Bolt properly because she believed that he had a special talent. She had learned at the Q theatre that the first steps one takes with a new play are extremely important and that whatever happens to a play afterwards happens in relation to that initial move. She told him that she only wanted to show potential producers a play to which they would be irresistibly drawn, and she would not put her name to a play which she did not believe in. Her high-mindedness impressed the tyro writer, who swiftly returned to work.

He turned three of the rejected scripts into radio plays and kept on trying to achieve his new-found ambition of writing a play that Peggy would judge worthy to be produced on stage, all the while cursing her for setting him on this new course only to obstruct it with her repeated rejections. She became in his eyes the barrier to his success, forever castigating his failure while whipping him on to further and greater efforts. He decided at least a dozen times that each play he was working on would be his last.

Robert Bolt, who was born in Sale, Manchester, in 1924, was an ex grammar school boy whose mother was a teacher and whose father ran a small furniture shop. They were not well-off, had modest tastes and had brought up Robert and his elder brother within a clear-cut Methodist morality. Robert had not enjoyed his formal education. He had drifted into doing menial tasks in an insurance office and then had attended Manchester University for a year, where he joined the Communist Party, before doing national service in the air force and the army. He returned to Manchester University from 1946-1949, left the Communist Party, got married and, in 1950, after a year at Exeter University, became a teacher in the west country, first at a village school and then at the expensive Millfield school in Somerset. He had been writing since childhood but had not tried plays until, in his first term as a teacher, he had to write a nativity play. He had then followed this up with his work for radio and some stories for children's TV.

Structurally, his writing was a mess, and Peggy addressed this short-coming with determination and force. She would describe plays to him as being like the arched ceiling of a cathedral and set him writing exercises to improve his skill. She advised him to read plays by superb craftsmen, like Ibsen or, nearer home, Somerset Maugham. Bolt remembered that in his many discussions with her he had to tolerate a lot of waffle, in which she might trail through any subject that came into her mind, from a disquisition on the wonders of the South African landscape, which Bolt had seen for himself during a wartime visit, to a synopsis of Gide's *Journals*. Bolt said that it was well worth being patient because the circum-locutions usually had a bearing, even if not immediately obvious, and suddenly she would throw up a hard truth from which he always learned a huge amount.

Peggy had considered trying to place *The Last of the Wine* with a management. She had contacted an old acquaintance, the director Murray Macdonald, to ask if he would approach a friend of his, Fay Compton, to see if she would be prepared to repeat on stage the performance she had given in the play on the radio. When it became clear that her work commitments would not allow this, Peggy had already switched her attention to wresting from Bolt a stronger new play that she could send out. It did not take long to arrive. *The Critic and the Heart* was delivered in the late autumn of 1955. She had lent Bolt £95 to help him while he wrote it and had told him to repay the sum by that Christmas, but, with two children in his family, he was unable to do so. Peggy, however, did not mind; she had the richer reward of a play that demonstrated Bolt was beginning to realise his potential.

The Critic and the Heart centres on the housekeeper sister of an eminent painter, who has devoted herself to his service, and her relationship with an art critic, who is writing the painter's biography, and a young couple, of whom the pregnant wife is likewise working to support her artist husband. Bolt's play implies that life is to be lived, that a balance needs to be struck between duty and desire, and that self-sacrifice, even if heroic, can be damaging: everyone needs to be very careful how they treat each other. Its subject of responsibility for talent and female sacrifice for the sake of the male artist touched Peggy closely.

The play, which Bolt modelled structurally on Somerset Maugham's *The Circle*, had its faults, chiefly, Peggy thought, that it tried to cover too much ground. Yet she desperately wanted Bolt to have the experience and encouragement of seeing a play of his produced professionally, as this would be the best way for him to learn about stagecraft. Peggy told her board that *The Critic and the Heart* was not going to be a money spinner but a reputation maker. In order to prove that her judgement was sound, however, she had to find a management that would agree to produce it. Peggy worked hard to elicit interest in the play and was extremely frustrated by the eighteen months it took to achieve a production. She did manage to arrange in late 1956 a non-professional showing of *The Last of the Wine*, directed for a single Sunday night performance in central London by Stephen Joseph, but this proved to be Bolt's only theatre experience since he had begun writing prior to the eventual appearance on stage of *The Critic and the Heart* in March 1957.

Peggy sent the play both to contacts whom she knew well and to those whom she did not know at all. The Arts Council drama officer dismissed the play, as she recalled, with 'scorn and contempt,' John Perry at H.M. Tennent Ltd. read it twice before rejecting it, and the Royal Court, where the newly formed English Stage Company was just about to open its first season, turned it down graciously. Peggy's dream was to be a part of this new enterprise. She knew of their interest in new plays and had heard that Peggy Ashcroft, her favourite choice for the play's female lead role, was due to join them soon. It had been read by John Osborne, then an actor in the company, whose play *Look Back in Anger* had been announced for the opening season and was already in rehearsal. Osborne was helping out as script reader. With a diplomatic reply that might have come from the practised hand of a veteran literary manager, he wrote that the play was not quite suitable, although there was much of interest in it, and that he would rather like to meet the author. Peggy replied very straightforwardly that Bolt 'is not really yet capable enough of rewriting this play. What we want is to get this one on so that he may learn more about the theatre, about which he knows nothing at the moment.' She wished Osborne well for *Look Back in Anger*, 'which we are looking forward to enormously.'

To Campbell Williams at the Arts Theatre, who was prevaricating about whether or not to accept *The Critic and the Heart*, she wrote: 'If a play is good enough for you to want to do it, you should do it. If it isn't, you shouldn't . . . I'm not only pleading for my play, I'm pleading for *every* play which is good.' To Toby Rowland, she cajoled: 'I am sure that this author is going to be "*something*" – if you *knew* how he has grown since I first met him six months ago.' She also sent the play to three leading actresses, Edith Evans, Flora Robson and Elisabeth Bergner, a friend and neighbour (and included in the package to Bergner Joyce's *Exiles* and Beckett's *Watt* simply because she thought they would interest her).

Eventually the play was taken up by Jack Minster, an old colleague of hers whom she had helped enter into management and for whom she used to read scripts. He and his partner E.P. Clift bought a six-month option on the play but then let it expire. Peggy badgered Minster to renew it, which he did. She put him in touch with the Oxford Playhouse, which had recently come under the management of Meadow Players run by Frank Hauser, whom Peggy knew from the Q theatre. Hauser had a policy of staging new British plays and new translations of European plays with which he was to become an important figure in the regeneration of the British theatre. Hauser wanted Bolt's play in his new theatre and Peggy was glad to let it go there instead of to the Arts.

Peggy developed a good working relationship with the Playhouse through its manager Elizabeth Sweeting, a former lecturer at the University of London. Sweeting had changed the direction of her life by switching to theatre and had been the first manager of the Aldeburgh Festival, which she had helped to found. As often happened with Peggy, friendships began with a battle during which mutual respect was established; in this case, it involved Bolt's royalty deal. Peggy told Sweeting that she had looked after Bolt for two years without making any profit but did not mind because she deeply respected his talent: she argued that this was a good reason to improve Bolt's percentage of the box office take. After all, the play 'concerns our responsibility to talent,' said Peggy, adding in mitigation, 'Bolt could become one of the big playwrights, if he learns, develops and *survives*.' Hauser and his solicitor Laurence Harbottle became involved in the negotiations, and a mutually satisfactory compromise was finally agreed.

When *The Critic and the Heart* finally opened, with Margaret Vines and Robert Eddison leading the cast in Minster's production, it was the fourth production in a row at the Playhouse written by clients of Peggy's. If Bolt's fortunes had rested on *The Critic and the Heart*, however, then perhaps neither he nor Peggy's agency would have survived. The play sank and did not 'come in' to London. She could not even persuade Cyril Hogg at Samuel French to gamble on acquiring half the amateur rights. Peggy considered the production to be old fashioned and to have perverted the content of the play. Nevertheless, seeing it on stage she felt was beneficial to Bolt, who pleased Peggy by not succumbing to the despondency of failure. On the contrary, having *The Critic and the Heart* produced provided an enormous boost to Bolt's confidence and self-esteem, and he always retained a fondness for the play.

Survival, however, was about to become a worry of the past, although neither Bolt nor Peggy knew this at the time. She had managed to sell his next play before *The Critic and the Heart* had even opened, and *Flowering Cherry*, as it was called, changed both their fortunes.

One of the things that Peggy had told Bolt was that his plays were all splendid talk but too little action. As an exercise she had suggested that he 'write a play about inarticulate people, which blows up dramatically because they are unable to talk about their predicament'. She advanced the idea that his subject matter might be an old man fantasising. The result was *Flowering Cherry*, which was inspired by Bolt's hated spell of working for an insurance company; Jim Cherry is an insurance company salesman who dreams of owning an apple orchard in Somerset. His marriage is falling apart, he drinks too much, and he turns to lying and thieving after he loses his job, a fact which he cannot bear to admit to his family. His wife Isobel offers to sell their London house in order to buy a fruit farm and make the dream come true but Cherry has so lost his self-respect that he refuses; he would rather keep the dream as a dream and not face the fact that his life is a lie. Isobel, eager to escape ruin herself, finally leaves him; Cherry is left alone with his dream fading.

Peggy saw Cherry as a prototype of millions of ordinary office workers who live in the city but who really want to live in the country. She thought that this longing for nature was very English.

The first draft that arrived showed Bolt's growing command of play construction, although she was not convinced that he had fully resolved several of the problems he had set himself, particularly in his attempt to wrestle with a poetic style at the end of the play. The solitary Cherry tries to bend a poker across the back of his neck, as if testing his natural powers. He finally succeeds as the rear wall dissolves into light and the audience see an orchard in blossom. Cherry crashes to the floor and lies still, his life extinguished, as the orchard disappears.

Notwithstanding her private criticisms, Peggy believed that *Flowering Cherry* would be an ideal choice for H.M. Tennent. But she was wary of sending it direct because they had turned down *The Critic and the Heart*, which, on the surface, contained more interesting characters than the current crop of a failed insurance man and his family. Peggy was no utopian visionary intent on overturning the established order. She just wanted a better quality of play to be afforded the resources at the command of the major West End managers. To further this aim, she embarked on a gamble. In what turned out to be a shrewd if risky move, Peggy sent *Flowering Cherry* before it was properly finished to the actor, manager and director Frith Banbury, who had liked *The Critic and the Heart*. Banbury was one of the major postwar directors, who had directed nine shows for Tennent's non-profit arm, Tennent Productions Ltd., including N.C. Hunter's *Waters of the Moon* and Terence Rattigan's *The Deep Blue Sea*. Peggy had known Banbury when she worked with Peter Daubeny just after the war and had sent him plays before. She respected his judgement because he had championed new writing and supported playwrights like Wynyard Browne, Rodney Ackland and John Whiting.

In the case of *Flowering Cherry* she responded instinctively to a propitious moment. Banbury had happened to call her one Monday to ask if she had any new plays that he could read over the forthcoming weekend. Bolt's draft had just arrived. She knew Banbury liked quirky plays and sent him the script. The gamble paid off. Promptly on the following Monday, Banbury phoned Peggy full of enthusiasm to direct Bolt's play and to buy the rights too. 'It was rather raw but as soon as I read it, I knew I wanted to do it,' said Banbury.

Protocol would have required Peggy to send Bolt's new play to Jack Minster, who had taken the risk with *The Critic and the Heart* and was then in rehearsal with it. Peggy, however, did not think Minster would serve either the new play or Bolt's development very well. He had taken more than a year to stage *The Critic and the Heart*, and both *Flowering Cherry* as well as Bolt needed a quicker response. She had also promised Bolt's next play to the Oxford Playhouse but told Elizabeth Sweeting that she had sent the play to Banbury on impulse and had never expected him to respond immediately. When he did, she was stuck. She minded less about jeopardising her relationship with Minster and the Playhouse than endangering her reputation as a trustworthy agent this early on in her career where it mattered most for her, among playwrights.

When Minster discovered he had been snubbed, he was furious. Peggy apologised and took all the blame. She justified her opportunism under the banner of service to the play, and, in an attempt to placate him, said that *Flowering Cherry* was not as interesting as *The Critic and the Heart*. She added: 'Over Bolt I suppose I am a bit emotional – I feel that his talent comes before anything else – I have such belief in him! . . . I shall not have anybody in the world talking to me soon, but the alternative is to play the managers' game and betray the authors. (Perhaps this is the only thing possible in the West End?).'

Peggy talked to Banbury about his ideas for a production and urged him to get the backing of H.M. Tennent in order to put Bolt in the top league. Banbury was not convinced at first. He finally agreed to try but said that, as Bolt was a newcomer, it was imperative that they could offer Tennent something attractive, like a star or two in the cast. He thought Celia Johnson would be ideal for Isobel – he had directed her in *The Deep Blue Sea* when Peggy Ashcroft had taken a break. Johnson agreed, on condition that she approved of the leading man. Top of both Johnson's and Banbury's lists for Cherry was Ralph Richardson. Peggy agreed that Banbury should fly the script to Sir Ralph, who was appearing in New York; he, too, agreed. Richardson further strengthened Banbury's hand by insisting that Binkie Beaumont, Tennent's managing director, should be approached to co-produce the play, which was exactly what Peggy and Banbury had intended. Armed with this commitment from his two stars, Banbury approached Beaumont to see if he would share the risk of pro-ducing the play, Banbury to put up half the money and the other half to come this time from the profit-making arm of Beaumont's empire. Beaumont judged the deal to be worth backing, especially as the pro-duction would mark the return of Richardson to the English stage after an absence of more than a year. An 'out of town' tour was planned prior to a West End opening at the Theatre Royal, Haymarket. The pieces of the jigsaw had all fallen into place quickly and with remarkably little fuss.

Beaumont's participation confirmed Peggy's fine tactical sense as well as offering her the perfect introduction to the most powerful manager in the English theatre. For Bolt, it was the stuff of a novice playwright's dreams come true.

Flowering Cherry was of a singular importance to Peggy and her every fibre was committed to its success. She kept a guardian eye on every part of the process. On the one hand she wrote eagerly to Harold Hobson about the play, while on the other she complained to Banbury about the pub-licity, which to her mind implied that the play concerned an incompatible old couple rather than depicting the damage done to them and their marriage by inhabiting a barren metropolis in a competitive world. She saw the production in each of its pre-London venues and wrote extra-ordinary letters to Banbury, assessing the cast's capabilities with a detached eye, weighing the play's strengths and weaknesses, defending its non-naturalistic ending as essential to its emotional need, and offering sugges-tions as to how the play might be more effectively staged.

There was much discussion over the ending, which perplexed the cast and the director. Peggy had her reservations but she liked the ending because it broke the rules. She did not try to interpret it. Its difficulty was part of the excitement and challenge of presenting a new play She supported Bolt in his arguments with Banbury and the set designer Reece Pemberton, whom Peggy represented briefly, and, offering practical suggestions, argued that the ending be realised properly as intended. She recalled a production of *Faust* from her days with the Carl Rosa Opera Company, in which a gauze had been made transparent in order to reveal Marguerite at the spinning wheel; she also cited the design of Büchner's *Woyzeck* by the legendary scenographer Caspar Neher, which had just been seen in London during a visit by the Theater am Kurfurstendamm from Berlin.

At the same time, Peggy confided to Barbara Bray that, while she was fond of the play, she did think it rather lowbrow and had higher expectations of Bolt in the future. 'I am rather alarmed,' she wrote, 'that with the stars and the grand theatre and management, people will imagine that this is a peak of a career, instead of a beginning.'

She hoped that Banbury's production would provide the launch that Bolt had missed at the Oxford Playhouse and thereby prepare the ground for better things to come. Her anxiety was the opposite of what might have been expected from a relatively new agent representing an unknown writer on the verge of a prestigious West End opening, namely that the production appeared to be a commercial success in embryo but not an artistic one. To this end, she wrote to Banbury:

'I'm taking my courage in my hands (as they say) and writing to you to tell you what has been growing inside me since I saw the play at Liverpool, and though it was wonderfully improved at Oxford, it still doesn't quieten this inner voice! It's quite baldly this: as agent for Bolt it's his career I care about, not just this one play. If I thought this play as it stood would be an artistic success and a commercial failure I would think your money well lost! But it CANNOT be an "artistic success" – the play is a straightforward play of emotion and relationship. The set is in the tradition of the modern American play and breaks no new ground, the music doesn't startle in its originality, it isn't as angry as Osborne, or as poetic as Fry and Tennessee Williams, or as avant-garde as Ionesco.'

Peggy's letter then switched to the issue of feeling, for her the key to the play. 'We must feel, that is everything. We must feel as a brute beast feels, and knows that it has felt, and knows that each feeling shakes it like an earthquake,' she wrote, quoting Maupassant. In support of her cause she went on, moreover, to quote Quiller-Couch, Tennessee Williams, Marlowe, Baudelaire and Villon (both in French), Havelock Ellis, Ovid (in Latin, with translation), Gide and D.H. Lawrence, and to cite Racine's *Phèdre*, Lorca, Verlaine, Thomas Wyatt, Heine, Propertius, Pirandello, and Ronsard.

'Can you forgive this outpouring?,' she asked at the end. 'I'm simply pleading for the maximum amount of feeling to be drawn out of the play, and every possible weapon used in order to allow the characters to reach out to us over the footlights, telling us that we are not alone in the world; that other human beings live, suffer and play the fool.' She signed off at the end of her four-page torrent – 'Next time I'll try and write a proper letter.'

Peggy copied the letter to Beaumont, which did not endear her to Banbury. He felt that her 'charming eccentricity' was dangerously close to becoming irritating interference and banned her from attending the remaining pre-London performances.

As it turned out, Johnson received terrific notices and Richardson's performance was hailed as a triumph. *Flowering Cherry*, which opened at the Theatre Royal, Haymarket, on 21 November 1957, became an immediate West End hit, playing until December the following year before embarking upon a fourteen-week UK tour. Ironically, a play which Peggy had seen as an anti-heroic and off-beat portrayal of how the average person can lose their sense of identity in an age of materialism, succeeded precisely because Cherry was played by a star who was incapable of being Mr Ordinary. Richardson had transformed the 'average' into 'the moving, mysterious, important and wonderful', in her words, and Peggy always remained thankful to him for this because in so doing he established the name of Robert Bolt.

Bolt readily acknowledged the debt he owed to Richardson, despite some worries that had arisen during rehearsals over his grasp of the lines. Bolt was also exasperated by Richardson's habit of extemporising in front of an audience. He had even disturbed the balance of the play, according to Bolt, by giving a star performance that emphasised the idiosyncratic fantasy rather than the mundane reality of the piece. Nevertheless, Bolt had learned from him an enormous amount about theatre, about timing and pace, about what worked and what did not: Richardson had brought Bolt out of his study and on to the stage.

Bolt himself received a pretty good batch of reviews, though not outstanding. Milton Shulman in the *Evening Standard* called the play 'a *Death of a Salesman* with a Clapham accent'; Kenneth Tynan, in the *Observer*, thought that 'Mr Bolt's spiky, provocative play dissolves into abject melodrama'; Harold Hobson, primed by Peggy, devoted the whole of his *Sunday Times* column to *Flowering Cherry*, and, while pointing out some of the play's faults, commended Bolt as 'plainly destined to become a distinguished dramatist.' The overnight success of *Flowering Cherry*, however, led Bolt to be likened in some quarters to John Osborne, who had been catapulted into theatrical fame the year before with *Look Back In Anger*. Derek Granger, writing in the *Financial Times*, described Bolt's 'fine sad play' as 'the best thing by an English playwright' since Osborne's.

Flowering Cherry brought Bolt the Evening Standard Award for the Most Promising Playwright, the first of twelve of Peggy's clients to win the award in the following two decades. The play's success also persuaded Bolt to give up his teaching job, a decision that alarmed Peggy at first, although she admired its boldness. *Flowering Cherry* proved to be a turning point for Peggy's agency as well as for Bolt; it was the firm's first long run in the West End, bringing in regular income, putting a new writer in the spotlight, and, through the published text, providing useful publicity for Margaret Ramsay Ltd.

It also began Peggy's professional relationship with Binkie Beaumont. They were both thoroughly practical theatre people with a streak of ruthlessness. He was a little afraid of her but admired her fighting instincts and knowledge. Peggy respected him hugely as a manager and became quite childlike when she was first permitted to call him Binkie. She praised his adherence to principle when he resigned from the board of the Royal Shakespeare Company because the publicly subsidised company had acquired a London base in the commercial West End and he did not believe it was fair competition. Peggy was always thankful for his support of Bolt yet, by the early 1960s, when he had presented Bolt's next three plays, she became anxious about Beaumont's judgement and taste. She told Bolt that Beaumont was now favouring the banal, which 'ill equips him for your progress as a writer'.

Operating at this level brought with it new strains. Peggy's attitude to contracts in general could border on the cavalier, and things could, and sometimes did, go wrong. She was distraught, for example, when she realised that the deal she had agreed with Frith Banbury for *Flowering Cherry* in New York gave Bolt worse terms than those approved by the American Dramatists' Guild. She had just posted the contract to Banbury when she realised this, so early the next morning, after a sleepless night, she rushed round to sit on Banbury's doorstep in order to explain her mistake before he opened the mail.

In June 1958, during the run of *Flowering Cherry*, Wendy Hiller replaced Celia Johnson, a change that gave rise to very bad behaviour from Ralph Richardson, who had wanted his wife, Meriel Forbes, to play the part. She did take the role subsequently, when the play went on its tour in 1959. Later that year, a New York production of *Flowering Cherry* was set up but by then Richardson was appearing in another show in London. The role of Cherry was taken by Eric Portman while Wendy Hiller returned to play Isobel. Portman, who had become an alcoholic, arrived drunk at a New York press conference called to publicise the play and, on stage, ruined the show. It closed after four performances. Bolt, who had been raised to the heights in London, was now dashed to the earth. He sloped back to England by boat severely chastened. Peggy, unhelpfully in Bolt's view, thought this failure to be salutary in teaching him the hard lesson: not to enjoy success too rapidly or too readily. There was always a price to be paid, she cautioned.

After *Flowering Cherry*'s success, Frith Banbury had asked if Bolt could be put under contract to him. Peggy rebuffed this notion imperiously; writers had to be free in order to write, and, in any case, because Bolt was developing fast as a playwright, she did not want to tie him to any one director for his future work. Banbury, nevertheless, made a sound claim to be shown Bolt's next play. Bolt was more than happy to repay him for his work on *Flowering Cherry*, so when in early 1959 Bolt finished *The Tiger and the Horse* (then called *Forests of the Night*) Peggy sent it to Banbury. Peggy was caught in a dilemma because she found *The Tiger and the Horse* rather embarrassing and self-conscious; both the story and its milieu were too intellectual and dry for her taste, yet she could not refuse to send it out, because she could see that it could work on stage.

The Tiger and the Horse – an allusion to Blake's *Proverbs of Hell* – has a rarefied Oxbridge setting and tells of a Master of a college, an outstanding astronomer turned ordinary philosopher, whose prospects of becoming vice-chancellor are threatened by his wife, Gwen, who wants to sign a petition for unilateral nuclear disarmament that is being organised by their youngest daughter's boyfriend. Gwen, unloved in the marriage, takes the sins of the world on her shoulders. She begins to crack up and slashes the college's prize possession, a Holbein portrait of the founder and his family, to which she pins a copy of the petition she has just signed. The incident jolts the Master into a degree of self-realisation; his saint-like behaviour and lack of emotional commitment has driven his wife into this state. He decides to sign the petition and share the blame for the destruction of the painting with Gwen, thereby ending his chances of promotion.

Peggy knew how important the subject of nuclear disarmament was to Bolt yet she also knew that she must tell him of her misgivings. Later, after the play had opened, he came round to her point of view. Meanwhile, Frith

Banbury had found the play fascinating and wanted to direct it. Peggy concurred. She thought Banbury's taste would be a counter to the play's shortcomings and would be an advantage in the casting. Bolt had written the play with Michael Redgrave, the epitome of the 'angst-ridden intellectual', in mind as the Master. Bolt also wanted Redgrave's daughter Vanessa to play the part of the Master's youngest daughter. Banbury knew the Redgraves well; he had directed them as father and daughter in *A Touch of the Sun* by N. C. Hunter, which happened to have been the next production of Banbury's after *Flowering Cherry*. Michael Redgrave was duly dispatched a copy of *The Tiger and the Horse* and loved it. Vanessa Redgrave, who was then appearing in Stratford-upon-Avon, also accepted. She has written that it was this play and Bolt's influence during rehearsals that awakened in her an interest in politics. Catherine Lacey played Gwen.

Rehearsals were delayed for seventeen months because Michael Redgrave was already committed to appearing in his own adaptation of Henry James' story *The Aspern Papers*, which then proceeded to run for 350 performances. When rehearsals for Bolt's play finally began, it was clear that Redgrave was going to have trouble remembering both his lines and his moves. His drinking was affecting him badly. During rehearsals, he also decided to change tack and abandon his truthful portrayal of the slightly haughty and reserved Master in favour of a more sentimental interpretation in which he would be loved by the audience. Peggy again complained to Banbury and to Binkie Beaumont, who had agreed to co-present the production, as he had *Flowering Cherry*. Peggy this time was pushing at an open door but little could be done. Redgrave, knighted the year before, was his own man.

The Tiger and the Horse opened in Brighton in July 1960 without mishap and went to Manchester where Redgrave's slow delivery added fifteen minutes to the production's running time. Against Peggy's better judgement, Bolt persuaded Banbury to leave the show alone when it visited Leeds and allow Bolt to rehearse Redgrave in an effort to put him back on the right road. Banbury obliged, but Bolt failed to make any impact. The production transferred to the Queen's Theatre in Shaftesbury Avenue on 24 August 1960 – the theatre in which Redgrave had scored a hit with *The Aspern Papers*. It received good notices but business began to drop after a few months and the production came off at the end of Redgrave's six-month contract. The decline was due partly, Bolt believed, to Redgrave's performance, which, by offering a portrayal the opposite in temperament to that which the role required, was confusing to the audience, and partly to the success of a production in the adjacent Globe Theatre.

This was not only another H.M. Tennent production: it was another play by Robert Bolt, and it became not only his greatest triumph on stage but also one of the the most successful plays of the century, *A Man for All Seasons*.

It had begun life in 1951 when Bolt had conceived it for radio, and it was broadcast in 1954. Bolt tried his hand at a television version in 1957 when Peggy advised him to re-write it for the stage. In the play, Bolt is once again fascinated by the ethical conflict between strict morality and indulgence; this time the quandary is faced by Sir Thomas More, Henry VIII's Catholic Chancellor, when the King decides to divorce Catherine of Aragon and marry Ann Boleyn. The martyr More sacrifices his position, his family and ultimately his life for the sake of his conscience.

Peggy's main influence on the play's development was not on content but on structure. Bolt had been struggling in all his stage plays with certain formal problems. The central one sprang from the tension within him between a talent for naturalistic writing and a desire to express his ideas with a sharpness and effectiveness in non-naturalistic ways. In *A Man for All Seasons* he found a balance.

Bolt discounted reports that it was Peggy who suggested the creation of the Common Man, who acts as a commentator on the story and became the subject of much debate by the critics, both for and against. 'She never told me what to write but would say things like there were too many characters for me to handle, or not enough, or that I hadn't gone far enough.' The Common Man, in fact, seems to have a mixed parentage. Peggy said that she urged Bolt to read Thomas Mann's *Death in Venice* because of the recurring narrative figure who runs through it. It was after this, she recalled, that the Common Man first appeared, a character, who, in Peggy's view, transformed the play, which otherwise was in danger of remaining an old fashioned costume drama. Bolt said that he had looked to Brecht for inspiration, having admitted that he had been rather timid dramaturgically in *Flowering Cherry* and *The Tiger and the Horse*. Bolt's overall assessment of his intention in *A Man for All Seasons* – that he tried 'for a bold and beautiful verbal architecture' – is, however, a distinct echo not of the author of *Mother Courage* and *Galileo* but of Peggy Ramsay.

Peggy played a part in several of the crucial production decisions. The first was to find a director. Banbury was ruled out because he was tied up on *The Tiger and the Horse*. (Banbury was deeply disappointed that he did not direct *A Man for All Seasons*; nevertheless, he did invest in the production.) Peggy suggested Noël Willman, a friend from the Bristol Old Vic days with whom she was now sharing the same house. Bolt met Willman and accepted the idea. Peggy and Bolt then persuaded Binkie Beaumont to sanction the choice. Willman had directed several productions since the war, including *All's Well That Ends Well* at Stratford-upon-Avon in 1955 and *The Devil's Disciple* in New York in 1956, yet he was still something of a risk.

For the role of Sir Thomas More, Beaumont was arguing for a 'heavyweight' star like Laurence Olivier to take the role. Peggy was not against stars, and upbraided Bolt for being condescending towards them, but she was aware that they brought problems and that, with certain types of writing, stars could divert attention to their own personalities at the expense of the meaning of the play. Bolt's fame owed much to stars yet his experience had not been all glowing. Michael Redgrave's availability had agonizingly delayed rehearsals for *The Tiger and the Horse*, and his interpretation had then run counter to the play's intention; Ralph Richardson had caused considerable heartache in the course of making *Flowering Cherry* a success; and Eric Portman had destroyed the New York production of that play. Peggy believed that *A Man for All Seasons* needed a brilliant actor capable of considerable emotional depth and detail who, most importantly, could work with the other characters on stage as part of the team, albeit the major part.

Peggy and Willman believed that this could be achieved by Paul Scofield, whom Willman had directed in the 1946 Arts Theatre production of Christopher Fry's *A Phoenix Too Frequent*. Peggy had admired Scofield in Willman's production and had met him when he was playing Tybalt to Bill Roderick's Mercutio at Bristol two years before that. There was a problem, however. Scofield was currently appearing with Ralph Richardson in a Tennent hit, *The Complaisant Lover*, and, therefore, strictly speaking, was not available for the new play; and Binkie Beaumont would not be too pleased if he discovered someone approaching one of his own stars behind his back. Peggy and Willman nonetheless agreed that they should try to get Scofield to read the play and then, if Scofield were interested, persuade Beaumont that he was the right choice. Peggy recalled how Willman delivered the Bolt script by hand in a plain brown envelope to the stage door of the theatre where Scofield was appearing, which, by a pleasing coincidence, happened to be the Globe Theatre, the hub of the Tennent empire.

Scofield liked the part, and so, with Bolt in full support, Willman persuaded Beaumont. Other considerations, of which Peggy and Willman were not at first aware, came into play. Scofield had already talked of leaving *The Complaisant Lover* in order to go to Stratford-upon-Avon but had abandoned that idea because it would have meant an impracticable drop in his earnings. Also, the show was coming to the end of its West End life and Scofield did not want to tour with it. Beaumont, however, held the rights to another historical drama, Anouilh's *Becket*, and wanted to avoid competing with himself. He was also conscious that competition loomed in the shape of Christopher Fry's own Henry II-Becket play, *Curtmantle*. Scofield was then offered the role of Becket in the New York production of the Anouilh play and accepted. He asked Bolt if *A Man for All Seasons* could wait. Peggy and Bolt had been in this position before, with Michael Redgrave, and were not keen. Meanwhile, Beaumont was dealing with the Royal Shakespeare Company to sort out the London dates of *Becket*, which he was going to co-present with the company at its newly-acquired Aldwych home. As it turned out, Laurence Olivier took the part of Becket in America, thereby releasing Scofield for Bolt's play, which opened before *Becket* (in 1961) and *Curtmantle* (in 1962), both presented by the RSC. Leo McKern took the part of the Common Man in *A Man for All Seasons* and design was by Motley.

After a try-out at Oxford's New Theatre, *A Man for All Seasons* came to the Globe Theatre on I July 1960. The notices were generally positive, if polite. Scofield, like the play itself, was praised for a latent power, and several critics regretted the lack of full emotional throttle. *The Times* caught the mood: '*A Man for All Seasons* is a play that has obvious weaknesses as entertainment but has dramatic integrity and quiet distinction.' Philip Hope-Wallace in the *Guardian* wrote 'it is distinguished, respectable, worth the watchful attention it continuously exacts from its audience.' Harold Hobson welcomed the fact that 'Mr Bolt writes in a style which avoids pedantry on the one hand and vulgarity on the other.' Yet he found it 'disconcerting that *A Man for All Seasons* is not more theatrically gripping.' Kenneth Tynan saw an analogy between More and the witnesses who took the Fifth Amendment before the House UnAmerican Activities Committee but unfavourably compared the play to Brecht's *Galileo*. 'For Mr Bolt, in short, truth is subjective; for Brecht, it is objective.' Bolt was roused to answer Tynan, who was subsequently allowed his riposte, grandly asserting that Bolt's premises 'expose, quite poignantly, the limitations of our Western approach to historical drama'.

This was a far cry from the roistering reception that had greeted *Flowering Cherry*. Noël Willman learned the verdict of the daily critics from Peggy at dawn the morning after the first night. 'Barely light, she stole thunderously into my bedroom with this enormous load of newspapers,' he later told Bolt's wife, Jo. "We must all remember Schopenhauer," she said, "and we must all live without hope".' Binkie Beaumont was un-nerved and talked immediately of when he might take the play off. Peggy and Willman argued strongly that he should give *A Man for All Seasons* a chance. Audiences did build but Beaumont had one eye on his plans for *Becket*. *A Man for All Seasons* came off in March 1961, three months before *Becket* opened, having run in the West End for 315 performances – 120 fewer than *Flowering Cherry*, although it became by far the more famous play. *A Man for All Seasons* failed to win any *Evening Standard* prizes, at the time the sole prestigious theatrical awards in Britain. Both Bolt and Scofield were overlooked (Bolt in favour of Harold Pinter's *The Caretaker*). Ironically, the following year both *Becket* and Christopher Plummer in the eponymous role won their respective awards.

A Man for All Seasons, however, did conquer America. With Willman directing again and Scofield making his Broadway début, it ran for 637 performances in New York, where it was voted by the critics Best Foreign Play of 1962 and picked up five Tony awards, including the one for Best New Play. It also enjoyed a successful US tour. The play was translated into dozens of languages, was sanctified a classic as a set text in school examinations, and became widely popular through Fred Zinnemann's 1966 film, which won six Oscars, including Best Screenplay for Bolt.

When *The Tiger and the Horse* had opened at the Queen's alongside *A Man for All Seasons* at the Globe, Bolt had found himself with two plays running next to each other on Shaftesbury Avenue only four years after he had seen his first play produced. He had succeeded Terence Rattigan as Tennent's 'house dramatist' and his earnings had risen from £18 a week as a teacher to £400 a week as a playwright. He had swapped his aged west country cottage with no running water, a well in the garden and an outside lavatory behind an elderberry bush for a near-mansion in west London; and he was able at last to indulge some of his expensive tastes. At the same time, with his liberal views, he became a public touchstone on various issues, taking up many column-inches in the press. In theatre circles and beyond, Bolt had become a major national figure.

Fame brought its own rewards; it also led, however, to much tension in his relationship with Peggy as their paths began to diverge. In this case, it was Peggy who was unwittingly the architect of the major cause of the strain, and paradoxically it related to Bolt's unwilling entry into a world of which Peggy was very suspicious, that of film.

It was Peggy who received the letter from film mogul, Sam Spiegel, asking if Bolt would be interested in re-writing the dialogue of a screen-play about T.E. Lawrence called *The Seven Pillars of Wisdom*. Spiegel was looking for an 'upmarket' name; Moura Budberg, a well-connected film script writer who moved in elevated literary circles and whom Peggy had heard of as a former lover of Maxim Gorky, had seen *A Man for All Seasons* and had recommended Bolt to Spiegel. On the telephone, Peggy was told that the author of the original screenplay, Michael Wilson, was a drunk and had walked off the project. Spiegel needed the script rewritten quickly, in six to eight weeks at the outside. Could he meet Bolt?

Peggy said she would ask Bolt, who was not keen on the idea of polishing up someone else's script. He had managed to attain an enviable position in the theatre world; Peggy had won for him control over producer, director, leading actors and designer, and he was earning handsomely. He wanted to consolidate his reputation by finishing the play he was working on, *Gentle Jack*. Bolt also suffered from an ingrained snobbery, which led him to dismiss films as not a serious arena for real writers. 'I was both insulted and yet I was also intrigued,' recalled Bolt. Oddly enough, while Peggy shared his view of the cinema, she was fascinated by Lawrence. The film was to be directed by David Lean, whose work she admired, and Peggy thought the discipline of a short, sharp burst of concentrated writing might be a beneficial challenge for Bolt. She persuaded Bolt to attend at least one meeting with Spiegel.

According to Bolt, Spiegel asked him to write some 'classy' dialogue, especially for the Arab characters, who needed a more exotic treatment than Wilson had provided. Bolt turned down the idea, and then Spiegel mentioned a sum of money. Bolt said no more but agreed to read the existing script, which he did on the tube on his way home. He found the script dull and in places unintelligible, and this further convinced him that he should not take on the job. Peggy read the Wilson script and was convinced that Bolt could do much better. She advised him to change his mind, but Bolt was reluctant. He telephoned Spiegel to say he was declining because of his views about the script. Spiegel replied that he could start from scratch and offered what to Bolt was so much money that Bolt, alarmed that he was out of his depth, said they should meet again, this time with Peggy present. A deal was then concluded, with seven weeks to go before shooting was due to start. Bolt said that Peggy won him double the original offer, and put the final offer in the region of £10,000 – a huge sum then – although this figure has not been corroborated by any records.

Lean was in Jordan choosing locations for the film. When Wilson, faced with demands from Lean for rewrites which he found unacceptable, said he was pulling out, Lean had no option but to let Spiegel find the successor. Spiegel had already hired two other writers to work on the film; David Garnett, the Bloomsbury author and Lawrence expert, annotated Wilson's script but none of his comments was ever used; Beverley Cross, who was to become known as the book author of the musical *Half a Sixpence*, went to Jordan as a continuity writer to provide scenes that Lean could rehearse while Bolt, oblivious of the role of these other two authors, finished his work. In Jordan, Lean himself was ignorant of Spiegel's approach to Bolt until he delivered his script.

By the time Bolt had finished the initial assignment, he had become hooked on the Lawrence film and was frustrated at the prospect of having to yield to another writer, who would finish the script with Lean on location. When he did discover the existence of the other two writers, he demanded he become the sole author of the screenplay. Spiegel extended his contract, and paid him a further £15,000 for another twenty weeks' work. In all, Bolt was to spend a year on the film. He was shipped out to Spiegel's luxury yacht, which was moored off the Jordanian port of Aqaba, to write for two months while Lean was shooting, and then he was returned to London to finish the screenplay.

Neither Bolt nor Peggy knew very much about films, and it turned out to be a bumpy ride, not only because of the exacting demands of the fastidious David Lean but also because of Bolt's temporary inability to meet them anyway, since he landed in prison before he had finished the script. Bolt was arrested in Trafalgar Square as he took part in a mass civil disobedience protest along with other members of the Campaign for Nuclear Disarmament's Committee of 100, including Arnold Wesker, John Osborne, Vanessa Redgrave and Bertrand Russell. Bolt, in common with the others who were arrested, refused to be bound over to keep the peace and was given a one month prison sentence.

Spiegel was furious because the film was already running into problems. It had always been a high risk, given that it was a film about Arab struggle, shot in an Arab country on the border of Israel, financed by Columbia, a studio which was run by leading members of Hollywood's Jewish community; now, Spiegel had news that building the remaining sets in Jordan would be very difficult. Most important, the film's budget was soaring perilously. On top of this, Bolt's imprisonment threatened to add considerably to the production costs – no script, no filming. Spiegel bombarded Bolt in prison with telegrams, pleading with him to recant but Bolt refused. Spiegel drove in his blue Rolls-Royce to Drake Hall, the open prison in Stafford where Bolt was being detained, and persuaded him face-to-face to bind himself over so that he could leave gaol and finish the picture. After serving half his sentence, Bolt signed the good conduct statement and was duly released. Bolt immediately regretted his decision. The parallel with his most famous character, Thomas More, was not lost on him: More had refused to sign and lost his head – Bolt had signed and, as Peggy rather cruelly put it, had won a fortune for every one of Lawrence's seven pillars. Bolt always maintained that he was swayed to break ranks only by Spiegel's claim that all the cast and crew had ceased to be paid because of his action and would be put out of work if he stayed in prison.

Bolt felt so ashamed that he gave some of the money he earned on the film to Centre 42, Arnold Wesker's trades union cultural project, and later donated generously to the Campaign for Nuclear Disarmament. He never forgave himself, however, for getting out of gaol while his colleagues remained inside, although there is no evidence that they held it against him. Bolt was especially wrathful when he discovered that Spiegel had been lying about the cast and crew. On the day when Bolt betrayed himself, Spiegel had already just shut down production in Jordan and was preparing to move the entire film team to Spain, where Columbia believed the shooting of the remaining parts of *Lawrence of Arabia*, as the film was retitled, would be easier and cheaper.

Peggy described the prison episode as the greatest crisis in Bolt's life. Of Spiegel, she commented: 'He has great charm but he is a real corrupter in the most diabolical way. He is the nearest thing to Mephistopheles I have ever met.' When David Lean asked Bolt to work on his next film, *Doctor Zhivago*, Bolt agreed with the one proviso that it was not produced by Sam Spiegel.

Lawrence of Arabia, which had its première in December 1962, marked a turning point for Bolt in more than one sense. The film pushed his already troubled first marriage to a point almost beyond repair. Working on *Doctor Zhivago* finished it, although Bolt was not finally divorced until 1967, a process he charted for Peggy in agonising detail. (Bolt moved in with Noël Willman for while, downstairs from Peggy.) *Lawrence of Arabia* also robbed Bolt of his self-respect, yet, at the same time, introduced Bolt to a new life style, that of the film star, and rewarded him with the means by which he could afford to live it. He moved to a secluded farmhouse in Hampshire where he enjoyed acting the lord of the manor, complete with chauffeur and silk smoking jackets. The tussle between the moral and the material world exercised Bolt for the rest of his life, and Peggy played the role of nagging conscience.

The film won Bolt a new reputation as a top-class screenwriter, although not the expected Oscar. The issue of the screenplay had become complicated by a demand from Michael Wilson, made to Bolt a month before the film opened, that they share the writer's credit. Wilson had faced this problem before because he had been 'blacklisted' in America; most recently, he had been denied a credit, and, as it turned out, an Oscar, for the screenplay of Lean's film *The Bridge on the River Kwai*, which Spiegel also produced. A clause in Wilson's contract for his work on *Lawrence of Arabia* allowed Spiegel to deny Wilson a credit for the American distribution of the film but opened up the possibility of a credit in Europe, although this too was refused. The Screen Writers' Guild, which awarded Bolt its prize that year for Best Dramatic Screenplay, investigated Wilson's claim and found in his favour. Bolt admitted Wilson's contribution to *Lawrence of Arabia* but refused to issue a statement that implied their work was of equal value. A year after the film opened, the Guild gave Wilson an identical award to the one they had given Bolt. Wilson's name, however, remained absent from the film.

Lawrence of Arabia launched Bolt on an extraordinary career; along with *Doctor Zhivago* in 1965 and *A Man for All Seasons* the following year, for both of which films he received the Oscar for Best Screenplay, it was to make him the cinema's highest-paid script writer and an internationally recognised name – a unique achievement for an English author.

Bolt could not decide whether to thank Peggy or not. They both had to cope with a culture that was alien to them and with new fortunes that made Bolt's considerable West End earnings seem modest. Peggy was shocked at the amounts because she had lived her adult life with very little money and had a strong streak of the puritan in her. In one of her first film deals, in 1960, she had been on the telephone to Rome and was told that the film in question would cost a million. 'Dollars?' she asked. 'Good gracious, no. Pounds, of course,' came the condescending reply. She was made to feel even smaller when she passed on the information to an agent in New York with whom she was negotiating, only to be told, 'Oh, it's a low-budget movie then.'

Peggy had not become an agent to make money nor to haggle over the minutiae of a contract, yet she learned quickly – and had to, because she and Bolt were now moving in the big league. She sought help and advice from her solicitor Laurence Harbottle and others. In a deal brokered by the American agent Irving P. Lazaar, for example, Bolt earned $200,000 for writing *Doctor Zhivago*. He then earned an additional $6666.66 per week for five months because the script took longer to complete than expected and the late delivery was not Bolt's fault. These were huge sums at the time and strategies had to be devised to gain Bolt the maximum benefit. He had to live as a tax exile for certain periods, and a company, Robert Bolt Ltd., was set up to arrange his income in a more advantageous way. For royalties that were earned from the stage rights of *A Man for All Seasons* a trust was established for Bolt's children. With the screen rights of *A Man for All Seasons* Peggy waited before selling in order to make a killing. They garnered Bolt $200,000 on their own, the screenplay another £50,000, and, as part of a complex arrangement, he was granted 24% of the profit after the film had recouped all its costs, a very high percentage at the time.

Peggy seemed indifferent to making money herself and disliked discussing it in private conversation, yet she did enjoy negotiating a 'deal' with tough film producers. She found their piratical verve both repulsive and thrilling, and in return she earned the kudos of being respected by some of the most powerful men in American cinema such as Dino de Laurentiis and Sam Spiegel.

Bolt's success changed Peggy's life as well as his own. She was at last able to realise her initial ambition of becoming independent as an agent. By 1963 she was able to buy out the original shareholders and at the same time purchase a production company called Amethyst Productions, which technically owned the new agency. She wanted to return to her Q days of producing and, in collaboration with Robert Bolt and Noël Willman, drew up plans for another production company, to be called MANFAS (*Man for All Seasons*), which, as well as presenting plays, would also find premises that could be turned into a social meeting place. Peggy liked the idea of creating a hub of debate and gossip, but her work for her other clients, which was becoming more exacting, and personal differences between her and Bolt over money matters meant none of these ambitions came to anything.

Their arguments over money stemmed, as ever, from Bolt's increased involvement in cinema, which was of much less interest to Peggy than his work for the theatre. With the failure in 1963 of his play *Gentle Jack*, she believed that his heart had been lost to celluloid. Peggy had a soft spot for this curious and idiosyncratic play about the pagan spirit of nature which re-united the *A Man For All Seasons* team of director Noël Willman and producer Binkie Beaumont. It had a star cast again that included Kenneth Williams and Edith Evans, who played a part, Violet Lazara, in which Peggy saw something of herself. Violet is a self-possessed businesswoman, charming but dangerously angry, by turns 'delicately gentle and shockingly coarse'; her wealth gives her power over people but it is a barren, uncreative power. Peggy thought that Violet was the 'cruellest and sharpest drawn' of Bolt's characters and liked her 'because she doesn't kid herself, tells the truth and takes her punishment without whining'.

While Peggy saw the failure of *Gentle Jack* (it confused the critics and played only 75 performances) as another salutary lesson for Bolt, saving him from the canker of self-importance, he never enjoyed his subsequent time in the theatre as he had before.

Bolt turned again to *The Critic and the Heart*. Following a revival in Dundee in 1961, he decided to rework it, and in 1967 a new version appeared, now entitled *Brother and Sister*, at the Liverpool Royal Court, presented by Binkie Beaumont. Flora Robson and Nigel Stock led the cast, Noël Willman was the director. Bolt, unhappy with the new version, resisted – with Peggy's support – pressure from Willman and Beaumont to bring the production to London. Bolt rewrote it again and Val May directed this latest, and last, version at the Bristol Old Vic the following year. Bolt still felt that he had not unlocked the secret to the play but decided to let it rest.

By this time his new children's play had been staged by the Royal Shakespeare Company. At its founding in 1960, the artistic director, Peter Hall, had offered Bolt a commission to write a play on a large scale, as he had other writers such as John Arden and John Whiting. Peggy did not like the idea of commissions because they restricted the freedom of the playwright and Bolt was then more than content with the standards of production and remuneration afforded him by the commercial sector; he was happy to decline the comparatively poorly paid commission from the publicly-subsidised RSC, saying he owed his next play to Beaumont. Bolt, however, gladly accepted the RSC's offer to stage his children's play, *The Thwarting of Baron Bolligrew*, which had begun life in the 1950s when Bolt had written a short version for Children's Hour on television. The RSC presented Bolt's play at Christmas time in the Aldwych Theatre in 1965. It played in the afternoons, had a fairly low budget and had to fit onto the sets of several other productions which were performed in repertoire in the evenings. Bolt, who was very fond of *The Thwarting of Baron Bolligrew*, felt that its young director, Trevor Nunn, 'was unusually enthusiastic and inventive'. It was revived the following Christmas. Bolt even agreed to let the RSC have his next play, which was called *Remarkable Women* and was subsequently re-titled *Vivat! Vivat Regina!*. His recent experiences with *Gentle Jack* and *Brother and Sister* had led to disenchantment with the commercial sector, and he now enjoyed the contrast that the subsidised theatre offered to the extravagant film world he mostly inhabited.

Vivat! is another chronicle play and in some ways a sequel to *A Man for All Seasons* in that it deals with the quarrel between Henry VIII's daughter Elizabeth and her rival claimant to the throne, Mary Queen of Scots. The

RSC was to present the play in a co-production with Binkie Beaumont, who had not been deterred by *Gentle Jack* or *Brother and Sister* and had hopes of transferring Bolt's latest offering to the West End. Peter Hall was the designated director. Negotiations dragged on for a long time; the fate of the play became enmeshed in the internal problems of RSC planning. Several factors came into play, notably, Hall's availability, the overall needs of the RSC repertoire, and a guarantee the RSC was seeking from the Arts Council to cover a tour which would be undertaken while the Bolt play appeared in the Aldwych. The delays began to irritate both Beaumont and Peggy, who complained to the RSC that there was no one in the company who seemed to be empowered to negotiate. Peggy's frustration affected Bolt, who panicked and resolved to pull out, even though he risked a break with Beaumont. Beaumont in fact stayed with the play when Peggy, returning to the commercial world, then placed it with John Clements, the actor-director who was running the Chichester Festival Theatre.

Peggy had originally suggested the title *Extraordinary Women*, which Bolt had altered slightly to *Remarkable Women*, and now Clements was insisting it be renamed *Vivat! Vivat Regina!*, much to Peggy's annoyance. 'I want to add RAH RAH RAH to this title,' she told Bolt, 'because to my mind it is public school amateur dramatics.' Bolt, however, went along with Clements. The production, directed by Peter Dews, opened in the summer of 1970 with Eileen Atkins playing Elizabeth and Bolt's current wife Sarah Miles playing Mary. It transferred in October to the West End and chalked up Bolt's longest run there of 442 performances.

The only new play by Bolt to be performed after *Vivat! Vivat Regina!* was *State of Revolution*, commissioned by Peter Hall when he took over the National Theatre and seen there in 1977. The play is a further exploration of history, this time through the leading characters in the Bolshevik political experiment. Peggy and the theatre in general had moved on beyond Bolt by this time. His middlebrow writing had been overtaken by tougher fare, frequently by other playwrights whom Peggy represented, although she defended Bolt against those of her clients who sneered at his plays while also holding him up as an example of what not to become. She was fond of him for not being a 'modern' and for resisting theatrical fashion, yet she was at the same time his most unforgiving critic. She felt that as a playwright he had committed the cardinal sin: he had not fulfilled his potential.

Peggy and Bolt shared a relationship that was marked by the intensities of both love and hate; they often corresponded with the almost unbearable candour of family. Bolt felt the need to expose his life to the protective but stern figure of Peggy as if she were all-knowing and all-seeing; not to confess something would be a sin that she would already have discovered, and therefore confession became important to sustaining the faith. She became his beacon and had a hand in directing his life in both the large and the small areas. His divorces and his four marriages – twice to Sarah Miles – the issue of whom the children should live with and where they should be educated, his lifestyle, his health, his complex financial arrangements as he became more successful, all were the subject of Peggy's advice.

When Bolt's first marriage broke down, Peggy told him not to worry, even though she was sympathetic to Jo. Peggy mistrusted the partners of her clients on principle, and she felt that what followed with Bolt proved her point. He met Sarah Miles, 18 years his junior, at a party that was held as filming began on *A Man for All Seasons* and became infatuated with her. So much so that he wrote a film, *Madame Bovary*, for her, which, recast in an Irish setting, became *Ryan's Daughter*. He conceived the role of Mary Queen of Scots in *Vivat! Vivat Regina!* for her. (Worried about her confidence to play the part, he asked someone to stand on the first night and applaud her entry on to the stage. Bolt had overlooked the fact that Miles, who had not asked him for the part, was not altogether happy with it.) And he wrote the film *Lady Caroline Lamb* for her. Disastrously, he directed it himself too. After two weeks of shooting, he and Sarah Miles were not speaking and they separated shortly afterwards.

Peggy was outrageously blunt about what she saw as the shortcomings of Sarah Miles, even on one occasion referring to her as 'that witch'. Peggy believed that she was draining Bolt's creativity – the most heinous of crimes – and despised her for it. Peggy's most extreme reaction came at a time when Bolt was no longer married to her. He was working with Lean in Tahiti and she was living in Los Angeles with their son, Tom, about whom they were in frequent contact. It was a difficult time for Bolt as a writer, and Peggy was aggressively attacking anyone whom she felt was an obstacle to his artistic progress or a competitor for his attention. Yet, when Peggy was dealing with Sarah Miles directly, her jealous protectiveness of Bolt was set aside and the two women were on the best of terms, especially later, when she and Bolt had remarried. Peggy had helped her as she was somewhat reluctantly preparing to play the role of Mary in London, and when Miles sent Peggy her first play, she received the positive response, 'you're a real writer'. Paradoxically, Peggy even offered assistance during Bolt's long spell abroad in Tahiti, particularly with her one-woman show, *Smiles*. This mixture of ravaging honesty and supportive action Bolt described as 'a typically Ramsayan combination'.

Peggy's overriding concern, however, was the deleterious effect that Bolt's rich lifestyle was having on his writing. She once told him he would have been better off if he had stayed in Manchester. 'Success when indulged in saps people's character and drains their true potential talent away,' she wrote to him. After Bolt had won his second Oscar, she warned him against playing the grand old man. 'My feeling is that you are still at the beginning of a very big career with many new plays and films yet to be written. We need to work and fight for your career as never before. The couple of Oscars are not in the least helpful; I spit on them. I want us to struggle as if from square one.

'I am voicing my real true feeling about your career. I shan't hide my worries because I want to spur you to take this business incredibly seriously. I feel sometimes as if I'm trying to talk to some kind of sybarite who has eluded me. Why do I feel this? It's not just puritanism, it's based on some area of fact!!!!!!! Of course I'd really like you back to no running water and the lavatory a bog at the end of the garden. No, I don't wish this, but I'm always aware that a career can turn full circle, and Norman Hunter [author of very successful plays in the early 1950s], for instance, is indeed back in some tiny cottage in some tiny village and I turned down his last two plays. So, Bob, let's pull the collars of our overcoats up over our ears, and let's pull our hats over our heads, and grimly GO FORWARD. If we don't do this, we might go *back*.'

Peggy believed that as an agent she should not act like a mere hireling who was afraid to speak out; she had a duty to tell her client the truth as she saw it. 'Once an author has become successful and famous,' she wrote to Bolt, 'it becomes more and more difficult to speak the truth, and this is why people like Rattigan become bloodless, because, in time, people fear to give them anything but lip service for self-preservation's sake. In addition, as soon as an author lives a "privileged" life (hotel suites, chauffeurs, etc) he cuts himself off from Jung's "collective unconscious" and begins to stop communicating.'

She was critical of David Lean's influence on Bolt in this regard. Lean took an opposite view to Peggy's on what she called 'the corruption of the Grand Hotels'. Lean encouraged Bolt to enjoy his wealth and, for example, applauded Bolt's decision to buy a Rolls-Royce. If you are going to buy a new car, he said, why not buy a Rolls if you can afford it? Peggy thought this attitude deplorable. She saw Lean as the bad angel tempting Bolt into the hell of success and self-importance. She saw Bolt as a lost spirit, declining in a never-ending spiral of spiritual decay. 'The trouble is,' she wrote to Bolt, 'no author is rich, because the more he earns the higher his station in life becomes. Motor cars are bought, garçonnières are booked and wives are given the mink treatment.'

Her antagonism to Lean was tinged with a little jealousy. Lean, whom Peggy found in his work to be selfish as well as demanding, had come to play an influential role in Bolt's artistic development and life, particularly when Bolt and Lean were working abroad on a script. This implicitly challenged her authority and her access to Bolt, which was primarily by letter or on the telephone. Lean did not view Peggy as a competitor; she did not figure in his thinking, other than as the traditional protective agent. He did once seek her intervention in an artistic dispute with Bolt, but in vain. Lean and Bolt were at loggerheads over the interpretation of Lara in the *Doctor Zhivago* script. Peggy kept her role to a minimum, and that was to advise and support Bolt. She wrote to him: 'Insist your scene is best but write Lean's alternative as well so he can't go on dreaming of the scene you refuse to write.'

Peggy's dislike of Lean reached its nadir in the late 1970s when Bolt agreed to work on a project for him that involved writing two film scripts about Captain Bligh and the mutiny on HMS Bounty. Bolt had always been interested in the sea but he admitted to Peggy that he had accepted the offer primarily to earn a large sum of money. Peggy and Bolt reached near breaking point as she engaged in negotiating a bruising deal with the producer Dino de Laurentiis, who owned the scripts. She felt that, under Lean's sway, Bolt was now completely in thrall to mammon. As the years had passed, Bolt had come to have less practical need for Peggy and she had increasingly left him alone to become snarled up in the film world while expostulating at the loss of his artistic soul. She felt his decline personally.

The Bounty episode represented a sad moment for Bolt, who, on the edge of departure from the agency after more than two decades, told Peggy how much he owed her, to which she replied forthrightly that the reverse was true. In a handwritten reply, she wrote: 'If I hadn't heard from you personally, I'd have suggested we said "goodbye" and thanked you for your endless loyalty to me. If you'd like to go, you should do so, as you owe me nothing – I owe you far more for the years I've been associated with your extraordinary artistic developments.' She warned him once more about the hardening of the artistic spirit and the blunting of his sensibilities yet, disarmingly, spent the last two pages of the letter discussing the work at hand, as if the parting had been completely forgotten. Bolt did not, and never did, leave the agency, although from a business point of view, he could have done so at any moment.

Peggy's anger at the Bounty project was exacerbated when Bolt, working with Lean in Tahiti, suffered a heart attack. Bolt was advised to go on a diet, take regular exercise and cut out smoking and alcohol. He returned to work in Tahiti and caught malaria. Two months later, he was in Los Angeles at Lean's insistence because of a worsening heart condition. He was staying with Michael and Shakira Caine, awaiting treatment, when he became ill and was rushed to hospital. He was given an immediate triple by-pass heart operation. Two days later, while still in intensive care, he tried to climb out of bed and fell. He hit his head on the floor and suffered a stroke, which disabled him down one side of his body and left him unable to speak or write. Two years later he had another heart attack. With fierce determination, Bolt did manage to speak again, albeit with a drawl, but he could never use a pen again. Technology came to his aid, however, in the shape of the word processor.

Peggy believed the operation to have been unnecessary and blamed his condition on what to her was the indisputable fact that he now only cared about being rich. Greed was the culprit and Lean its midwife. Lean paid the Santa Monica hospital bill of $24,644.90 because he did feel some responsibility for Bolt's condition, but subsequently he thought that paying the medical bill might be interpreted as his accepting all the blame. He asked Peggy to return the money, only to find that she had already done so. Despite her view of Bolt's demise, when she visited him during his recovery from the stroke, she was, recalls Bolt's first wife, Jo, 'at her most kind with Bob. Peaceable, even gentle.'

After the stroke, Bolt wrote no more plays and, although he worked on many film scripts, had only one new film script produced: *Thumbs Up: The James Brady Story*, a TV movie released in 1991 about Ronald Reagan's press secretary who was shot in the head during the attempted assassination of the President and had a stroke. Two earlier scripts were also released as films, but both flopped. Following Lean's departure from the Captain Bligh film, it was finally released in 1984 as *The Bounty*, based on the first of the two scripts that Bolt had written. An idea Bolt had sold to Paramount of adapting a play by Fritz Hochwälder, about the Jesuits in South America in the 18th century, became in 1986 *The Mission*. Directed by Roland Joffé with Robert de Niro and Jeremy Irons, it won many plaudits but failed at the box office.

Peggy liked Bolt as a person because he made a lot of mistakes; she saw something of the child in him. She stood by him even though she found him 'so difficult to love' and had severe misgivings about the direction his life and work took. To some extent, he always remained a schoolteacher, responding in turn to the schoolmistress in Peggy. Their exchanges on this were often painful and even bitter. She was tough-minded, yet, Bolt believed, meant what she said kindly. He did not feel that she was rude or malicious. 'You couldn't cope with the chastisement if you didn't see the truth in it,' was his verdict. In spite of her exasperating frankness and however hard he tried to break away, something in him always pulled him back. Bolt accepted Peggy's siren role because she never gave up on him, and, while he acknowledged that she was deeply suspicious of success, he knew that she was none too keen on failure either.

'I don't know how best to express what effect Peggy had,' said Bolt. 'She was a controlling figure but somehow did not interfere. She fought like a veritable tigress for me. There was no one in her class. There's no one else's opinion I'd rather seek. Her early support was crucial. Far and away she's at the head of the list of people who influenced me.'

Fittingly, it was Bolt who spoke at the ceremony in 1984 when the British Film Institute celebrated her contribution to its art. As he said on that occasion: 'In the middle of some letter of complaint or praise there is always something, which, if one stuck to it, would have the same effect on one's life as those little bits in the *I Ching*. And I do not refer to those bits of worldly wisdom vis-à-vis the managements. But bits of wisdom regarding one's life.'

Chapter Four

Iron in the Soul

*'I have no interest in my work as such at all (if we are talking about
my firm), nor have I any interest in either the theatre or the cinema,
or TV as such. To me the only interest is in life, and these arts
(stage, cinema etc), like painting and all the rest, are reflections of
life and should enhance and enrich life. They are nothing at all in
themselves, except that creative people (which I am not) have
got to forget that they are operating reflections. But none of us
should love the reflections without living the actuality more. Most
people I know in this business seem to love the theatre as such.
I have no religion, but I imagine that the phrase about worshipping
graven images could apply here!'*

PEGGY was thrilled by the way the theatrical landscape opened out in
the mid-1950s just as she was establishing herself as an agent. A new
dramatic language was being developed by playwrights and, in their own
disciplines, by actors, directors and designers too. All kinds of people who
previously would not have considered becoming playwrights were
writing for the stage and, without being constrained by the inhibition of
tradition, were trying out new and exciting things.

Change was in the air; they were exhilarating times. Against a background of postwar recovery and an expansion in higher education, many
cultural and political influences were at work, from jazz, rock 'n' roll and
cinema to the emergence of political commitment as a valid rallying call.
In theatre, new ideas flooded in from all directions. From abroad, there
was the impact of the Theatre of the Absurd, of the new emotional realism
of Arthur Miller and Tennessee Williams, and of Brecht and the Berliner
Ensemble, which first visited Britain in 1956. At home, there was Joan
Littlewood and Theatre Workshop, which in 1956 made the first of several

explosive transfers to the West End, and there was George Devine and the English Stage Company, founded at the Royal Court also in 1956, just eighteen months after Peggy had become an agent.

Devine's original aim was to revitalise the theatre by running a permanent company in Sloane Square that would play in repertory a mix of classical revivals and new plays. The emphasis would be placed on the new writing, the main source of which Devine believed would be novelists, whom he wished to coax to the stage. Although the company soon discovered that it could not sustain a repertory system and that most novelists proved stubbornly resistant to the glories of the stage, the success of John Osborne's *Look Back in Anger* in the first season shaped the future of the Royal Court and established it as the standard bearer of new British playwriting.

Peggy knew how important it was for such a development to happen, not only for the theatre in general but for her as an agent specialising, she hoped, in new talent. She believed in a quasi-mystical way that the English Stage Company had to be born because a John Osborne figure had to arise. Without him, she felt the Company would die, not necessarily in the literal, but in the artistic sense. 'Any major talent is more powerful and potent and more important than any theatre,' she said.

When Osborne asked Devine if he could recommend an agent, Devine told him that there were only two agents from whom he should choose: Margery Vosper (the agent of Ronald Duncan, one of the co-founders of the English Stage Company) and Peggy Ramsay. Devine said that he could not see Osborne and Peggy tolerating each other for long. Osborne duly chose Vosper but later declared that Peggy, with whom he stayed in frequent contact, was 'the best agent I never had'. He observed in his autobiography that, for Vosper, being an agent meant not asking too much, 'which homely caution meant being well-nigh supplicant to managers'. Peggy held the opposite view, and this attracted Osborne, along with her curmudgeonly independence of judgement and disdainful disregard for other people's opinion of her. In many respects, they were kindred spirits.

Peggy was devoted to Osborne at first. 'We owe everything to him,' she would say. She even suggested him for work (with due consideration of Vosper's feelings), although she did not represent him. In the '60s, when he wanted to leave Vosper and come to Margaret Ramsay Ltd., Peggy rebuffed him with a rejoinder that loyalty should be paramount. By then she may also have recognised that Osborne as a dear acquaintance was one thing, whereas Osborne as a client, already past his best, might be madness; moreover, she never had any interest in servicing the famous. As with her own clients, she cooled towards him after the initial enthusiasm, and by the late '70s she was indifferent to his fate.

She did enjoy ticking him off and took a hard line when he came to her to complain about his writer's 'block'. Once, when he was about to leave her office, he asked a young writer who happened to be present – John McGrath – to call him a taxi. McGrath enquired where Osborne was going. On giving the destination, Peggy intervened, as if hurling a thunderbolt directly at Osborne's heart: 'There's a perfectly good bus service to take you there. As long as you indulge yourself in such luxuries as riding by taxi, John darling, you will never be able to write properly again.'

Peggy was not as closely involved in the early days of the English Stage Company as she would like to have been. She had tried unsuccessfully to place Robert Bolt's first stage play in the company's inaugural season yet did manage that year to sell to George Devine Ionesco's *The Chairs*, which had to wait until 1957 for production. It was followed six months later by a version of *Lysistrata*, by an American client, Dudley Fitts, which transferred to the West End.

A decade later, by the time that John Arden and Edward Bond had joined Peggy, she represented the bulk of the Royal Court's important new writers.

Of the first wave of English Stage Company playwrights, Peggy represented only one, Ann Jellicoe, who was also the only female writer to make a breakthrough at the Royal Court until Caryl Churchill, another of Peggy's clients, in the late 1970s. This was ironic, considering that Peggy's views on women as playwrights left many an unreconstructed man looking dangerously liberal.

Peggy first met Jellicoe when she was running the Cockpit Theatre, Westminster, which she had founded in 1951 after being commissioned to study the relationship between acting and theatre architecture. This study had led her to favour an open stage, playing on three sides, which was then an advanced theatrical idea. Peggy was impressed by the Cockpit, which deployed this configuration, and described it as the first open stage theatre in London for 150 years. Jellicoe wanted to present *Danton's Death* there, and Peggy was fighting with great vigour for her to use the translation by John Holmstrom, which Peggy represented. Jellicoe eventually adapted the play herself. When she wrote her first full-length play, *The Sport of My Mad Mother*, and needed an agent, she remembered how stoutly Peggy had defended Holmstrom and thought that she might do the same for her.

The play won joint third prize in an Observer competition, which had been expected to attract around 500 entrants rather than the final total of 2,000. The paper's critic, Kenneth Tynan, described Jellicoe's unconventional, ritualistic play about a London teenage gang as a '*tour de force* that belongs to no known category of drama'. Jellicoe says Peggy never believed *The Sport of My Mad Mother* would be produced; she liked its quirkiness but doubted whether any management would want to risk producing it. Devine, however, promised a production and stayed true to his word.

The Sport of My Mad Mother was a *flop d'estime*, one of the Royal Court's more famous, playing on one occasion to only two people. The play has since entered the history books as a seminal modern work. 'Failing noisily then was fine,' comments Jellicoe. 'The Court was new and there was still not that much happening in the new play world, so you were noticed.'

Jellicoe briefly became the new name to be fêted at Sloane Square. She revised her earlier adaptation of Ibsen's *Rosmersholm* for Devine, which became the hit of the Royal Court's 1959 season, transferring to the West End, with Peggy Ashcroft as Rebecca West. Jellicoe's next full-length play, *The Knack*, owed much to the work of the Royal Court's Writers' Group, which was led by the director William Gaskill and one of Devine's assistants, Keith Johnstone. Jellicoe was a regular attender, along with David Cregan, Edward Bond, John Arden, and Arnold Wesker, all of whom, with the exception of Wesker, became clients of Peggy's. Despite its origins, Devine turned down *The Knack*.

Peggy considered its story of three young men sharing a flat too slight and the comedy too light, although she did like the central character, Tolen, whose ability to attract and seduce women gives the play its title. Nonetheless, she was convinced the Royal Court should present the play and badgered Devine to give it a chance. In the end, it opened for a week in Cambridge, as part of a regional project in which the Royal Court was involved. The production was co-directed by Jellicoe and by Keith Johnstone, who later was also to become one of Peggy's clients as a writer. *The Knack* then played in Bath and came into the Royal Court for a limited run of 29 performances, averaging 60% at the box office. There was no chance of a further life because Devine, who never believed the play would be a success, had let its lead, Rita Tushingham, sign a film contract, which rendered her unavailable.

Jellicoe was upset that Peggy had not secured a better deal for the play; Jellicoe had wanted an open-ended run or nothing at all. Peggy felt this approach would have been self-defeating and that, in the circumstances, she had achieved a victory in getting the play on at all. She had interested

the producer Oscar Lewenstein in the play and had used his close connections with the Royal Court as leverage on Devine to obtain even the
short exposure that the play enjoyed. Subsequently *The Knack* was picked
up by the American director Mike Nichols and it ran in New York for two
years, during which time the film version was released. Jellicoe believed
that Peggy had sold the film rights to Oscar Lewenstein too cheaply, not
out of dishonesty or even incompetence, but simply out of insanity. In
riposte, Peggy argued that it was the film, adapted by another of Peggy's
clients, Charles Wood, that had made Jellicoe's reputation. The film,
indeed, became emblematic of the 'liberated' 1960s and of London's new-
found fame as the centre of fashionable existence.

Jellicoe and Peggy crossed swords several times. Peggy became exasperated when Jellicoe was lionised by the intellectual avant-garde and put
her down as 'just a girl with a fringe'. Perhaps she and Jellicoe shared too
much in common to get on well; both were warm yet explosive, and both
liked to be left alone. In Goodwin's Court, Jellicoe's nickname was Ann
Bellicose. 'Ann isn't easy,' Peggy confided to Oscar Lewenstein at the time
of *The Knack* deal. 'I'm really surprised that she and I haven't fallen out.'

They did, in the early '70s, when Peggy showed her a letter from John
Arden, whom Jellicoe had introduced to Peggy. The letter from Arden to
Peggy was marked 'Confidential'. Jellicoe felt this to be a breach of trust
and left the agency. Later, she said that she departed because she was
bored with Peggy and 'all her chat. She never nailed anything down.'
Jellicoe became quickly bored with her new agent too and returned to
Peggy.

'She was infuriating,' recalls Jellicoe. 'When I was offered a television
adaptation of *Catch 22* Peggy was dead against it. She said it would be
interrupted every five minutes by ads and she made me feel ashamed
because I wanted to earn some money for once, and yet she was right.'

Jellicoe remembers another perspicacious piece of advice. An American
director wanted to film *The Sport of My Mad Mother* but to precede this
with Jellicoe directing the play in a New York warehouse. Jellicoe, who
was then 38, was pregnant and felt that if she went ahead she might lose
the baby. Peggy said the decision was up to Jellicoe, but that if she did
want to go to America then she must not tell the producer that she was
pregnant or he would call the whole deal off. Jellicoe did tell him and
Peggy was proved right; the deal fell through, the play was never filmed,
but the baby survived.

*

Peggy

'Running your own business puts iron in the soul,
strengthens the will.'

Within only a couple of years of setting up as an agent, Peggy had built a considerable reputation inside the profession. At the beginning of 1958, she sent the Stage Year Book a list of her clients, which comprised: Arthur Adamov, Nigel Balchin, Barbara Bingley, Franklyn Black, Guy Bolton, Robert Bolt, Rosemary Casey, Kenneth Cavander, Campbell and Dorothy Christie, Dudley Fitts, Horton Foote, Rex Frost, Roger Gellert, Ibsen/ Michael Meyer, Eugène Ionesco, Ann Jellicoe, Fay and Michael Kanin, Leo Lehman, William Marchant, Edmund Morris, Joseph O'Conor, Dorothy Parker, John Patrick, Edward and Lilian Percy, Pol Quentin, Armand Salacrou, Christopher Taylor, Cedric Wallis, Donald Watson, and Alwyne Whatsley. Peggy was only too aware, however, of how little indigenous talent she had unearthed; she still saw an uncertain future.

She travelled a great deal outside of London in the early days and was as pleased to have a production in Scunthorpe as she was in the West End if it was good. She nurtured fruitful contacts with regional theatres and their directors, such as Willard Stoker at the Liverpool Playhouse, where in 1958 four plays in a new play season were written by her clients; Frank Hauser and the Oxford Playhouse, where Robert Bolt was given his début; and Val May, first at the Nottingham Playhouse and then at the Bristol Old Vic, where successful plays she represented, like *A Severed Head* and *The Killing of Sister George*, were originally seen. She felt, however, that towards the end of the 1950s the bottom was dropping out of the regional repertory system, and by the 1960s there was little room for adventure beyond the capital.

In London, managers were unsettled by the Royal Court revolution; it was changing audience's tastes while proving to be a financial disaster. The so-called 'well-made play' was going out of fashion, but the new wave was not yet able to replace it commercially. Public subsidy had yet to become available on the substantial scale that was required to create a new and vital theatre culture which had new plays at its heart.

Television was becoming voracious in its demand for more 'product', a situation which, while it provided work for writers, in Peggy's view destabilised playwrights because it was the wrong kind of work for the wrong kind of rewards. Nevertheless, much of the agency's assets by this time lay in television writing. In 1959 she reluctantly expanded her now full-time staff, from two to three, in order to become more efficient in the TV world. At the same time, she worried that she was over-reaching and might face the prospect of having to retrench by losing staff and cutting back her client list.

That she did not have to do so was due partly to Robert Bolt, and partly to her discovery of a bright new talent whom she came across through radio, just as she had done with Bolt.

Her friend John Holmstrom, who was working as a radio announcer, had to introduce a play called *The Dock Brief* and thought that Peggy might be interested in the author, John Mortimer. It was his first play, a two-hander set in a prison cell, and in it he had drawn on his experiences as a barrister in a humorous, touching and imaginative way. Peggy immediately liked Mortimer – or Mortimaire, as she called him – and agreed to represent him. The following year, 1958, she had sold *The Dock Brief* to television and had secured a stage production of it as a one-act play. It was later made into a film with Peter Sellers and Richard Attenborough.

In the first years of Mortimer's playwriting career, Peggy was especially keen for him to develop his craft skills. She regularly commented on his first drafts and rewrites. By 1960, when he had been successful with several more short plays and his first full-length play, *The Wrong Side of the Park*, had run in the West End for six months, she felt that he had mastered stage technique, but she was now worried that the plays were too lightweight.

Peggy spoke most openly about this during the birth pangs of *Two Stars for Comfort*, which charts the decline of Sam Turner, a libidinous hotel proprietor. It was directed by Michael Elliott in the West End in 1962, with Trevor Howard in the lead. She confided in Elliott that 'the trouble with Sam is that there is too much periphery and not sufficient indication of what he IS. This is what makes it so tremendously hard for Trevor to play him. Yes, he's unsympathetic, but so is Iago; the latter is riveting because one sees the movement of his mind. We should see more of the movement of Sam's. This is, actually, Mortimer's big failing to my mind. He himself hasn't got a true philosophy and wouldn't know, if you asked him, where he *stands*. In the old days it didn't matter in the theatre, because we were only interested in surface, but now we want to try and see how people tick . . . The only thing I'm really interested in is *what drives a man*, and it's discernible in quite a short time in real life.'

She broadened her critique into what would become a familiar complaint. 'Mortimer's big weakness is a passion for success and the trappings of success, and the awful part of it is that success, when indulged in, saps people's character and drains their true potential talent away – the people who love successful people exploit them, take them up, throw them away, and sometimes only a shell is left. Mortimer has a rare and touching talent, a remarkable sense of atmosphere, deep sympathy and a moving plaintive voice – he could be a superb artist, not merely a successful one, and it's this which makes me sad.'

Peggy lost real interest in Mortimer's development as a writer at this point, although she continued to represent him for the rest of her life. She thought that his writing for the screen was better than his writing for the stage, and, indeed, he became a highly successful television and film writer. She always retained an affection for him, and shared his libertarian instincts and espousal of the anti-censorship cause.

For all of Peggy's artistic anxieties about Mortimer, he proved not only to be economically very valuable for the agency but, more importantly, to be the catalyst for two crucial developments in the firm's life.

The first of these brought to the agency a prestigious list of new clients and the second engendered one of the most influential relationships in contemporary British theatre, that of Peggy and a new young producer, Michael Codron.

Mortimer, who had written five novels by the time he wrote *The Dock Brief* in 1957, was represented for his fiction by the noted agent, A.D. Peters, who had given up handling plays a few years previously because of a number of disappointments. Chief amongst them had been the desertion of Terence Rattigan, whom he had represented since the mid-1930s, occasioned by his dislike of Rattigan's latest play, *The Sleeping Princess*. Peters felt that this was poor reward for having helped establish Rattigan before the war when he was struggling to make his name, by taking him up as a client and adding his personal financial backing to Rattigan's first play, *French Without Tears*. Peters had also had trouble with another client, J.B. Priestley, with whom Peters had been in partnership as a producer. So, when Peggy made contact with John Mortimer, Peters was happy to let her take over the representation of Mortimer's stage writing.

Peters also saw, however, that, following the Osborne breakthrough at the Royal Court, playwriting was coming back into fashion, and this meant more theatrical work in the offing. He asked Peggy if she would like to enter into a partnership with him. She discussed the proposal with both Campbell Christie, as chair of her board of directors, and with John Holmstrom, whom she had been considering inviting to become a partner in her agency.

She decided against both moves. Instead, she put a counter proposal to Peters. This was to establish a new firm altogether, run by her from Goodwin's Court. The independence of both 'parent' agencies would be guaranteed by keeping them intact and completely separate. Christie had been in favour of the amalgamation with Peters because his was the more secure of the two agencies. Christie feared that if a new firm were to be set up on its own he would be excluded from it, both as a client and as a director.

In spite of Christie's opposition, Peggy went ahead with her own idea, and in January 1958 the firm of Peters and Ramsay was founded, with an interest free loan of £500 from Peters. Peggy was paid 5% commission for the work as opposed to the normal 10%, the other half going to A.D. Peters Ltd. They shared all profit equally, and Peters bore any losses. This arrangement helped Peters by encouraging the dramatic exploitation of the work of his clients as well as bringing some financial gain from this to his agency. It helped Peggy by adding more clients to her list, and notable ones at that – the two dozen names she inherited included J.B. Priestley, Stephen Spender, and John Whiting. It also allowed her to learn a great deal from Peters' experience as an agent, which was especially useful in film matters. Her secretary unexpectedly won a rise from the deal too.

Peters came from the 'old school' and had a reputation as a difficult man. Peggy found him a little cold and unimaginative but co-operative. She had impressed on Peters before he agreed to her idea how vehemently she felt about plays and that she had her own way of being an agent. She had laid down two conditions; one, that the new firm should be established without any publicity, and the other, that no play or playwright be taken on by the new agency without her consent. She had to be certain that he understood her attitude in order to prevent anything in the arrangement from destroying her reputation. Peters agreed to both. The first test came in the shape of a play that arrived via Peters, written by Wayland Young (later to become the Social Democrats' foreign affairs spokesman in the Lords), which dealt with promiscuity, lesbianism, and abortion. Peggy was offended not by its subject matter but by its lack of truth. It did not get recommended. Having started as she meant to go on, Peggy ran the firm with little interference from Peters to the general satisfaction of them both.

Priestley, the grand old man of English letters and a national institution, was the senior figure to come into Peggy's life through the Peters route. She did not deal with 'JB's' backlist, which would have been lucrative, on the grounds that she had not put in the work at the time and should not, therefore, benefit now. The first play of his that she represented, in 1963, turned out to be his last, ending an illustrious theatrical career that spanned three decades. It was a collaboration with Iris Murdoch on the dramatisation of her novel *A Severed Head*, which transferred from the Bristol Old Vic to the West End for a remarkable two-and-a-half year run.

Peggy's main concern with 'JB' was coping with his deep sense of grievance that the theatre world had passed him by. In any other European country, he claimed with some justification, several of his plays would have earned a permanent place in the national repertoire. He felt out of touch and wanted Peggy to bring him up to date. In 1962, she organised a huge party for him so that he could meet the best of the new playwriting talent. The hundred-plus guest list reads like the proverbial entry for a standard reference book on contemporary British theatre: there were the directors from the Royal Court, Lindsay Anderson, George Devine, John Dexter, Bill Gaskill and Anthony Page, and other notable directors, Frith Banbury, Michael Elliott, Val May, and Peter Wood; producers Peter Bridge, Michael Codron, Peter Daubeny, Oscar Lewenstein, Toby Rowland; writers Peggy did not represent, Bernard Kops, John Osborne, Harold Pinter, Arnold Wesker, as well as her own clients. They ranged from the designer Tim O'Brien and the composers Carl Davis and Ron Grainer to her Peters and Ramsay writers – John Mortimer, Bill Naughton, Stephen Spender, John Whiting along with Iris Murdoch and A.D. Peters himself – and those on the books of Margaret Ramsay Ltd. itself – Dannie Abse, Barry Bermange, Caryl Brahms, Robert Bolt, Donald Howarth, Ann Jellicoe, Leo Lehman, Henry Livings, David Mercer, Michael Meyer, Peter Nichols, Alan Plater, David Rudkin, James Saunders, Ned Sherrin, and Charles Wood.

'JB' was totally bemused by the party and, when told who all the people were, was horrified because they were the very ones in the theatre who appalled him.

Peggy generally found Priestley over-demanding of her – and disliked his attempts at flirting – yet, against the odds, they did develop a friendship. Although she found him lowbrow, the common ground they shared was culture and an interest in the arts, which they discussed animatedly. Her main regret was that in this, as in other matters, she had not managed to prod the great 'JB' into a proper understanding of the world as it had become.

The most interesting writer in Peggy's view to come to her via A.D. Peters Ltd. was John Whiting, whom Peggy described as 'one of the nicest and most honest men I have ever known'. His playwriting career, however, was in the doldrums. Like Peggy, a former actor, his early work only ever found favour with a small group of enthusiasts within the profession. He was swimming against the tide of postwar conservatism in the English theatre, which dubbed him disparagingly 'Small Fry', in reference to the vogue for poetic plays associated with Christopher Fry. Whiting, a precursor of the new drama yet to come, never fully recovered from this rejection. The turning point was the failure in 1954 of *Marching Song*. It was the third of his plays to be seen in London, to excite interest and even controversy, and then to fade. He retreated into writing film scripts and theatre criticism.

Peggy was delighted when his fortunes changed with *The Devils*, the play about demonic possession among the nuns of a 17th-century priory that put his name back on the theatrical map and finally won him recognition beyond the profession. A vibrant, muscular adaptation of Aldous Huxley's *The Devils of Loudun*, it reached new depths of understanding for Peggy, who felt that Whiting had at last been able to match his vision with a substantial dramatic structure and powerful, imagistic language. The play was commissioned by Whiting's champion Peter Hall for the newly-founded Royal Shakespeare Company. Hall wanted to tempt Whiting back to the theatre and, more generally, to offer contemporary playwrights liberation from the restrictions of the commercial stage. A great deal depended on *The Devils*, both for John Whiting personally, after years in the wilderness, and for the RSC, which was to include it in the company's inaugural season in the capital, itself a high-risk undertaking.

After some negotiation to gain the necessary approval from the Lord Chamberlain's office, *The Devils* opened at the Aldwych Theatre in 1961, directed by Peter Wood and designed by Sean Kenny, as the first new play ever to be presented by the RSC. The reviews were mixed but enough of them praised the ambition and epic scale of the venture to vindicate Whiting and Hall. This encouraged the RSC and the incipient National Theatre, which was launched two years later, to promote new and large-canvas drama. In its next season, the RSC revived *The Devils* and added to the repertoire Whiting's earliest performed play, *A Penny for a Song*. Whiting died, aged 45, the following year from cancer, and Peggy took on the representation of the estate.

In 1965, in a unique tribute to a playwright, the Arts Council established an annual award that bore Whiting's name, for 'writing of a special quality, of potential value to the British theatre, and of relevance and importance to contemporary life'. He had served on the Council's drama panel from 1955 until his death. In the first decade of the award's existence, ten out of the 16 winners were clients of Peggy's. Although Peggy did not approve of awards, she felt pleased that it was Whiting who had been so honoured: 'He was one of the few authors I will never forget,' she said, 'and I miss him greatly.'

With the death of John Whiting, and the increasing employment of John Mortimer in film and television, Peggy's Peters and Ramsay clients ceased to be primarily theatre people. J.B. Priestley was both a novelist and a playwright but was no longer active in the theatre. Iris Murdoch was a novelist with a passing interest in the stage. Peggy considered Iris Murdoch to be a Margaret Ramsay Ltd. client whom she placed with Peters and Ramsay for the stage adaptations of her two novels, *A Severed Head* and *The Italian Girl*.

Peggy was curious about the crossover between the theatre and the novel and had once shared George Devine's belief that novelists would furnish the British theatre with the new playwrights of the future. Although she no longer held this view, she remained interested in the two forms; she read voraciously in both, and she did represent several novelists who also worked briefly in theatre – such as Brigid Brophy, whose short novel, *Flesh*, in which a woman turns an academic virgin into a Rubensesque figure through sex, was a favourite of Peggy's; David Caute, whom Peggy admired because he was tackling epic, political themes when it was unfashionable; Colin McInnes, whose novel, *Absolute Beginners*, she discussed with the director John Dexter as the possible basis for a musical; and Muriel Spark, who became the most notable of this group because of the enormous success on stage, film and television of her novel, *The Prime of Miss Jean Brodie*.

Brodie became a by-word in the language for a particular type of sharp-tongued, independent-minded female teacher. Peggy shared some of the characteristics of Spark's pedagogue, an interest in the self-liberation of others, a string of affairs, a love of truth and art, and a spirit of militancy and wit, shrewdness and innocence. Brodie even had an airman poet – the controversial proto-fascist Gabriele D'Annunzio – as a fantasy lover, another echo of Peggy herself. It is worth noting, though not surprising, that so many of the famous plays she represented reflect aspects of her own persona.

To Peggy, the most intriguing of the novelists she represented was Enid Bagnold, who was already a playwright of distinction when she joined Peggy in 1967, aged nearly 80, following the death of her previous agent. She was best known for her novel *National Velvet*, which had been adapted into a play and a film, but her passion remained theatre. *The Chalk Garden* had been one of Binkie Beaumont's major successes. Peggy for years had been drawn to Bagnold as a figure, with her military background, her affairs with famous men like H.G. Wells and Frank Harris, and her fear of death. She had also known the writer Maurice

Baring, who had died in 1945 and whose work was a private passion of Peggy's.

When Bagnold came to Peggy she had written a draft of a new play, *Call Me Jacky*, which Peggy urged her to finish. It was a disaster on its pre-London tour and did not make it to the West End. Bagnold was devastated. Reliant on morphine, she became close to Peggy but hardly wrote anything more, except to dabble in her autobiography, in which pursuit Peggy greatly encouraged her. She made Bagnold buy a copying machine (which Peggy loathed) in order to prevent the loss of the manuscript, which Bagnold always carried around with her and was in danger of leaving somewhere or, in desperation, burning. She also rewrote *Call Me Jacky*, which played in the United States as *A Matter of Gravity* with Katherine Hepburn; it was attacked critically but proved popular. It was Bagnold's last play. She died in 1981, aged 91.

Bagnold was another client of Margaret Ramsay Ltd., who, like Iris Murdoch, was listed under Peters and Ramsay, although by the time *Call Me Jacky* was produced, Peters and Ramsay had shown clear signs of having outlived its purpose and had fallen into desuetude.

The main problem for Peggy was that Peters and Ramsay did not bring her any new talent. Nor was it making her great sums of money because it only handled a few authors. A.D. Peters Ltd. mostly dealt with their TV, film and publishing rights, unless they related directly to a play. Peggy's successful handling of those few clients led to several of them, notably John Mortimer, wanting to leave A.D. Peters altogether in order to join Margaret Ramsay Ltd., which had become acknowledged as the country's leading play agency.

Peggy talked seriously to Peters of formally ending the Peters and Ramsay arrangement. He had not taken too much interest in the firm after its initial establishment and, on looking more closely at the books, realised that he was in effect paying tax twice under the deal he had made with Peggy. They both agreed to finish with the firm, and it was finally wound up in 1971, two years before Peters died. The accounts were closed in 1974. Margaret Ramsay Ltd. continued to pay A.D. Peters Ltd., which later became Peters, Fraser and Dunlop, for contracts covered by the original Peters and Ramsay deal.

*

Peggy

'There is a kind of destiny in any play which should
be left to fate, I suppose.'

John Mortimer had proved to be both the original hook for the Peters and Ramsay deal and, through his desire to join Peggy full-time, the catalyst for its demise. Mortimer had also been the unconscious progenitor of another of Peggy's collaborations, which, in its effect on British theatre, turned out to be much more far reaching than the modest contribution made by Peters and Ramsay.

It was Mortimer's play, *The Dock Brief*, that provided the occasion for Peggy's initial contact with Michael Codron, an Oxford graduate who had worked for the eminent impresario Jack Hylton and had branched out on his own as a producer in 1956. Two years later Codron, then 27, took over the Lyric, Hammersmith, with David Hall. For their first season Codron wanted to present the stage première of *The Dock Brief* but needed another short play to accompany it. Peggy came up with a second Mortimer play, *What Shall We Tell Caroline?* The resulting double-bill, directed by Stuart Burge, whom Peggy had known from her acting days, successfully transferred to the Garrick Theatre. Codron subsequently produced Mortimer's *The Wrong Side of the Park*, *Two Stars for Comfort* and *A Voyage Round My Father*.

Codron and Peggy quickly became very close associates. They enjoyed a productive if occasionally tempestuous professional relationship that resulted in some of the English theatre's most distinguished and challenging productions: after Mortimer, the long and impressive chain of Peggy's clients produced by Codron includes Alan Ayckbourn, Christopher Hampton, David Hare, Henry Livings, Frank Marcus, David Mercer, Joe Orton, Willy Russell, James Saunders and Charles Wood.

She encouraged, admonished and supported Codron (known to Peggy as Codders, Codfish or Cod) and helped him to become the most innovative producer of the 1960s and '70s, urging him to present not what he thought the public would accept but to risk producing what he himself liked.

Peggy believed Codron succeeded because of his 'great tenacity'. She described him as 'small, frail and quiet' and recognised that he needed 'warm' handling but said, 'I don't find this difficult, as he never annoys me, is always available, works very hard, and, most important of all, has really good taste allied to genuine modesty . . . This métier is so hard and so hurtful from time to time that people who survive in it do so by a kind of stoical endurance, and if possible, the retention of some kind of inner life. There is not much happiness from the career itself, except hard work, which is a good disciplinary hair-shirt for us all.' The last two sentences applied to her just as much as they did to Codron.

The 1958 Lyric season which included the two short Mortimer plays is most famous now for the brief appearance and swift demise of the première production of Harold Pinter's *The Birthday Party*. Peggy did not represent Pinter, whom she said she had first met when they were both actors, but she was obliquely involved in the production. She recalled recommending Richard Pearson, an actor she had known at Q, for the part of Stanley, and calling Harold Hobson, who had missed the opening night, urging him to see the play after it had received disastrous reviews in the daily newspapers. Codron himself, who had been alerted to Harold Pinter by Hobson's review of his first play, *The Room,* in Bristol, also called Hobson to make the same plea. Codron closed the play the night before Hobson's review appeared, but his notice, nonetheless, proved to be a turning point for Pinter.

In the same season, Codron lost £20,000 on the musical *Valmouth* by Sandy Wilson, adapted from the works of Ronald Firbank. Codron decided to quit the Lyric, where he had found it difficult to experiment.

As well as the Mortimer plays, Peggy by chance represented the opening play of that Codron Lyric season, Ibsen's *Little Eyolf* in a translation by Michael Meyer. It was directed by Caspar Wrede, who had directed a play of Meyer's, *The Ortolan*, at Oxford where Codron had seen and liked it. Meyer had been asked to translate *Little Eyolf* from the Norwegian for radio on the strength of his translation of a Swedish novel, and he accepted in order to secure a much needed fee, pretending that the two languages were more similar than they are, even though he had never read a word of Ibsen's native tongue. With the help of a bilingual friend he cobbled together a version and only later, when he had mastered Norwegian, did he recognise how bad his first attempt had been. He then rewrote *Little Eyolf* completely.

Meyer had heard of Peggy from Caspar Wrede, who had come across her while searching for the rights to *Danton's Death*, and his Swedish agent was Lars Schmidt, who was on the board of Peggy's firm. Meyer wanted to be a playwright and approached Peggy in the hope that she might be able to secure a production of *The May Game*, a dark farce that had been rejected by two West End managements and had been abandoned by his current agent. Peggy agreed to try but failed both with the farce and with the earlier play that had been seen at Oxford. She felt that she might have stood a better chance if she had been guiding Meyer from the start. 'My idea of hell,' she told him, 'is trying to sell plays that have been soiled by other agents.'

It was, however, Meyer's translation work rather than his original writing that took off. Peggy loved Ibsen's plays and felt a palpable thrill when she read them in Meyer's typescripts, imagining they were newly-minted, unknown. She particularly liked *The Lady from the Sea*, which happened to be the other Ibsen play that Meyer had translated when he came to her.

Michael Meyer became the doyen of Ibsen and Strindberg translators in the theatre, as well as their biographer; yet, in a phrase that would not have sounded odd coming from Peggy's lips, he has described himself as simply 'the least bad' of those who practise this craft. Meyer became a mainstay of the agency and brought it a constant and steady income because of the tremendous interest in Strindberg and Ibsen in the English-speaking theatre.

In the early years, Peggy took on a number of translators and adaptors – such as John Barton, Barbara Bray, Kenneth Cavander, Richard Cottrell, John Holmstrom, Dmitri Makaroff, Derek Marlowe, Peter Meyer (Michael's brother), Derek Prouse, Donald Watson, Simon Watson Taylor, and Barbara Wright. Most of them Peggy agreed to represent because of her interest in the plays they were translating. Often she represented the translators for one or two titles only. In general, she found representing translators and adaptors to be too much trouble for too little spiritual reward and once described it as 'part of the chores of my profession'; it was bread-and-butter work for her, although this did not usually diminish the zeal with which she tried to secure a better deal for her translators.

'I prefer my writers alive,' she would say – and gave this as one reason why she turned down the opportunity of representing the prestigious and remunerative Brecht canon, along with the horror of having to deal with the relatives who controlled his estate. She thought his work had been perverted by the current trend for 'morality package deals' and deserved better than the available translations, most of which she thought very poor. She would chastise her own living playwrights such as Christopher Hampton when they seemed to her to be spending too much time working on translations and adaptations rather than writing their own plays. On the other hand, she felt that playwrights could learn something from an intimate acquaintance with gifted forebears. In seeming indifference to the fact that she represented several of the foremost translators of the time, she said on more than one occasion that only playwrights should undertake this kind of work. It was they alone, she believed, who, for their audience, could properly enrich the original play textually and imaginatively through writing apposite and speakable dialogue.

Peggy's involvement with translation rights led her into a tangential connection with a new venture, which was called the 59 Theatre Company, named after the year of its founding, and which was the genesis of the Royal Exchange Theatre, Manchester, a decade later. Caspar Wrede wanted to form a company that would mount Strindberg's *Creditors* and Ibsen's *Brand*, both to be translated by Michael Meyer, as well as *Danton's Death* (but not in John Holmstrom's version). Peggy discussed with Wrede the proposed company, which traced its roots back a few years to a one-off season in Manchester when it was known as the Piccolo Theatre Club. She supported his wish to establish the new company at the Arts Theatre Club in London and argued in his favour with the theatre's owner Campbell Williams, who, however, would not agree.

At the same time, she advised Wrede that he would need a solicitor if he were going to found a theatre company, and recommended a young man called Laurence Harbottle. She knew he was good because 'I lost a case to him once' – a reference to a skirmish over rights in which Harbottle represented Frank Hauser and Meadow Players at the Oxford Playhouse. Peggy insisted that Harbottle see Wrede, whom she described characteristically as 'this intolerable young man'. Instead of the Arts, through Harbottle's contacts, Wrede eventually secured the Lyric, Hammersmith, which had been vacated by Michael Codron and David Hall, and the 59 Theatre Company's season went ahead. When the company re-formed in Manchester as the 69 Theatre Company, Harbottle became its chairman and continued to serve as such when it was transformed into the Royal Exchange.

Harbottle, who had become Peggy's solicitor following their Oxford Playhouse clash ('you were so awkward, dear, would you come and work for me?'), established himself as the English theatrical profession's leading legal figure. He represented many major companies and individuals, and served on the boards of a number of important theatrical organisations, often as chairman.

Despite losing the argument with Campbell Williams over Wrede, Peggy continued to enjoy a close association with the Arts Theatre. It was very close to her office and had become a favourite spot of hers at this time. It functioned as a social meeting place because of its restaurant and bar where young theatre people, including several of her clients, often gathered. It was a club theatre, which did not have to submit its plays to the Lord Chamberlain for approval, although in practice it usually did so. The actors were paid no more than a bare minimum but were attracted by the plays and by the theatre's profile; being close to the West End, the critics always came. The Arts reminded her of her days at Q.

It had never been quite the same since the 'golden' period of Alec Clunes following the war, when his mix of classical revivals and new plays, championing Shaw in particular, earned it the sobriquet of a 'mini' National Theatre. Campbell Williams, a former managing director of the Keith Prowse ticket agency who had married a wealthy wife, bought the lease to the theatre in the winter of 1953, just as Peggy was setting up her agency. He had sustained the reputation of the Arts for innovation at the cost of the gradual erosion of a personal fortune. Peggy described Williams as 'a comparative amateur in the theatre though very nice'.

In 1955, Williams had installed as artistic director Peter Hall, with whom Peggy used to discuss the repertoire, including *Waiting for Godot*. On Hall's departure she found his successor in Peter Wood. Clifford Williams took over for 1959-60 and, from 1961 to 1964 the driving force was Michael Codron, with the RSC making a brief but important visit in 1962. Peggy had encouraged Codron after he had left the Lyric, Hammersmith, to look for another base where he could exert a continuous artistic influence and concentrate on presenting new plays.

From 1956, when Peggy first had a client's work produced at the Arts (Horton Foote's *The Trip to the Bountiful*), through to the end of Michael Codron's reign in 1964, she represented 28 plays that were seen at the theatre. During the Codron years, she was responsible for nearly a third of the output, ranging widely from comedies by John Mortimer and Muriel Spark to breakthrough plays by Henry Livings, James Saunders, Charles Wood, Frank Marcus and Joe Orton.

In the RSC's experimental season at the Arts, she was involved as an agent in four of the seven productions and indirectly, through her friendship with the director Anthony Page, in one other. She represented Derek Marlowe, who adapted Gorky's *The Lower Depths*, Simon Watson Taylor, who translated Boris Vian's *The Empire Builders*, David Rudkin, who wrote *Afore Night Come*, and Henry Livings, who wrote *Nil Carborundum*. Except for Harold Pinter, the vanguard of the RSC's new playwriting force in its opening years – Whiting, Rudkin, Livings, and David Mercer – were all Peggy's clients.

The lease of the Arts was taken over in March 1962 by Nat Cohen, who renamed it the New Arts, with Michael Codron as its managing director. The theatre was redecorated after the RSC left and was re-launched with a play by another of Peggy's clients, Muriel Spark's *Doctors of Philosophy*. In the mid-sixties the Arts, which reverted to its old name in 1966, was to change its identity again, owing to a combination of an emerging new fringe and occupation of the theatre in the afternoons by Caryl Jenner's Unicorn Theatre for children – which, incidentally, revived Franklyn Black's *The Heartless Princess*, the first play Peggy had represented. In the evenings regular programming continued but, without a permanent artistic presence, the theatre had become just another small-scale venue housing shows by a variety of producers.

But in the early '60s, with Codron at the helm, his programme of modern plays at the Arts created great excitement in the world of contemporary writing and helped build an audience for challenging new work. Codron, for example, kept faith with Harold Pinter and staged the première of *The Caretaker*, transferring to the West End where it ran for a year.

The set-up at the Arts suited both Codron and Peggy very well. Codron opened a new production every month, which allowed flexibility and experimentation but also required a ready supply of high-quality scripts, for which he looked first to Peggy. Peggy, in her turn, had just what she needed – a fully professional showcase for her writers, free from the demands of the star system that was strangling the West End.

After the RSC season, Charles Wood and James Saunders both ended a period of frustration with productions at the Arts which led to a joint Evening Standard award for Most Promising Playwright – Wood for three plays collected under the title *Cockade*, and Saunders for *Next Time I'll Sing To You*.

Saunders had begun his theatrical writing with a panto when he was attending Southampton University following wartime service as an electrical mechanic on a navy cruiser. He became a chemistry teacher and wrote several plays for radio. He tried different styles but when he turned to absurdism in 1958 with three short plays, his agent dropped him. He approached another agent, who returned the plays with a nondescript refusal and, in error, the reader's report. Saunders' friend from college, Leo Lehman, suggested he try Peggy, who replied quickly, though not effusively. She proved to be efficient in dealing with the business aspect of his work and encouraged him in his experimentation, so he stayed.

Next Time I'll Sing To You was suggested by a book called *A Hermit Disclosed* written by Raleigh Trevelyan, managing director of the publishers Michael Joseph whom Peggy knew socially. The book tells the story of Jimmy Mason, a man who became a recluse in East Anglia at the beginning of the century. He died, aged 84, in 1942 in Essex. Peggy introduced Saunders to Trevelyan, but Saunders put the idea of a play aside when the BBC said that it was not suitable for them. Peggy passed her copy of the book to Henry Livings, who did write a TV play from it, called *Jim All Alone*, which in turn influenced his later stage play *Kelly's Eye*. The book also fed into Edward Bond's writing of *The Pope's Wedding*.

Saunders, meanwhile, returned to the story for the innovative amateur theatre group, Questors, based in west London where Saunders lived. In this way he was able to write *Next Time I'll Sing to You* free both of commercial pressure and constricting audience expectations. He produced a dramatically bold investigation into the paradoxes of existence, using the device of actors reconstructing the hermit's life to question the nature of reality and role playing. Codron asked Saunders to re-write it for the New Arts Theatre from where it transferred to the West End in 1963. Tom Stoppard has acknowledged the debt he owes in the creation of *Rosencrantz and Guildenstern Are Dead* to *Next Time I'll Sing to You*, which earned Saunders a justified reputation as a distinctive voice, intelligent and eloquent.

Peggy was very fond of Saunders, a prolific writer of considerable diversity who followed his own path and was not constantly at her elbow seeking help. She did not suppose that his plays would ever make huge waves. In 1964, however, she invested money in his play *A Scent of Flowers*, something which Peggy did only rarely, when it was presented by Codron and Richard Pilbrow in the West End. It marked Ian McKellen's début there. She did not care that she did not recoup her financial investment because she admired the play, which pieces together with great emotional depth the story of a young woman who has comitted suicide.

Like many of her clients, Saunders was extremely gifted but did not occupy a high profile. Much of his work was first produced by small theatres, such as Questors, Inter-Action or the Orange Tree. For this reason, Peggy often baited him with the accusation that he was only toying with theatre, yet she was happy as long as he was. Moreover, despite her predilection for the West End, she often found she preferred the productions of his plays in what she called the 'coterie' theatres to subsequent productions in larger venues; she liked, for example, the simpler, more direct, interpretation of *Bodies* at the Orange Tree rather than the baroque version in the West End. She was pleased, however, when, having suggested Saunders to co-adapt with Iris Murdoch her novel *The Italian Girl*, it went from the Bristol Old Vic in 1967 to a long run at the Wyndham's Theatre the following year.

From time to time she would suggest ideas for plays without putting any pressure on him to pursue them. 'One Christmas,' he recalls, 'Peggy sent me a volume of Kleist stories. "If you don't have any Kleist on your shelves you should have," read the inscription, "and if you do, then you can never have too much".' In due course, Saunders did, indeed, write a play based on Kleist's *Michael Kolhaas*.

By her standards, Peggy handled Saunders gently. Theirs was a quiet relationship which survived until she died. 'She treated me as a tender plant and an odd fish,' says Saunders. 'She was keen on new writers when she found them, then would fall out of love with them. I never looked to her for affection or congratulations. She respected me without saying she liked my plays all that much. I stayed with her because of her name and my inertia, but I came gradually to realise her importance.'

When the agency to which Charles Wood belonged closed down in 1962, he had to his credit two television plays and one for radio but none for the stage. His friend Peter Nichols, who was already with Peggy, suggested he write to her. She had heard the radio play, *Cowheel Jelly*, and agreed to represent him. He was waiting for BBC-TV, which had broadcast one of his army plays, *Prisoner and Escort*, to respond to two more. After what amounted to a delay of more than a year, Peggy decided to change tack. She contacted Michael Codron. Within two days of receiving the two plays plus *Prisoner and Escort* he had agreed to produce the trio at the New Arts.

Wood's theatrical critique of the military was devastating, and brought him constant battles with the Lord Chamberlain's office. National Service had only finished the previous year; no one had told the truth about life in the army quite like this before. Wood signalled the rise of 1960s iconoclasm, and Peggy relished his sabre blows.

The success of *Cockade*, as the three plays were collectively known, opened up a new world to Wood. The RSC staged another short army play of his, *Don't Make Me Laugh*, in an experimental evening at the Aldwych Theatre in 1965, but more significantly *Cockade* introduced him to Oscar Lewenstein.

Peggy had become a close associate of Lewenstein's since they first met during rehearsals of Ionesco's *The Chairs* in 1958. She had been involved as an agent in several Lewenstein productions: she represented Ionesco and his translators for *Rhinoceros* and *Jacques*, and Harry Cookson, who wrote the book for *The Lily White Boys*, a Brechtian musical satire about a group of Teddy Boys with lyrics by Christopher Logue – three productions all at the Royal Court. She also represented Carl Davis, who had composed the music for a revue, *Twists*, by Stephen Vinaver, at the Arts. She and Lewenstein would work together again as agent and producer on plays by Joe Orton and Colin Spencer, as well as during the period from 1972-75 when Lewenstein was artistic director of the Royal Court. At one point, she began interviewing him on tape, material which Lewenstein used much later in his autobiography, *Kicking Against the Pricks*.

With Peggy's encouragement, Lewenstein was responsible for starting Wood on a distinguished career in the cinema by employing him as the screenwriter on the film adaptation of Ann Jellicoe's *The Knack*. (This was fitting, as it turned out, because Wood had been turned on to playwriting in the first place by reading Jellicoe's *The Sport of My Mad Mother*.) After *The Knack*, there followed Lewenstein productions of three Charles Wood plays in association with the Royal Court. The first, *Meals on Wheels*, was directed by John Osborne at the Royal Court in 1965 and was a disaster. Osborne has described the play, which deals with being old, as a 'bizarre comic extravaganza of such inventiveness that nobody understands it,' adding that neither did he; Peggy came to rehearsals and was very supportive. A West End theatre, the Vaudeville, had to be taken over in 1967 for the second, William Gaskill's production of *Fill the Stage With Happy Hours*, because the Royal Court was occupied by a visiting show from the US, Jean-Claude van Itallie's *America Hurrah*. Originally seen in Nottingham, *Fill the Stage With Happy Hours*, was a favourite of Peggy's; set behind the scenes of a faded small-town rep, it captured the self-delusion of a world she remembered so vividly from her time as an actress. Two months later, Lewenstein produced at the Royal Court Wood's next play, *Dingo*, which earlier in the year had been staged at the Bristol Arts Centre after the National Theatre had dropped it when it ran foul of the censor. The Lord Chamberlain had refused the play a licence, so it had to be presented at the Royal Court under club conditions. This debunking attack on war and the mythologising of World War II was a companion piece to Wood's film, *How I Won the War*, which was produced by Lewenstein and directed by Richard Lester, who had made *The Knack*.

Wood's blistering writing on the army made him a natural choice to write the final screenplay for another film Lewenstein was producing, the much-troubled *The Charge of the Light Brigade*. In the pre-production period, Lewenstein had a disagreement with the director, Tony Richardson, and pulled out, as did the original screenwriter, John Osborne. Osborne had been charged with plagiarism by Laurence Harvey, who owned the rights to the book in question, *The Reason Why* by Mrs Cecil Woodham-Smith, considered then the definitive account of the Crimean campaign. Richardson struck a deal with Harvey, which included Harvey getting a part in the film. The problem was that this was the part that was due to be played by Osborne, who split with Richardson over the issue. When the trouble began in earnest Wood was approached, but he had fallen out with Lewenstein too and told Peggy he would not take on the job. Osborne then rang him and urged him to accept because the alternative would be the hiring of a Hollywood hack. Wood agreed because it was Osborne who was asking. Wood reworked the script and stayed on location during the shooting, a remarkable experience which gave him great comic material for his plays *Veterans* and *Has Washington Legs*?

Wood's twin obsessions, the military and the theatre, stemmed from his own upbringing in a theatrical family and five years' service in the 17/21st Lancers. Peggy responded readily to obsessions and to these in particular because they were central to her earlier life. She liked Wood's off-beat humour and bold dramaturgy but felt that he was losing his way after *H*, a wild, poetic epic on the Indian mutiny of 1857 (performed at the National Theatre in 1969) and *Veterans*, a 'cinema' sequel to *Fill the Stage With Happy Hours* that brought together John Gielgud and John Mills at the Royal Court in 1972 and won Wood that year's Evening Standard Award for Best Comedy.

Apart from *The Knack*, Peggy had shown little interest in Wood's films, and now he entered a period when many of his film scripts were not getting made. His TV work she saw as merely a means to an end. In the mid-70s he decided, therefore, to leave Peggy in order to give himself a new start with another agent and to earn some more money. She wrote to him: 'Trying to make money is just as difficult as trying to be the greatest writer in the world. To write a really bad play, or a really bad novel, requires all the author's talent because it has got to be written with sincerity.'

Looking back, Wood says that his first ten years with Peggy formed 'the most important decade for me, because of the encouragement I got when I was starting out, when you really need a good agent. I hadn't realised how important her letters were – you took them for granted – and her warmth and her care about my work. In a way, she's the only agent I've ever had.'

Henry Livings experienced a similar whirlwind start with Peggy to that enjoyed by Charles Wood and yet also left a decade after joining, when he felt his relationship with her had run into the sands. In 1961, his first full year with Peggy, Livings had his first radio play and first two television plays broadcast, which, he says, he had more or less sold himself, as well as his first two stage plays – *Stop It, Whoever You Are* and *Big Soft Nellie* –

both produced by Michael Codron. It was an extraordinary year and, to cap it, he won the Evening Standard Most Promising Playwright Award.

Livings, born a few miles outside Manchester in Prestwich, Lancashire, was an actor, who, among other things, had been a rail porter, a hosiery knitter, and a pastry cook as well as a student of Hispanic studies at Liverpool University. His national service had been in the RAF. His plays expressed a working-class spirit of fun, mixing farce and fantasy, and brought with them a desire to make social connections with the audience that was characteristic of Joan Littlewood's Theatre Workshop at Stratford East, where he had been an actor. Codron took *Big Soft Nellie* to Stratford East, which Peggy believed provided just the kind of strong actor-audience relationship his plays required and which was difficult, if not impossible, to find in the West End.

Peggy interested the recently-founded RSC and the Royal Court in Livings, who was quickly establishing himself as a distinctive new talent. His RAF comedy, *Nil Carborundum*, was included in the RSC's 1962 experimental season at the Arts. The following year, the Royal Court presented *Kelly's Eye* in association with Codron, and in 1964 the RSC put Livings on its main London stage at the Aldwych in Peter Hall's production of *Eh?*, a comedy set in the boiler room of a dye factory. The main character, Valentine Brose, was played by David Warner, while in New York the part was taken by Dustin Hoffman, in a production by Alan Arkin, that led directly to Hoffman being cast in *The Graduate*, the beginning of his prestigious career in the cinema.

Hall went on to choose *Eh?* for his first foray into films, and Livings looked set to follow the pattern of Charles Woods' success. Disaster struck, however, when Livings fell out with Hall over the film script and was replaced as screenwriter by another of Peggy's clients, Jeremy Brooks, who was Hall's literary manager at the RSC. Peggy advised Hall against this move, yet he proceeded.

The film, which was released in 1968 as *Work Is a Four-Letter Word*, turned out to be a flop. Peggy denounced Hall's judgement as ludicrous. 'He got a very sprightly and original script from the author [Livings] and threw it out, to get a completely unfunny, deadly "decent" one from his dramaturg . . . which was one of the sensational failures of the year.' Unfortunately, it was still associated with Livings' original play and he felt that it damaged his reputation. Livings believed that Peggy had let him down, although there was very little that she could have done other than argue with Hall, which she did, as there was no contractual obligation on Hall to remain with Livings.

Whereas only a year or so before, all doors seemed to be opening for Livings, they now all seemed to be firmly shut. Peggy appeared to have become indifferent to his work and when, in 1969, she did not know the details of a radio adaptation he had written of Gogol's *The Government Inspector*, Livings determined to leave the agency. 'I have never been sentimental about theatre,' says Livings, 'and I was very upset when I left her, but once I'd decided, it acquired a finality and I couldn't go back on it. Others change wives at 40. I changed my agent, much to my own disadvantage as it turned out.'

Livings recalls Peggy as a great iconoclast, satirising the 'Royal Shaggers Company' and even stripping her friend Hall to pieces for being machiavellian and megalomaniacal. 'Her job was to put you with the right management and she was very good at placing plays. The RSC were frightened to pick up the phone if they knew it was her because she wasn't a diplomat. She didn't like the money being made by the subsidised theatre when the writer was being paid so little in advance. She was encouraging to me as a writer. "If they say you go too far," she would urge, "go further." She was very quick and responded fast, but I was more interested in the opinions of people who would pay me, not hers. She had the wit to leave me alone and therefore, I suppose, the indifference was really mine. She dropped people when there was no more to offer, and she was not useful when you tumbled. But you have no right to expect endless commitment. It is sad that she was right so often.'

Peggy liked Livings' down-to-earth, anarchic characters and his truculent sardonic philosophy, summed up in the meaning of *Nil Carborundum* – 'don't let the bastards grind you down.' Yet, despite the serious tone of a play like *Kelly's Eye*, in which a man who has escaped from life offers an unexpected and inexplicable vitality to a naive young woman, Peggy thought that Livings' flamboyant cartoon style was not developing properly. Livings was caught in a limbo between the prevailing naturalism of the establishment and the experimentation of the avant-garde. Peggy was unable to help him pursue his work in the comic popular tradition. She was finding it increasingly difficult to envisage his plays working in the London theatre. For Peggy, this problem stemmed from Livings' origins in the North of England.

Livings was a Lancastrian but to Peggy all northerners blurred into one. 'Get back up north,' she would say to him, 'and leave us in the shit.' She had the idea that northerners were forever festive because a few of her northern clients would take her out and get drunk. To her the industrial north was another country, with its own values and culture quite removed from the world of Shaftesbury Avenue. Her clients who hailed from this far-off land formed a special category in her mind and included other Lancastrians Bill Naughton (born in Ireland but raised in Lancashire), Jack Rosenthal and later Willy Russell, from Yorkshire David Mercer and Stanley Eveling, Peter Terson from Northumberland, and Alan Plater from County Durham.

Never one to surrender a strongly-rooted opinion to recalcitrant reality, Peggy enrolled honorary northerners in this élite club, such as C. P. Taylor, who was born and raised further north in Scotland, and Alan Ayckbourn, who was born and raised in the south. They had both moved to the north of England (Newcastle and Scarborough respectively) and themselves became closely identified with their chosen domiciles.

What seems like snobbishness in this regard was to Peggy a matter of telling the truth as she saw it. She insisted that she was a 'northern fan' and loved the directness of the 'northern' emotions that she seldom found in the ossified south. She especially liked the working-class writers because they broke through the effete culture of the West End, along with a new generation of northern directors and actors who no longer felt obliged to ape Home Counties pronunciation and behaviour. Nevertheless, she equally strongly feared that London audiences would not accept 'northern' plays and declared this as simply an uncontrovertible fact of commercial life.

For Peggy a 'northern' play could be defined either by content or form, or both. Often it was less a matter of geography and more a matter of 'provincial' versus 'metropolitan' taste. She was a firm believer in non-London productions, whether from Leatherhead or Leeds, being re-thought for the capital because plays that had been wonderful in their home town often came over as crude or exaggerated to a London audience. Some of Peggy's clients, such as David Mercer, transcended the north-south divide by virtue of the sensibilities that Peggy saw in their writing; others, such as Alan Plater, in her view never managed to bridge the gap successfully, while a few, such as Bill Naughton, straddled the chasm by depicting the north in ways that found favour down south.

Bill Naughton had come to Peggy as a Peters and Ramsay client. With *All in Good Time* and *Spring and Port Wine* in the early 1960s he placed working-class family life in Bolton squarely on the southern map before becoming even better known for his Cockney Don Juan character Alfie, who began life in a radio play, became sharpest in his 1963 stage incarnation and then appeared in both a novel and a film. When Naughton left A.D. Peters Ltd. in 1968 he pulled out of Peters and Ramsay too and decided not to have an agent thereafter. He subsequently relented, however, and did return.

Alan Plater approached Peggy in 1961 on the advice of Henry Livings, who was acting in Plater's first play on radio. Plater sent her what he describes as two 'modest' radio plays, with an accompanying plea that he wished to work in theatre, TV and film, and needed someone to sell his plays. The telephone rang by return. 'Darling,' came Peggy's reprimand, 'I don't sell plays! My writers write plays and other people want to buy them!'

During the introductory stage of their relationship, when Plater was still living in Hull, she wrote 'one should have only North Country authors, they are such a blessing', yet only a few weeks later she was inviting him to consider taking his plays to another agent because she had responded bleakly to his latest offering, a TV script that was never produced. 'I feel I must tell you the truth,' she wrote to him, 'yet you could be quite justified in saying, "very well, if you don't like the play, I can go elsewhere".'

But Plater stayed put. He was being needled and nudged by her in a way that was too stimulating to reject, although she persisted in her view that his writing would not catch on in the south. She wrote about one script: 'Lennie's Nine Lives is a very ambitious play which I think needs considerable revising. It is difficult to judge for the south because it is pretty harsh and awkward, whereas down here we try and pack our plays with spurious charm.' The play tells the story of a frustrated and alienated young man who seeks a more fulfilling life, which he is convinced he will one day find somewhere. It eventually became *A Smashing Day*, which was televised in 1962 and, in a rewritten form, staged in 1965 at Stoke-on-Trent where it was seen by Brian Epstein, the Beatles' manager. He decided to bring it to the New Arts Theatre in London. The director fell ill and Epstein took over. Despite a first-night audience that included Cilla Black, Ringo Starr and John Lennon, the play, as Peggy had predicted all those years before, was not a success, although the composers of the music, Ben Kingsley and Robert Powell, went on to become famous actors, as did Hywel Bennett, who was given his break in films on the strength of his portrayal of Lennie.

Plater enjoyed his biggest theatrical hit in Newcastle upon Tyne in 1968 with *Close the Coalhouse Door*, his popular adaptation of mining stories by Sid Chaplin with music by Alex Glasgow. Peggy thought it was revolutionary but believed that it would not work in London – and she was again proved right, up to a point; it played the Fortune, a small West End theatre, for only four months, unlike the working-class plays from the London-based Theatre Workshop, which enjoyed much longer runs in larger theatres.

Peggy and Plater corresponded a lot on non-theatrical matters, such as the state of the nation, and Peggy would challenge his view that the south was living off the fat. She accused him of confusing the south with London, which, she said, lived off tourists. The real south, she insisted, was more like Brighton, where she lived at weekends; it was almost derelict.

Although Peggy was the conduit for Plater's fruitful collaboration with the pioneering TV police series *Z Cars*, Plater's distinguished TV writing career was mostly self-generated, with the agency merely providing the business support. His attempts to make a similar mark in theatre – and he was prolific for the stage – were obstructed in Peggy's view by a trait he shared in common with other northern writers: an obsession with theatre-in-the-round. She blamed the two figures who were central to the development of playwriting in the north at this time, Stephen Joseph, who had formed a company in Scarborough in 1955, and Peter Cheeseman, who, with Joseph, had founded the country's first permanent theatre-in-the-round in Stoke in 1962. Ironically, one of Peggy's most successful playwrights, Alan Ayckbourn, came from precisely this stable.

In Peggy's view, Plater's *A Smashing Day* was a typical example of a play that was well-suited to theatre-in-the-round but which suffered in the conventional end-on, proscenium form. The day after it had opened in London, Peggy wrote to Cheeseman, who had staged the play in Stoke, explaining her disappointment in what she considered to be the poor production at the Arts.

'The play has enormous quality, but it's a series of scenes and isn't written fully for the stage. This shorthand doesn't show in-the-round, it's almost an advantage. A closely-knit proscenium play is a bit too "thick" for the round, I think . . . You are a brilliant help to a new author – discerning and recognising their talent immediately, you do fascinating productions in your theatre – a real asset to our profession. But people come up and see what you do and imagine it's easy as pie to do exactly the same. What they don't understand is that a play in-the-round is essentially freer and more oblique and more subtle than the proscenium, which needs enlarging and needs projecting, so that everything "holds". One doesn't need this in-the-round.'

Peggy believed that the in-the-round configuration was too hypnotic; she thought it seduced the audience into valuing everything with too much and equal weight, a small gesture like lifting a cup seemingly becoming just as meaningful as a murder. Plater saw this as a strength, but Peggy preferred the formality and discipline of the proscenium.

An insoluble paradox for writers such as Alan Plater, or Jack Rosenthal, a fellow member of Peggy's northern club who came to Peggy already established in TV, was their inability to match on stage the immense popular appeal they enjoyed on television. This tension added to Peggy's disenchantment with TV; her obsession remained theatre, as did theirs. Nevertheless, she exerted considerable influence in the world of television and, despite her anti-TV rhetoric, worked very hard for her television writers, who wrote some of the most impressive and innovative plays ever broadcast in the medium. As well as Plater and Rosenthal, her clients included many writers well-known for their contribution to TV, such as Tom Clarke, Ray Jenkins, John Bowen, Stephen Poliakoff, Hugh Whitemore, David Hare, John McGrath, Peter Nichols, and David Mercer, who redefined TV drama much as Peggy redefined being an agent.

David Mercer was another of Peggy's northerners, but for Peggy he was different. She felt his writing was less imprisoned in the north because he was writing about escape from roots and subsequent loss of belonging. She did help Mercer directly in his TV career, which, while internationally recognised for its creativity, never won him the popularity that other clients achieved. Mercer became one of Peggy's favourites, though at first she was characteristically circumspect about defining his potential whilst being adamant that it existed.

She was drawn to him by his response to the toughness of his life, which in Peggy's romantic view was the very stuff of being a writer. It began in 1928 in a strict, upper working-class environment in Wakefield in the West Riding of Yorkshire. He left school at 14, worked as a laboratory technician, joined the navy for three years, where, among other things, he treated sailors for venereal disease, returned to school and matriculated. He attended Durham University, switching from chemistry to fine art at a college in Newcastle, where he began to read about politics, psychiatry, history and philosophy. He saw himself as a Communist who had no illusions about Stalinism and never joined the Communist Party. He lived in Paris for two years with his first wife in order to be a painter and, on realising that he was not going to be a good artist, burnt all his canvases and began instead to write novels, which he later destroyed too. Mercer returned to London in 1955 and started to earn his living as a supply teacher. His first marriage broke up, he suffered a nervous breakdown and he was accepted as 'a suitable case for treatment' under the radical psychoanalyst R. D. Laing at the Tavistock Clinic in north London.

Peggy

It was while he was undergoing psychoanalysis here that ideas began to occur to him in the form of images and speeches. He went to see Shelagh Delaney's *A Taste of Honey*, thought he could do better and wrote his first play, *A Death in the Family*, a partly autobiographical story set in Yorkshire in which a family gathers on the death of the mother. The widower, an engine driver like Mercer's father, comes to recognise that he has lost not only his wife but his two sons, who have become middle class.

Mercer was destitute and neurotic when Peggy first came across him, which, in the best possible way for Peggy, was completely by accident. The Aldwych Theatre's general manager, John Roberts, had asked a wine merchant he knew to give his son a job. In return, the wine merchant had asked Roberts to look at a script that had been written by his lodger, who was stereotypically starving. Roberts thought the script was awful and asked Peggy as a favour if she would write a non-committal report that would keep the wine merchant sweet. The writer was David Mercer; the script was *A Death in the Family*.

Peggy summoned Mercer to Goodwin's Court. She found him very frightened and shy but under the nervousness she felt him snorting like a bull. 'There was a tremendous latent, dangerous element,' she recalled, which attracted her in an almost Lawrentian way. She thought Mercer could become an excellent writer but needed to learn a great deal about the theatre. She did not think that his first play should be seen on the stage without considerable rewriting, which Mercer set about undertaking. Peggy once told another client that she first met Mercer at a party, subsequently read his novels and then told him to become a dramatist. The detail of Peggy's first encounter with his work is less important than the fact that there was never any doubt in Mercer's mind that it was Peggy who gave him the self-confidence to persist as a playwright and guided him through his subsequent career.

In his first year with her, 1960, she obtained commissions for him in radio and television, and sent him a TV play by her client Rhys Adrian as a model for Mercer to study. She also sent him Büchner's *Woyzeck* and *Danton's Death* so that he could learn more about stagecraft. She showed a revised version of *A Death in the Family* to a few contacts, including Jack Minster, who offered £100 to take out an option on it, but Peggy refused because by this time Mercer had already written a second play which she thought showed even more promise.

Peggy had been closely involved in the early development of this play, *The Buried Man*, in which a factory worker who has a breakdown chooses to return to mental hospital because his family find him insufferable after his release. Mercer sent the play to Peggy scene by scene for her comments, waiting for her response before being able to continue. Accompanying one scene, he wrote a note in the form of a poem:

Am I being wet-legged?
feeble-minded?
fragile in the dorsal region?
by asking for more of your time?
Perhaps I should see a head shrinker.

Peggy found *The Buried Man* 'full of remarkable things', a 'bit stodgy' (in terms of form) but with 'a strange sense of feeling coming through'. Several London managements took out options but did not produce the play. Peggy felt they were too scared. It was emotionally very direct and more disturbing than other contemporary writing about working-class life.

When *The Buried Man* was eventually produced, in 1962, by the Library Theatre, Manchester, Mercer had already moved on as a writer. Also, Peggy thought the play had been spoiled because Mercer had rewritten it every time it was rejected and in each draft had supplied answers to the questions that had been raised by the rejecting managements. 'Life is unresolved,' she said to him, 'and so plays should be.' She warned him not to retreat into symbolism. 'Non-realism, as in *The Bald Prima Donna*, is terribly real.' By the time of the Manchester production Peggy did not want the play to be seen in London and sold it instead to a commercial TV station, Associated Television. It was broadcast in 1963, two years after his TV début, with some of the ambiguity re-introduced.

Mercer's route to television was circuitous, as these things often are, and involved another of Peggy's clients, Don Taylor. Taylor had sent Peggy a play in 1958 when he was an assistant to Frank Hauser at the Oxford Playhouse, and she had taken Taylor on as a writer and adaptor. Taylor had attended a BBC-TV trainee director course and had become a full-time TV director in 1960. While he was directing Robert Shaw that year in a TV play (*The Train Set* by David Turner), Shaw showed Taylor David Mercer's play *The Buried Man*. Shaw had been given it to read by Oscar Lewenstein, who had taken out an option on the play.

Taylor read it, liked it and noticed from the script that Mercer was also represented by Peggy. He telephoned Peggy to find out more about Mercer and was greeted by a blast from Peggy who was furious with Shaw because *The Buried Man* was under option to Lewenstein and therefore not available for television. She agreed to send Taylor another play of

Mercer's, the earlier *A Death in the Family*. Taylor told Peggy that he would like to work on it with Mercer and turn it into a TV play. Peggy agreed, Taylor and Mercer duly met, and Taylor persuaded Michael Barry, Head of TV Drama at the BBC, to let him direct what was now called *Where the Difference Begins*. It was broadcast in 1961 and became the first of Mercer's innovative trilogy of TV plays, *The Generations*, which were all directed by Taylor.

When Mercer finally made his London stage début in 1965, he had been acclaimed for half a dozen TV plays, had won the 1962 Screenwriters' Guild Award, and was established as one of Britain's leading writers for TV. Sadly, his mighty reputation, which was enhanced by a further 18 plays for the medium, was not sufficient to prevent the BBC from destroying much of his output in their routine culling of the archive. Peggy was outraged, and was particularly upset at the loss of *A Suitable Case for Treatment*, which, in terms of storytelling, cutting and editing, showed Mercer at his dazzling and inventive best.

It is not surprising that it was in television that Mercer emerged as a writer; following his first TV play, the medium had responded to him with alacrity, and therefore money. In the theatre he had met only delay, and his radio commission, *The Governor's Lady* – a fable about loss of empire in which the mentally distraught eponymous heroine imagines her dead husband resurrected as a sexually rampaging gorilla which she shoots – had been banned because it was deemed too offensive. (It was eventually broadcast in 1969.)

Peggy did not regret encouraging Mercer to write for television, in which he found a liberation denied him in the theatre. She recognised that television had kept him alive; it had given him 'self-respect and a new mistress.'

His irrepressible desire to be recognised as a stage playwright, however, reflected Peggy's own preferences. Yet it took her until 1965 to secure him a return to the stage, in two productions both seen in London; *The Governor's Lady* was rewritten for the RSC as part of an evening of new plays at the Aldwych Theatre and, later that year, Michael Codron presented at Nottingham and then the Piccadilly Theatre *Ride a Cock Horse*, a play about the decline of a successful working-class novelist whose guilt at the way he treats the three women in his life corrodes his sense of self. Directed by Gordon Flemyng, it starred Peter O'Toole, who had become one of Mercer's drinking partners, and played to full houses during its run.

Mercer may have been exasperated by the delay to his London stage début but it was worth the wait; he won the Evening Standard Most

Promising Playwright award that year for *Ride a Cock Horse* – a tremendous boost to his confidence.

Through the championing of David Jones, who had directed *The Governor's Lady*, Mercer became, along with Harold Pinter, something akin to a resident dramatist of the RSC. Five more of his stage plays were performed by the company, four of them at the 1,000-seat Aldwych, including *After Haggerty*, the first RSC new play to transfer to a commercial West End theatre, where it ran for five months. Directed by Jones in 1970, it covers familiar Mercer terrain: a left-wing but traditional theatre critic confronts the contradictions of family, sexuality and politics when the flat he is living in is visited by a radicalised American woman and her infant, the child of the flat's former occupant, James Haggerty. The critic's father arrives, a working-class Yorkshireman, thus adding another generation to the mix and completing a new kind of family in which their various attempts at self-expression knock against the confines of blood-ties and convention.

For all Peggy's formidable nurturing skills, she could not bring Mercer to fulfil his potential for the stage, which was a source of constant anxiety for him and disappointment for her. He felt this more keenly because of his success in television and on film, not only with his two cinema versions of TV plays – Karel Reisz's *Morgan* (in 1966, based on *A Suitable Case for Treatment*) and Ken Loach's *Family Life* (in 1972, based on *In Two Minds*) – but also with his 1973 adaptation of Ibsen's *A Doll's House*, directed by Joseph Losey, and in 1978 his script for Alan Resnais' only film in English, *Providence*. Resnais had decided upon Mercer to write this elusive, extraordinary film about an ageing novelist after seeing his play *Duck Song* at the RSC. Starring John Gielgud, Dirk Bogarde and David Warner, *Providence* was one of Peggy's favourite pieces of work by any of her clients.

One of Mercer's great sadnesses was that he made only one film with Losey, a friend who was his best man at his third wedding and who had known Peggy since the mid-50s. Mercer and Losey collaborated on several projects which came to nothing, the most exciting being one very dear to Peggy, a seven-part TV serialisation of *The Magic Mountain* by Thomas Mann, which was abandoned when the producers wanted to cut it back and turn it into a feature film.

Peggy and Mercer enjoyed a mother-son relationship of highs and lows, of rebuke and forgiveness. She adored him but expected his devotion in return. Mercer put his career entirely in Peggy's hands and did not make any important moves without consulting her. The few times that he neglected this principle he regretted it.

'I have no doubt that I shall be ten times the writer working with you than I would be on my own or with anyone else,' he wrote to her at the outset. After receiving his first royalty cheque (for £42) he was childlike in his response: 'I have never received so much money before . . . It's an experience I'm quite sure I wouldn't have had at all if you hadn't "taken me over".'

Mercer wanted to believe that he was a great writer; this made him an ideal client for Peggy. She was possessive of his talent and justified this possessiveness by the inspiration she afforded him. She advised Mercer to read Strindberg, who became his master, yet she also told him to be lighter and to write something funny and wild. This piece of advice led directly to *A Suitable Case for Treatment*.

She thought Mercer had a tendency to be over-literary and suggested that he put more of his own personality into his plays. She admired his courage for doing this, which, she felt, put his early plays outside Osborne's range and made them tougher and sharper than Wesker's. She felt Mercer's time spent as a patient of R. D. Laing was extremely beneficial to his writing.

Peggy was wary of those who in her view admired him extravagantly. When she criticised the central character in *The Buried Man* for being too passive, she told him: 'This is the whole problem of your bloody play and the same is true of your career. Things are happening to you and you are not making things happen.'

She intervened ruthlessly in Mercer's relationship with Don Taylor. She valued loyalty and recognised Taylor's role in establishing Mercer as England's premier television writer but believed that the relationship with Taylor was hindering Mercer's development. After six TV plays together, Peggy helped Mercer prise himself away from Taylor in 1965. Although Taylor was one of Peggy's clients too, she knew where her priorities lay. She also wanted Taylor to develop as a writer himself. She realised that the introduction of a new producer system in TV drama would diminish the power of a director such as Taylor.

That same year, 1965, saw the beginning of Mercer's association with David Jones – he directed four of Mercer's stage plays and one TV adaptation – about which Peggy was similarly uneasy. For Peggy, a settled relationship not only spelled complacency in the work of the writer but threatened her own power too.

She encouraged and prompted Mercer, and often had to goad him into work when she thought he was being lazy. She fuelled his self-belief, much helped by his association with other famous writers in her agency, but warned him against being egotistical. 'With his beard he thinks he's Balzac,' Peggy would say deprecatingly. On one occasion, as a newcomer to the agency, Mercer telephoned Robert Bolt to tell him what dreadful things Peggy was saying about him. 'You've got to do something to muzzle her. You should hear what she's saying about your play,' said Mercer. Bolt, the old hand, laughed. Mercer continued in the same concerned vein; it was no laughing matter, he insisted. Bolt calmly replied, 'You should hear what she's saying about yours.'

For his part, Mercer brought class-consciousness and left-wing politics into Peggy's life. Long before she met Mercer, she had warmed instinctively to the outsider, the rebel, the dispossessed, and was generally 'against the system' in a moral and individual rather than a social and political sense. She had little faith in the capacity of human beings to organise rationally, although she did attend one Aldermaston peace march. Mercer argued at length to try to persuade her that organised political action did have meaning. She even took out a subscription to the revolutionary magazine *Black Dwarf* with which Mercer was involved, and enjoyed the idea that an editorial he wrote might be vetted for subversion by MI5.

Mercer was often frustrated with her over money; she was only too aware of how badly Mercer wanted it but wary of its destructive effects on him. She stuck to her philosophy that material wealth spoiled a writer while trying her damnedest to negotiate for him better deals, without losing her or his respect. 'I have as much dubious lust for success and money as the next man,' he wrote her, 'but it will either come or not. To do what one only can do is not a moral achievement, but to live out the necessities of one's temperament.'

Despite these noble sentiments, his spending capacity was voluminous and ruinous, particularly when drinking hard. A very emotional man, he was wayward in drink as well as in money and, after bouts of indulgence, would seek confirmation of Peggy's continued love, often to receive a scolding for his pains. Peggy did not approve of Mercer's drunkenness and was occasionally fearful of it, even if at times she thought it could be instructive. She urged Mercer and other clients to tap into their sub-conscious, but there were limits to her love of abandonment. She felt it was self-defeating, and demeaning, to embrace excess through a complete loss of control. When Mercer was drunk he was difficult to get close to, which she disliked, and yet she responded to the life force that drink could release; a drunken Mercer hit a radio producer at a Writers' Guild function and the next day remembered nothing of it. Peggy, perhaps sensing an echo of a fight she had been involved in on a tour, felt that Mercer's action had shown a true expressiveness and vitality.

Their relationship was frank and intimate, though not physical. It was frequently sexually blunt; what he called his primitive male urges continually challenged his attempts to wrestle intellectually with feminism, and, when angry or drunk, or both, his misogyny could rise to the surface, sometimes violently. Peggy's attitudes were more like those of a disinterested male, and the vocabulary they used together was more like that employed by two male friends. They enjoyed a jokey familiarity; Mercer would often find her in the office with her legs up on the desk, and sometimes without knickers. 'Put your fanny away, darling,' he would say with a smile, and Peggy would cackle in delight. When he was abroad once he wrote to her about romance. In a typically anti-sentimental reply, she wrote back: 'Have you not considered the fact that you are still very adolescent as far as women are concerned. You still have these absurd romantic illusions. After all, they are just a bit of cunt and you should keep your friendships and emotions separate from your sexual desires. However, we wouldn't get such good stage plays from you.'

Peggy saw many women come and go in Mercer's life. During the collapse of his second marriage in the early 1960s he wrote to Peggy: 'Do you still love me? I suspect there is a new generation of wet-eared youngsters ready to climb upon the shattered necks of the pioneers. Ho hum.' His drinking worsened as the marriage ended, and he moved in briefly with Peggy, to be sheltered and to receive her wisdom. This led him to admire her 'self-containedness' all the more. 'One day I shall grow up too – shall I? Is it conceivable?' he asked her. Peggy would tell him that the women were temporary but the talent should not be.

None of his female partners were as important to him as was Peggy, until perhaps his third and last wife Dafna, whom he married in 1974 and with whom he was eventually to settle in Israel. From there he wrote Peggy long letters about love and politics (for example, he hangs on to being pro-Palestinian but says that 'any non-Jew is doomed to feel unauthentic'). To Peggy, his life with Dafna signalled the end of his creativity.

Mercer died aged 52 in Israel in 1980. He had weaned himself off alcohol, although too late to live to a good old age. Peggy was wilfully harsh about him after his death, as if to convince herself that she continued to be right about her assessment of his fate; 'I'm glad he died,' she said, 'because he wouldn't have written any more good plays. He drank himself to death because he knew he'd written himself out. It was desolating for him.' She blamed the fame and the money it bought him, which had fed his drink problem. 'Mercer survived failure but not success,' was her final judgement.

As soon as she heard the news, Peggy telephoned David Hare to tell him that Mercer had died. Not being close to Mercer, Hare asked who else she had called. No one else, she replied. He was the first because she needed to know what to do with the body, how to get it back from a foreign country. He had written about this in *Plenty*, and all he could suggest was for her to contact the British embassy, which is what happens in the play. And Peggy did. As it turned out, her help was not required; Mercer was buried in Haifa. The episode had a distancing effect for Peggy, which she needed in order to maintain her own equilibrium. Sentiment had no place where art was concerned; talent existed for her over and above the individual who embodied it.

At the same time as Peggy was attempting to corral the talents of David Mercer she was conducting a similarly intense mother-son relationship with another David, David Rudkin, who was in many ways the antithesis of Mercer, yet they ploughed a common terrain. Both wrote as if they were setting out on a spiritual expedition into the unknown; as Mercer said, there is no point in writing a play if you know what it is about from the outset. But whereas Mercer had a wild emotional quality, to Peggy there was a repressed tightness about the Oxford-educated Rudkin, who was eight years Mercer's junior. Both had a puritanical background (Rudkin's father was a revivalist pastor) and, in their different ways, were struggling intensively with the politics of the psyche, to Peggy's intense fascination.

As president of his college drama society at Oxford University, Rudkin (on behalf of an undergraduate, Michael Billington) had written to Peggy to obtain the rights to perform Ionesco's *The Bald Prima Donna*. He recalls that she replied in an extraordinary way for an agent receiving a request to stage a client's work: 'What are you bright young Oxford boys doing pissing around with Ionesco, for fuck's sake? Why don't you write plays of your own?'

The college production of *The Bald Prima Donna* went ahead, but Rudkin also responded to Peggy's challenge. He sent her a short play, which she passed on to John Holmstrom to read, who recommended it to Peggy. She was cautious, as was her wont with new talent, but recognised its merits as well as the author's potential. Rudkin was invited to Goodwin's Court. He remembers the visit in 1959. 'Peggy wore flyaway glasses, came in like a whirlwind and said, "Ah, someone young". She offered a mixture of the put down and the pick up, saying, "You won't write anything for years but you will one day".'

131

J.D. Rudkin, as he was known then, was 23. He was born in London, educated in Birmingham, and did national service in the Royal Corps of Signals before going to university. Peggy found him too serious, pompous and clever, but admired his unflinching honesty and high work rate. He sent her a couple of plays very quickly, which she pronounced unstageable. However, she sold a radio play of his, *No Accounting for Taste*, to the Midlands BBC in early 1960 and tried, though unsuccessfully, to interest BBC Radio in London in two other plays that year. Rudkin organised in Oxford a reading of a new play of his, *Afore Night Come*, which he felt was his first real play. Peggy surprised him – the first of many chastening surprises she was to administer to him – by saying: 'I hope you don't have any more like this to get off your chest. Put it away.'

A group of fruit-pickers on a farm in the Midlands turn on an outsider, a cultured Irish tramp, and ritualistically sacrifice him as if in expiation and revenge for their own individual and collective inadequacies. Peggy responded to its rich, sinewy language and found its savage murder startling yet its menacing tone a little too dark. '*Afore Night Come* is VERY uncommercial, and very odd, but *extremely* talented,' she said. John Holmstrom, who was by now literary adviser to Peter Hall at the newly-founded RSC, liked the play even more than Peggy – the published text is dedicated to him. Holmstrom asked Peggy if he could show the play to Hall when the idea arose of the RSC mounting an experimental season. She agreed that this would be ideal. Hall read *Afore Night Come* and decided that he wanted it to form a part of the season. He met Rudkin in Stratford-upon-Avon with Peter Wood, whom Hall had chosen to direct. A production was agreed but then postponed for many months to fit in with Wood's dates and the setting up of the whole season.

Peggy was furious at the delay but powerless. She was sure no commercial management would produce the play, so the RSC was her only hope. Yet when rehearsals were finally due to start, the situation spun further out of control. Wood fell ill and Hall approached a new director, Clifford Williams, whom he had taken on as a staff producer to keep an eye on shows at the Aldwych once they had opened but on the absolute condition that he would never direct a production of his own. Hall's chagrin at having to retreat was compounded by Peggy's ire. She threatened to shoot the new director if he began rehearsing Rudkin's play. 'Manslaughter would have been a mild price to pay for the destruction of an author,' she said.

Wood recovered and then, two days later, he fell ill again. Williams said he was still prepared to take over. Peggy reluctantly agreed because she now knew that Wood was actually under contract to Binkie Beaumont to direct a production in the West End. The fact that hardly any of the play had been cast and there was no design ready when Williams took over suggested that the illness had been convenient. Peggy's rage did not abate, and yet, despite reminding everyone that her threat to Williams had been serious, she was grateful to him in the end. He opened *Afore Night Come* in the RSC's season at the Arts Theatre in 1962 and later transferred the production to the Aldwych Theatre.

It marked a stunning debut for Rudkin – Kenneth Tynan likened its impact to that of Osborne's first play, *Look Back in Anger*. Rudkin won the Evening Standard Most Promising Playwright award and gave up teaching to become a full-time writer.

For Rudkin, it was a move that promised much but yielded a bleak period of deep self-doubt which tested him to the extreme. He had to wait a decade before he saw his next full-length original stage play produced. Peggy encouraged him to keep working during this time, and, in order to sustain him while he wrestled with his stage work, she was happy for him to diversify: four TV plays, two radio plays, a translation of a libretto (for Peter Hall's production at Covent Garden of Schoenberg's *Moses and Aaron*, which caused a scandal because of nudity in the orgy scene), a piece for the Aldeburgh Festival, a ballet scenario and two produced screenplays. For these, which Peggy set up, she put Rudkin in touch with Robert Bolt, who made him a tape of helpful tips on writing films.

The first, *Mademoiselle*, was being directed by Tony Richardson with Oscar Lewenstein producing. The screenplay was by Jean Genet, but he had disappeared, leaving his script incomplete. Rudkin worked in French and generated a few scenes, though he did not receive a credit. Peggy thought of Rudkin for the second, *Fahrenheit 451*, directed by François Truffaut, because Rudkin shared with Truffaut a love of Alfred Hitchcock's films. Rudkin had to work very quickly on this project and in two languages, English and French; he was responsible for the English spoken text. There were also two screenplays from this period that Rudkin wrote but were not filmed. Both came via Peggy again and were for the same director, Fred Zinnemann, whom she knew well from Robert Bolt's film, *A Man for All Seasons*. Rudkin worked on *The Dybbuk* for three years, and, although it was never made, it proved to be the most useful of his screen experiences then. It was pulled when the management of Columbia, the studio which owned it, changed hands and the new regime decreed that they could not countenance both *The Dybbuk* and *Fiddler on the Roof*. The other screenplay, adapted from the John Fowles novel *The French*

Lieutenant's Woman, Zinnemann considered too anti-romantic, though Rudkin believes Fowles always wanted Harold Pinter, who eventually wrote the film that was made by Karel Reisz.

Peggy felt that Rudkin's troubles in the theatre were due to a mix of reasons. While she always warned against the seductions of early praise and easy success, she felt that the uncertainty surrounding the programming of *Afore Night Come* as well as the rejection of Rudkin's second two radio plays had been unjust and had affected him badly. A proposed television production of *Afore Night Come* had fallen through (owing, she believed, to the director Anthony Page letting Rudkin down), and this meant that the play had never been filmed, which Peggy thought a great shame.

His problems with the theatre then took on a more complex hue; she introduced him to George Devine at the Royal Court and they had a positive meeting but Rudkin was unable to follow this up with a new play. There was interest at the National Theatre but it came to nothing. For Binkie Beaumont, Rudkin agreed to write an adaptation of Roger Vitrac's *Victor*, which had been sent to Beaumont by Jean Anouilh. Peggy was wildly and eccentrically enthusiastic about this play. After reading it, she proclaimed: 'I realise that, apart from Jarry, Vitrac is the greatest innovator in the theatre in this generation' – an opinion that she believed utterly at the time and just as utterly contradicted on other, later, occasions. Rudkin was both tardy in his delivery and unsure of his work. It was not a good translation, and the play was finally produced in another version.

Rudkin embarked upon a new play of his own, a marathon effort which at first had the title *The Sea* and would have run some eight or nine hours. Subsequently called *The Sons of Light*, it was postponed by the RSC several times, pushing Rudkin to the brink of abandoning the stage altogether. It is a fantastical, mythical play structured in five acts like a symphony and set on a Celtic volcanic island ruled by a repressive religion. A new pastor arrives with his three sons, two of whom die in a fierce and bloody struggle which results in the third descending into the island's pit to destroy its dehumanising industrial network. The slaves are freed, the island is united and, mirroring this process of making whole, a schizophrenic young woman regains an integrated identity. Peggy thought this complex, many-layered work to be the most extraordinary of all Rudkin's plays. Each time the RSC postponed its production, Rudkin would rewrite and wrestle further, both with himself and with his leviathan play.

The strain told on the relationship between Peggy and Rudkin, which was very intense and personal, reaching, as had her relationship with

Mercer, to the very core of Rudkin's being. He was grappling to come to terms with himself, his politics, his culture, his upbringing; he had chosen a challenging profession for a boy who was brought up to view public entertainment as a sin. Peggy was enthralled by his rigorous exploration of self and sexuality, and encouraged him to dig as deep as possible. He felt that he was going through a process in his late twenties that most men went through in their teens – growing up into adulthood and selfhood. He identified both homosexual and heterosexual desires within him, but did not want to be ghettoised by attracting a specific sexual tag, just as he did not wish to be labelled politically. He wanted the work to speak for him. All this inner turmoil is indeed refracted in his stage writing, which runs in parallel with the progress of his psychological state.

To Peggy the confessional aspect of their relationship was important, because she believed that a writer's life and his or her creativity were seamless; the writer's emotional state affected what the writer was able to create, and this is what interested her above all. Rudkin agonized with her to such a degree of scalding self-scrutiny that she became anxious in case the liberating aspect of his investigation gave way to mere self-destruction – an issue that touched her deeply as she believed that she shared this tendency with him, even though to many she appeared to be the opposite.

Rudkin approached the tenth anniversary of his stage début with his only other theatre credit an unusual children's play, *Burglars*, which Peggy found esoteric. It was produced in 1970 following rejection by its commissioners, BBC Children's TV, who had not liked the notion of children burgling a house and hunting down the owner, who enjoys the deaths he causes by spreading oil on the road outside. In the anniversary year itself, 1972, Rudkin was given a lunchtime fringe production of his play about the demonic aspect of anality, *The Filth Hunt*, in which a self-appointed Pornography Commission joins forces with their supposed antagonists, the Pornographers. Peggy found this play 'blasphemous and excremental'.

The early '70s saw Rudkin come through his dark period, though not centre stage as Peggy had hoped, and not without the relationship between him and her reaching near-breaking point. He was developing two ideas simultaneously, both in their different ways dealing with the political context in which the individual finds him or herself. With *The Sons of Light* in an agonising limbo, Rudkin became even more frustrated when Peggy found it difficult to place these ideas. One, which concerned the Ulster Protestant hero Roger Casement and the price he paid for expressing his homosexuality, Rudkin wanted to offer as a film but Peggy said that she did not trust film companies with biographical material of his order. The other idea, which revolved around the problems of conception faced by an infertile couple, Rudkin wanted to offer to TV but Peggy said no TV company would touch the subject and advised him to write it for the stage.

Given the difficulties that he had suffered in the theatre he felt this was insensitive and unhelpful. This feeling was exacerbated when she told him: 'The trend at the moment is to cushion people from the truth if it is unpleasant, and this is why the West End is completely unimportant and trivial – and people are flocking to see the rubbish that is being shown.' She added with a sobering dash of realism that 'if plays are too painful [like the ones he was trying to write], there is a possibility that they won't go on because people may be frightened.' She was not asking him 'to veil the truth, or water it down' but was trying to act as an honest guide. She wanted him to find his true voice and to hold firm to it but, equally, she wanted him to recognise that this might mean his voice would not be listened to or heard.

The Casement idea became *Cries from Casement as His Bones Are Brought to Dublin.* It was the first play by the Anglo-Irish Rudkin to address the issue of Ireland head-on, and this made him more than usually upset at Peggy's failure to find it a home. She told him he should change agents if he thought this would help. He replied that he had no intention of so doing. 'You are the ONLY agent. I just want you to understand that my impatience on *Casement* is *not* a literary or vainglorious impatience; it is a moral, and political, one . . . You must imagine how I feel, now that everybody is jumping onto the Irish apple-cart and writing his English-liberal-conscience play. I am terrified that I shall be overtaken by a lot of well-intentioned nonsense. That's why I feel you should nag more people about it.'

She did, and the play was broadcast on radio in 1973 and staged by the RSC that year during another of the company's experimental seasons, this time at The Place near King's Cross. Peggy, however, felt Rudkin had not moved forward in the intervening decade from a similar début with *Afore Night Come.*

The idea about fertility was transformed from his own experiences with his wife Sandra into *Ashes*, a stark drama that powerfully welded together several of Rudkin's favoured themes, personal dilemma, the nature of existence and English-Irish politics. Rudkin had taken Peggy's advice and written it as a stage play. 'It stopped me in my tracks,' said Peggy when she read it. 'It shook me.' She responded in a total, physical way to all artistic experience; she gave herself up, not passively but openly and critically, to the experience, hence the power of her reactions, either in favour or against. The unsentimental candour of *Ashes* affected her profoundly; she felt extreme pain when she read it but believed that the play had to be seen.

It was commissioned by Charles Marowitz for the Open Space Theatre in London, but he could not include it as intended in the 1973 season. Rudkin's German contacts heard of it and asked if the play were available, and it opened that year instead in Hamburg. *Ashes* made its British début at the Open Space the following year and won for Rudkin the prestigious John Whiting award.

When *The Sons of Light* finally appeared, in a production by Keith Hack for the Tyneside Theatre Company at the University Theatre, Newcastle-upon-Tyne, in 1976, nine years after Rudkin had first begun work on the play, Peggy felt as if her client child had grown up at last and left home. This release into the world was sealed for Peggy when the following year, after some more revisions, the RSC eventually produced the play. Rudkin rewrote it for the last time for its publication.

Rudkin guided his own career after that – he had six more plays produced by the RSC, one at the Birmingham Repertory Studio Theatre, and two at the Almeida Theatre, north London, and he continued to write for television. Peggy managed the business side and maintained her interest but not at the same level of intensity that had been the case hitherto.

'I had been adopted as a surrogate son,' says Rudkin, who was called Rudders or Squirrel Nutkin by Peggy, a whimsicality seemingly at odds with the seriousness of their project but consonant with her attempts to make him embrace life in its fullness. She would frequently chide him for his earnestness. 'I think humour comes with time,' she would assure him. 'If one were serious altogether about life it would be unsupportable.' She had enunciated at the outset her cardinal principle – her battle cry – which she reiterated to all those clients whom she nurtured out of a protected existence: 'One must be *available for life*, this is the important thing. And one mustn't betray other people. For the rest, one should plunge into life easily, try and enjoy and experience all feelings and sensations and no harm need come provided one plays the game with some kind of ethical honour – never exploit or corrupt other people, that's all one needs to be aware of.'

In Rudkin's view, he was striving to become 'a man writer, and not a brilliant apprentice, while she made me feel that I had to measure up to other clients, and that I was never good enough.' She saw him as a special case. His problem was not the usual one of being seduced by success –

'he's incorruptible,' she wrote – but the opposite. She thought him an astonishing writer who was so completely committed to his own vision that he frequently could not stand outside of his work sufficiently to rescue it from being either obscure or too private. Just before *The Sons of Light* was first produced, she summed up her feelings: 'I think I care more passionately about his talent than any other author's, and I care about his future and believe in his future (though we may all be dead before he gets his deserts).'

Rudkin felt that she was hard on him compared to the way in which she mollycoddled other clients, for example giving them rail tickets to go on holiday, whereas she would not give him an advance when he was hard up for the simple reason that he had asked for one. 'She wasn't a shoulder to cry on. She was abrasive. We all seemed to expect that she would have time for each one of us alone, as though each of us was her only problem child.'

When he asked Peggy to Newcastle to see the first production of *The Sons of Light*, she told him that he would have to earn the train fare as well as the cost of her hotel. It grew worse. As she was introduced to the artistic director of the Newcastle theatre, she said, 'So lovely of you to invite me to Liverpool' and then, instead of going out to dinner after the performance, disappeared to her hotel. Rudkin decided not to invite her to Birmingham when *The Triumph of Death* was playing, yet Peggy came, at her own expense, and took Rudkin and the director Peter Faragó back to her hotel where she talked until 2 o'clock the next morning.

Like many of her clients, Rudkin did not look to her to find him work but to offer him guidance, both spiritual and material. The advice could be literary (she once told him that Thomas Mann was someone that '*you must have read!*') or it could be practical. She was involved in many of the vital decisions concerning the production of his plays, ranging from which producer and director should be approached to the suitability of venue and casting. For example, she suggested Ron Daniels to direct the RSC revival in 1974 of *Afore Night Come*. This led to an important relationship for the RSC, embracing five productions at the company's small Stratford theatre The Other Place, of which Daniels was the artistic director, including Rudkin's superb adaptation of *Peer Gynt*.

Once, however, when Peggy believed she had mishandled a revival of *Ashes*, she offered to cease being Rudkin's agent, as she had done when he was dissatisfied with her response to his Casement play. The original actor was contracted to appear in a TV series and was not available for the revival; Peggy thought, given the intensity of the play, it would be unfair for a new actor to have to work with the original actress and insisted that the producer, Michael Codron, find a new man and woman to replace the initial casting. Rudkin again refused to leave her.

For all their intimacy, however, Rudkin never considered himself to be part of her fold in the way that Mercer was, in regular contact on the telephone or always visiting the office. 'I think she went through lists regularly to purge people, though none of us ever had contracts with her,' he recalls. 'Your relationship just hardened or dissolved.' Yet, throughout the fluctuations of their relationship, she remained for him, as she did for many others, a lodestar, whether actual or in his mind forming a benchmark against which to judge his efforts, steering him both in life and in work.

'If anything happened to you,' he once wrote to her, 'the shit would *really* hit the fan, and we might as well give up. It sometimes looks, and other people get the same impression, that you alone are holding the theatre together.' His estrangement from the theatre since her death might seem to underline this point of view. He comments: 'My position in the theatre is as it is because of who I am and what the theatre is. An agent can't make theatres do a play if they don't want to. Her death is a sore loss because she was the last of the participatory agents who was interested in your development as an artist.'

*

'Authors are just people who happen to write'

Peggy was rising to the height of her profession in the early 1960s with her unique blend of good taste and commercial nous. Her eclectic embrace gave her an unprecedented range of established and promising clients. After Bolt and Mortimer she had been drawn to the stronger meat of Mercer and Rudkin. Yet, because she did not judge plays ideologically, at the time she was nurturing their savage talents Peggy also took on board two of the British theatre's great entertainers, Peter Nichols and Alan Ayckbourn, who, nevertheless, were not without their own dark sides.

Peter Nichols joined Peggy in 1959 when he was 32. A former barman, waiter, cinema commissionaire, park keeper, actor and teacher, he was one of Peggy's most successful clients in both the commercial and the subsidised sectors – he won four Evening Standard awards, the John Whiting Award and two Society of West End Theatre Awards as well as an anonymous award for Best Impersonation of Your Agent. He was well known for his rendition of Peggy's foibles and recorded her inimitably, though not necessarily accurately, in the character of Nancy Fraser in his autobiographical play *A Piece of My Mind*.

Nichols insists that he was poached by Peggy when he was lying in hospital with a collapsed lung. He describes how she arrived on the ward bearing cheese and pâté, looking like a peacock on a council estate. (Another visitor that day was Kenneth Williams, so the other patients got their money's worth on the NHS.) As Nichols had only three TV plays to his name – *Walk on the Grass*, *After All* (co-authored with Bernie Cooper), and *Promenade* – his interpretation of her visit is hardly credible. In fact, Robert Bolt had told her that Nichols was unhappy with his current agent and that he had advised Nichols that she should represent him. Peggy recalled that when she heard that Nichols was in hospital she felt sorry for him – she had a particular hatred of hospitals and the medical profession – and decided on a mercy trip. The end result was that Nichols, poached or not, did join Peggy's agency.

Nichols wrote prolifically for television, which did not interest Peggy much. She urged him to write for the theatre, only to find that she was not too keen on the results. A stage play about his father, *The Continuity Man*, Peggy found insufficiently wicked: 'There's not enough vice in you. That's why your lung collapses all the time.' She could not place the play, so Nichols turned it into a television drama that was broadcast in 1963.

Maybe Nichols could not turn on wickedness like a tap, but his own life provided a bitter experience that allowed him at least to be brutal. He mines autobiography in all his writing, and in *A Day in the Death of Joe Egg* he came to terms with a particularly traumatic personal tragedy which, unexpectedly, caught Peggy totally off-guard. Michael Codron had read a novel about a couple with an autistic child and had suggested to Peggy that it might make a good play. She had given the book to Nichols, who told her he had thrown it the length of the room because it was untrue. He was determined to write his own account. He had bought himself the time to do so by writing a film about a pop group, the Dave Clark Five, which he was offered by the director, his friend and fellow Bristol inhabitant, John Boorman. *Joe Egg* broached with jocular bravado and deep pain what was at the time a taboo subject, the brain-damaged child. Essentially, it told the story of Peter Nichols, his wife Thelma and their daughter Abigail.

Peggy was shocked, both because she had represented him for several years without realising exactly what his home life was like and because he had presented his private grief with such disturbing power on a public platform. Disability had yet to become a convenient metaphor for the problems of society. The directness of Nichols' writing embarrassed her and, in a curious way, made her own body feel uncomfortable and vulnerable. Nichols had struck deep and somehow undermined her grip on mortality. In spite of her desire to be astonished by plays, she responded to this one conservatively. She knew that it was an important play but she felt that she could not send it to any potential producers, even though she risked losing Nichols as a client.

He recalls her response. 'What do you want me to do with this?' she asked. 'Get it on,' he answered, and offered her a list of potential interested parties. 'These are very busy people, darling' came her less than encouraging reply. Codron tried to set up the play but none of the directors he approached wanted to take it on. Peggy fared no better, which is not altogether surprising given that she herself was not convinced it should be staged. Nichols made another list of people to whom he thought the play should be sent, including this time regional theatre managers. The same negative response was registered and Nichols was left to place *A Day in the Death of Joe Egg* on his own.

Nichols was a good friend of the actor Michael Blakemore, who had joined the company at the Citizens' Theatre, Glasgow, and had recently become co-director there with another actor, Michael Meecham. Blakemore asked if he could try out the play at the Citizens. Nichols agreed and wrote another draft with input from Blakemore. When Nichols saw a run of the first act he found himself crying at his own play.

He was aged almost 40, had been writing for a decade and was now a major, if unsung, TV writer, yet *A Day in the Death of Joe Egg*, which opened in May 1967, was only his second play to be staged – the first had been an extended version of a television play, *The Hooded Terror*, that had been given a brief outing in Bristol in 1965 in what he admitted was a token season of local plays. In Glasgow, he had arrived with his own voice, and at considerable personal cost.

Peggy remained unhappy. She flew up to Glasgow with Michael Codron to see the production, and during the return flight was pleading with him 'please don't do it'.

Following Ronald Bryden's *Observer* review of the production, the National Theatre made an offer for the play, as did Albert Finney's company, Memorial Enterprises Ltd. run by Michael Medwin. Nichols chose the latter because the deal they offered would keep intact the original cast and director, and repay the Citizens for its commitment to the play. (Medwin made Blakemore, as a new director, a poor offer, and it was Peggy who secured its improvement.) Memorial Enterprises, in an arrangement with two other managements, Bernard Delfont Ltd. and Tom Arnold Ltd., brought the production to the West End, with Joe Melia and Zena Walker repeating their performances as the father and mother. It ran for only about four months but made Nichols' name. He won the John Whiting Award and Evening Standard Best Play Award that year, although, unfortunately for him, the show had closed by then. Albert Finney played the father in New York, and a film of the play was released in 1971, the same year that Abigail Nichols, the real-life Joe Egg, died.

Peggy did not change her mind even when the play was a success, although she did prefer the screenplay because it made possible all sorts of scenes that were not possible on stage; it deepened the characters and made them more sympathetic and interesting.

Nichols felt that Peggy was never entirely happy with any of his work. She enjoyed his playfulness in the theatre – the soap opera pastiche of *The National Health*, splitting the main character into two roles in *Passion Play*, the army troupe motif in *Privates on Parade* and the subversion of panto-mime in *Poppy* – but she thought he remained a boulevard writer who was beset by jealousy and cared too much for money. The nearest he recalls her ever coming to paying him a compliment was when she said that *The National Health* was '*nearly* a work of art.'

Nichols says Peggy did not systematically help his career, although she could on occasion be useful, almost by accident. He remembers, for in-stance, when she took Michael Codron to see *Born in the Gardens* in Bristol in 1979. Codron said that he would bring it in to London, so Nichols went on holiday as planned to France. He received a cable there from Peggy telling him that Codron had now gone cold on the idea. Nichols returned to London for a meeting with Codron in the office of another producer, Eddie Kulukundis, who attended along with Peggy. Codron said he thought the play too local to Bristol to be acceptable in London. Peggy turned to Kulukundis and said with great panache, in a tone that brooked no demur, 'Then *you'll* just have to do it, Eddie.' Which he did.

Over the years, Nichols left Peggy, then returned and then left again. Money was one of the reasons but not the only one; he could not accept her romantic view of the inspiration to be derived from poverty, especially when she herself lived very comfortably. When he challenged her with this contradiction, she protested that she did not live any better than her writers – a declaration that did not bear much scrutiny for the majority of her clients. He was fed up with her lack of enthusiasm for him, but, when he did leave, what he missed most was the excitement of being with her, in comparison with which all other agents he found were a bore.

His portrait of Peggy as Nancy Fraser, which was originally written for a TV play that was never made, captures this quality superbly, although it in no way offers a rounded view of her. In the play, a once successful writer, Ted Forrest, has an agent, Nancy Fraser, who mistakes people, as did Peggy, and who steamrollers them in her uninterrupted and uninterruptible flow, not allowing reality to deter or divert her. Her comments echo several that Peggy made to Nichols, including the advice that Fraser gives to Forrest: 'Sign on with a tramp steamer. Smuggle arms to terrorists. Forget the kitchen sink . . . At the very least have an affair, find an obliging little tart, darling.'

Nichols says that whenever the phone went at home and he knew that it was Peggy, his stomach knotted – 'it was not exactly like the police calling' – but he also knew that whatever else happened, good or bad, it would not be ordinary. 'She was great fun. She was a character. She was so indiscreet that she wasn't really being indiscreet. It was so over the top, you didn't know how much to believe. She appeared to tell you everything but kept you in the dark. She was cruel, shrewd and scatty. I resented her yet loved her. She liked to take us down a peg or two, but I was on a low enough peg already. She used to bemoan Alan Ayckbourn's fate to me – "poor Alan, five plays in the West End, two at the National," and so on, and I'd think, "what about poor me?"'

'Poor' Alan Ayckbourn joined Peggy a couple of years after Peter Nichols. She was sent an Ayckbourn play, *Standing Room Only*, which had been seen in Scarborough in 1961 and in Stoke-on-Trent in 1962. She received the play in March that year from the producer Peter Bridge, whom Peggy had known since she started out as an agent. Bridge had taken out an option on the play for a possible production in Bristol and maybe a transfer to London. Ayckbourn simultaneously had approached her through Peter Cheeseman, who was artistic director of Stoke's Victoria Theatre where the play had been revived – in-the-round, of course – and where Ayckbourn was his associate.

Ayckbourn, born in London in 1939, left school at seventeen and became an acting assistant stage manager for Donald Wolfit. He worked his way up through the repertory circuit to become a stage manager and subsequently an actor. He had written plays while he was at school. After complaining to the director Stephen Joseph about a part he was playing, he took up Joseph's challenge to write a better one. Joseph directed the result, *The Square Cat*, in 1959.

Standing Room Only, the play sent to Peggy, was Ayckbourn's fourth to be produced; all had been seen at Scarborough and all had been written under the pen-name Roland Allen. When Bridge took out his option, he asked Ayckbourn if he had an agent. Ayckbourn said he did not because all his plays had been produced at the same theatre where he was a member of the company. Bridge was urging Peggy to represent the twenty-two-year-old Ayckbourn for the putative London transfer while seeking at the same time another writer to improve Ayckbourn's play. Peggy was incandescent with rage at Bridge. She agreed to act for Ayckbourn, reduced Bridge to tears as she rebuffed his suggestion of engaging another writer, and won her newest client a better fee instead.

Peggy made some comments to Ayckbourn about the play, which was set in the future on a bus that is caught in a traffic jam in Shaftesbury Avenue. She loved the first act but did not think the whole play could be sustained in the same location. Ayckbourn rewrote several times but the Bridge production never happened.

Standing Room Only was the last play that Ayckbourn wrote as Ronald Allen. There was an implicit understanding, marked by his joining Peggy, that he had graduated into the ranks of the 'proper' playwrights and was going to have a writing life beyond Stoke and Scarborough. He was, however, still uncertain about his future and sought Peggy's advice as he tried to steer a course between the competing ambitions of acting, directing and playwriting.

Following a disastrous attempt at a Christmas play, the first that Cheeseman tried at Stoke, Ayckbourn's next play, *Mr Whatnot*, convinced Peggy of his originality and inventiveness. It is a tribute to Buster Keaton, in which a piano tuner, who remains silent throughout, is called to the country house of a cartoon-like upper-crust family where he causes mayhem at a mimed tennis match, a fantastic tea party that turns into a bout of trench bombardment, and a farcical dinner during which he swops around the glasses of all the guests. He woos and wins the affianced daughter of the house, even after she has been married to her drone of a husband.

Ayckbourn sent Peggy a script and she thought it 'a quite stunning exercise in mime, the most unusual I've ever read.' Her worry was whether or not it could transfer to a proscenium stage in London. Having seen it in-the-round at Stoke, where it was successfully directed by Ayckbourn himself, she was more concerned still about the problems of a move to the capital. There was talk of taking it to the Royal Court for a production with Clifford Williams, who had a background in mime; but he turned out not to be available at the right time.

Peter Bridge wanted to take the play to the Arts Theatre, which at least was intimate. Peggy told Ayckbourn that he was unlikely to earn any royalties at the Arts – it seats only 350 – and that Bridge would lose money unless the show proved to be a big draw. She was not keen on selling the option to Bridge; she felt he too often bought plays and then abandoned them, as happened with *Standing Room Only*. On the other hand, Ayckbourn felt a certain loyalty to Bridge, who did have a definite production in mind and at an available theatre. As Peggy had said that the play was too risky for the West End, and Ayckbourn did want a London production, then to his mind, Bridge was worth the risk.

With largely a new cast and a new director, *Mr Whatnot* opened at the Arts in August 1964, Ayckbourn's first play to be seen in London. The production had lost the spontaneity and charm of the Stoke original and was duly trounced by the critics. Ayckbourn was ready to give up being a playwright but Peggy shifted up into her encouragement gear and he pulled through.

Ayckbourn did give up being an actor, however, and from 1964-1970 was a producer with BBC Radio, Leeds, a job he landed by chance through Peggy. She was in her office with the senior Leeds radio producer, Alfred Bradley, who wanted her to represent him as a writer, when Ayckbourn telephoned looking for commiseration over the reception of *Mr Whatnot*. Bradley, not wanting to lose valuable time with Peggy, interjected brusquely: 'Get him off the phone. Tell him to apply for the job.' Ayckbourn did, and got it.

He was persuaded to write his next play in 1965 by his mentor Stephen Joseph, who wanted something for his Scarborough theatre. Ayckbourn responded with a conventional 'well-made' play, *Meet My Father*, which he described as 'all French windows and people sipping coffee'. A comedy of mistaken identity revolving around male angst at presumed female infidelity, it was bought by Peter Bridge for a London production but opened only after he and Peggy had had a serious disagreement over Ayckbourn's royalty, which Bridge wished to reduce. Peggy rejected this suggestion with customary robustness, which elicited from Bridge an angry rebuke. He was dismayed at her rudeness to him, complained of her persistent attacks on him and reminded her that it had been he who had introduced Ayckbourn to her in the first place. She replied with characteristic forthrightness. On the last point, she thanked him for wanting to do her a good turn, and, without a trace of irony, assured him that this was not invalidated by the fact that Ayckbourn had already approached her, courtesy of Peter Cheeseman. Nor did Bridge's recommendation buy her loyalty to him where Ayckbourn was concerned. 'You would be the first person to agree that you weren't trying to bribe me,' she said.

Peggy explained her 'rudeness' to Bridge as 'my attempt to speak the truth to somebody I have known ever since I started as an agent. The alternative is hypocrisy – much practised in the theatre, when everyone is lying to one another face to face, but oh boy, are they tearing each others' reputations to pieces behind their backs.' She dealt with the 'attacks' in similar fashion: 'I make persistent attacks upon all the London managers . . . Recently I outraged Michael Codron by demanding that he should let me buy back a play which I felt he was destroying, and I recently accused Binkie [Beaumont] of dishonesty because he wanted me to give him a play which belonged to somebody else. Maybe the true answer is that I am a very bad agent, since I have to wage these wars against Managers. Perhaps lies to their faces and innuendoes behind their backs would be another method, but I think it would be contemptible.'

Peggy won the day and the play enjoyed West End success in 1967 as *Relatively Speaking*, running for 355 performances. It was surpassed in 1970 by *How the Other Half Loves*, starring Robert Morley, in which Ayckbourn deftly cuts back and forth between two dinner parties held on consecutive evenings in two separate households. It ran in the West End for 869 performances. Ayckbourn had arrived as a first-rate comedy writer, a decade after he had embarked on his writing career.

Ayckbourn's early plays Peggy felt were charming but not sufficiently nourishing; she told him in her best school-ma'am tones that one good idea did not make a play. 'A writer needs three or four ideas and they have to intersect.' She was concerned that he was too often caricaturing human beings rather than characterising them. She urged him to paint pictures instead of drawing cartoon strips and to spend more time on character because nobody in the theatre could outstrip him technically on the formal side of the craft. 'I hope you aren't disappointed or disconcerted in my interest in your "development" of characters – I know you can do all the rest as only you can,' she wrote him. 'What I really want so much is for you to be fully estimated. A really successful author is often underestimated critically – the prizes tend to go to the boys who write characters and can't write a plot if it killed them.'

As had become Ayckbourn's custom, his plays were first staged at Scarborough, mostly directed by him, before they transferred to London or elsewhere in a new production. This was a useful system but also a confining one, Peggy believed, because it was tying Ayckbourn to the star vehicle formula. In order to advance his writing, Ayckbourn needed to break out of this straitjacket, and such an escape could only be effected if he left his producer, Peter Bridge, who was in any case becoming seriously ill. She thought Bridge a sweet, kind but talentless man and as a manager rather 'pre-war': honourable and endearing but lacking in discrimination and in the belief that authors were as important or more so than stars. 'Putting them on the same plateau would do to start with,' she said.

In the pursuit of liberation, she steered Ayckbourn towards Michael Codron, to the outrage of Bridge and Eddie Kulukundis, who, at Peggy's behest, had co-produced with Bridge *How the Other Half Loves*. Peggy told Bridge bluntly: 'The choice of a Manager must be made absolutely ruthlessly . . . Michael [Codron] has been entrusted with at least half a dozen of our new writers and has handled them with consummate delicacy as well as efficiency.'

In fact, Codron's first attempt, *Me Times Me Times Me*, did include stars. A revised version of an earlier play, *The Story So Far*, which had already been seen in Scarborough, it had a pre-London run but did not come into the West End. Peggy believed the play needed more work (and it later surfaced as *Family Circles*) but also felt once more that the stars had not helped. She insisted Codron take a new approach for the next play, *Time and Time Again*, which she considered a step forward because it explored character rather than being dominated by an intricate clockwork plot.

Ayckbourn directed the Scarborough premiere and, for the London production, Codron, with Peggy's agreement, hired as director Eric Thompson, an actor who had just made his directorial début with a sensitive production of the anti-war play, *Journey's End*. Thompson's cast featured excellent actors, such as Tom Courtenay, but they were not stars of the Robert Morley mould. (Peggy on Courtenay: 'I hope he isn't being too cute – he needs to play against this side of his character. The pixies must remain strictly in the garden.') The result: Ayckbourn felt that *Time and Time Again* was the best presented play of his that he had experienced so far.

For his next play, *Absurd Person Singular*, Peggy advised Ayckbourn to retain the same team and he readily agreed: Codron as producer, director Eric Thompson, designer Alan Tagg (a client of Peggy's) and lighting by Mick Hughes. Set on three consecutive Christmas Eves, *Absurd Person Singular* shows from the vantage point of the kitchen three couples celebrating in each other's homes, unable to acknowledge the pain that is clearly present. Ayckbourn himself has described it as 'an attempt to write a truly hilarious dark play', and, although he felt that Thompson went his own way on the production and altered the emphasis of the piece, it turned out to be a watershed for him. It played in the West End for 973 performances, won him his first Evening Standard Award for Best Comedy and enjoyed a long run on Broadway.

Peggy

It has been said that the character of Marion in the play (who electrocutes her husband on the Christmas tree) is based on Peggy, but Ayckbourn denies any conscious similarities, except possibly in the first scene. Peggy was neither stupid nor drank to excess. Ayckbourn accepts that certain phrases of Peggy's might have stuck and been used in several of his characters. There is certainly a whiff of Peggy in Marion's first few lines:

MARION (*bending to read the dial on Jane's washing machine*). What's this? Whites – coloureds – my God, it's apartheid.
JANE: Beg pardon?
MARION: What's this? Minimum icon? What on earth is that?
JANE: No, minimum iron.
MARION: Don't tell me it does the ironing too.
JANE: Oh, no, it . . .
MARION: Ronnie, have you seen this extraordinary machine?
RONNIE: Yes. Yes . . .
MARION: It not only does your washing and your whites and your blacks and your coloureds and so on, it does your ironing.
SIDNEY: No, no . . .
JANE: No . . .
The doorbell chimes.
MARION: Oh, good gracious. What was that? Does that mean your shirts are cooked or something?

When Peggy was asked about Marion, who has the habit of opening other people's cupboards and drawers, she replied that she could not remember ever doing it 'but it sounds like an awfully good idea.'

It was after *Absurd Person Singular* had been successfully transferred to London that Peggy felt Ayckbourn was properly launched. He had matured as a writer. Peggy said of the play: 'I am glad to see that a little irony and firmness is creeping into the writing of AA!' She found that by now he was creating sharper characters and his plays were less dependent on brilliantly executed tricks without being any the less dazzling in their craft.

He had reached a position where he was able to write his most complex achievement to date, a trilogy of full-length plays with the collective title of *The Norman Conquests*, dealing with the same characters in the same house during the same weekend, and have Codron transfer them all, after Scarborough and via Greenwich, to the West End. It was an audacious move and Codron had taken some persuading to bring in all three plays at once. ('Please don't whimper, Codron,' she would say.) Peggy backed Ayckbourn's wish that the trilogy should transfer as one, although she herself when first presented with the three plays had reacted, only half in jest, 'I don't have to read them all, do I?'

After the success of *The Norman Conquests*, Peggy recognised that the Ayckbourn-Codron partnership had been secured. She observed to Codron, 'That was a plum that landed in your lap.' The following year, 1975, Ayckbourn broke a record set by Somerset Maugham and Noël Coward with five plays running at the same time in London. All were produced by Codron.

Ayckbourn continued to experiment (for instance, in *Sisterly Feelings* there are four possible versions, depending on the toss of a coin at the end of the first scene and the decision of one of two actresses at the end of the second), and his plays continued to take on darker tones. He became not only an associate director of the National Theatre as well as the artistic director of the Stephen Joseph Theatre in Scarborough but also the most performed living writer in Britain, with his own category in the statistics compiled by the Arts Council. In recognition of such achievement, he was knighted in the 1996 New Year's Honours list.

Ayckbourn acknowledges that it was Peggy's encouragement early on that counted, even when it was characteristically unorthodox and unintentional, as happened the first time they met. During Ayckbourn's induction in Peggy's office, the phone rang and it was Eugène Ionesco. This was heady stuff to a shy 22-year-old actor who had dreams of becoming a great writer. He became even more impressed when she then took a transatlantic call from the film director Otto Preminger and finished it with a kindly flourish, 'Oh, piss off, Otto.'

It was something of a come-down when she failed to recognise Ayckbourn the second time they met, although he soon discovered that this was routine with Peggy. Nevertheless, he did feel out of place because her other clients seemed mostly to be far out on the other theatrical wing. Gradually, as he became more confident, he began to feel at home with the agency. Also, Ayckbourn did not live in London – he was an honorary member of her northern club – and was not, therefore, part of her regular court. Peggy herself, though, never made any distinction between him and her other playwrights; she challenged him just as she did everyone else. He says she had no reason to take him on except her instinct. She admired his technical boldness and liked his point of view (acerbic on marriage and masculinity, sympathetic towards the underdog). She saw in the very first plays a wilder writer than was evident in the author of West End successes like *Relatively Speaking* or *How the Other Half Loves*, and one who was in touch with human suffering. She did not tell Ayckbourn to write plays of greater 'relevance' but did nudge him in the direction of his darker side and responded favourably to his more serious suggestions.

While Ayckbourn's writing career was not directly influenced by Peggy, he did respond to her philosophy, particularly in relation to success, and indirectly to her hints and oblique prompting. 'She's refreshing in a fast buck world,' Ayckbourn says, 'but early on is where she counts when you have no money.' She would say in admonition to him when he was gloomy in the first years of struggle, 'Any fool can be a failure,' followed by a timely afterthought: 'The more you take out of theatre, the more you ought to be putting back in.' She used to send him books – by writers such as A.E. Housman or Siegfried Sassoon, or volumes on diet when she thought he was getting plump and sluggish.

He keenly sought her approval in the early days but felt that she became less interested, and therefore less perceptive, the more skilled and established he became. She gave him self-confidence when it mattered. 'Be generous with your talent,' she urged, 'and keep writing.' She offered him the wisdom of her many years' experience, on managers, actors, directors and designers. He was glad that she was on his side in negotiations: 'She would sound off like a fifty-one-gun salvo; you didn't point Peggy at any-one unless you intended to use her.'

His commitment to Scarborough and, for a short period, to Stoke, meant that he could experiment away from the glare and distortions of London. Ayckbourn needed Peggy for the transfers to London and abroad, not for guidance on how or what to write. She admired him for staying in Scarborough rather than succumbing to the fleshpots of the metropolis. She felt, however, that from the mid-1970s on he was too comfortable there and that it was stopping him from developing beyond the middlebrow. She believed he had become trapped and was unable to challenge his own limitations severely enough. There was a tendency in the Scarborough productions, she thought, to play up the cruder aspects of the work at the expense of their subtleties. Despite this, Scarborough was one of the few places out of London that Peggy felt comfortable in and which she enjoyed visiting; despite her touring background, or maybe because of it, she experienced most theatre-going 'in the provinces' as if she were a delicate bud who had just stepped out of a Turgenev novel.

As well as agreeing to be a director of his commissioning/producing company Redburn, she contributed generously to the building of the new

Stephen Joseph Theatre-in-the-Round in Scarborough, which opened in 1976 when it moved from the local library to the ground floor of a former boys' high school, with Ayckbourn as the theatre's artistic director. She joked that her donation was a bribe in order to be able to negotiate a better deal for Ayckbourn with his own theatre.

Ayckbourn's affection for, and debt to, her was made manifest in 1988 when he decided to organise a tribute to the nearly 80-year-old Peggy in response to the refusal of the Society for West End Theatre to honour her. Ayckbourn learned that a proposal to award her a special achievement prize had been vetoed at a SWET meeting by certain managers who did not think that an agent, let alone the belligerent Peggy, should be thus acclaimed. So, unknown to her, he wrote to her clients asking them to contribute to a silver salver which would bear their signatures. It was presented to her at a surprise gathering to which she had been inveigled by Michael Codron under the pretence that she was attending a welcome party for the National Theatre's new artistic director, Richard Eyre. It was fitting that the ceremony to honour her should have taken place at the National, attended by the cream of British playwrights, and that the doyenne of British agents should be presented with the gift by the man whom she had helped to become Britain's most popular and prolific living playwright.

Chapter Five

The Ruffian on the Stair

'It's only fucking show business, dear'

IN 1963, Peggy gave to the theatre magazine *Encore* what for her at the time was a rare interview. The magazine described her as 'one of England's leading play agents', who 'happens to figure in one way or another in practically every worthwhile theatrical undertaking in the London theatre.'

In the interview she said: 'It is up to us [the agents] to create the theatre of the future. If the theatre shrinks instead of expanding, it is *our* fault . . . One mustn't do in the '60s what could just as easily have been done in other decades. It's misusing the present.'

The start of the 1960s, the 'swinging' decade, saw her rise to preeminence as an agent. Her client list had expanded beyond the likes of Bolt and Mortimer to include Rhys Adrian, Alan Ayckbourn, Peter Barnes, Caryl Churchill, David Cregan, Stanley Eveling, Donald Howarth, Henry Livings, Frank Marcus, John McGrath, David Mercer, Peter Nichols, Alan Plater, David Rudkin, James Saunders, Peter Terson, Hugh Whitemore, and Charles Wood. Peggy was becoming synonymous with new writing. There was something in the 1960s its exuberance, its spirit, above all its youthfulness – that chimed with Peggy, whose energy and vitality belied her own age, which was only eight years younger than the century itself.

Peggy had become so busy that she had considered expansion, either by taking on more assistants and offices or by amalgamation. On reflection, she decided that it would not be advantageous to her or her authors and, in a characteristic switch, plumped for the other extreme – to purge her lists and take on no more clients.

Just as typically, she did neither, yet she did declare this intention to her staff in December 1963. One day that month while Peggy was out to lunch, a would-be client climbed the stairs at 14a Goodwin's Court, eager to hand in an A4 envelope containing a playtext. He was just about to be shown the door by the secretary, mindful that Peggy did not want to read any more unsolicited scripts, when the young man said that he had just had a play accepted by BBC Radio and was hoping it would be broadcast soon. Knowing Peggy's respect for radio, the secretary decided that this information changed matters, accepted the envelope, and said goodbye to the caller. On Peggy's return, the secretary gave the envelope to her, who decided to have a quick look at the play there and then. Peggy shut the door of her office and within minutes was engulfed in shrieks of laughter.

She wrote to the author, Joe Orton, and asked to see him. He appeared as he had before, wearing a plastic mac and a peaked cap and carrying a khaki knapsack. As was her way, she was hard on him, precisely because she felt that he was talented. She repeated what she had said in the letter, that she liked the play he had left at the office, *Entertaining Mr Sloane*, which appears to be a conventional West End drama set in a single room-to-let, but which, by the end, has turned this world upside down. Peggy, however, felt that the play was slight, derivative – of Pinter – and might not sustain a whole evening. She did not like the play's shape or its convenient ending, in which the landlady's father is murdered. Orton took the criticisms well and promised next time to write her a better play.

Orton told Peggy that it was his radio producer John Tydeman who had steered him to Goodwin's Court. Peggy knew of Tydeman from his Cambridge days when he had directed *The Bald Prima Donna* but without applying to her for a licence. He had received a fearsome letter from Peggy saying that he had broken the law. The drama society paid up and she decided to go and see the show, and liked it. He was also involved in a programme of plays by undergraduates, which she had been to Cambridge to see as well, two of which were written by future clients, Richard Cottrell and Ray Jenkins, and which she had helped bring to the Arts Theatre.

Tydeman had rescued Orton's radio play, *The Boy Hairdresser*, from the 'old biddies,' as he put it, who were the BBC script readers under the head of sound drama, Val Gielgud. He had shown it not to Gielgud but to his assistant Donald McWhinnie, who was known for his direction of Beckett and who agreed that the play was worth pursuing. Tydeman had called Orton in, told him he liked the play but said it needed rewriting and a new title. Orton did three sets of rewrites. In December 1963 he returned to see Tydeman, bringing with him the final rewrites, a new title, *The Ruffian on the Stair*, which had been suggested by his partner Kenneth Halliwell, and a script of *Entertaining Mr Sloane*, which Orton explained to Tydeman was not written for radio but for the theatre. Orton said he had been inspired to write the stage play by the interest that the BBC was showing in *The Boy Hairdresser*, following years of rejection of his writings. Tydeman read the first few pages of *Entertaining Mr Sloane*, recognised its merits and asked Orton if he had an agent, which he did not. Tydeman suggested Peggy.

Orton quoted Tydeman to Peggy: 'She can be a bit of an old cow, but if the chemistry is right, it will be terrific.' Peggy, listening to this tale, immediately picked up the telephone at this point and phoned Tydeman at the BBC. Without announcing herself she boomed, 'Tydie, you've been calling me a cow all over London. I may be an old bitch but I am not an old cow.' Tydeman denied that he ever said such a thing and inquired who had been making these allegations. 'Oh, a charming young man here,' she replied, and turned to him. 'What's your name? – a Mr Orton says so.'

On this first meeting, Orton had come without his partner Kenneth Halliwell, though Orton described *Entertaining Mr Sloane* to Peggy as 'our play', and asked if his friend could come next time he visited the office. Thereafter Halliwell was ever present.

Peggy was very taken with Orton; she liked his 'cool detachment, charm and confidence'. She found him fascinating and, in a typically Peggy observation, noticed how clean he was. Despite her criticisms of the play, she was struck by its luminous, spare and sharp quality. She was sufficiently convinced to send the play to the manager Donald Albery, whom she had known from her days at Q and who had brought the Murdoch-Priestley play *A Severed Head* into the West End where it was still running. Peggy saw that Orton occupied similar territory, in that both plays dealt with unconventional sexual couplings, albeit among different classes. Albery sent the play to Joan Littlewood, whose productions of *A Taste of Honey*, *The Hostage* and *Fings Aint' Wot They Used T' Be* had made him a great deal of money and were, to his way of thinking, set among the lower orders, as was the Orton play.

Peggy heard nothing from Albery for two weeks and, impatient as ever, telephoned Michael Codron, who was running the New Arts Theatre and always needed new plays to sustain his monthly turnover of productions. She sent *Entertaining Mr Sloane* to him along with a copy of *Formation Dancers* by Frank Marcus. Codron read and bought both plays immediately. His quick decision took even Peggy by surprise. The Marcus play appeared first, that March, and *Entertaining Mr Sloane* in May, before Orton's radio play was broadcast.

Marcus was to be linked to Orton in several ways, not least because they became well-known for writing about sex. Marcus, named Frank after the

German playwright Frank Wedekind, had been running his own company, functioning as director, designer, actor and translator, and had written half a dozen plays but without much success before he was introduced to Peggy. A mutual friend, Hugh Cruttwell, soon to become Principal of the Royal Academy of Dramatic Art, dropped Peggy a line about Marcus and she agreed to read his plays. 'About a week later the telephone rang,' Marcus recalled. 'The voice at the other end was sharp, fast, and unfamiliar. There was no introduction or self-identification. She began, 'Darling, in that scene in the Chinese restaurant, would the little girl have asked for "Egg Foo Yong"? Just wanted to check . . . Byee' . . . and hung up.'

He was soon to learn that the way Peggy said things was as important as what she said, and that she wielded a considerable armoury of coded communication. Her telephone call actually meant that she had read the plays and had agreed to become his agent. He stayed with her until she died, by which time he had had four plays in the West End, including *Formation Dances*.

Peggy would extol Orton's virtues as a goad to Marcus and vice versa; she told Orton to see *The Killing of Sister George* in order to learn about play construction. Much to Orton's annoyance, it won the Evening Standard Best Play Award (along with John Osborne's *A Patriot for Me*) in preference to *Entertaining Mr Sloane*. Orton found the Marcus play middlebrow, light-weight and unimaginative. Nevertheless, its picture of a lesbian couple was considered sufficiently offensive to have been booed, and at a matinée of the play Orton attended some women walked out at the point when George makes her lover drink the bath water.

This was a moment that Michael Codron, the play's producer, also did not like, but Peggy had urged him not to change it. 'It's only value is in its little claws,' she said of the play. 'Don't extract its teeth!' Compared to Orton's work, however, Peggy thought it mild, though it tickled Peggy's sense of the absurd to discover that, unlike homosexuality, lesbianism was legal in that it was not specifically prohibited and its portrayal on stage was acceptable to the Lord Chamberlain, even if not condoned.

Peggy was brim full of Orton. She wrote to Robert Bolt on the day that Codron bought *Entertaining Mr Sloane*: 'I suppose he is the answer to Pinter (NOT Bolt) but his influence is Firbank and Genet, instead of Beckett. The author has just come out of Wormwood Scrubs, for thieving and bodily violence, but I'd trust my life to him or any of my possessions. He is 25.' Peggy's enthusiasm was razor like, even if she did not have a grasp of all the personal detail – in fact, Orton and Halliwell had been in prison for stealing and defacing library books and they had been out for more than a year before the meeting with Peggy. Of course it was likely that Orton himself had been dissembling a little, not unlike his new mentor. (He frequently lied about his age, as Peggy did. For the production of *Entertaining Mr Sloane*, he wrote two programme notes; one gave his correct age of 31, the other 25, and this latter was the one that was used, making him seem, as his biographer John Lahr says, even more promising.)

Peggy also wrote in similarly positive terms to the critic Harold Hobson, asking him to attend *Entertaining Mr Sloane*. She reported that she had tried to help Orton financially but he had refused; he had even turned down her offer of a TV set, although he was to relent later when she said he needed one in order to learn about the craft of television writing, as she had done. Peggy told Hobson that, just as Orton was leaving their first meeting, Peggy had inquired what he was living on and he had replied that since leaving gaol he had survived on national assistance of £3.10 a week. 'I'm much struck with a young man who doesn't want to exploit people, who is prepared to live on £3.10 p.w., who doesn't whine, or tell a hard luck tale.' Contradictorily, Peggy also used to report to other clients that at their first meeting Orton 'touched me for a fiver'.

Entertaining Mr Sloane had to pass the Lord Chamberlain's strictures, which, ironically, as Orton pointed out, involved cutting all the heterosexual references and keeping in all the homosexual ones. Theatre, like life, was still operating a code as far as sexual identity was concerned. The real point for Orton, which the censor had missed, is that the lodger Sloane, although homosexual, is an ordinary man, and that gay sex did not automatically involve pathetic misfits or camp queens.

At Michael Codron's suggestion, Donald Albery was invited to come in on the production of *Entertaining Mr Sloane*. The swiftness of the decision to present the play was followed by an uncharacteristic haste to pay the option even before the contract had been signed. They also doubled Orton's advance. Codron had a hunch that the play might have the same commercial possibilities as Pinter's *The Caretaker*, which had transferred from the Arts to the West End and run well over a year. Unbeknown to Orton, Peggy put in £250 via MR Ltd. Investments. Peggy did not expect to make any money out of the play, she simply liked Orton enough to want to get it on.

Peggy only rarely invested in shows, although she often said she would have liked to become more involved in production by backing and even producing shows. As early as 1957 she had considered forming a production company but abandoned the idea because there were too few plays of quality around. Her only previous investments had also been in Codron shows, first with Mortimer's *Two Stars for Comfort* in 1962, followed in 1963 by Livings' *Kelly's Eye*. In 1964, as well as supporting *Entertaining Mr Sloane*, she invested in *A Scent of Flowers* by James Saunders, in 1965 another Orton play, *Loot*, and in 1974 David Hare's *Knuckle* – all Codron productions. Her only other recorded investment came in 1971 at the behest of the producer Robert Swash who needed backing for *The Dirtiest Show in Town* in which actors featured naked. After seeing the show, she commented, 'well, darling, one cock is very much like another'.

Peter Wood was due to direct *Entertaining Mr Sloane* but had to pull out because of prior commitments, although not before he had made suggestions, following Peggy's lead, to change the play's ending. He also helped Orton push the play more towards irony and an exploration of the relationships within the family, so that the idea of sexual sharing became more central. The production was designed by Peggy's client Tim O'Brien and directed, at Peggy's suggestion, by Patrick Dromgoole, who had been responsible for Charles Wood's *Cockade* at the Arts the year before.

Orton did not take to Dromgoole's approach and expropriated his surname as a pejorative adjective to stand for the liberal middle class who are at root very conservative. (In his film script *Up Against It* Orton retaliates further in the shape of a prissy character called Miss Drumgoole who wears a starched apron.) Peggy was likewise critical of the direction, which she felt mixed up too many styles and lacked edge, and she turned against the man whom she had originally promoted.

Nevertheless, *Entertaining Mr Sloane* captured the spirit of the times and caused a stir, earning praise from theatrical celebrities with whom Orton had nothing in common and for whom he even had a certain contempt, such as Ted Willis and Terence Rattigan, who thought it the most exciting and stimulating first play that he had ever seen. He backed up his judgement with an investment of £3,000, which ensured that the play transferred to Albery's West End theatre the Wyndham's; Albery had needed convincing because the reviews had been mixed and the play had lost money at the Arts.

Typically, Peggy disappeared on the opening night immediately after the show, even though it was the first in the West End for her new client. She left Codron standing on the pavement with Orton to go backstage on their own.

Not long after the transfer, a public brouhaha, which became known as the 'dirty plays' row, broke out over the alleged ill health of London's theatre, with Orton's play in the eye of the critical storm. Peter Cadbury, the head of London's largest ticket agency, and the impresario Emile Littler spearheaded a 'clean up the West End' campaign aimed against a certain sort of play, typified by *Entertaining Mr Sloane* and David Rudkin's *Afore Night Come*. The RSC, which presented the Rudkin play, was the subject of much vituperation, especially for its Theatre of Cruelty season and the Peter Brook production of Peter Weiss's *The Persecution and Assassination of Jean-Paul Marat as Performed by the Inmates of the Asylum of Charenton under the Direction of the Marquis de Sade*. There was an element of revenge in Littler's attack; he was a governor of the RSC and had offered its artistic director Peter Hall his theatre, the Cambridge, as the company's London base. Hall had used this offer as a bargaining ploy in his bid to gain the Aldwych, dropping Littler's theatre as soon as he was successful. The RSC was also in constant dispute with the censor. The row allowed some of the aggrieved commercial managers who had opposed the RSC's entry into the West End to strike back, and it offered them a little respite from a poor summer at the box office. Michael Codron, the commercial manager most closely associated with the plays under fire, resigned from the executive committee of the management body SWET, of which Littler was the president.

The publicity for Orton's play exploited the row: 'The persecution and assassination of *Entertaining Mr Sloane* is still taking place at the Wyndham's Theatre. Warning – this play is not suitable for the narrow minded.' Yet Albery wobbled in his commitment and, three months into its run, replaced the show with a conventional farce presented by Brian Rix. *Entertaining Mr Sloane* was moved to the Queen's and lost some momentum. The production closed just over a month later, having at least made a small profit.

Orton loved being at the heart of the outrage; he had even jumped in first himself just after *Sloane* had opened by writing a letter of complaint to the *Daily Telegraph* in the guise of his alter-ego Edna Welthorpe, whom he had used since the mid-50s to send up various institutions. But he was furious that the 'dirty plays row' had prevented him from winning an Evening Standard Award – at least that was how he saw it. According to the newspaper's critic, Milton Shulman, Orton was not, in fact, a serious contender in the Best Play category – won by Edward Albee's *Who's Afraid of Virginia Woolf?* – and the jury did not regard *Entertaining Mr Sloane* highly enough to justify the opprobrium they knew they would attract if they had chosen him as the Most Promising Playwright. For the first time, the award was not given; the figure of Sloane, however, went on to become an icon of the era.

Orton had completed a short play, *The Good and Faithful Servant*, just before *Entertaining Mr Sloane* opened in the West End; it was subsequently broadcast on Rediffusion Television in 1967. He then moved straight on to writing *Loot*, then with the title *Funeral Games*, which he promised Peggy would be better than *Entertaining Mr Sloane*, particularly in its construction. His subject this time was the all-pervasive, hypocritical authoritarianism of the English, and he had chosen to go on the offensive through farce: the story revolves around a coffin and a corpse which has to be hidden in a cupboard. Where *Entertaining Mr Sloane* had subverted the form of the well-made play, *Loot* satirised the whodunit, as reflected in the new title, which Halliwell once more had suggested.

Codron was to be the producer again, in what was to be an uneasy partnership with Albery that proved problematic for the production as the two men pulled in different directions. Peggy advised Codron to move on from Dromgoole as director to Peter Wood, the original choice for *Entertaining Mr Sloane*. This time Peter Wood was free, although, as it turned out, Peggy turned against him too. Unfortunately, he was very busy in the period leading up to rehearsals and much of the necessary script work was left until then. Codron was keen to move quickly because he wanted to capitalise on Orton's name while it was still in the public mind. A six-week, pre-West End tour was arranged, beginning in Cambridge in February 1965, and a starry cast was assembled that included Duncan Macrae, Geraldine McEwan, Ian McShane, and Kenneth Williams, for whom the central part of Inspector Truscott had been intended after Codron had introduced Orton to him during the writing of the play.

Both Peggy and Codron saw a problem with the casting of Williams once they had read the script, but Orton was enthusiastic and Codron was pleased to have an actor of Williams' standing lead the company to boost the production's box office chances. There were two main areas of concern. Orton had skewed the play to make Truscott more important than the original main protagonist, Fay, and yet, for Truscott to work, the role needed to be written as less of the parody than it had become.

Peggy was worried, both about the script and about Wood's lack of availability prior to rehearsal. When rewrites finally started arriving during rehearsals, they did not address the play's major problem of structure, and they were exhausting for the cast. Peggy believed that Wood was aiming at the wrong style, which was too high flown.

The tour opened disastrously in Cambridge; 'nauseating', 'rubbish', 'shapeless', 'boring' said the local critics, confirming the worst fears of the actors. Orton returned to London and delivered huge rewrites, much to the anger of the cast, who had to perform the existing flawed script each night while rehearsing what was radically new material during the day.

Peggy thought the production had improved by the time she saw it in Brighton – 'very much slicker and more professional . . . this play is already better than *Sloane* at any time' but she thought that the play was 'beginning, very slightly, to lose Joe's unique personality and voice'. In Oxford the show neared collapse. Orton, following Wood's prompting, was writing better and had achieved a near-farce form which could handle his ideas, but it was now too late to sort out both the play and the production. Codron and Albery were disagreeing about the rewrites; Orton and the cast were drained; morale was at rock bottom.

At Golder's Green, north London, Peggy's curt response to the tired and lumbering production was 'no comment'. Orton had turned bullish and believed the play would succeed in London. Her attitude enraged him. He wrote to her: '*Loot* is in far better shape than when we sold it to Michael. I wanted to write a farce. The nearer I come to it, the unhappier you are. I have not turned "an interesting failure" into a second-rate farce; I've turned a failed farce into a successful farce . . . If *Loot* folds through no fault of its own, I'll wash my hands of writing. Don't imagine that failure will stimulate me. It never has done yet.' He continued, succumbing to paranoia and exaggeration: 'That you hated *Sloane* I can forgive. Dromgoole's production, plus the acting, left a lot to be desired. But if you dislike *Loot* as well, perhaps it is the essential me as a writer you dislike. And we both of us better think seriously of parting company.'

Peggy soothed him, and they did not separate. It was a very depressing situation, she recalled. She gave a candid assessment and said she was not convinced that the show should come in to the West End. Nevertheless, rewrites continued as the production moved on to Bournemouth, where the internal problems were exacerbated by audience walk-outs, which were reported in the local newspapers as a protest at the moral tenor of the play. Word obviously spread to the next port of call, Manchester, because police were in attendance following objections from the local Watch Committee.

Peggy's increasing concern at the prospect of a West End showing was shared by members of the cast, the director and Donald Albery. When *Loot* arrived at Wimbledon, its final destination before the West End, Codron announced that he could not find a West End theatre to take the show. The première production of *Loot* died at the end of that week – subsequently to enter the theatrical history books as a legendary fiasco.

Peggy had seriously disagreed with Codron and Orton over the production, the failure of which had left Orton feeling humiliated and still resentful. She said she had only let the tour progress as far as it did because this was what Orton had wanted but she found such 'negative good behaviour' stultifying and uncreative. Finally Peggy had insisted Codron stop the tour. She and Codron had never experienced such a profound rift between them before, and, coming as it did at the same time as they were having disagreements over *The Killing of Sister George*, it marked the nadir in their relationship.

Orton believed Peggy was destroying his career and received from Peggy by way of appeasement a promise that she would arrange a production of *Loot* in London within six months. The strain of the traumas that had accompanied the tour had told on Peggy. Miserable and isolated, feeling denigrated and cold-shouldered by colleagues, she saw this as one of the worst moments of her professional life.

Peggy's promise to Orton was heartfelt but rash. It is never easy to pick up the pieces after a disaster, especially within the short space of time that she had set herself. Yet she also did believe that Orton was capable of carrying out his threat to give up writing and felt that such an urgent commitment was the order of the day; the further risk, however, was that a second failure with *Loot* could finish Orton as a playwright forever.

Her attempts to mount the revival were not helped by the failure in New York that autumn of *Entertaining Mr Sloane*, despite – or perhaps because of – the production being much more truthful to the play's intentions than had been the case in London. Orton had been denied a visa to enter the US because of his prison record. Peggy had persuaded him to write about this, but the magazines she approached turned the article down. It never appeared, adding to Orton's sense of paranoia about his future. He was finally granted a visa and wrote to Peggy from America full of praise for the director Alan Schneider, to whom Peggy had introduced him, and for the production. The critics, however, slated it; the show closed after thirteen performances.

Peggy was still trying to interest managements in a second production of *Loot*, without any success. Its notoriety proved a stumbling block. Codron still believed in the play and contacted a 22-year-old Oxford University graduate Braham Murray, who had successfully taken a university revue, *Hang Down Your Head and Die*, to the West End and New York the year before. Codron asked if Murray would be prepared to mount *Loot* at the Hampstead Theatre Club if Codron could set it up. Murray had just accepted the post of artistic director of Century Theatre, which itself had recently become the resident company at the University Theatre in Manchester. He read the play and told Codron that he would be happy to stage it, but only if he could do so in Manchester. Peggy was not convinced. She wrote to Orton: 'I honestly don't know whether he can be entrusted with it. We can't make any second mistake in the production of this play and we must be QUITE sure.' She did not know enough about Murray to judge whether or not he might help or hinder Orton's cause, nor did she relish Codron's involvement. She was holding out for a top-flight London production and, even though her six months were nearly up, she refused.

The six-month deadline passed without the promised production. Peggy's efforts turned a corner when she sold an option on the play to Oscar Lewenstein in January 1966. She and Lewenstein had met to discuss a different project concerning Orton – to write a short film script for Lindsay Anderson, who was looking for a modern *Bacchae* set in a holiday camp. Anderson recalled that Peggy had suggested Orton – Lewenstein that it was his idea. The upshot was that Orton wrote a treatment, which Anderson did not like because of its high camp. Orton turned the material into a TV play, *The Erpingham Camp*, which was broadcast in June 1966 and staged the following year at the Royal Court.

At her meeting with Lewenstein, Peggy told him the grisly details of the terrible tour of *Loot* and let him have a copy of the script. 'It was one of the funniest plays I'd ever read,' says Lewenstein. But he was busy working on a film, so needed a partner in order to present *Loot*; after approaching Michael Codron first – who, according to Lewenstein, insisted on any new production taking on the losses of the tour, a deal which Lewenstein found unacceptable – Lewenstein asked Michael White, with whom he had collaborated on several shows at the Theatre Royal, Stratford East. White, a former assistant to Peter Daubeny who had become a producer in his own right in 1961, agreed.

With no immediate prospect of a London production, the Manchester option re-appeared. It would allow Lewenstein and White the luxury of a try-out away from the glare of the capital. Orton worked with Murray on the script and made the play more compressed, focused and real. Murray's production opened in April and London theatres were approached to take it in. The production gave new life to *Loot* and renewed interest in the play in London, but the curse of the original tour still kept all doors firmly shut.

Orton, who was on holiday with Kenneth Halliwell in Tangier, wrote to Peggy for news. She told him that both the National Theatre and the Royal Court, now under William Gaskill, were in the hunt. Nothing, however, was definite. Orton became more frustrated; Peggy had to keep him as calm as possible: '*Loot* will go on some way or another.' She knew more about the way the theatre worked than Orton did and about the time certain plays take to find their level. An immensely practical woman, she nevertheless held to a belief in a kind of transcendental destiny; a play had its own fate and any play of real worth, she was convinced, would come to the surface and be recognised sooner or later. It was not a passive view, however, and she never gave up her quest to relaunch *Loot* properly.

In June 1966 this still seemed like a long way off. Peggy had to tell Orton in Tangier that William Gaskill, after all, was not taken with *Loot*. He thought Orton an amoral writer and not suitable for the Royal Court. Peggy took Orton's line that 'morals go much deeper than sexual appetites and real immorality has little to do with promiscuity.' She told Gaskill that the impetus behind Orton's work was, in fact, puritanism. Gaskill was not moved.

Orton wrote back scornfully. He was sick of the theatre and if Lewenstein's option ran out with no sign of a production being imminent, Orton would refuse Lewenstein the opportunity to renew his option. 'I shall throw the play on the fire. And I shan't write a third stage play. I shall earn my living on TV,' Orton wrote to Peggy. 'Of course, I know you're doing your best. All the foregoing isn't including you. As they say, "I've every confidence in your abilities".'

Peggy's patience was finally rewarded. Lewenstein struck a deal with the London offshoot of the Edinburgh Traverse Theatre, run by the avant-garde American director Charles Marowitz, who was to present a season at the Jeanetta Cochrane Theatre in central London. The deal was that Marowitz was to direct the play, not Murray. Peggy was suspicious of Marowitz but admired his entrepreneurial streak and willingness to tackle the new – 'those tiny wrists and ankles brought out the Oxfam in me,' she recalled. 'But, *oh God*, his theories!' For Lewenstein and White, Marowitz offered the opportunity of a relatively cheap London showing, which, if it failed, would not be too much of a catastrophe for them.

Marowitz did not impress Orton or the cast, which included Kenneth Cranham, Sheila Ballantine and Michael Bates as Truscott. Yet Marowitz did exude a confidence which infected the work he did with Orton on the Manchester script. Lewenstein had serious doubts about the whole venture and ten days before rehearsals were due to begin, he asked Orton if he wanted to cancel the production. Orton asked if there would be any chance of a new show and, on hearing that Lewenstein could offer no guarantees, decided Marowitz represented his best, if final, bet.

When *Loot* opened in September 1966, both Peggy and Orton were less than overjoyed at the production. They found the set dull and the direction too deliberate. There were some benefits in not having any stars in the cast, notably in the greater truth that ensemble playing allowed, though Orton felt more experienced actors might improve on the delivery of the comedy.

To Peggy's and Orton's astonishment, the critics responded positively to the play: Ronald Bryden in the *Observer* believed that *Loot* had 'established

Orton's niche in English drama'. The production transferred to the West End, where it ran for 342 performances, and won Orton his much-desired Evening Standard Best Play Award. The rehabilitation of *Loot* was complete; Peggy said she knew of no other play that had suffered such a mauling the first time round and then had resurfaced so soon with such a triumph.

Orton dedicated the published version of *Loot* to Peggy, 'for services rendered,' as she said. It was a kind and forgiving gesture from Orton, made in recognition of the promise she had kept, even if the resulting London production had taken a little longer to achieve than anticipated.

Orton took Peggy as his guest to the Evening Standard Award ceremony, at which the table plan described them as 'Mr and Mrs Orton'. They both chuckled as Orton had originally intended to come with his partner Kenneth Halliwell, who had decided not to attend; in 1966, it was a bold gesture for a man to take a male partner to such a public gathering, even in the theatre world, and Halliwell and Orton had always lived together in seclusion. Frank Marcus made a speech in praise of Orton, the former RADA student, assistant stage manager and part-time chocolate factory worker from Leicester who was now set to become a star. For all his cool exterior, Orton was extremely pleased to appear on the front page of the *Standard*, receiving the statuette, though less than enamoured by a TV programme which broadcast excerpts from the ceremony. When his name was announced, the sound was off, and when he appeared, there was still no sound and the credits were rolling over his face. 'Then the sound came on for the other winners,' he wrote in his diary. He felt as if there were a conspiracy to rob him of his moment of victory. 'The whole had the effect of the man with the bladder hitting the Emperor on the head as he rode in triumph.'

However bruised his ego may have been, Orton had indeed become a celebrity, and he hit the headlines with *Loot* again when the papers announced the sale of the film rights to Arthur Lewis and Bernard Delfont for £100,000, an enormous sum then for a play. In fact, the sale figure was £25,000, with a future royalty deal possibly accounting for the higher amount. According to the records, Orton received £9,720, a handsome return, nevertheless.

Peggy clinched the deal late one Friday when she should already have been on the train to Brighton to see the opening of a play by John Mortimer. She had received several inquiries about the film rights when Lewis telephoned her. Not entirely convinced that he was serious, she said he could have the rights if he came round with a cheque for £20,000 before she caught the next train 'otherwise you'll have to join the queue on Monday morning.' This was hardly the reality, but it had the desired effect.

Lewenstein, who was to get his share as the play's producer, was in her office and said to Peggy 'See what happens if you ask for £25,000.'

When Lewis arrived, she put the price up, and Lewis paid up, £18,000 then and another £7,000 on signature of contract. Orton discovered this when he arrived that evening at Peggy's Brighton house to watch himself on a TV show *Call My Bluff*. He was suitably chuffed at the film deal, especially as the play was in no way suitable for the cinema, as the filmed version proved when it was released in 1970. *Loot* was also a flop on Broadway, in 1968, a failure Orton foresaw with mature equanimity and summed up in advance by quoting Peggy: 'Reputations are made in London, only money is made in New York.'

Orton at this point in his life was very busy. By the time of the sale of the film rights to *Loot* in February 1967, he had finished a new TV play with a title he had toyed with before, *Funeral Games*, which was broadcast in 1968, the first draft of his farce *What the Butler Saw*, and he was revising *The Erpingham Camp* for the Royal Court, which, in spite of Gaskill's reservations, had eventually come to schedule an Orton play – in fact, a double-bill. Following a Sunday evening production without décor by Peter Gill at the Royal Court in 1966 of *The Ruffian on the Stair*, Gill was set to present that play again in the summer of 1967 alongside the new version of *The Erpingham Camp* under the umbrella title of *Crimes of Passion*. Orton had also been asked for a piece 'to do with sex' for Kenneth Tynan's revue, *Oh! Calcutta!*; this kind of liberal exhibitionism did not interest Orton, but he obliged by writing up a pornographic sketch that he had devised for Halliwell as a private joke.

Such was Orton's new-found fame that he seemed the ideal writer when the Beatles were searching for a follow-up to their two jokey films, *A Hard Day's Night* and *Help*. Orton was sent a script they had already commissioned and proceeded to transform it by borrowing both from the first, unpublished, novel he had written with Halliwell, *The Silver Bucket*, as well as from Orton's final novel, posthumously published as *Head to Toe*. Peggy saw the script, entitled *Up Against It*, as merely a piece of fun. She may even be recorded in it in some way as it includes a character called Jack Ramsay (Jack was the name Orton had sometimes used as a writer before he met Peggy). Ramsay, at one point during a battle, drives an ambulance with his colleagues into an oncoming lorry – an echo perhaps of Peggy's wartime exploits? Mayhem ensues; one colleague kneels, dumb, the other sobs, but Ramsay 'shrieks with maniacal laughter and begins to leap about in a kind of glee'.

Peggy sent the new script to the film's producer, Walter Shenson, and heard nothing for a month when it was returned without comment or explanation. Oscar Lewenstein stepped in and bought it. He set up a meeting with Orton and the film's prospective director, Richard Lester, who had made the Beatles' two previous films. On the day of the meeting, Peggy telephoned Orton at his flat to see if there was anything he wanted to discuss with her before he saw Lester, but there was no reply. She then received a telephone call from Lewenstein's chauffeur, who had been sent to drive Orton to the meeting; he told her that no one had answered the door when he had called at the flat to collect Orton. The chauffeur had first phoned Lewenstein, who had told him to try again; he did so, twice. He then looked through the letter box and saw a naked body lying apparently asleep. He had called Lewenstein again, who told him to phone Peggy. She said, 'Call the police.'

Peggy went to the flat – in Noel Road, Islington. She remembered entering the room where Halliwell had bludgeoned Orton with hammer blows to the head before killing himself at Orton's side by taking an overdose. She was so nervous that the only way she could bring herself to enter the room was by going in backwards. Once inside, she felt quite cool and dispassionate. Orton's body, she said, had already been taken away. She looked at Halliwell and felt nothing. She did, however, ask her secretary to buy her a bottle of brandy on her return to the office. Peggy had to identify Halliwell for the police because there was no next of kin available. Douglas Orton identified his brother.

There were two inquests and two funerals, and Peggy was the only person present at all four functions. Halliwell's funeral in Enfield, north London, was held the day before Orton's. The service, which Peggy arranged, was conducted by a clergyman with hymns and an organ playing. Other than Peggy, the only mourners were three of his relatives who had not seen him for years. Orton's funeral at the north London Golder's Green Crematorium was, in contrast, a non-religious theatrical affair, which became unintentionally ludicrous, as undoubtedly would have amused its subject. Douglas Orton had asked Peggy to organise the funeral and she in turn had left the detail to the TV producer Peter Willes, who doted on Orton and was desperate to be in charge of his send-off. It was not a huge crowd: Orton's family, members of the *Loot* cast, a contingent from the Royal Court, a smattering of the profession who knew Orton, and Peggy with some of her staff. None of the mourners knew when to stand or remain seated. They took the sedentary option as the coffin was borne down the aisle to the strains of 'A Day in the Life', Orton's favourite Beatles' song, played on a crackling tape with the psychedelic passages crudely excised. There was an agonisingly long pause before Harold Pinter and then Donald Pleasence each read a poem, the latter completely inappropriate, and yet another embarrassing gap before the coffin finally slid out of the chapel into the arms of the crematorium workers beyond. Despite the longueurs, the service was completed in the brief slot allowed for such occasions, at the end of which everybody was politely but firmly moved on. 'It was all false pomp,' said Peggy, 'a badly stage-managed affair. I hadn't the heart to tell Willes that funerals were not his speciality.'

Peggy brokered a secret deal to mix Halliwell's and Orton's ashes after one of Halliwell's relatives had suggested this to her. She asked Douglas Orton, who agreed, he said, as long as nobody in Leicester heard about it. The film about Orton and Halliwell, *Prick Up Your Ears*, written by Alan Bennett, picks up on this incident and has Orton's sister, Leonie, inexpertly mixing the ashes and saying, 'I think I'm putting in more of Joe than I am of Kenneth.' To which Peggy replies in an apt if not an actual Peggy riposte: 'It's a gesture, dear, not a recipe.'

When Orton was killed, he had already been discussing with Peggy and Lewenstein the plans for his last play, *What the Butler Saw*; it was 18 months, however, after his death before the production occurred. As with *Loot*, the production turned out to be a fiasco, yet, like its predecessor, the play has subsequently become a modern classic, thus to Peggy's mind, confirming her theory of the destiny of talent.

Orton had wanted a top-notch West End production for *What the Butler Saw*. He had relished the prospect of turning the tables on what he called the 'old theatre of reassurance'. Orton had dismissed the idea of Lewenstein partnering Michael White again, unfairly blaming White for *Loot*'s failure in New York. Peggy and Lewenstein believed that, in order to obtain the right theatre and the right cast, the best person to achieve this was undoubtedly Binkie Beaumont, who had shown some interest in Orton's work. He needed to be persuaded, however. According to the producer Toby Rowland, who met Orton through Peggy, it was he, Rowland, who interceded and secured Beaumont's involvement. The production that finally emerged should have been the ultimate triumph for Orton – a star-studded cast, led by Ralph Richardson, Stanley Baxter, Coral Browne and Julia Foster, playing in a Shaftesbury Avenue theatre under the banner of the commercial establishment's most powerful figure.

Sadly, it was not to be. Again the direction was wrong – Robert Chetwyn was better suited to smooth productions of West End comedies – and Stanley Baxter was mis-cast, just as Kenneth Williams had been in *Loot*, as a doctor who runs a private clinic that specialises in mental disorders. At the start of the play, he is interviewing a prospective secretary whom he orders to undress, thus beginning a farcical spiral of cross-dressing and mistaken identity into which strides Dr Rance, played with bemusement by Ralph Richardson, who has come to inspect the clinic. Orton had discussed some of the principal casting; he thought Richardson too old and preferred Halliwell's idea of Alistair Sim but Lewenstein was set on Sir Ralph. Orton and Lewenstein had both wanted Arthur Lowe to play Baxter's part but Peggy and Beaumont had taken against this idea. Lewenstein recalls this as the only serious artistic disagreement he ever had with Peggy.

When Peggy saw the pre-London showing she became very concerned and wrote of her anxiety to Lewenstein: 'There is far too much mouthing of the text. Joe's style can now surely be left to look after itself, and a little more speed, ease and enjoyment could creep in. There is no feeling of enjoyment or zest or expansion, and I think the actors have all become tense . . . To me it simply struck a chill'. She thought the reason Richardson was appalling was because he was terrified. He was messing up his lines and ruining the play, but she knew that he was not cowardly enough to leave the show. She found this production worse than the original production of *Loot*.

Orton's death had made him the most notorious figure in the theatre world and cast a huge shadow over all of his work. In Brighton, this fuelled hostility in the audience to *What the Butler Saw*, particularly from those who felt a grand old actor like Ralph Richardson had demeaned himself by appearing in such a play. In the West End, a hostile clique booed *What the Butler Saw* from the gallery on its first night. Amidst a general critical drubbing, it was Frank Marcus, now the drama critic of the *Sunday Telegraph*, who championed the play: 'I think it will survive and tell people more about what it felt to be alive in the 60s than almost anything else of the period.'

There were further castigations of Ralph Richardson, who replied in a dignified manner to all the letters of complaint he received. Stanley Baxter recalled that Richardson had at first turned down the part and, then, having accepted, came to believe that he was taking part in a dirty play, but, as a professional, he had stuck with it. Peggy gracefully thanked Richardson for his solidarity and said she believed it was important for leading actors to support new writing. She told him Robert Bolt always said that, but for Richardson's performance in *Flowering Cherry*, Bolt would still be a schoolteacher.

Peggy insisted that she was guided in everything she did concerning the production by a fidelity to Orton, even if he had been misguided. 'Joe was wrong in his decision over the original production of *Loot* [to let the tour proceed so far],' she said, 'and over his instructions concerning *What the Butler Saw*, which were carried out after he was dead. But they were his wishes, and we tried to do what we feel he would have liked.'

The text of *What the Butler Saw*, however, was a different matter. Peggy had told Orton the play was 'the very best thing you've done so far. And technically in advance of *Loot*.' It was, however, unfinished, and Orton always rewrote in rehearsal, a conjunction of circumstances that brought Peggy into action on two fronts – one successfully, the other not. She resisted the demands of the director and designer for a share of the author's royalty for the whole period of copyright if future productions used what they termed the production script, which, necessarily, incorporated changes that were made without Orton's contribution. It was, however, the changes that were the problem. She and Lewenstein discussed cuts and alterations, several suggested by Ralph Richardson; some were agreed while others were not. The most important departure from Orton's script came at the end of the play when a missing fragment of a blown-up statue of Winston Churchill is found. The piece is the great war leader's penis – Orton's symbol of liberation and anarchy – but, even in the absence of the now defunct censor, Richardson insisted on changing the phallic object to a cigar. He also took the last lines of the play, instead of their being spoken by Stanley Baxter's character, who should open and close the play as the cycle of life is disconcertingly re-established.

The American production by the comedy director, Joe Hardy, went further in neutering the play and, probably as a result, gave Orton his first New York success. Binkie Beaumont was unrepentant in his support for the American version: 'My pleasure in seeing the play in New York and reading the glowing notices,' he wrote to Peggy, 'was in the great feeling of relief that we had been able to achieve Orton's desire – a commercial success. I personally wish we had done the play in the Joe Hardy version at the Haymarket, and it may be then we would have given Orton what he had set out to do.'

Peggy, however, was delighted when Lewenstein was later able, as he puts it, to 'make amends' by presenting an Orton season during his time as artistic director of the Royal Court, including an important revival of *What the Butler Saw* by Lindsay Anderson that restored Orton's original textual intentions.

Orton's life, because of his death, has been so well documented and publicised in biography, diaries, plays and on film that, like Peggy's, it has become inseparable from its own myth. It was in fact Peggy who helped the myth into being by giving crucial assistance to Orton's biographer, John Lahr, and in allowing publication of the diaries, which she had encouraged Orton to write in the first place. Orton's death affected her deeply, and she later regretted the access she had given Lahr to Orton's diaries.

When she was asked by the publishers, shortly after Orton's death, if a tribute to Orton could be carried in a forthcoming edition of *Loot*, she refused and said that she hoped the events of his private life would be forgotten as soon as possible. She despised what she saw as the exploitation of Orton, who, in the way of modern times, had been appropriated and turned into a commodity like James Dean, Marilyn Monroe, or Che Guevara, albeit less ubiquitously. All Peggy's comments and judgements on Orton and Halliwell after their deaths were coloured by her dislike of this phenomenon, especially as the diaries emphasised the sexually rampant and irresponsible Orton, which was not the Orton that Peggy, or many others who knew him well, remembered.

Peggy wanted Orton to be seen as a serious person and a working playwright; her memories presented him as sweet, well mannered, bright, humorous, benign, puritanical; he did not smoke tobacco, only drank socially and looked after his body. He led a spartan existence with Halliwell, even when they could afford a more expensive lifestyle. (She had to persuade Orton to have a telephone because sending telegrams was becoming tiresome.) She recalled him as loyal, yet she also saw him being heartless, manipulative, vain and calculating.

To Peggy he was both ambitious and carefree, seduced by his own success and yet capable of giving it all up. 'He would have been happy to go off to North Africa with a plethora of boys and leave me to earn enough from his work so that he could live there with his harem,' she said. 'The theatre is a mere reflection of life, but it's life that's the important thing. The theatre throws it back, enhances it with a good play, makes life wonderful. Joe was never kidded that it was more than a reflection.'

Mostly, she saw a little boy; she liked the insecurity that lay beneath the bravado – it was a saving grace – because she recognised people's masks and was not shocked by his exhibitionism. The little boy also shared with her an inability to love and a horror of continuous personal commitment – he from a childlike desire for permanent adventure, she from the pain of experience. This gave him a streak of ruthless self-sufficiency, to which Peggy was drawn. It made him strive to be a consummate artist, 'better than practically every author we've looked after,' she said.

Nevertheless, she still saw Orton as a minority writer, which was not meant pejoratively. Public taste had simply not caught up with him; none of his plays had been a thoroughbred commercial success. She had little interest in whether or not his plays had pushed back the sexual boundaries of the theatre; playwriting not pioneering was her concern, and, in that regard, she thought he should have concentrated more on content. She would defend Orton if others criticised him, because she saw that as her prerogative, yet she criticised Orton to other clients, as she did with all the playwrights she represented. She tended to play down his standing in exact relation to the growth of his myth, partly because she was generally iconoclastic and sceptical, partly because she was irritated because she could not control the myth, and partly because she felt genuinely sorry for his partner Halliwell, the real 'author' of Orton.

Halliwell, born in the Wirral and seven years older than Orton, had created Orton the writer, had educated and sustained him and written several unpublished novels with him. Orton had seen his role as educating Halliwell in sexual matters but, at a time when homosexuality was illegal, the more Orton was exhilarated by promiscuous adventures, which often began in public lavatories, the more scared Halliwell became for him; police entrapment, 'queer-bashing' and possible scandal all threatened the privacy of their relationship.

They had met at RADA in 1951 and had lived together since then, for over a decade as the only family each of them acknowledged. Halliwell's mother had died when he was eleven and his father had committed suicide when Halliwell was 23. He became both Orton's older brother and lover, and in every way his mentor. Then, after accepting *Entertaining Mr Sloane*, Peggy had taken over this role, with Orton's blessing; she had opened the door to a new world of theatrical success, an alien world to him dominated by a different class and its tastes yet one which Orton both loathed and desired. Halliwell's contribution, which continued to the end, was gradually being buried.

She kept in her 1968 scrap book – the year after their deaths – a cutting from a local newspaper, the *Hackney Gazette*, dated 18 May 1962, presumably given to her by Orton or Halliwell, or found by her among their belongings. It was a simple report of 'Kenneth Leith Halliwell, 35, invoice clerk, and John Kingsley Orton, 29, a lens cleaner' being sentenced by Old Street magistrates to six months' imprisonment, carried under the main headline 'Stole and Damaged Library Books' with a smaller heading below it, 'Two Men Gaoled'. 'A Senior Probation Officer said both men were frustrated actors and authors.' Peggy saw the book defacing as a strange form of artistic expression, and the cutting signalled the moment when they experienced the beginnings of a life apart from each other; after being sent together to Wormwood Scrubs, Orton went to an open prison in Sheerness, Kent, and Halliwell to one in Arundel, West Sussex. Orton used his time in prison to try to write on his own for the first time; prison proved a kind of liberation. It was there that his work developed a distance that, for Peggy, was to become his hallmark. For Halliwell, prison was a nightmare.

Peggy recalled that at her first meeting with Halliwell he had terrified her. He was pompous and exhibitionist, but what shocked her, for some reason, was his baldness because it affected his behaviour. His hair had receded badly by the time he was twenty, and he had gone completely bald before he was thirty. With the first money that Orton earned he bought Halliwell a wig. This, Peggy remembered, transformed his personality. Halliwell was ashamed of his baldness but with his wig on became reasonable and nice. When she had to identify his dead body she remarked that the wig gave him a certain grandeur, 'like a Roman emperor'. He looked then as if he were finally satisfied, she observed.

She felt great sympathy for Halliwell because, although he was the prime mover in the relationship with Orton, he was actually the underdog, the weaker partner, and, most importantly, he was the failure. She found him somehow repulsive – brittle and ludicrous yet also psychologically more complex than Orton. She had suggested that, for tax reasons, he become Orton's personal assistant, and Halliwell had satirised his subservient role by wearing an apron and calling himself Orton's secretary. Halliwell lacked vision, said Peggy, and had a cold wit but he had made this extraordinary emotional commitment to and investment in Orton, which Orton's success had undermined.

Halliwell consulted Peggy about his own talents and gave up his attempts at stage writing on her advice. A year before his death, she damned his latest and last offering to her: 'The first scene sent me into such a well of boredom that I had to struggle to continue which I did in a kind of abstract anguish!!!' When she was urging Orton to write a diary of his visit to Tangier, she suggested that if Orton did not wish to do so then Halliwell might. She did not think that he lacked talent; the problem was he did not know how best to apply it in a way that was uniquely his. He asked her if the answer might lie in the artistic collages he liked making, of which the defaced library books were merely one example. He made her a black and white collage screen, featuring her favourite animal, the cat, which she kept in her London flat.

It was through her that Halliwell came to exhibit his collages in a shop in the King's Road owned by her acquaintance from wartime touring days,

Freddie Bartman. She had lent Bartman money in order to help him set up his antiques business in the Portobello Road in west London, before he graduated to the King's Road. Bartman saw the screen in Peggy's flat and was so impressed that he asked if he could see more of Halliwell's work. Orton and Halliwell took about twenty collages to the shop. Bartman refused to exhibit two of them for fear of prosecution; one was a nude Venus and the other a collage of sections of young men cut from physical culture magazines juxtaposed with flowers and views of houses. 'Freddie B. is a nervous twit,' wrote Orton in his diary. 'Like all the middle classes. Too nervous to live . . . 'As though,' Kenneth said, with some truth, 'anybody will go and see the pictures stuck away at the wrong end of the King's Road'.' Peggy's view was that Halliwell's pictures were 'very talented and very unpleasant'. None was sold.

Halliwell had purchased the flat in Islington in 1959 and dreamed that he and Orton would live together as a couple for the rest of their lives. He wanted a conventional 'marriage'. In a homophobic society, it was an achievement to have survived together for so long. But, when Orton's fame threatened this stability and Halliwell believed he was going to be abandoned by Orton, the only way he could make his dream stay true was to kill his partner and then himself. Peggy, who knew from her own experience about the tussle between family and freedom, believed that Halliwell slew Orton not out of revenge or hatred, or even love, but out of a kind of selfishness – he could not go on living himself without Orton and he could not bear to leave Orton behind. Mutual death was the only way that Halliwell could guarantee that no one else would have Orton and that they would remain together forever.

Peggy was intrigued by Orton and Halliwell and was moved by their relationship. Yet she took an essentially tragic view of life and believed in a destiny; in confirming her view, their deaths seemed to her both an awful and exhilarating parable of existence.

Orton's death would have been sufficient to create a myth around the young writer, but it was his diaries, written at Peggy's prompting, which gave the myth its particular contemporary edge and provided the detail for the myth to take hold as an emblem of the times. It is, necessarily, an ambiguous emblem, capable of different interpretation. Orton arouses salacious voyeurism as much as literary adulation; he is a decadent destroyed by his deviation as much as a source of gay pride.

Orton was not the first client whom she had urged to keep a diary – others included David Mercer and David Rudkin, though only Orton's has been published. Orton himself had already kept several diaries, as a child and young man, but either stopped in the mid-50s or destroyed his later efforts. Peggy had made her suggestion to Orton after the initial failure of *Loot*. She had hoped that he would record his trip to north Africa, a favourite spot of Peggy's, in the manner of Gide, who wrote a series of personally revealing *Journals*. In fact, Orton began them some six months later.

Peggy did not interfere in Orton's private life but was fascinated by it. As with all her clients, she believed it had a decisive bearing on his writing. She and Orton both loved candour and hated humbug, and in conversation they were uninhibited and discussed intimate details of sex. It is not surprising that Orton's sexual activities and imaginings are explicitly reported in a diary written at Peggy's behest – so much so that it is not always possible to distinguish between fact and fantasy. Furthermore they were both involved in showbiz; there is little sense when reading the diaries that Orton was writing for private consumption and every sense that he had an audience in mind. Orton was a performer, and the diaries are another of his shows. The emphasis in the diaries on sexual exploits and gossip, combined with their general lack of routine, mundane detail, and the way Orton talked about the diaries to his friends, with a definite view of them, supports this supposition.

Peggy and Orton had even discussed possible publication, and, as is clear from Orton's correspondence with her, he was aware of the effect that this frankness about sex and about certain named individuals might have. He acknowledged that his revelations might mean a delay in publication until long after his death.

Orton kept diaries from December 1966 until his death in August 1967. They fall into three periods; his time in London, until May 1967, in Tangier during May and June, and the last days of his life back in London from July onwards. They range in subject from his changing theatrical fortunes, to his mother's funeral, from fellatio in public lavatories to buggery in unknown flats, all underscored by the ebb and flow of his partnership with Halliwell. As a chronicle of a moment of social change caught in snapshot, they can be wicked and very funny, and in their celebration of the temporary respite to be found in instant gratification, they can be unintentionally sad.

The diaries also contain their own mystery, which has added to the Orton myth, and it is fitting that it is a mystery that links Peggy to their fate. Orton was a meticulous author and wrote a complete entry pretty well every day, yet the diaries end in mid-sentence at the bottom of a page while he is in Leicester, relating his sister's account of the birth of her daughter. The date is 1 August. Orton died on 9 August. The missing pages containing the entries for the last days of his life have never been found.

Halliwell left a note, which was discovered by the police, that points to their significance:

> If you read his diary all will be explained.
>   K.H.
> P.S. Especially the latter part.

Whatever Halliwell meant precisely by the 'latter part', he would certainly have included Orton's accounts of the crucial days leading to the horrific murder. These were the pages that were not available to explain anything. If they had been, the entries would have probably picked up at Orton's return to London from Leicester on 4 August, necessarily missing out Halliwell's plummeting towards suicide in the intervening days of Orton's absence. Halliwell, who had tried to commit suicide before, had visited the Samaritans, who were unable to offer immediate help, had twice seen his doctor, and, for succour, had gone backstage at the Criterion Theatre where *Loot* was playing. On the day before the murder, Halliwell returned to see the doctor, who was about to go on holiday. The doctor recognised that Halliwell needed specialist psychiatric help but offered no assistance other than to increase Halliwell's prescription to more powerful anti-depressants. He agreed to arrange an appointment for a specialist on his return from holiday.

While Halliwell was waiting for the prescription to be made up, he visited Peter Willes, who lived nearby. Only ten days before, Willes had insulted Halliwell at a dinner party given by Willes, calling Halliwell 'a middle-aged nonentity'. Worse, Orton had just gone to a party of the musical comedy star Dorothy Dickson's organised by Willes, but he had gone without Halliwell, one of the first open signs of Orton's disloyalty.

John Lahr reports Willes as saying that, when Halliwell visited him while waiting for the chemist, he was distraught and talked of himself and Orton separating. Halliwell, however, reversed the likely roles; he being the one to walk out and Orton begging him not to. Willes telephoned Orton after Halliwell had left to collect his prescription and advised Orton not to leave Halliwell 'for a moment'.

That evening was their last. Although Halliwell had fatally injured Orton, it was Halliwell who died first, from his overdose, while Orton, presumably unconscious, lived on for an hour or so more.

Peggy claimed that the police took the last few pages of the diary and that she tried unsuccessfully to retrieve them, first from the police and then from the coroner. Several people close to Peggy believe, however, that she herself took the last pages from the red, loose-leaf folder in which the diary was kept, in order to protect people associated with the final breakdown of their relationship.

Apparently, Willes had offered to become Orton's patron; Orton should leave Halliwell and live with Willes, not as a lover – though Willes was certainly infatuated with Orton – but in order to liberate him from his claustrophobic partnership with Halliwell, who was seen increasingly by Orton's new circle of friends as an impediment to Orton's future. On the day before the murder, Halliwell telephoned a mutual friend of his and Peggy's to rail at Willes' intervention. At Orton's inquest it was said that Orton had already found another lover – Orton had considered living with a novelist whom he had met recently at a party and on the Saturday evening before the murder Orton had appeared at the Criterion without Halliwell but had told one of the cast that he was not alone. It seems clear that Orton had, in fact, decided to move on.

When the diaries were published in 1986, the editor John Lahr and the publisher Methuen worked from typescripts of the handwritten originals, which, by then, had been deposited by Peggy in a bank, along with a juvenile diary Orton had written. Although Peggy was known subsequently to have shown the original diaries to close acquaintances, after her death the originals could not be found. After some searching, the Tangier diary was discovered by Simon Callow tucked behind one of Peggy's bookcases, but of the juvenile diary and the final diary there was no trace.

In another bizarre twist, the Orton estate ended up in the mid-1990s suing the Peggy Ramsay estate for their loss. Maybe the documentation for the bank deposit had been lost in a fire that occurred in Peggy's offices. Maybe Peggy had destroyed them. No one knows, and the whereabouts of two of the diaries continues to be as much of a mystery as the fate of the missing pages.

The situation following Orton's death was unusual; Halliwell and Orton had made each other their beneficiary but, because Halliwell pre-deceased Orton, their two estates passed as one to Orton's next-of-kin. It was unlikely, however, that Halliwell's family would have been able to benefit from Orton's estate had Orton died first, because under English law the family of a murderer cannot benefit from the murderer's victim.

Peggy asked Orton's family, whom she tended to patronise – she called them 'little people' – if they wished her to act as the agent for his estate, and they agreed she should. She suggested they read the diaries and decide what should be done with them. They were happy to take her advice. A fortnight after the murder, Peggy had said of the final diary, 'I do not think that it is publishable or money making in any way. It could, perhaps, after legal advice, be valuable for someone who might possibly and remotely wish to write a biography of Orton.' Three weeks later, Peggy was telling Douglas Orton that the earlier diary covering Tangier was 'very interesting'. She was 'fascinated by it' and thought that it could be published. 'The main problem would be whether it could be published with Joe's name. It would cause something of a stir.' The entries in the final diary, however, were 'very "indecent",' she thought, 'but, as with everything Joe did, marvellously truthful and detached' – although later she was to change her opinion.

'We must read both together,' she wrote to Douglas Orton, 'and then if you think we might try and do some careful publishing, I could ask one or two of the publishing experts.' At this point, in September, the final diary was still held by the coroner, although Peggy thought the lawyers had been given it. It was returned to her in May 1968 when the estates had been settled.

In October, Peggy was corresponding with the writer Christopher Logue (whom she briefly represented) about a possible revision of Orton's film script *Up Against It* and the fate of the diaries came up. Logue, who had known Orton, reminded her that families of writers – he cited as examples the wives of Büchner, Rimbaud and D.H. Lawrence – often destroyed such documents, for understandable reasons, but in his opinion this should not be allowed to happen in Orton's case. Genet's *The Thief's Journal* had become a classic, he pointed out, and advised her to obtain copies of the diaries as a safeguard.

She did have the originals typed up, and in November sent a copy of the Tangier diary, in confidence, to Harold Hobson, who wanted to write a piece on Orton. The motive, however, may have had as much to do with Hobson's private passion for erotica as with his plying the trade of journalism. 'I think you will be immensely bored and sad,' she wrote him, 'because you will possibly feel, as I do, that for our tastes this would be a most boring way of spending a holiday [sex and drugs] one could possibly contrive.' Whatever his interests, Hobson broke the confidence later, in May 1968, by mentioning the diary in a review of Brecht's adaptation of the Marlowe play, *Edward II*, while writing about the practice of men kissing each other on the mouth.

In December 1967, Charles Monteith at Faber and Faber approached Peggy about publishing a book on Orton and Halliwell, and Peggy in reply told Monteith about the diaries. Orton and Halliwell had sent Monteith their writings in the 1950s. Monteith had found their work fascinating but had to turn it down because he did not know what to do with it at the time. He had befriended the authors and even threw a party for them once, disastrously as it turned out, because they were socially very ill at ease. They had sat on a couch and ate chocolates Orton had stolen from the factory where they worked.

Peggy was keen on the idea of a book and discussed it with Monteith. 'A book on Orton and Halliwell should and could be written . . . I doubt, however, whether a really first rate writer would want to do their lives. Would Emlyn Williams perhaps?' Monteith preferred John Bowen, a client of Peggy's who had met Orton and Halliwell at Monteith's party. Bowen was approached but declined because he could not afford to accept on the money that was being offered. Oscar Lewenstein joined in the discussion and suggested Frank Marcus, but Peggy felt he would produce a middle-class documentary. She favoured Edward Bond, who had recently joined her and who would understand, among other things, the class dimension of the story. He declined; he had known Orton, thought him vain, and could not contemplate all the research such a book would entail.

These discussions ran in tandem with a growing interest within the publishing world in making the diaries public. Geoffrey Strachan at Methuen, who had published Orton's plays, made an approach in May 1968. 'They're very highly personal and private,' she replied. 'At the moment it would be considered either obscene to publish them or wouldn't be permitted by the people who are mentioned.' Truman Capote expressed a wish to help edit the diaries and to write a book on Orton and Halliwell. Peggy had thought of him in conjunction with Orton but had to stall him (through his agent) while she continued exploring possibilities with Faber, who next suggested Julian Mitchell, whom Peggy met. Peggy gave him the juvenile and Tangier diaries to read, but he recalls that she was not keen on having them published and was very off-putting. The idea fizzled out, he says, and was not followed up.

John Lahr entered the fray in May 1970 through his writing in America on Orton, which was sent to Peggy by Jack Hutto of the William Morris Agency, who handled Orton's American affairs. She admired an article Lahr had written on Orton but was shattered by his criticism of the New York production, and of the intended publication by Grove of *What the Butler Saw* in its bowdlerised form. (The original Methuen edition had reproduced the altered ending without any dissent from Peggy.) Lahr, who was then the literary adviser to the Lincoln Center's Repertory Theater in New York, wanted Grove to publish the original text, and his intervention through Peggy succeeded in securing this. She became irritated by him, however, when later that year a Washington production, which used the original text, became as she saw it an excuse to attack the London and New York productions, as well as her. She pointed out to Lahr that Orton used to revise heavily during rehearsals for both stage and TV plays, and as he had been unable to do so for *What the Butler Saw*, it was wrong to view the original as gospel. 'We simply can't take a totally academic and righteous stand.'

She complained that Lahr's tone 'sounded tremendously superior as if saying all the words in the right order was going to ensure a successful production.' What deeply upset her was 'the impression that managements, stars and directors are either without talent or deliberately seeking success at the cost of the play, and that I am frivolously allowing Joe's play to be bowdlerised.' Lahr had clearly touched a nerve. She agreed that the final scene should have been staged in New York as originally intended and that a programme note should have detailed changes in the play. 'What I am deploring is the subsequent unkindness and unpleasantness, and the way well-meaning people's careers are being hurt for the future . . . Let's see how Washington do it in all its glory.'

It was a foretaste of disagreements to come. She said she loved Lahr at the time 'for his passion for Orton and his purity. He reminds me of those young people in Anouilh's plays who set out in purity and innocence until Life corrupts them. I hope Life will not do this to John Lahr.' In her view, she was to be disappointed.

In their correspondence in 1970, she mentioned the Tangier diary to Lahr, who said he wanted to write a book on Orton. Peggy replied that if he were to do so, then Halliwell's role must be acknowledged. She recounted their life together in a three-page letter and concluded: 'I am not being sentimental when I say that Joe wouldn't in the least mind being killed by Kenneth.'

Prior to Lahr's arrival in England that summer, he and Peggy continued to discuss a possible book. She agreed to let him read the diaries, which, she wrote to him, are 'infinitely boring for the most part, because they are a day-by-day account of the really trivial life they led when they were in Morocco – up in the morning, picking up boys, and a rather detailed description of the narcissistic nature of the main event of the day [i.e. sex]. They could never give you anything substantial. What I found interesting was that there was a dress rehearsal of Joe's death – obviously in Morocco they were getting on each other's nerves, and Joe was beginning to resent Ken's domination, and Ken was beginning to dictate to him about his boyfriends, which, of course, was probably more irritating than Ken's advice over plays. In the Diary there is a very graphic description of Ken beating Joe over the head, and with great difficulty Joe avoiding it and staying alive.

'From my point of view, there was one interesting entry, which told me where Joe went after a dress rehearsal of *Crimes of Passion*. We had a rather boring dress rehearsal and then Joe got a bus to Holloway, and you will read what he did that evening.' [Peggy is actually referring to Orton's activities on the opening night of the production when he picked up a man in a public lavatory and went back to the stranger's flat. It was the fact that Orton found 'fucking an Irishman' more satisfactory than enjoying a first night which interested Peggy.]

Peggy noted that the diary becomes 'somewhat petty, and very much less likeable' as Halliwell becomes spiteful again. 'I think the subject is really . . . how two people are destroyed – one by success and one by failure.'

She had come to the conclusion that the final diary showed Orton in a bad light. She did not like its sneering quality nor its portraits of certain people who deserved better: Kenneth Williams with his 'stupid camp talk', for instance, or Peter Gill, the director of *Crimes of Passion*, whom, she felt, Orton had described as 'a kind of hysterical queen'.

Lahr was pushing hard to write the biography, and Peggy responded to his passion. She had also enjoyed his biography of his father Bert Lahr, the vaudeville actor who played the cowardly lion in the film of *The Wizard of Oz*. Peggy thought that a book on Orton would be 'enormously advantageous to Joe's reputation as a writer' and agreed that Lahr could write it because 'you would be writing about his work as well as his life. I think the tone would be very important, because Joe was absolutely unromantic and unsentimental, and he only had one overwhelming relationship allied to complete loyalty and that was to Ken.'

Peggy helped Lahr prepare the book, opening her files to him and giving him invaluable introductions to Orton's collaborators. She gave Lahr press cuttings, different versions of the plays, unpublished novels, photographs and a bundle of his diaries – the ones detailing the last eight months of his life, and boyhood diaries from 1948, '49 and '50. (One diary detailing theft and illegal sexual practices had gone missing during their 1962 trial for defacing library books.) At her solicitor's advice she had removed a few passages from the copy she had made of the final diary before showing it to Lahr. (For example, a reference to a rumour that Peter Willes had been responsible for a lover's death was taken out.) Lahr asked after the missing pages of the final diary and was told by Peggy's solicitor that the police had been approached but without any luck.

In making all this material available to Lahr, Peggy was acting on trust and took no precautions concerning their safe-keeping or return. Her prime concern was for plays and their production, not the value to the scholar of the first draft, the niceties of original documentation or the practicalities of archival conservation.

When Lahr began working on his biography in 1970, Orton's reputation as a writer was completely overshadowed by his death. The film of *Loot* came out in 1970 and did not enhance his standing. Peggy found it a 'very ugly psychedelic version': Richard Attenborough as Truscott was a 'disaster', and the film 'just isn't funny'. The screenwriters Ray Galton and Alan Simpson, best known for *Hancock's Half Hour*, had altered Orton's play for the worse. Peggy had no control over that, but she did prevent the 'novelisation' of the screenplay from appearing.

Peggy had also come across Orton's own novel, *Head to Toe*, among his effects and had sold it to Anthony Blond. He published it in 1971, with line drawings by Patrick Procktor, but it proved to be no more than a footnote to the Orton myth.

Oscar Lewenstein had been wanting to mount a season of Orton's full-length plays at the Royal Court since 1970, and he succeeded in 1975 in his last days as artistic director. Apart from making amends for the *What the Butler Saw* fiasco, the season established Orton's credentials as a playwright. *Loot*, directed by Albert Finney, was the weakest production of the three. *Entertaining Mr Sloane* was well cast with Beryl Reid and Malcolm Mac-Dowell and played to 91% of the box office. Roger Croucher's production transferred to the West End, as did the strongest of the three, Lindsay Anderson's rehabilitation of the original *What the Butler Saw*, which paved the way for the play's current status as a cherished part of the national culture.

In 1976, when Lahr was nearing completion of the biography, Methuen published a volume of Orton's *Complete Plays*, with an enthusiastic introduction by Lahr, which quoted at length from the diaries. This led to a serious spat between him and Peggy. An agreement had been reached back in 1970 for Lahr to quote from the diaries in his biography, but it did not cover use elsewhere, such as in the introduction to the plays. Peggy was further angered when she discovered that Lahr had received £400 for his introduction but the Orton estate had received nothing. She approached Methuen and the estate was paid the same sum. A similar situation arose with the American publishers of the plays, to whom Peggy said that she would allow publication only if the estate were paid whatever Lahr was paid. This gave rise, she said, to an accusation from Lahr that she was trying to stop him earning any money from the introduction.

The relationship between Peggy and Lahr was to fluctuate over the next decade, during which Peggy became more dismayed the more that Lahr's literary efforts led to the near canonization of Orton. The scuffle over the introduction grew into a major row over the Orton biography, then called *A Revenger's Tragedy*. The 1970 agreement had never been formalised and no contract had been signed. There was a tussle over the percentage to be paid to the estate but the main point of contention was the extent to which Lahr was able to quote from the diaries. Peggy was very distressed at the tetchy and lengthy legal negotiations.

Peggy by now believed that Lahr was set on exploiting Orton through his use of the diaries. She considered him 'very talented but ruthless' and told Douglas Orton she found him 'so devious and positively secretive and unreliable'. Lahr had taken seven years to write the book; in that time he had written two novels and, as Peggy put it, travelled round the world, often being out of touch for long periods. She believed that this was a deliberate tactic on his part to keep control of all the material and to mini-mise any contribution from others. But she still helped him while being angry at him. Matters were made worse when Lewenstein complained of inaccuracies in the introduction to the plays which he wanted corrected for the biography but was told it was too late.

Peggy even thought of trying to stop the biography coming out. She sought David Hare's advice, by sending him proofs of the book. He con-firmed her fears. 'The final effect,' said Hare, 'is very cruel.' On Orton's life and plays, Hare commented that they 'just don't bear the scrutiny Lahr brings to them; the more he overpraises them the more they shrink.' Peggy, however, felt Douglas Orton was as much on Lahr's side as on hers and decided against either trying to prevent publication or actively interfering any further. Now called *Prick Up Your Ears*, the title that Peggy had sug-gested to Orton for *Funeral Games*, Lahr's biography was eventually pub-lished in 1978 to great acclaim.

Exasperated and resigned, she wrote to Lahr. 'We trusted you, and therefore in 1970 I gave you all my papers, quotations, Joe's diaries, photos, and asked Douglas, as Administrator of the Estate, to do all in his power to help you write a book on Joe. You took everything away, and nobody was allowed access or information from that day to this.

'When the proofs were ready, you sent them to Douglas, telling him not to show them to me. He sent them to me at once, with your message. I threw them on a shelf unread, and posted them back to him when he asked for them. You sent me via your Publisher a copy of the printed work. I put it aside unopened. Did you think I would *read* it?

'You have used me as far as I was useful, and then you deliberately told people not to get in touch with me . . . You never knew Joe. He was honourable and loyal. He would have been disappointed in your behaviour. I do not regret giving you access to all the material, because you are a talented writer. I feel only disillusion.'

At the root of their rift lay the diaries. Lahr pointed out with justification that Peggy had never seen much of value in them. She had discussed them with him in terms of pornography, on which account they were of only minor interest. He, on the other hand, had found value in them as a critic and had demonstrated their value in the biography, which drew on them extensively to comment on the plays. In so doing, Lahr felt that he had given Orton his due weight as a playwright and had increased international awareness of, and demand for, Orton's work.

Peggy felt that she had let Orton and Halliwell down, as well as the estate and those who had helped Orton who were mentioned detrimentally in the diaries, by not ensuring stricter control over Lahr's use of them. She felt Lahr was both credulous and ambitious, had diminished the role of Halliwell and created a voyeuristic image of Orton that left a nasty taste in the mouth.

Lahr himself believes that his crime was two-fold – to take Peggy on in a battle and best her, and to shatter Peggy's sense of omnipotence. Until then she had been the keeper of the Orton flame, which, after the shock of his death, was fading; it was Lahr who revived it (a scenario which ignores the catalytic role played by the Royal Court season of three plays in 1975, before the publication of the *Complete Plays*, the biography or the *Diaries*).

Peggy was upset that Lahr acted as if he had invented Orton, and she rejected his interpretation of their differences. She wrote to her solicitor that Lahr 'imagines there is some ulterior motive for my concern about the diary, i.e. perhaps he thinks I am jealous of him or I want power over Joe – in fact, all the things inside himself he is transferring to me. If I were jealous of writers, it would certainly not be of someone like Lahr, since we have so many creative writers here of whom I could be jealous, were I such a person. Nor do I have any particular feeling for Joe – I liked him as a person and I liked his plays a great deal. I did not think he was a genius.'

She did not like the publicity and self-advertisement surrounding what she came to see as Lahr's Orton industry and was angered when Lahr's then wife, Anthea, wanted to produce Orton postcards. 'Lahr is becoming a kind of octopus where Orton is concerned,' she said. With much regret, she had come to the conclusion that, just as Halliwell had linked his name irrevocably to Orton's through death, Lahr was doing the same.

Despite such feelings, Peggy supported Lahr as the best person both to write the introduction to the published script of the Orton screenplay *Up Against It* in 1979 and to edit *The Orton Diaries*, which were finally published seven years later. Methuen's drama editor, Nick Hern, had renewed the company's interest in publishing the diaries in the late 70s but Peggy had refused until the mid-80s, when a film based on the biography was already under way. Peggy even became the protagonist in the process, urging Methuen not to delay. She put aside her feud with Lahr and fulsomely praised his editing of the biography in order to speed Methuen on. Her championing of him, however, did not prevent another dispute with Lahr breaking out.

Lahr scripted a short play based on the diaries called *Diary of a Somebody* – the title Orton had given to his final diary. The play was first seen at the National Theatre's small Cottesloe auditorium in 1986 as a Platform Production. Peggy appeared as a character in the original production and asked that her name be removed when the expanded text was produced at the King's Head Theatre, Islington, the following year. A character called Nichola Webb spoke her lines instead. Peggy then demanded that the whole character be dropped for future performances; she did not like the tone of the piece, which, she thought, made Orton out to be selfish and callous, but was particularly upset at the way an incident concerning her and a fake fur coat had been portrayed.

The moment in the play is taken from an entry in the diaries which related to a meeting Orton had with Charles Marowitz, Michael White and Oscar Lewenstein to discuss possible casting for the New York production of *Loot*. The meeting over, they stood on a street corner before departing. Lewenstein said to Orton: 'You look very pretty in that fur coat you're wearing.' Orton replied, 'Peggy bought it me. It cost thirteen pounds nineteen.' 'Very cheap,' Michael White said. 'Yes,' continued Orton. 'I've discovered that I look better in cheap clothes.' Lewenstein wondered what the significance of that was, to which Orton answered, 'I'm from the gutter. And don't you ever forget it because I won't.'

Peggy remembered the occasion. She had offered him anything he wanted, and it was Orton who had chosen the ridiculously cheap fur coat as a joke. He had, in his way, been mocking Peggy the bourgeois. Peggy thought the play smeared her by implying that she had bought Orton a cheap coat, and, therefore, considered him to be cheap too.

Lahr insists that it was Peggy who suggested the idea of the play to him in the first place and who subsequently suggested he extend it into a fuller version. Peggy, however, hated the whole thing and thought the play

185

exploited and harmed Orton and Halliwell. 'Joe *wasn't* as brutal; he was driven to, what seems in the play, heartlessness because of Ken's nagging, and the nagging was to try and save Joe from scandal,' she wrote. 'They *loved* each other. There is no *love* in the play. I mean the kindliness of affection, the camaraderie of all their years together, and the fun they had.

'I now realise why the British in earlier time flocked to Tyburn to see the hangings . . . I think it was one of the saddest evenings I have ever spent.' She told Lahr that perhaps he wanted it to be depressing. However 'all the yuppies and everybody else simply loved it, and I am sure you will make money. We have asked that our commission on the Estate's share goes to charity. I imagine AIDS would be most appropriate.'

As if drawing a line under their 17 years relationship with each other and Orton, Peggy wrote to Lahr when the *Diaries* were published: 'We still remain beholden to you for all the critical help, and even the dubious publicity you have given to Joe. I do hope now that this is the end of all the ways of exploiting this poor dead boy.' Lahr's reply thanked her for giving him the opportunity to write Orton's life and edit the *Diaries*. 'The inevitable hubbub about the "Orton Industry" will die down soon enough,' he wrote. 'It doesn't mean anything, except that we've done our jobs well. More people know about Orton and read and perform his plays now than we ever could have imagined back when this all started in 1970. That was always the point of the exercise.'

For Peggy, it had not been. The final irony was that Lahr's labours in the Orton industry had the effect of making Peggy herself better known to a wider audience beyond the theatrical profession when she was played by Vanessa Redgrave in the film of Lahr's biography, *Prick Up Your Ears*. Written by Alan Bennett and directed by Stephen Frears, it came out in 1987.

Lahr had begun thinking about a film as soon as the biography had been published and by 1980 a script was ready but the deal with the film company fell through when it became clear that they wanted to make an English *Cage aux Folles*. Bennett says the script was very unwieldy at this time, and revolved around Lahr writing the biography. It included Bennett writing a screenplay of the biography and much of Orton and Halliwell's life told in flashback. A couple of years later, a new company became interested and, in 1984, Alan Bennett wrote a new script with Peggy as the narrator.

Three days were spent filming at Goodwin's Court where Peggy talked to the cast about her memories of Orton and Halliwell. Bennett recalls her flirting with Gary Oldman, who was playing Orton, just as she must have done with the real Joe a quarter of a century earlier. Peggy said Oldman was excellent as Orton but felt that Halliwell as played by Fred Molina 'was not like that' but it is 'much the harder part to pull off, dear.'

She claimed to be indifferent to Vanessa Redgrave's portrayal of her but did rather enjoy the accompanying celebrity. She playfully recalled the various casting suggestions that had preceded the approach to Redgrave – Irene Worth, Catherine Deneuve, Jill Bennett, and Jeanne Moreau (suggested by Lahr, to whom Peggy replied, 'the part would have to be a bit more interesting for her to play it'). Peggy herself fancied 'a young Edith Evans', but, of the real possibilities, she plumped for Maggie Smith, who, unfortunately, did not like the script. Vanessa Redgrave visited Peggy before the filming began. Peggy was happy to talk to her and admired her for coming. Playing real people can be forbidding; she said the actress who had portrayed her in the Lahr play, *Diary of a Somebody*, had declined to meet her. Redgrave was reported as being surprised at how beautiful and delicate Peggy was. On seeing the film, Peggy felt she should have been played as a little more eccentric. She was not an English rose – she was more fun, more earthy, less intellectual, but she thought that Redgrave had 'got the legs right'.

Redgrave's name came up in conversation some time later when Simon Callow was directing her in a film. Peggy paused and said to him with a mischievous twinkle, 'I played her once, didn't I?'

Peggy, as might have been suspected, had certain objections to the script, namely that she did not steal the diaries and that Orton's body had been removed by the time she arrived at the flat. She proposed the credit should be 'drawn from' instead of 'based on' the biography. The final version was 'adapted from'. Her judgement on the film was 'sweet' but 'inaccurate'. Employing a favourite technique of exaggeration, she claimed there was not a true word spoken in the film, which applied to her own character as well, of course, but this flowed from 'ignorance not wickedness'.

Orton came to symbolise the decade in which Peggy reached her apogee as an agent, and his life and death confirmed her in her philosophical opinions; he was a young lad from the lower classes finding fame and dying for it in the most savage of ways, but his talent survived in his work.

Violence, sex and ritual fascinated Peggy, and all three elements were combined in Orton's work as well as in his death. After the murder, she wrote to the poet James Kirkup, whom she had met briefly at an Orton first night. Kirkup had dedicated a book of poems to Two Joes – Ackerley and Orton. Peggy had known J.R. Ackerley slightly in relation to his play *The Prisoners of War*. She corresponded with Kirkup about Japanese culture, in which those same three elements of violence, sex and ritual are also constantly mixed, and in particular about the work of Yukio Mishima, who killed himself in ceremonial hara kiri in 1970.

Peggy's attitude to death hardened after the Orton experience. In a response that was repeated when David Mercer died, she became very cold, as if cut off or pushed away by death. It brought a callousness to the surface, which was the obverse side of her tremendous loyalty and commitment. Throughout her life she had set her face against death, and yet she embraced it for Orton and Mercer.

She had been thinking a great deal about death during the sixties – the era of ebullient vivacity. She wrote early in the decade: 'I find I no longer see things through the close-up side of a telescope but through the longer ones, which is really rather disconcerting and because of this most people don't know what I'm talking about. No doubt it's nature's way of preparing one for the grave.'

She had a fear of death as a victory over her own mortality and a spiting of her own will. Decay was not subject to the power of the mind or of the emotions. Death reminded her that the flesh was frail. She had a concern for a healthy body and a nutritious diet, and she disliked doctors and conventional medicine. She once sent a postcard to the wife of a client showing the human anatomy on which she had ringed all the parts of the body that had troubled her.

Orton's death reminded her once again of her stoical solitude. She saw life as essentially paradoxical; one constantly struggles for fulfilment, but fulfilment is an illusion except in death. Death solves the conundrum of life, but it represents the complete denial of life, existence rubbed out.

Yet Orton showed that it is death, rather than life, that confers hero status. She understood the imperative to live life as if every minute were the last, as well as its corollary, that to die *in extremis* was preferable to living ingloriously. Orton was the first of her surrogate sons to die, and, in spite of herself, she felt it was the perfect end for him, and that horrified her. She believed that there were no unwritten masterpieces and that a writer wrote what he or she was destined to write. In that sense, as with Mercer, Peggy said Orton's death was best thing that happened to him; she did not take the view that a promising talent had been cut short but that he had written himself out. That distressed her and left her feeling even more alone.

Chapter Six

Queen Bee

'Most of one's work is trying to get bloody people to do theirs'

ALAN PLATER tells an anecdote that sums up Peggy in her prime. A tough, rival agent meets Peggy in the street and asks sarcastically, 'How are the world's greatest writers?' Peggy's lightning quick reply: 'They're well, darling. How are all the others?'

It had taken Peggy just under a decade to reach the position of pre-eminence in a world she described as 'utterly ruthless, competitive and needs enormous drive and decision and strategy. Thousands of plays are being pushed on a handful of managers, and all of them never have less than four or so on option and there are always dozens of people fighting for a theatre. The rewards in reputation and money are big enough to make this formidable.'

Her drive towards independence had involved a hard struggle, in which she had denied herself and the agency by restricting spending – on business lunches, taxis, equipment, wages. She had not earned much, and had supplemented her pay with a little remuneration from her Peters and Ramsay work. In her interview in *Encore* magazine in 1963, the year she eventually bought out her shareholders, she summed up what it had been like.

> But it's hell to start up as an agent. I began with no authors, knew nothing about the job, and on borrowed money. When I first set up shop, cars looked like prams and gramophone records played at 78. When I came up for air, the cars looked like mouth organs and there was something called hi-fi (and I couldn't afford either). I didn't exactly starve, thanks to petty cash. I still find that late at night I have to calm myself by reading Schopenhauer. I have only to look at his little worried face to feel happy.

Peggy

Peggy had begun to earn both kinds of reward as the 1950s gave way to the 1960s, which meant that she was not only ready but almost able to make her company truly her own. She had opened a separate deposit account in 1960 in order to accumulate funds from which she could repay the original investors. The firm, however, had been set up in such a way that straightforward repayment of the shareholders' investment was precluded.

Peggy began to discuss with her solicitor and accountant how she could achieve her goal of independence as well as limiting further financial interest in the agency by other parties. There were inevitably difficulties in calculating how to remunerate the investors, yet, at the AGM of Margaret Ramsay Ltd. held on 27 March 1963, it was agreed that Peggy should form a new company, of which she would be the sole owner and director. The new firm would buy all the shares of the existing company and thereby own and control it.

As well as being paid the cover price of their shares (i.e. the face value of £1 per share), the shareholders in the original firm would also be paid a 10% dividend in respect of the 1962 accounts, which showed a reasonable profit (of £2,514). Peggy was paid an additional £1,000, a sum which she needed to help her buy outright a house in Brighton.

Some anger was expressed by the Christies at the AGM at what was seen as Peggy's lack of gratitude. A discussion ensued about further payment. The board was divided, with William Roderick and Edward Sutro arguing against the Christies on the grounds that, apart from the original investment, the shareholders and directors had been idle while Peggy had worked tremendously hard to turn the venture into the success it had become. Differences were settled by a deal that involved the firm paying a one-off fee to its directors. This fee brought the return on their investment to an overall figure of 5% per annum during the period of the investment. The fee ranged from £87.10 to £100 depending on the original investment.

Edward Sutro and William Roderick waived this fee. In addition, Sutro, who was very rich and, as Peggy put it, suffered from supertax, also waived his 10% dividend and gave Peggy his shares as a present.

At the time when the deal was completed, Peggy had established herself not so much at the top of her profession but in a league of her own, fully formed at last and in full flight. Yet, despite her joy at becoming independent, Peggy remained darkly realistic. This is how the premier agent recorded her feelings when profit had at last allowed her to gain her freedom in the maverick world in which she operated: 'No amount of money I've made (and we've made a lot) can recompense me for the miseries and pressures we've suffered . . . Everything has to be paid for, and the price is always too high . . . Had I known the horrors of the job, nothing would have induced me to become an authors' agent.'

Just as she was gaining her autonomy, Peggy was privately wanting to soft-pedal on the agency and put her energies into becoming a manager. In April 1963, she bought for £1 from her solicitor a new company for this purpose called Amethyst Productions Ltd. A year later, a new Memorandum and Articles of Association was drawn up for Margaret Ramsay Ltd., making the agency a wholly-owned subsidiary of Amethyst for tax reasons – the losses of the production company could be set off against the profits of the agency. Peggy effectively controlled all 4,000 shares in Margaret Ramsay Ltd., 850 shares in her own name and 3,150 shares in the name of Amethyst Productions.

She looked upon the prospect of becoming a manager as fun. She had abandoned the idea of branching out in this direction in 1957 because there were too few good plays being written. That situation had changed now, hence Amethyst. She even speculated with Robert Bolt and Noël Willman about establishing another production company, called MANFAS (an acronym taken from *A Man for All Seasons*, which, she said, had been lucky for them all). It would co-present plays with Amethyst. As it turned out, Peggy was absorbed in her agency work, the MANFAS project fell apart because of personal clashes, and Amethyst remained a paper company.

Peggy, however, sustained an unrealised interest in producing, and in the light of this, her solicitor advised her to reverse the relationship between Amethyst and Margaret Ramsay Ltd., so that, were Peggy to become a producer, it would now be the wholly-owned subsidiary that would be taking any production risks. Peggy still toyed with the notion of producing as late as 1969 and would have taken the plunge with Bolt's *Vivat! Vivat Regina!* that year if it had involved a smaller cast and lower production costs. Peggy, in the end, never did move into management. In the early 1970s, Amethyst was incorporated into Margaret Ramsay Ltd. and finally dissolved in 1985.

It is not surprising that Peggy did not find time for anything other than being an agent. In 1963, she had more than 100 clients on her books, and she was inundated not only by the efforts of would-be scribes hoping to swell her famous ranks but by the approaches of larger agencies – for example, Jimmy Wax's ACTAC, Jonathan Clowes Ltd., Curtis Brown Ltd., London Management, and from America, the William Morris Agency – constantly wooing her to amalgamate with them.

Ever since she had established Peters and Ramsay in 1958, the size and growth of her workload had been a major issue for her. Her successes built up the pressure on her to expand, both internally and externally, and this drove her to despair because she could not do any of the obvious things that would have made life easier, namely merge, delegate, reduce the number of clients or stop taking on any more.

She was often tempted to amalgamate, especially when she was bored or exhausted. She thought that she could become a more efficient agent by making the firm bigger and off-loading all the administrative work in order to leave her free, either to look after the writers or to move more into management. There was a flurry of near mergers in the mid-1960s once the agency was hers to dispose of. In February 1964, the year her tenancy on Goodwin's Court was due for renewal, she came very close to joining forces with another agency, Gregson and Wigan, among whose clients was the playwright Giles Cooper. The amalgamation would have involved an expansion for her into new offices, with only half the staff remaining at Goodwin's Court. 'If the room you allot me has a window,' she asked Gareth Wigan, 'may I have a small cat?'

A celebratory party was being planned when Wigan and Richard Gregson sounded out Peggy to see if she would be interested in a take-over by the Grade family. She had an instinctive distaste for huge firms or near-monopoly organisations like those run by the Grades, three powerful brothers – Lew, Leslie and Bernard Delfont – who between them controlled theatres, clubs, cinemas, film companies, and the Associated Television company, as well as entertainment and actors agencies with top billing stars on their books. 'These big machines have to have fuel, I suppose,' she observed, but she found their 'constant drumming up for business deplorable'. Peggy called the family the 'monster Grades', and was both fascinated and repelled by them and their Jewish immigrant showbiz background, with some of which she identified.

She pulled out of the deal, but Gregson and Wigan went ahead and joined the Grades. In the September of 1964, the Grades approached her themselves. They wanted to take over both Margaret Ramsay Ltd. and London Management, an agency which handled actors as well as the British representation of those American playwrights, among them Tennessee Williams, who were with the Ashley Famous agency in New York. Peggy rejected the proposal of working with London Management but gave some consideration to a counter-proposal from the Grades that she develop a play department for them whilst being free to run her own agency, along with Peters and Ramsay. The Grades were willing to leave Peggy alone artistically as long as they retained ultimate control. She was flattered by the offer but was anxious that the Grades wanted to split the work of the authors up into separate departments, for theatre, film, TV and radio, whereas she had always dealt with the plays of her authors as a whole.

When Leslie Grade tried to cajole her by pointing out how much money she would make, Peggy, in her sharpest Lady Bracknell tone, replied disdainfully: 'I believe this is called a "killing"!' She was even more angry when he then told Peggy that everyone had their price. 'This is a statement that I challenge. If I had, I ought not to be an agent,' she said. 'If I were selling *goods*, perhaps I wouldn't mind having my market picked for me, but with talent – thank you, no.'

She finally called the deal off; if the writers were to be as free as possible, this would be best achieved by her retaining sole ownership of her own agency.

'I just don't have really enough ambition to see that it [amalgamation] might well be in my interest,' she confided to Audrey Wood, the *grande dame* of the Ashley Famous agency. 'My only concern is that it might, in some obscure way, NOT be in the interests of my clients. They seem happy as they are, and as none of them have left me to go to the Grade Organisation, I take it that we have as much to offer them as the Grades have. I must be doing something right.'

Amalgamation would have meant defeat, as if everything that she had stood for had meant nothing. She would have done what everyone else does, which was to join up to a bigger and economically more powerful firm, and this, she believed, was both a form of surrender and greed. She told a friend that before ditching the deal she had consulted the *I Ching*. It had told her what she had known in her bones all the time – say 'no'.

Instead, Peggy renewed her tenancy at 14a Goodwin's Court for a further seven years. The only physical growth the agency enjoyed, with the exception of a brief expansion in the 1960s into a ground floor office next door at No 12a to accommodate an accountant, came in 1968 when Peggy took on a second floor in No. 14a. She had considered moving, to Soho Square or Oxford Street, and also had thought of renting other offices in Goodwin's Court (Nos 1, 5, 6 and 9 were possibilities at one time or another) but, in the end, she always stayed in the building where she had started the agency and where it still was when she died.

Peggy never wanted to open offices abroad. When she succeeded in selling a play overseas, she would approach an agent in that particular country to represent her client on her behalf. But she always worked on a play by play basis, thereby maintaining flexibility and a degree of control. She would share any resulting commission 50/50 with the overseas agent. Even though she sacrificed some earnings by using this system, since it was she who had sold the play in the first place, she felt that her authors should have someone 'on the spot' to look after their interests.

While Peggy did not see her agency as a global institution, she had no intention of being a bit player, either. She looked upon the agency business as a dynamic cottage industry; small in size did not mean small in status. Early on in Peggy's career, another agent, Margery Vosper, had said to her, concerning a successful West End play, 'That's not for the likes of us, dear.' This attitude had angered and upset Peggy. How could she serve her clients if she was not as important a figure as the other agents? The problem was to earn this position without compromising her beliefs.

In her view, agents were too often satisfied with simply carrying out the mechanics of the job. 'If I were only to be a booking agent, it would be more fun to run a bookshop or a travel agency,' she said. 'Agents are not merely licensors for authors. We are supposed to be protecting their artistic interests. If it were merely a case of giving a licence to anybody for anything, we could all retire to the country and let some computer do it.'

For a writer, an agent was successful if that writer was successful; conversely, if the writer was unsuccessful, an agent was perceived as being bad. For her, there was no such thing as a successful agent, only a success-ful writer. 'I'm not successful,' she said. 'I'm still here. I've survived. You survive when the authors are successful. I'm supposed to be "lucky" for authors, but, of course, my "luck" is merely their own talent, which *I've* been lucky enough to be allowed to handle.'

There was no reason for the writer to take any notice of, or even to know about, the amount of work an agent carried out unseen in the background. 'A writer will think I do nothing for him when I've just had the 100th script of his returned,' she once said. 'Agents aren't just there to do the things authors can't do, or can't be bothered to do, but to do things they wouldn't or shouldn't do, like risking all for the best deal. Sometimes I think the job I do is worth more than the 10% I demand.'

It was her writers who kept her going. Exaltation, however, was less in evidence than tedium. 'What I need is to be told *how not to get bored*,' she said. 'Alas, it's not the administrative drudgery which tires me,' she once wrote – although she frequently did complain of the office treadmill – 'it's the endless plays, the endless try-outs . . . and the exhausting first nights and the lunches which are a depletion of the spirit . . . I suppose I ought to rejoice at my luck, instead of finding the whole thing so meaningless and boring.'

This 'depletion of the spirit', as well as overwork, led her to make peri-odic attempts to purge her client list, which had expanded enormously around a core of treasured playwrights to encompass a sizeable assortment of 'fellow travellers'. This ranged from the distinguished professor of English I.A. Richards and the novelist Francis King, to the future film censor James Ferman and even John Lennon (seeking help to sort out the dramatic rights to *In His Own Write*). Peggy often felt she had too many authors and that, through their collective success, her clients ended up competing with each other. She would determine to uncouple certain established writers, such as Benn Levy, in whom she had lost interest. She would tell the staff that she was going to cut back and not take on any new clients. There was always a proviso, however; she would except from this prohibition those writers of such outstanding worth that it would make a nonsense of her being an agent if she were to refuse the opportunity to represent them. A few clients might fall away, often because of her indifference rather than as a result of an actual shove, but most hung on, usually by keeping a low profile or by direct defiance, insisting they were staying put.

Peggy would inevitably surrender to the lure of new and especially young talent, and the cycle would continue; pressure on her time would be renewed, which meant that quite a number of clients felt hurt and neglected because she could only spread her energy so far.

The strain did tell on Peggy, and she frequently considered ways of easing the load. Her solicitor suggested she appoint a trustworthy office manager, but she did not like this idea. 'I need a better and fresher *me*,' she replied. At various times she wondered about the wisdom of finding a partner or successor. She gave the distinct impression to several staff at different moments in the agency's history that she was in some way grooming them for the role, though it was never articulated clearly or explicitly, as if she could not bring herself to make such a commitment and always required the safety net of ambiguity. She would lose interest and the hint of a promise would fade or vanish. Peggy seemed to become increasingly paranoid about the intentions of some of those whom she had encouraged, especially in the late 1960s and after. She was for them, understandably, a role model – how better to learn the business of being an agent than at the feet of the most famous exponent?

In the 1970s, Peggy did, in fact, off-load some of her burden onto the broad shoulders of an assistant called Tom Erhardt. He joined the agency in July 1971, having worked in his native America for the New Dramatists' Committee in New York and for the agent Lucy Kroll. He had first come to Britain briefly in 1966 as assistant to the producer Peter Bridge and through him had met Peggy's client Alan Ayckbourn. Back in America, he had looked after Ayckbourn and had been assistant to the director Gene Saks on

Ayckbourn's *How the Other Half Loves*, which was co-produced in New York, as it had been in London, by Peter Bridge and Eddie Kulukundis. Erhardt came to London after the show opened and decided he wanted to stay. A grateful Kulukundis put him in touch with Peggy, who asked Ayckbourn about Erhardt before hiring him. She made Erhardt a director of the agency three years later. She did not offer him any explanation of why she had given him a directorship, and he did not realise until later that she had never done this before with any of her staff. The only difference was that he could now sign cheques on the clients' account in Peggy's absence.

Erhardt dealt with foreign rights and worked with Peggy as London representative of her foreign writers, such as Günther Grass, Tancred Dorst, Shusako Endo, Boris Vian, Joshua Sobol, Manuel Puig and Václav Havel, the future president of the Czech republic who had come via her associate, Klaus Juncker of Rowohlt, which represented most of Peggy's clients in Germany. Erhardt handled the rights for Peggy's American dramatists, too, like Israel Horovitz, Larry Kramer and Wallace Shawn, as well as for the Tennessee Williams estate. Erhardt was also the agency's initial contact for David Wood, whom he first met when he was working for Peter Bridge and who became the leading British writer of children's plays. Following Erhardt's introduction, Peggy wrote Wood: 'The idea of reading a play with characters like the Plum Pudding Flea and the Runcible Spoon is irresistible.'

*

'The most disgusting word in the English language is agent'

Until the early 1960s, Peggy's life was completely absorbed in running the agency seven days a week; from then onwards, she worked in London from Monday until Friday, her commitment undimmed, and spent the weekends in Brighton. When in London, she lived in a flat, first in Mornington Crescent near Euston, then Victoria, Sloane Square, and finally Earl's Court. She worked long hours in the office, staying late and coming in early, often by 6am, to read, write letters or make telephone calls. She was always fresh at the dawning of the day, just like several of the moguls whose work rate and productivity she admired, such as Winston Churchill, Peter Hall, Sam Spiegel, or Margaret Thatcher. With advancing years she began to ease up on the early mornings and late nights but she continued to put in a full day at the office right until the last months of her life.

Come Friday, she left the office at 4pm to catch the train to Brighton. Her parents had died there and with the money she inherited, plus £1,000 voted to her by the directors of the agency, she bought an 1830s terraced house in the town's bohemian North Laine area near the railway station, which she filled with a cornucopia of *bric-a-brac* and *objets d'art*. In the next road she also bought a primitive railway cottage, which she called the Hut and which she let her clients use – David Hare wrote most of *Licking Hitler* and *Plenty* there as well as *A Map of the World*. It was ideal for writers because it had no telephone but was close to London.

Peggy knew Brighton from her rep days but she avoided the theatrical set who lived there. (One of its leading lights, Laurence Olivier, she used to liken to a bank manager.) The only exception was Oscar Lewenstein, who lived in Hove and whom she did see socially.

She enjoyed her cats, her garden and her non-theatrical reading. She also enjoyed driving her Morris 1000 fast and erratically along the seafront. She passed her driving test, aged 56, just after she bought the house in Brighton. She never lost the disconcerting habit of looking at her passenger rather than the road ahead and once, as a result, knocked over a policeman. She was a regular visitor to the town's many antique shops and art galleries, and had her hair done every weekend in Brighton. She had rows of dresses, expensive shoes and hat boxes, but she lived comfortably, not extrava- gantly. She made occasional visits to a health farm in Sussex, drank little and hardly smoked – and when she did it was usually in company and she did not finish her cigarette. She did have a weakness for Pernod but she said it was too expensive in Britain. When she visited France, she would buy a bottle of pastis, take a nip and put the top back on in order to get through customs. She kept herself to herself, living in this weekend cocoon with Bill Roderick, who kept the domestic side of things running smoothly and so that, having taken an early train back to Victoria, she could spring back into work at Goodwin's Court on Monday morning.

Peggy deliberately kept her private and professional lives separate. Nevertheless, there was not a separation between her private self and her professional self. The agency was Peggy and she was the agency; the office was more important to her than home. Peggy truly came to life in the office, and the office in turn became renowned for the stream of theatrical lumi- naries who were to be found there visiting Peggy. Away from Goodwin's Court, Peggy might choose to behave deferentially or to play the scatty female. Not so in the office. There she was undisputed monarch. She was not averse to primping and preening on occasion when she felt it to be politic – she dressed up like royalty when Marcello Mastroianni called in to discuss doing an Alan Ayckbourn play in Italy – but mostly, overwhelmingly, she was just Queen Bee, instructing, ordering, arranging, re-arranging, swirling like a typhoon.

Peggy ran a tight ship at Goodwin's Court; even she observed that working there was like being in a forced labour camp. The hours were set firmly and were strictly adhered to; 10am until 6pm with an hour and a half for lunch, because she felt one hour was not enough. She would have a snack or go to Cranks, a health food restaurant a couple of streets away. For more formal lunches, she was spoilt for choice in that part of London. The fish restaurant Sheekeys was a favourite, but certain places, such as the Empress and the Elephant, she thought stuffy and designated them 'enemy' territory where she would not go 'with my own gang'. ('Visiting these joints tends to make me revolutionary.') Tea and biscuits were taken at 4pm, and Peggy would make the tea herself if she were free. She allowed three weeks holiday, though she herself often only took two because of the demands of work. She liked hot and simple environments, like the Greek Islands, in its pre-tourist boom days, and North Africa.

She was tough on staff who were late or absent, and she preferred them to be unattached so that their loyalty to her and the agency could be wholehearted. She felt betrayed when staff wanted to leave and dealt with this apostasy by cutting the guilty party out of her life.

Peggy kept staff numbers to a minimum; they all helped out to keep the office ticking over, answering the telephone or typing when required. She mainly recruited by word of mouth but did occasionally place advertisements. She wanted her staff to be interested in writers, and would let them read scripts if they asked, but only she decided whether or not the agency would take on a writer or a play and only she would be their representative. Her staff had their functions, e.g. handling foreign and amateur rights, keeping the accounts, logging the scripts that came and were sent out, or – the toughest assignment of all – being her personal assistant. Even when her client list was at its most onerous, she would not delegate her duties or share out clients to be dealt with by another member of the agency, which was the common practice in other firms. With the onset of Alzheimer's disease towards the end of her life, however, other members of staff had perforce to look after clients' affairs. The staff were discreet and allowed Peggy to go on believing that she was still determining everything.

Staff were always a worry to Peggy, who never really wanted to be responsible for anyone other than herself but did feel a duty towards them as their employer. She did not believe that there was a rigid 'them and us' division in the office because they worked in such close physical proximity and everything had to be shared in order for anything to get done. She was even paid weekly in cash as were the others. She had not bothered with employment contracts, job descriptions or pensions schemes until the late 1960s when staff made her realise that these things were important to them. This overwhelmed her. It made her feel like giving up and selling the firm. But with the help of her solicitor, Peggy set to and instead re-organised the terms and conditions of working at the agency, using a contract borrowed from Oscar Lewenstein, and even made provision for the staff in her will.

Her concern for her staff extended to their health – she insisted for a time on their drinking honey vinegar and taking Royal Jelly – but not to their wages, which, in common with the rest of the arts world, were very low. She was, however, generous, although unpredictable, with gifts – she unexpectedly bought one of her assistants an expensive coat from Harvey Nichols and one day came to the office with an umbrella for everyone purchased at Harrods.

Generally the staff were long suffering and knew what was at stake and what was expected. Unsung, they contributed an enormous amount to the work and success of the agency. They were not only a great memory bank for her, but also a barometer of the outside world, especially useful for Peggy as a way of keeping in touch with younger generations. This was a responsibility they took to heart in 1971 when, much to her delight, they gave Peggy cannabis as a birthday present.

The staff had to keep up with Peggy's whirlwind temperament as best they could, despite the difficulties posed by her individual way of doing things and by her emotional volatility. She acted the tyrant, snapping at gasping secretaries who had been given no clue as to what she wanted. She could frequently be heard issuing instructions even as she was still coming up the stairs from the street. In such circumstances, with Peggy at the centre of affairs, the staff, like others in her life, learned to operate on the periphery.

It was not uncommon for her to enter the office without warning, already dictating at speed, arms gyrating like a windmill. She would continue to dictate in an uninterrupted stream as she paced the room without giving anyone a moment to pick up a pencil and would then exit just as abruptly as she had arrived. Later, when she read the typed-up letter, it was quite likely that, however accurately the letter reflected her dictation, she would declare aghast, 'I would *never* have said that, dear. Do it again.' On one occasion she came to the end of a particularly infuriating script and, without pause, bellowed, 'Dictation. Dear So and So. Don't ever bother to put pen to paper again. Yours sincerely.'

Peggy

It could be hard for staff to follow Peggy's relationship with clients because in many cases it was highly personal, stretching far beyond the normal business side of an agency. Peggy conducted much of her relationships on the telephone as well as by postcard or letter, which would often be hand-written or self-typed. If she wanted to write or type a letter herself she would shut the door of her office, or she would come into work early or stay late. She used two fingers to type and such letters often bore the rubric 'This note is self-tippped'. One even carried the additional but superfluous warning, 'so anything could happen.' Spelling and punctuation went awry and spidery handwritten emendations or accretions would veer into the margins at all kinds of odd angles and directions. When carbon copies of such letters were made, Peggy filed them along with business letters, and staff had to maintain an unusually high level of discretion in handling the often intimate details revealed therein.

Staff had to monitor Peggy's behaviour in case it could inflict unintended cruelty on lesser mortals. They would tactfully alert Peggy to the possible harm she might have caused. She might telephone the wounded client and either act as if nothing had happened and 'normal service had been resumed', or apologise in such an exaggerated way that the client was made to feel even worse for being so pathetic as to have been upset.

Primarily the staff had to keep the business side of the agency well oiled. Peggy, who made up most of her business practice as she went along, was shrewd, scrupulous and practical but not always accurate, particularly when it came to detail.

Even when the firm began to deal in fortunes, she loyally remained with the same local bank branch where she had opened an account when she first began the agency; she stayed until it shredded a week's Broadway takings of *A Man for All Seasons* by mistake. She was keen on financial propriety, although she herself could forget to sign cheques. She ensured that monies were properly paid, and from the correct accounts; money in advance, for example, could only be taken from the deposit account because the current account only contained what was necessary for the firm to survive. Peggy often did her own filing and might inadvertently throw the system out of kilter; her physical confusion of clients might sometimes be mirrored in administrative error; a royalty cheque destined for an impoverished Alan Ayckbourn once ended up on Alan Plater's breakfast table, and *vice versa*. (Ayckbourn's eye was caught by the noughts, not by the name that followed Alan on the cheque. The phone rang. It was Plater, who was writing successfully for television and earning relatively well. He said he would send Ayckbourn's cheque on in the post. Plater put the phone down with the words, 'I'm very sorry.')

For all Peggy's dislike of business, she could drive a hard bargain. A film producer who wanted David Mercer to write a screenplay for him was taken out to lunch and then invited back to Goodwin's Court as if for coffee. He was locked in her office and told that he would not be released until he had signed a cheque, which duly was slipped under the door. She introduced Christopher Hampton to David Lean and advised Hampton to sign a contract for a flat six months regardless of what else happened and then insist on being paid on a weekly basis thereafter. She negotiated the deal and Hampton ended up working for a whole extra six months on a handsome weekly fee, just as Peggy had anticipated.

Peggy believed that her tough behaviour never lost her a deal, yet James Saunders tells the story of how a producer telephoned her to discuss the possibility of making a film of his play *Neighbours* and found her so difficult that he gave up. She was hard on her writers, too. She made Ayckbourn pay back a BBC commission when it became clear that he was not going to write the play. 'You'll be worth a lot more anyway later on,' she told him, rightly, as it turned out.

She negotiated emotionally rather than logically and sometimes won the day because the other party just could not cope with the onslaught. Michael Meyer recalls her responding to BBC-TV in fury over an offer for his translation of Strindberg's *The Ghost Sonata*. She railed at them, scandalised, comparing the offer unfavourably with what Meyer had received for Ibsen's *The Lady from the Sea*, which, she stated accusingly, was only half as long. Meyer should therefore be paid twice as much. In fact, she had got it completely wrong, but the BBC agreed to a rise in order to get rid of her.

Peggy would also subordinate the business interests of a deal to the artistic interests of the writer. She would rather something did not happen than it happen on terms that she found unfavourable. David Rudkin was fiercely disappointed when she turned down an apparently exciting RKO video deal for his stage adaptation of *Peer Gynt*, though he had to admit that she was right; the contract was terrible, what she described as a preemptive buy-out, allowing no artistic control for the writer after an initial payment had been made and no other exploitation of the text for a considerable period.

She was even known to refuse work for a client without consulting the client concerned if she thought it disadvantageous, as David Hare discovered after going to see the film *Julia*. He happened to mention his visit to Peggy, and she matter-of-factly told him that the director Fred

Zinnemann had approached her to enquire if Hare would consider writing the screenplay.

'I told him you should be writing for the theatre and not to waste our time,' Peggy said. Hare sheepishly replied that it would have been nice to have been asked.

'Why?' queried Peggy. 'You wouldn't have done it, would you?'

'Probably not,' said Hare.

'Then I was right, wasn't I?'

Her natural habitat when working through a contract was not her desk but the floor. Desks were never big enough for her and were of much greater use as a place to rest her legs. She would spread out contracts before her like a picnic cloth and get on her knees to push papers about as if piecing together a giant jigsaw. Sometimes she would just leave her sifting of the papers to continue with something else and then forget to return to the contract. Sometimes she would become exasperated and fling all the papers in the air, maybe hoping they would fall back to earth in the right order. The staff knew, therefore, that they had to double check all the paperwork, especially TV and film contracts, which interested Peggy least of all.

She spent little on office equipment, heating and furniture, and she kept the overheads extremely low. She even failed to insure the contents of the office. Nothing was hired; it was all bought and as a consequence nothing would be replaced until it was completely clapped out. This hub of Peggy's universe stayed as near the same as she could make it throughout her long career as an agent. Many a foreign visitor arrived at the famous address expecting swish décor overflowing with supernumeraries only to discover a handful of slaves sweating away at wobbly desks with ancient type-writers in a poorly heated clump of ramshackle Dickensian rooms up a rickety staircase off a narrow alleyway. In a curious way, this ramshackle arrangement rather impressed many of the powerful figures with whom Peggy had to deal, and gave her a canny psychological edge over them.

Her carefulness stemmed from the early days, when she had been very hard up. She always nursed a fear of running out of money, an anxiety that returned in a more extreme form towards the end of her life. She was extremely pleased, therefore, when the company making *Prick Up Your Ears*, the film about Joe Orton and Kenneth Halliwell, had the office repainted before filming there. Her thrift was reinforced by a dislike of 'new technology', which was always more expensive than her existing equipment. She especially did not trust the photocopier, as if it destroyed the soul of the object it was copying by making originality and uniqueness redundant. When she sent a script to a large theatre organisation, such as the RSC or the NT, she seemed both angry and surprised that more than one person was reading the play at the same time, thanks to the copying machine. She instinctively felt that a misdemeanour was afoot; she had only sent one script and no one had been given permission to make a copy. Even when her own staff photocopied a play it bothered her; she kept a close eye on who was to pay for each copy and was justifiably nervous about piracy and copyright – technology seemed to be capable of taking things out of her control, and when that happened she was always unhappy.

The telephone was the one piece of technology that she was at home with. Not the dialling, however, which secretaries frequently did because she could not remember numbers and could not be bothered to look them up. She demanded instant action: 'Get me Bolt', 'Get me Ayckbourn' came the shout, and when she picked up the phone she would launch straight into conversation with the confident assumption that Bolt or Ayckbourn would be on the other end.

If the office was the hub of her universe, then the telephone was the heart of the office. She loved both its immediacy and its distance. She could surprise someone with an unexpected call and she could terminate it at the moment of her own choosing. Frequently it was Peggy who initiated the calls. When people tried to ring her, the phone was often engaged; for much of the time there were only two lines into the office. She was so attached to her telephone that she constantly resisted the periodic requests from staff to update the system. Only in the late 1980s did the office have a tie line installed which allowed calls to be switched from one phone to another without, as before, the person for whom the call was intended having to get up and walk over to the apparatus on which the call had been received. Peggy disliked this innovation because it removed the spontaneity of the unplanned response, and on one occasion she smashed it to the ground as if it represented a threat to the future of civilisation itself.

Peggy on the phone was quite a sight; she was a mass of nervous energy. Animated even when seated, she would thrust her glasses up onto her forehead, shift her legs about and continue to gesture all the time, waving her free arm like a mad conductor.

The telephone became an extension of her personality, her means of plugging into her clients wherever they were. It was a crucial working tool, and she used it with clients and managements alike as a formidable weapon. She would pattern her day via her calls. She would begin early with a call to a favourite client. 'So you're not working then, dear,' Peggy would say to the playwright whom she has just woken at 6am. Her day would escalate on a roll from one call to the next and so on, with each setting the context for the one that followed.

She had a habit of not announcing herself, which could be strange and unnerving to the unwary recipient of the call. If you had not been party to whatever earlier conversation had triggered the call, which was usually the case, you had to catch up quickly and grasp the thread. She treated all calls as she did her life, as part of one continuous monologue into which other people came and went at her behest. She would sustain a fierce flow of free association in which the couth and the uncouth were mixed in equal measure and the penetrating insight jostled with much of dubious worth.

Peggy often forgot whom it was she had asked the secretary to get for her and would address the person on the other end of the telephone as someone else, just as she could mistake her clients in the flesh. Mortimer might be Mercer, Ayckbourn might be Plater, or Wood might be Nichols. (It sometimes took her two years to learn a client's name; she preferred to use the simpler, all-purpose 'that child' or 'that boy' instead. Some clients believed, however, that the confusions were deliberate.) Jack Rosenthal received an early morning call congratulating him on winning a writers' award for *Educating Rita*. When Rosenthal mildly suggested that Peggy probably wanted to speak to the play's author, Willy Russell, the phone went down without apology or farewell.

One day, when Peter Nichols was in the office, she was in the middle of a conversation with him about John Mortimer, whom she was calling a tart. 'I said to John – darling, you're just a *whore*. You're a harlot of literature. At least . . . ' and the telephone rang. She picked it up and continued without pause, but now speaking directly into the mouthpiece, 'if you're going to be a whore then at least before you open your legs make sure you're properly paid. Hello.' The bemused caller, appropriately enough, turned out to be Sam Spiegel.

Even when she remembered or bothered to shut the door to her office she conducted her calls with such projection and crispness it made the walls seem as thin as tissue paper. This was true whether she were speaking on the telephone or face to face, and gave rise to many anecdotes concerning her liberated candour.

Christopher Hampton was visiting Peggy when she took a call from the Arena Stage in Washington DC about a different client. 'Oh, don't do *that* play, dear,' she said. 'He never got it right. He never solved the ending. I'm here with Hampton. Why don't you talk to him and do his play instead?' This exchange led to the first American production of *Total Eclipse*. On another occasion, however, Hampton arrived at her office to hear her on the phone admonishing another writer, 'You don't want to end up like Hampton, darling. One success and he imagines the world owes him a living.' Hampton interrupted and made it clear he had heard what she was saying. She just waved at him and boomed rhetorically, 'Well, it's *true*, isn't it, dear?'

And Robert Bolt once overheard Peggy on the telephone answering an inquiry about the rights for a new play of his: 'Can't you think of anything more interesting than that, dear. You don't want that bourgeois crap.'

Peggy conducted most of her business on the telephone, more so than over lunch or through what became known as 'networking'. A telephone conversation, however, is as ephemeral as a theatrical performance and lives on only in the memory, if at all. It is a tribute to Peggy that a legion of witnesses offer vivid testimony to her unique telephone manner, and several account her one of the great verbal stylists of the age.

*

'I'll naturally pass on every bit of news as it comes in – call me Reuter!'

Client after client says that it was always worth visiting Goodwin's Court just for its own sake, because, however nerve-racking and unpredictable a meeting with Peggy might be, it was like taking a tonic, you fed off her adrenalin. She sent her clients away convinced that they were not mad in wanting to write plays, and that they must and should write. She made them feel not only that they were special but that they alone could save the theatre from the danger of imminent collapse.

It was important to Peggy that the front door at street level was always open so that her writers could call at any time. (This had to be changed after a fire in 1991, when the arrival of an entryphone marked a new, more safety-conscious era.) The open door was a reminder that the agency existed for the writers. This accessibility was in keeping with Peggy's informality, which was liberating for the clients, allowing them to jettison the protocol and enforced politeness that normally besets the agency business.

Past the front door, posters beckoned her visitors from the walls of the pinched stairway leading up and into the offices, which were festooned with further pictorial testimonials to her clients' achievements around the globe. In her own inner office, Peggy had surrounded herself with plants, scripts, books and yet more posters as well as a few of the many awards won by her clients.

She liked to see her clients in person from time to time because otherwise they became unreal for her, a genuine danger when playwrights had to disappear for long periods in order to write their plays. 'They are usually so much odder than characters in a play that if one doesn't meet them, for, say, six months,' she once wrote, 'I begin to imagine that either they or I are an invention.'

The writers might be delivering what in many cases would turn out to be a famous play that had yet to be read by anyone except the author. More commonly, they would be dropping in to recharge their batteries or to indulge in a bit of gossip. Visiting Goodwin's Court gave the clients a sense of identity, of retaining an individuality yet within a prestigious collective. This was especially important for the younger writers who were flattered by the association of belonging to Peggy's 'stable' of renowned names. Within the profession, in Britain and abroad, Peggy herself was more famous than many of her clients. Belonging to her agency was a passport to being noticed and taken seriously, and, most important, to having your play read by the managements. It was a high-class club carrying the most influential calling card in the business.

Paying court to her was both part of the privilege of club membership and part of the dues to be paid; staying away could be construed as a significant act – a meaningful silence or withdrawal of favour. Once at the office, the playwright had to negotiate a host of possible unseen eventualities. How would Peggy behave? Would she be angry or honey sweet? Would she remember who you were? Peggy had crushes and favourites. A lot could be read into which plays' posters were hanging up and where. Had one of yours been moved recently? Were you in favour or out? Would Peggy even see you?

Alan Ayckbourn, an out-of-town member, recalls a visit which began encouragingly enough with an enthusiastic greeting from Peggy. She then added disconcertingly, 'I'm so glad you've come, because John's here.'

'John who?' asked Ayckbourn.

'Why, John Arden, dear. I've got to make a phone call. I'll leave you two together. I'm sure you'll have *masses* to talk about.'

Peggy then shut the door, leaving the two somewhat reticent writers alone together. Not only had they never met each other before, they had never seen any of each other's work. Arden had only just joined Peggy after his previous agent had absconded with the firm's money and was at Goodwin's Court to try to sort out his resulting financial difficulties. Ayckbourn must have been the last person he wanted to talk to, and he did not. Ayckbourn, for his part, felt a little in awe of the author of *Serjeant*

Musgrave's Dance and did not think he could initiate a conversation with such a senior figure unless invited to do so, which he was not.

So, the two writers sat in silence for a quarter of an hour before Peggy thrust back in and exclaimed, 'So sorry to interrupt.'

James Saunders left his two children in the outer office while he had a meeting with Peggy in hers. The children heard screams and more screams coming from behind the closed door. They were shocked and terrified, fearful that father might not come out alive. When he re-appeared to be asked if he was all right, Saunders nonchalantly replied, 'Oh, I'm OK. That was just a normal chat with Peggy.'

Robert Holman was 24 when he made his first visit to Goodwin's Court. He and Stephen Poliakoff had both been asked to become resident writers at the National Theatre. Holman had been sent what he thought was a ridiculously long and involved contract, which his then agent was ready to accept. Still unhappy, Holman had phoned Poliakoff, who said *he* would check with *his* agent, namely Peggy. Peggy phoned Holman and asked to see his contract. She went to see Peter Hall, who was then running the National, and arranged for both writers to have a new and much simpler contract. When she and Holman spoke on the phone, he asked if she would read some of his plays. He sent two, and a few days later she asked him to come and see her.

When the day came, Holman was extremely nervous, both because of Peggy's reputation and because she had already arranged a new contract for him without officially representing him or even having met him. The only advice he received from Poliakoff was not to call her Margaret.

He was ushered in to her office. She had her feet on the desk and was flicking her knicker elastic. She talked about the National and said that she had known Peter Hall since he was in short trousers, which was why she had been able to sort out the contract. She told Holman all about Joe Orton and how he had died – this was before publication of the biography and diaries. She was fascinated to learn about Holman's upbringing on a farm in Yorkshire and about the details of his flat, which was fairly spartan – like Orton's. After half and hour there was still no mention of Holman's plays and he sat wondering if she would take him on.

Peggy invited him to have a drink with her at the nearby Salisbury Tavern, a well-known theatre pub with a large gay clientèle. Seemingly oblivious, she stood at the bar blithely continuing at the top of her voice to recount her stories about Orton's sexual adventures and his interest in the sizes of men's cocks.

Back in the office after lunch in the pub, there was still no reference to

Holman's plays. Eventually he plucked up the courage to ask if she were going to represent him.

'Of course I am, dear,' she said airily and promptly disappeared.

Holman was soon to discover that Peggy did not differentiate between the new and the established clients. If anything, she treated the former as more important than the latter. Still virtually unknown, Holman was at Goodwin's Court when Peggy's secretary announced the arrival of the much garlanded Peter Nichols. Peggy and Holman had not finished talking.

'Get rid of Nichols,' said Peggy to the secretary.

'I can't,' came the reply. 'He's bought you a Christmas present.'

'Oh fuck,' said Peggy, 'you'd better let him in I suppose.'

She quickly changed tone as Nichols appeared, took the present, cooed a 'thank you' and showed Nichols out with a half-apologetic, 'I'm in the middle of a meeting. Byee.' And she picked up the conversation with the embarrassed but strangely flattered Holman just where she had left off.

Peggy shrewdly stimulated competition between her clients, focusing especially on the young and relatively innocent men who were vulnerable to such manipulation. She exploited age and status skilfully to exercise her control in what she regarded as their best interests. She did not care whether her clients liked her – she boosted them and deflated them at the same time and used her frankness to keep them at arm's length. She was only interested in them writing better plays and the whole Peggy paraphernalia was dedicated to that end.

Few of the writers knew each other independently of her and many were shy and socially diffident. By talking explicitly about other clients' private lives and criticising one client to another, she was testing those on the receiving end of this candour. The writers often joined in the gossiping, know-ing all the while that they could be the target next time. Her indiscretions and damning judgements were applied equally to all – an egalitarian ab-rasiveness that proved comforting to her beleaguered and abused clients in the long term when the smart of the initial blows had worn off.

The shock came not just from her bluntness, and the expletives with which she peppered her conversation, but from the fact that they emanated from such a haughty, refined and influential figure. Writers could feel com-plimented when she was being vile about them; at least they were in the limelight and she was expending enormous energy on them. Being her client conferred status on you because your name was part of her infamous damning currency: have you heard what Peggy's saying about *you*?

She maintained a sway over both those whom she talked about and those to whom she talked. Her clients would feel indebted and in awe;

Peggy had let them into a secret. This made them feel special and made them believe she knew more about all the other clients than anyone else, even if, on closer scrutiny, what she had said turned out to be much less substantial than it had seemed at first. She encouraged openness in everyone save herself and had the knack of making people feel that they knew her well after the briefest of meetings though actually she had parted with very little personal information.

Despite her effusiveness, she could also be a splendid listener, utilising her fierce concentration to good effect. She induced collaboration and created a bond through the potency of the confessional. She established a power relationship, in which the inside knowledge of one elevates the status of the other and confers a privilege by the act of receiving it. This makes the recipient feel better and superior; having joined the initiated, there is an expectation of more privilege to come, and this leads to a kind of dependency.

Clients needed Peggy; they invented her, magnified her and deified her, and she did the same in return for her clients. It took great patience, artistry and vigour to handle all those creative egos, particularly on her own terms.

λ

'I like authors and agents to be near suicidal before a plays opens.'

For many of her clients the severest challenge, greater by far than awaiting the response of a director or the critics, was to please Peggy with a new play. She was her clients' most indomitable judge, jury and prosecuting counsel – and this was someone who was, technically, her clients' employee. Writers would picture her reading their script and imagine with alarm the dreaded moment when she found their play boring and her eyelids would close. 'If it's dead in the head,' she would say, 'it'll be dead on the stage.' A visit to the office to deliver a new script was almost as excruciating as waiting for the reply. She made her writers feel as if she were judging their play against the yardstick of Ibsen, Shakespeare and the Greeks, because that should be the standard of their ambition. Alan Plater recalls this expectation as being 'awesome but inspiring'.

If the script did not match up to a writer's capabilities, Peggy would be merciless. Her habitually tough response to many of her clients' plays can be summed up as 'not enough' – they had fallen short of what she thought they could and should achieve. Yet she was deeply upset if her objective criticism were misconstrued. It was not meant spitefully, she would say, and 'was no more malicious than Flaubert noting all the ugly details of the funeral of the sister he loved.'

She worried about the effect that her honesty might have, especially as for some clients it seemed as if she never had a good word to say about their plays. ' "Truth" is as distorting as lies or evasions and it throws every-thing out of perspective,' she observed, but 'I have no option but to con-tinue to respond in the only way that I can', even if her reactions were taken by her clients to be crude or tactless.

'When I cease to react when I read plays, I must stop being an agent,' she wrote to David Rudkin after a severe response to one of his plays. 'You can't expect me not to react – the only thing I can do is not tell you.'

It was this passion, and her care for the writer, that defined Peggy as an agent. It was not narrowly confined to her clients, however, as shown by her support of John Osborne, her championing of *Waiting for Godot,* or her recommending Tom Stoppard's *Rosencrantz and Guildenstern Are Dead* to Kenneth Tynan at the National Theatre after seeing it at the 1966 Edinburgh Festival. He had been alerted by Ronald Bryden in the *Observer* as well and within a week of Peggy's call had bought the play for the NT. (Stoppard said he knew nothing of her intervention. On hearing this, Peggy simply said he knew but had forgotten, adding 'It's not very important.') Peggy's eye for writing talent extended wide. She used to read the Jeffrey Bernard column in the *Spectator* and pronounced it would make good theatre some considerable time prior to the appearance of a dramatic adaptation in the West End. When she saw Antony Sher in David Hare's *Teeth 'n' Smiles* in 1975, she knew immediately that he was a writer and wrote to him after-wards, telling him this. It turned out to be prophetic; ten years later he was acclaimed for his literary début, *Year of the King,* his account of how he prepared for the role of Richard III and the prelude to a burgeoning reputation as a novelist.

Nevertheless, her main energy was focused on her own authors, and there was no other agent who identified so strongly with their clients' work as Peggy did. This dedication towered over her other attributes and put them all into perspective. For many, her ability to read a script was her chief talent, and in this regard she assumed the status of a contemporary sibyl, graced with amazing powers of prophecy and divination. When she was wrong about a play, however, it was her commitment that carried the day with the misjudged writer, who often forgave much because she was so evidently on the side of the angels.

She did have a 'nose' for a good script, the ability to visualise from the page how a play might work on stage, although, despite her papal reputation which was inflated by her acolytes, she was far from infallible.

Her practice was to read clients' scripts straightaway and to respond straightaway. She loved the feel of a new manuscript and would read it in bed, or at breakfast, or under the hair dryer. She also read plays in the office early in the morning or in the evening but usually not during the day because of the incessant interruptions. At her peak, she averaged a minimum of three scripts a day.

If a client had not heard from her by breakfast the day following the receipt of a script then it was likely that she did not like the play and a withering blast on the telephone could be expected at about 11am. She tried to keep her weekends free of reading but if a script by a client arrived on Friday it would elicit a response from Brighton on Sunday morning if she liked it or Monday morning from the office if not. Sometimes, if she were not sure about a play, her response might take longer, perhaps up to three weeks while she either asked a second opinion or worked out her own way to reply.

There were occasions when she sought the opinion of others about plays – notably John Holmstrom and David Hare – yet as a rule she did not use readers because she feared that they would recommend only the well-made plays that looked a safe bet. She would not invite any new writers to meet her unless she had read at least one play by them that she liked. She once said that all she looked for in an unsolicited play was one good line 'because if they can write one they can write another'.

Most of the unsolicited plays she was sent she described as 'staggeringly dull and bad'. Nevertheless, she claimed that she read the whole of a play and did not give up after ten pages. 'You would be lucky if five plays in a hundred were any good,' she commented, 'and three good plays in one year in the West End was very good.'

She admitted to blind spots in her theatrical taste. She disliked thrillers (and hated *Sleuth* in particular, not a play she represented). Light comedy (such as *No Sex Please We're British*) drove her 'suicidal' and farce she found 'an anguish to read'; no one could be 100% sound in their judgement, she felt, because so much depended on the actor in performance. She loved musicals – 'the last outpost of showbiz' – but admitted to a 'pretty sour and downbeat taste. I still wait for another *Pal Joey*.' When a proposal was put to her for a musical on the fashion designer Coco Chanel, Peggy replied: 'A musical on Cocteau would be more fruitful . . . because he had so many fascinating friends. He's kind of lightweight himself, so one doesn't have to genuflect.' As an agent, she was rarely involved with musicals, with certain outstanding exceptions such as Willy Russell's *Blood Brothers*.

Peggy

Her general taste was highbrow; Kleist, ee cummings, Zola, de Maupassant, Schnitzler, Thomas Mann, Kokoschka, Beardsley, the Secessionists. Of contemporary writers, she particularly liked John Updike. The Bloomsbury group she favoured because they stood for culture and a discriminating sensibility. She found them 'endlessly fascinating because they are big-time losers'. She would have liked to represent Molière. In art, as in life, she followed Keats – 'you have to be free to be inhabited by sensations,' she said, and acknowledged that this intoxication meant she could be prejudiced and wrong.

'A play agent's job is to judge a text, but the judgement isn't based on rules,' she wrote; 'it is based on emotion, intuition and faith . . . All of us are wrong sometimes and right sometimes.'

She knew that her own reactions might be unguarded or impetuous, but they were deeply felt and white hot. She likened them to a sexual experience and insisted on the link between carnal feelings and art. 'We're dead without these feelings,' she said, 'but to live them fully, to be available for life, you have to be prepared to pick up the bill afterwards – and there will be a bill.'

For Peggy, the way to balance life's credit/debit account was to live in 'harmonious conflict'. She scored in the margin of a newspaper article by the sculptor Henry Moore the following passage: 'No one knows anything unless he knows also the opposite. I personally believe that all life is a conflict; that's something to be accepted, something you have to know . . . One must try to find a synthesis, to come to terms with opposite qualities.' She used the metaphor of architecture for both life and plays, admiring the miracle of the arch, which is derived from the stability of opposing forces. She herself would veer between temperamental highs and lows, sometimes consciously wallowing in sensuality and then compensating with a period of arid, even despised, existence.

Good plays, Peggy believed, expressed this counterpoint and had, therefore, to be a reflection of life in some imaginative way. She often complained: 'Our theatre is not a mirror of life but a weekend substitute. People don't tell the truth in plays as a rule.' However inadequate or clumsy, theatre was a place to find recognisable portraits of life, but this would only be possible if writers transformed their experience through their art. While advocating that life should be lived to the full, Peggy knew that this alone was not sufficient; the key was still imaginative transformation. 'There's nothing wrong with limited "experience",' she said. 'There are millions of people going through the full cycle of life up to the hilt, but who could not give us one single piece of

212

information which might give us a better understanding of what it's all about.'

Yet she was not a proponent of social realism or a lover of formalism or abstract aesthetics, although she was moved by the purity of high art. She was steeped in aphorisms about life and art culled from her mentors and copied into her commonplace books. She knew about trends but did not follow them. She shared with modernism, for example, an interest in dreams and the unconventional, but she found modernism often too intel- lectually driven and not sufficiently spontaneous. She wanted to be able to take something away from a play in a moral sense, which was defined very broadly and not ideologically. In her view, religious, political or artistic '-isms' were a cover for individual weaknesses dressed up as moral principle.

Peggy had her own way of making meaning out of life, a kind of every- day mysticism that was highly active and found its parallel in theatre when plays revealed the marvellous in the mundane. She wanted to see in a play what she called 'the movement of the mind' in order to respond both to its emotional and to its intellectual structure, which, for her, were intertwined; we should feel with intelligence and think with passion. It was the form of the play, its shape, colour, drive, rather than its individual characters that comprised and yielded up its meaning.

'Each good play,' she wrote, 'carries the author's secret which isn't spoken by the characters. It must be listened to, heard and accepted by the audience individually – something that will shake their lives a little bit, a sort of terrible pain. A "god, yes" kind of recognition . . . A really good play ought to seem enormously simple and one should say to oneself, why has no one ever written this before.'

She saw in this effect a kind of universality which was directly related to the degree to which the artist had achieved impersonality as his or her life experience had been transmuted into art. But it had to be transmuted with intensity and urgency; with every new play, she wanted the writer to treat its potential audience as seriously as possible, imagining the words in that play to be the writer's last. It should be 'à la Whitman,' as she put it, as if the writer were whispering marvellous secrets to the audience which the writer might forget unless they were expressed at that very moment.

Were a writer to underestimate the audience, Peggy would warn against paying too much respect to art and not enough to life. 'If we are all fools, why write for us at all?' she would say. 'A writer had better look out if he thinks he's better than a factory worker or a carpenter, because he's writing for them.' It was an audience that made the theatre a live art form and gave it its force and physicality. She urged writers to use this immediacy, not to pander to the audience but to train them to appreciate the new.

This was important because each good new play bore its own stamp and was by definition unfamiliar. 'If the work is original the territory is uncharted and there is no compass.' Unlike an audience, however, or a critic, Peggy first met a play in an unaccommodated state without even the guidance of a production, and that was the way she liked it, unmediated and naked.

When she read a new script, she thought it should surprise, astonish, frighten and alarm her, maybe even become unbearable. 'All art comes from ignoble sources' was a favourite quotation, taken from Thomas Mann. She once wrote to the critic Harold Hobson: 'Those who follow make the new acceptable because they know what has gone before – if you are really creative, you do not know, so it is bound to be ugly.' Yet such ugliness, which was related to a remorseless quality she found in the best art, was to be distinguished from nihilism. She saw a belief in life beyond the apparent callousness of much original work – for example, Beckett's or Bond's; 'art is not created out of despair at life,' she said.

Peggy wanted to be disturbed by a play, but not for its shock value as a self-indulgence. She sought a distinct and unique voice in a play but knew that a strong sense of self could turn into the wrong kind of ambition and easily become a form of exhibitionism. Good writing should draw attention to the subject not the writer. She relished danger in a script but only if honed by dedication and hard work. 'Any good original talent should have something slightly daunting about it, even ugly, certainly not acceptable to everybody, or it would not be new.'

Her general advice to playwrights was direct and simple: 'The only way to learn to write plays is to write plays'. She had tried herself to write a play in the '50s, just to see if she could. This confirmed what she had already thought, that she could not, and that it was an exceedingly difficult discipline to conquer. She used to say to clients: 'Don't consider yourself a writer until you have written three plays and had at least two produced.'

Her tips were commonsensical. Make your characters believable; listen to the way people speak and catch the rhythms of their speech in your dialogue – she thought Osborne's 'marvellous ear' was his great secret; go to the theatre and watch how it is done. She advised against reading books on how to write plays and instead suggested a dip into a book on architecture. In the 1980s, concerned that the advent of workshops and collective creation had undermined the learning of the traditional skills of the author, she contradicted her own advice by helping the television script editor Stuart Griffiths to have published a book on playwriting, *How Plays Are Made*, which had begun life as a pamphlet for TV writers.

She took practical criticism literally by throwing a script of Robert Bolt's *Flowering Cherry* at Charles Wood after reading a new play of his. '*That's good writing*,' she said. It did not matter if she believed it or not, the effect was important. When she was not being brutal ('Burn it, dear, and start again') or bruising ('Have a wank and get on with it'), she could be helpful in a direct way. She gave one young writer, Richard Cottrell, whom she thought was strong on dialogue but weak on story, La Rochefoucauld's *Maxims* and told him to choose one a day and write the plot of a play from it until he had improved. Other aids included Flaubert's letters and Ernst Fischer's *The Necessity of Art*.

Peggy would point clients in the direction of her favourite writers, such as Schopenhauer or Gide ('of all people to find consoling, but perhaps it was because he made an ass of himself so often'). In keeping with her fondness for collecting sayings about art, she often responded to a play with a homily, for instance, 'comedy is constant small surprises'. Another strategy was to speak in code. On the phone to Peter Nichols, for instance, she told him that she had just attended the opening of the much-praised *Lawrence of Arabia*. There was a pause. 'Lovely camels, dear. Byee.' She often gave advice allegorically. She sent Howard Brenton a haiku, which meant his work was over-extended and he should learn to compress. When she sent him a leaf from Balzac's grave, the message was 'be prolific'. She dispatched a tape of Urdu love songs to David Hare. John Bowen said she might send a US paperback on Zen or an item torn from a newspaper accompanied by a message: 'What could you make of this if you let your unconscious rip?' scrawled on a bit of brown wrapping paper. Books she gave as first night presents were often the subject of much tangled interpretation – one view had it that the better the present the worse Peggy thought the play would be received.

She recommended an awareness of the other arts yet was frequently dismissive of playwrights' attempts to experiment formally. 'Robbe-Grillet [an innovative French novelist and film-maker] started a trend in literature which is really new but I see no sign of it in the theatre.' In reference to the debate about naturalism and modernism, she said it was easier to break the fourth wall than to write a good, conventional proscenium play, and she did not like Joan Littlewood's theatrical experimentation, in which the author's play became raw material for the director's playmaking.

In keeping with what might be termed her radical conservatism, she held strict views on the protocol of theatre, which many of her clients found old-fashioned and overly prescriptive; agents should stick to doing what agents do, managers should stick to doing what managers do, and writers should stick to what writers do. She was highly sceptical, for example, when some playwrights formed a management to present David Mercer's *Flint* in 1970. 'I'm not convinced authors banding together to become Managers make better Managers than Managers,' Peggy commented.

She saw one of her tasks as standing between the writer, who was vulnerable, and the management, who were risking their money, but she often disappointed clients when they were expecting support if she felt they had not done their own job properly. She could arrogantly and dismissively tell an anxious manager awaiting delivery of an overdue play that her client's play would come when it came, while at the same time reproving the culpable writer that if an agreement had been entered into then its terms should be met.

She chided John Arden for delivering a four-hour play that was not in a proper state of readiness; it is the responsibility of the author to prepare a text and it is not the business of managements, she told him. She similarly took Charles Wood, Peter Barnes and David Rudkin to task and would cite plays of theirs as examples of what happens when a playwright does not prepare the text adequately before rehearsals begin and relies on the rehearsal process to put it right. 'I wouldn't trust a director to shape a new play,' she said. 'Writers should cut more and not leave someone else to do the dirty work for them.' She did not, however, believe in rewriting for its own sake and found frequently that rewrites were as bad, if not worse, than what had gone before.

She gave more detailed textual responses when she first started out as an agent than later when she was established, although, even early on, she did not offer line by line dramaturgical advice; the logical or analytical method was not in her make-up. Rather she would comment on where a scene should be placed or where energy was lost and a climax missed. Her views on play construction and the vocabulary she used to discuss it were traditional and drew heavily on standard texts from Aristotle's *Poetics* to William Archer's *Play-Making*. Has a scene or a moment been properly prepared for? Is there an 'obligation' scene at the heart of the play? What is the force and clarity of its exposition? What is the nature of its 'revealment'?

The chance to influence a script before it was finished was a great thrill, and she was guided by a practical maxim: 'A play has simply got to be grasped by an audience sitting through it once.' Peggy adored being part of this process of preparing a play before it becomes public; she loved it, for instance, when the designer Alan Tagg, one of the few non-playwrights whom she represented, called into her office with his set models to discuss how the play he was designing might work in production.

Her advice was often of the most practical kind and ranged from discussing with managers and publishers the timing of the publication of a script to helping a client choose key collaborators, such as director, designer, or lead actors.

She gave sound counsel on all fronts, though her jaundiced view of actors often made her less reliable in this regard than, for instance, on directors. Peggy's wisdom on how to tell if an actor is in character was simplicity itself: 'Look at the feet, dear.'

Martin Sherman tells the story of how Peggy intervened to sort out a problem with the production of his play *Bent* at the Royal Court. There was a difficult scene change which had been a terrible mess at the technical rehearsal. Quite distressed, he had gone to see Peggy the next morning. 'You mean it's roaring like a lion when it should be purring like a kitten?' she asked, and, repeating this phrase, 'purring like a kitten' – a habit she had when she liked something she had said – she told him she would telephone the theatre. An hour later Sherman went to the Royal Court to find extra technicians on hand and seemingly the whole staff trying to sort out the problem, which they did. Afterwards, one of the stage crew went up to Sherman and said, 'It purred like a kitten'.

Comments would come back to writers as she attended rehearsals, run-throughs and previews, though these reports would mostly concern performance, design and direction rather than text. Her presence at such occasions was not always beneficial. At the opening of the 1966 try-out in Guildford of a revue, *Night is for Delight*, to which her clients Caryl Brahms and Ned Sherrin had contributed, Sherrin was approached at the interval by several producers who were attending with a view to bringing the show into London.

'Who is that extraordinary woman in the hat telling everyone not to invest in the show?' they asked.

Shamefaced, Sherrin replied: 'That's my agent.'

Whereas attending performances of a play before an opening night constituted work for Peggy, her presence at a first night she saw as a social duty and, therefore, of much less value. Early on, she went to first nights with Edward Sutro, one of her original backers, because he knew the London critics and she felt it was important to show that she was at the centre of things. She soon tired of this, not being one for the theatrical scene.

Peggy

In refusing to attend a first night party thrown by Binkie Beaumont for Robert Bolt's *Gentle Jack* she wrote: 'I know that you will understand when I say that I would rather just go home. I would love to celebrate on the 100th or 500th performance, but it's marvellous to be able to keep away from people on the first night . . . If one meets members of the cast, one is pushed into a position of insincerity which I know is something you have to do in your job, but, thank God, isn't necessary in mine.'

She told one client, Stanley Eveling, that he was mad to organise a first night party. She acknowledged that he would need sustaining and suggested an evening with Euripides instead. 'That's where you'll find the bombs of the imagination.' She herself would disappear after the show on a first night and telephone the author the next day. She might have tested her own views out on others by then and found what she thought was the best way to respond or even hoped that her comments to a third party would be passed on. Constant spontaneity and instant wisdom could be exhausting, both for her and the recipients.

Her authority for intervening came from her detailed knowledge of each part of the process of creating and putting on a play, and many clients found this aspect of her service to them the most useful. She was very sharp not only on how to place a play but where. 'A bad theatre today isn't as good as a good theatre tomorrow,' she would say. And while she believed that 'No really good piece of work lies undone and neglected', she was also aware that good plays can be rushed into the wrong theatre and badly spoiled.

Diaghilev-like, she enjoyed bringing complementary talents together. When it came to finding collaborators for her playwrights she cast her net wide across the generations and valued efficiency and practicality as well as taste, rating reliability more highly than erratic genius. She might be swopping jobs around within her own client list, passing, for example, a Christopher Hampton film project onto Robert Bolt or vice versa, or putting her clients in touch with her own contacts, like Ionesco and the director Peter Wood, or, when Robert Holman wanted to write a play about George Orwell, introducing him to Sonia Orwell, who made the play possible.

Peggy seemed endlessly patient with her writers as she shepherded them through the whole process. She recognised the need to get each link in the chain right and the importance of trust and integrity to make the process work at all. 'It is necessary to know all about the people you are to work with because the success of any venture is the sum total of all the talents, weaknesses and strengths of the people concerned,' she said. 'In the theatre people's careers are linked . . . If one of these links snaps, the remaining link [the author] has to pay the bill.'. This was why she recommended people whom she knew and in whom she had confidence.

The counter to that was her strictures to writers on the dangers of friendship in the theatre. In her experience the friendship of writers was usually exploited to benefit someone else's career, particularly directors. Peggy warned that directors ultimately would always put their own needs first, regardless of how personally close they might be to the playwright.

A final link in the chain was the critic. Peggy applied her usual commonsense, hard-nosed approach to reviews and reviewers, although, as with most things, she held bi-polar views on them. On the whole she had little time for critics, and was particularly wary of those who were unsuccessful authors – 'a dangerous combination,' she thought. Her relations were cordial with the critical community – she happily corresponded with Frank Rich, the *New York Times*'s 'butcher of Broadway', when he wanted to write an article on British theatre – and one of her clients, Frank Marcus, was a distinguished critic for ten years.

She favoured the sharpness of the immediate response required from the overnight reviewer to the more measured tones of the weekly columnist, who was more susceptible, she felt, to the distorting influence of theories, worldviews and the opinions of the other reviewers.

Critics by definition had to be punch-drunk with mediocrity because they saw so much bad theatre and, therefore, did not receive sufficient nourishment. 'They need food like the rest of us,' she said in their defence. 'I have great sympathy for them. On the whole they're OK and they hand out a kind of rough justice. They have to go to the theatre every night and see mostly awful things, poor buggers. I'd rather spend an hour reading a play than sit for two-and-a-half hours watching one.'

Therein lay the difference between the agent and the critic. One had to judge on the page, the other on the stage. She thought that it was easy to assess a play once it had been 'served up' and was stumped by the critics' frequent lack of comprehension; for example, she crossed swords with the *Daily Telegraph* critic W.E. Darlington, who announced to her at the first night of Pirandello's *Six Characters in Search of an Author* at the Arts Theatre in 1954 that he could not understand a word of what Pirandello was saying. She resisted the trap of trying to explain and rounded on Darlington with a plain declaration that carried the stamp of factual incontrovertibility, 'there's nothing difficult or complicated *to* understand'. She added that his attitude resembled 'a typist who "didn't understand" *Omar Khayyam*,' and then, she said, 'he really began to take notice, and I hope the *Telegraph* (which I don't read) profited by the encounter.'

Critical success, like all success, was to be treated with the utmost suspicion. When Robert Holman as a fledgling writer phoned her one day with modest pride to say he had received good reviews, she replied instantly: 'You don't deserve them.' Moreover, when her clients were on the receiving end of harsh words from the critics she might still side with the perpetrators of the hurt rather than her own authors. Depending on the play concerned, however, and the state of her client's development, she might offer words of comfort and lambast the critical community for being collectively as well as individually moronic.

In such circumstances, she advised writers not to become entangled with the critics – 'write better plays instead', she would say. However, she did argue with the critics in private on her clients' behalf if she felt it necessary, as, for example, over David Hare's *Knuckle*. She had no hesitation in approaching critics, especially in the early days of a playwright's career, and would on occasion invite a critic to meet an author. She took this step with a new Irish author, Thomas Kilroy, following the production at the Hampstead Theatre Club in 1969 of *The Death and Resurrection of Mr Roche*, his first play to be seen in London. Peggy summoned to the Café Royal Irving Wardle, *The Times* critic, who had been foolhardy enough to criticise the play. Kilroy and the play's director, Richard Eyre, were present. The conversation ranged wide and far, as was Peggy's wont, and she soon began to attack Brecht; what an awful writer, what terrible box office. 'Wardle tentatively pointed out that *The Resistible Rise of Arturo Ui* was doing rather well in the West End,' recalls Eyre. 'Yes, dear,' came Peggy's reply, 'but that's about Hitler and,' she added very loudly, 'Hitler's a fucking star!'

Peggy disliked the critics' insular mentality and felt most of them had a limited vision. Her general view of where critics went wrong can be summed up in a letter of hers to Michael Billington: 'It's no good accepting a flight in a hovercraft and then saying "Oh, how I long to fly in Concorde".' She despaired of their narrow demands for explicitness: 'Critics see truth only if it's spelled out whereas it's often elusive, "the echo of an echo". One must be prepared to allow oneself to receive these mysterious forces, and it's difficult to do this if one limits one's nourishment to the Greater London area.'

The two towering critical figures of her time were Harold Hobson and Kenneth Tynan. Tynan clashed publicly with two of her major clients, Eugène Ionesco and Robert Bolt, and, despite his endorsement of *Waiting for Godot*, flew the flag for Brecht rather than Beckett. Peggy did not find warmth in Tynan and disliked his dedication to self-publicity. Hobson was the critic with whom Peggy had the most dealings. Her intervention at the interval of *Waiting for Godot* was a defining moment in their relationship and she subsequently felt that, unlike the waspish Tynan, Hobson was someone to whom she could appeal when a new play required sensitive handling. In 1968, Hobson's review of the year included six plays written by her clients.

He and Peggy shared an interest in bridge and enjoyed unabashedly fervid discussions of art, creativity and the moral dimension of existence. Binkie Beaumont saw something sexual in their relationship, which, apart from Peggy's fascination with Hobson's collection of pornography, seems more likely to have been a recognition of the intensity which they were both capable of bringing to life.

*

'Lack of funds and lack of friends is good for a writer'

Bad critics, bad actors, bad directors, bad theatres, bad managers – all these, Peggy knew, could stifle talent but could not kill it. None was as lethal to talent as bad character. In a writer's temperament could be found either the life or the death of talent. A writer had to find, hold on to, feed and expand his or her inner voice. It would be a struggle, and if it was not, then something was wrong. 'Demand is enormous for talent and people must not bugger it about,' she told Alan Plater. 'Obstructions and prevarication must be circumscribed.'

Peggy saw that a writer was as much a slave to, as a master of, his or her talent and consequently recognised the importance of character in the exploitation of talent. She took an austere, almost sacramental, view of the life of a writer as one that should be utterly dedicated to that writer's talent, yet it was not a view that denied pleasure. She valued enjoyment and life experience generally in a writer but only because it kept the writer human and fed the writing. Extremes of pleasure, which fascinated her, were counterproductive if they became destructive, as when drugs, or drink, or sex detracted from instead of enhancing the writing. She was bright enough to recognise that excess and its self-destructive capacity, both of which she found in herself, had to be kept under control; her apparently puritanical response was not so much repression as a plea against prodigality, a desire for the proper use of what exists – in the writer's case, talent.

221

Peggy

Peggy preferred pleasure to come in short sharp bursts and to be balanced by a sustained period of hard grind at the writing desk. Her belief in constant work, however, was not measured by the volume of outcome but its quality. She warned against writing too much too quickly. Conversely, she did have a tendency to confuse working with being prolific, as if writers who were not producing regularly were being lazy and thereby not honouring their talent. Laziness was a cardinal sin in Peggy's catechism, which was driven by an almost Nietzschean zeal for perpetual, protean creativity. Laziness signified unfulfilled talent, and that struck Peggy as an immense spiritual, even cosmic, waste.

The problem, however, for most of her clients lay not in indolence but in the shortfall of their achievement. Peggy saw an inevitable and unbridgeable gap between a writer's ambition and its fulfilment. If a writer did achieve his or her potential, they would, in her eyes, be finished. There would be nothing left. Perfection was death; to arrive was to depart. Yet there was no choice for her but to spur the writers on. She knew they could not write marvellously every time, and they would falter. For the writers there was no alternative but, like Sisyphus, to keep pushing the boulder of their talent up the hill. 'Talent will renew itself if it is any good,' she said, 'or end when it has to'.

For Peggy, theatre was a harsh disciplinarian; the playwriting craft was 'very, very difficult – it takes time and focus. You might not earn much from a play for two years and you have to wait to reach your peak and then you're lucky if you can spend ten years there.' A playwright was the only begetter of a play but was then excluded from its life in performance. It was tough being both a god and a nobody.

Theatre, Peggy also recognised, was a limited medium 'because hardly anyone sees it', yet the nature of its process and its scrutiny meant 'it would be safer to be a novelist'. It took great courage to look foolish in front of an audience. Theatre is very public both in production and reception, and participants survive expecting their commitment to this art form to be tested continually in a series of trials, in which, more often than not, they will be deemed failures.

Playwrights tend to defend themselves by rationalising their failures – stupid critics, poor performances, overbearing sets, crazed direction – or indulging in aggressive behaviour which can compensate for their relative impotence. They often find themselves picking a fight in order to be heard, or simply to make a point, or even to make themselves unemployable, and thus complete the circle of paranoia. Some choose other defensive constructs, like the Playwright in Exile, or the Playwright for Posterity, or the Playwright More Honoured Abroad Than At Home. Peggy had to deal with all these, and more.

She did not consider writing a glamorous profession and took an austere view of the life a writer needed to lead. 'Plays must *cost* the writer; they must be *bloodied*,' she said. 'Writers must not sit alone all the time. They need outside attractions. That's what they write about, but this must not distract them.' Suffering was crucial, she believed. She thought Pinter was not as authentic as Beckett because he had not suffered as much. 'You need to suffer to be a good person not just a good writer, but you mustn't be embittered by suffering. You mustn't be petty or spiteful or jealous because of suffering, you must be compassionate.'

It was character and talent that supported an author through the buffeting both of the profession and the world at large. For this reason she admired the writers who stood up to her, like Stephen Poliakoff or, in a more wily manner, David Cregan. Cregan used to know when she did not like his latest play because he would receive a letter that began 'Dear Cregan.' He would write back, pointing out that she had obviously missed something, and her reply would then begin 'Dear David.' She liked a certain arrogance in a playwright as a necessary bulwark of the craft. At the same time, she believed that if an author never felt 'inferior' with a due modesty, he or she would never develop or grow wise. Eventually, she was convinced, a good writer would come through and find his or her own level, even if it did not happen as quickly as the writer might have hoped.

The biggest obstacle, paradoxically, was success. Failure brought its own problems but represented a test of character that Peggy thought allowed for growth. Success was much more harmful. Success was the serpent in her theatrical garden. 'You're not in danger of making money, are you dear?' she would say.

She was scathing about success in the material and public sense, although it was easier to handle in Britain because the rewards were so poor. She believed that success led to moral decay if not handled properly. She could be quite glitzy when she wanted to be and enjoyed certain of the trappings of success, like the award ceremonies; prizes, however, she considered 'shoddy though fun to win but valueless'. Critical acclaim was of 'dubious worth'. Money had to be used wisely and preferably not salted away – 'You can't buy happiness, pleasure or talent.'

The financial part of the equation was frequently a point of contention between Peggy and her clients, most of whom would gladly have earned more than they did. Despite her elevated position in the profession, it was not necessarily the most lucrative option for a client to be represented by her. For the last 25 years of Peggy's life she lived very comfortably without seemingly being aware of how much she was worth. This indifference to the cost of her own lifestyle, coupled with her stentorian lectures on the evils of wealth in her writers, roused several of her clients, most notably Peter Nichols, to insurrection.

Success, to Peggy, was a justification of one's own taste, which is why she saw it as dangerous. Success was sordid and ugly, and 'something "they" talked about, like *trade*,' she observed with a touch of snobbery. It was good for lesser talents like directors to be celebrities but not writers. She pointed to examples such as Osborne, Wesker and Bolt to support her contention that success was disastrous. 'I think we must all at least feel clean in only taking what comes to us and not buying our happiness or pleasure,' she once wrote. 'Success, such as it is,' she opined in an echo of her interest in Zen, 'is gained by not trying to get it.' '

She saw her role as 'jockeying and cheering' the writers and helping them 'try not to get it'. She devoted her energies to serving their talents, and that included offering advice on how to handle success and failure. There was little to interest her in representing a writer who did not need her help, a writer with insufficient talent, or one who was established and no longer growing. Before taking on a writer, she had to be able to 'see' the talent, to have an account of who the writer was, who the writer should be and how the writer might change from the one to the other.

The process was not as planned as it might sound, nor was it entirely random. Peggy responded instinctively but within her own moral matrix. Her relationships with writers were dialectical, the outcomes open. Inexperience and youth were obvious attractions because there was so much room for Peggy to do her shaping. She believed, however, that she was mostly drawn to writers because of their faults and weaknesses, in which she would recognise herself. ('I'm with the sinners,' she would say.) But it was axiomatic that the character flaws that attracted her would inevitably become the obstacles that she wanted the writers to overcome in order for them to be able to serve their own talent better.

'How the ordinary well balanced citizen manages to live life is astounding but those who have imagination are bound to *nearly* break from time to time,' she wrote to John Whiting. 'There's only one word anyone can give to anyone else and that's *endure*.'

Her advice to her clients on how to endure encroached in many cases on highly personal matters, which was inevitable because she had to remain in contact with the writer's inner life, the source of creativity, if she was to be of use; for the writer – unlike herself – she saw no distinction between the private and the professional, they were as one in her temple of talent.

Proprietorial is almost too light a word to describe her pastoral care, which assumed the all-seeing, all-knowing qualities of a matriarchal deity. Indeed, she treated her clients as if they were a part of a huge family that had Peggy at its head. Her clients were the children she never had. She was protective of them to the outside world and a scourge to them inside, directing their nurture, schooling, welfare, health and love life, knowing they would grow up one day and she would have to encourage them to leave home, while at the same time resenting having to do so.

Peggy's involvement in her clients' private affairs was determined by her view of each client's needs and the degree to which personal issues affected the writing.

Financial considerations were the commonest cause of a client's anxiety. This could be tricky territory. Peggy combined extravagant generosity with irritating meanness. She did not like writers who mentioned money – 'People must pee and earn money but let's not *talk* about it' – and she would not help out if a client asked directly. Yet she did lend money – to Robert Bolt and Howard Brenton among others, early on in their writing careers – when she knew they were hard up.

David Hare, a year after he had joined her, found Peggy pressing a perfumed wallet into his hand just before he set off to see *Knuckle* in New York, his first play to be produced there. Inside the wallet was $2,000. There was an ulterior motive. In true Romantic spirit, she wanted him to experience life and, despite being married at the time, entertain lots of women. 'Buy yourself a girl,' she advised. Being of a practical nature, Peggy knew all this social education cost money, and she was happy to provide it. Yet when, on being shown her holiday snaps and entreated to travel, Robert Holman had replied that he had always wanted to but could not afford it, her instant rejoinder was: 'You don't need money to travel, just the desire.'

Peggy often did help out, however, in other ways. When the agency was still quite new, she would assist needy authors by arranging for them to earn three guineas by preparing from the prompt copy of a play an acting script for the publishers Samuel French, the main conduit for the amateur market. Sometimes her help was directly utilitarian – writers were invited to use the Hut in Brighton to write in – or she might pay a client's telephone bills for a period. Peggy would not take the agency's commission from a writer's earnings, or she would pay it back, if she judged that the writer could not afford it. This may have been a material bonus to the writer, yet it also implied a lack of success, something which did not bother Peggy but might have exercised the already unhappy client.

Sometimes her help was apparently a caprice, as when she gave unexpected gifts. She might spontaneously buy a client books or an expensive painting, for example, but behind the gesture would have lain the idea that it was appropriate and helpful, and might stimulate further creativity. She liked giving and receiving presents, but abhorred the forced and, to her mind, false exchange of gifts at times like Christmas. Instead, she would bestow small mementoes on people such as the leading actors in plays by her clients (for instance, giving a groat to Paul Scofield on the opening night of *A Man for All Seasons*).

She often contradicted her admonition to her clients to 'live simply', recalls Howard Brenton, who was understandably astonished when she took him and two other clients, by taxi, to see Kabuki at Sadlers Wells (where she told them she used to screech from the stage), then to an expensive Japanese restaurant, and ended the evening by paying for them all to go home by taxi.

Beneath the good humour and élan of such minor extravagances, Peggy battled with an insecurity, a lack of roots, of not properly and securely belonging. She had gathered around her a new family of writers to replace her own family, which she had left behind a decade before the war, and, inevitably, she had a complex set of responses to this new kinship.

Her family comprised an extraordinary mix, embracing the differing styles of John Mortimer and David Mercer, or Edward Bond and Alan Ayckbourn, and public figures like John McGrath and David Hare as well as private writers like Robert Holman or Peter Gill. Beyond their talent, there is no common weave; she praised them all and damned them all.

Not all writers could form part of the family. Peggy was not a good agent for everyone and she did not have the Midas touch. There was no guarantee that being represented by Peggy would automatically transform a writer's fate. Alongside the recognised names in her ledgers are those of many who fell by the wayside. There were also those who suffered from her early pronouncement on their talent and found no escape from the pigeon hole into which she had crammed them. Stanley Eveling said she actively discouraged him from abandoning his absurdist vein; she seemed comfortable having discovered where she thought his talent lay and did not want him to disturb her. Peter Terson recalls her being fixated on his first play, *A Night To Make the Angels Weep*. 'You are a genius who must be allowed to mature,' she said, but every subsequent play he wrote she judged against that initial favourite of hers, as if wanting him to repeat the same play over again.

She could also be blinkered about people because of their perceived role; David Cook she treated as merely John Bowen's partner rather than as a writer himself, and the German-born Frank Marcus, who translated Schnitzler, she refused to accept was not Viennese. Hugh Whitemore, for some unknown reason, she considered to be a DIY expert and when she moved into a new flat she asked him to fix all the plugs. She would not be swayed by any amount of argument to the contrary.

Many writers with whom she had an awkward relationship survived within the agency by adopting their own strategies of peaceful co-existence. A writer like Peter Barnes, for example, was a regular visitor at Goodwin's Court on his way home from a day at the British Library, but there were long periods when he and Peggy hardly spoke. 'A brilliant writer,' she said, 'but his work is not easy to handle, or sell.' His apocalyptic plays appealed to her sense of the absurd and the obsessive, yet she found them naughty rather than wicked and lacking in eroticism; Peggy described them as 'Jacobean excess crossed with Laurel and Hardy.' His best-known play, *The Ruling Class*, she liked for its scope and ambition; it was tough, difficult and endearing, she thought, as well as scatter-brained and fuzzy. She was nonetheless determined to see it produced, which it was after she sent it to Stuart Burge at Nottingham Playhouse. Barnes, however, insists that he had already placed the play there. He concedes that she was an enthusiast who was worth listening to on practical theatre matters but he considered her views on life and art to be romantic tosh. Asked why he did not leave the agency, he replied: 'Changing agents is like changing deckchairs on the Titanic and about as effective.'

For those writers who did leave, the price was excommunication. Peggy engendered and expected loyalty from her new family, a loyalty in which the bonds seemed as strong as blood ties. It was a loyalty that exerted a terrific grip, and a loyalty that implied a willingness to avoid criticism of Peggy. This could lead to the dangerous practice of allowing her to expatiate without interruption or defiance because it was easier; she would then find her opinions confirmed, even if the client's complicity had been born of courtesy, embarrassment or fear. She handled individual challenges like a joust, and admired a spark of resistance as long as she remained in pole position. If the disagreement led to a writer leaving, this was seen as treachery. She had single-mindedly devoted herself at considerable emotional cost to the client and was now being abandoned. She tried to empathise with the client's predicament and to behave as well as possible, but, just as when staff departed, as soon as clients left, they were instant history; to Peggy they were as good as dead.

Writers who left the agency, like Henry Livings, Peter Nichols, Charles Wood, Hugh Whitemore, were cast into an outer darkness, although at every turn she would insist that all her clients were free to leave at any time they chose. But, as James Saunders says, 'How can you change your mother?' On hearing that a relatively new client, Sean Mathias, was intending to quit, Peggy enacted a parody of her own extreme reactions, jumped onto a window sill and threatened suicide.

Peggy's behaviour had little to do with the merits of the situation. Hugh Whitemore, for instance, had every reason to leave yet he was ostracised by her none the less. He had joined in 1963 when he was working as a TV continuity writer and was having no luck with any of his own plays. John Mortimer suggested he approach Peggy, who said she could not help. 'If you want to be a writer, be one,' was her reply. An angry Whitemore then managed to sell one of his plays to Don Taylor, a TV director who, as a writer, was a client of Peggy's. Whitemore proudly told Peggy of his breakthrough. She asked him how much he had been paid, told him the sum was outrageously low and took him on. He was never one of Peggy's intimates, but they became close and enjoyed the kind of relationship that reached beyond the lunches into the exchanging of books and visiting of art galleries together. In the early 1980s, he was having trouble writing a stage play and instead decided to adapt a TV play of his for the theatre. When he gave her *Pack of Lies*, his play about a suburban family caught up in the efforts of the British secret service to trap two Russian spies, she said, 'I can't read this rubbish. It's an old TV play you've rehashed.' She told him that he was only a TV writer and that she did not approve of anything he had ever written. After 18 years with the agency, he left.

'It was worse than divorce', he remembers. 'Peggy would not speak to me. At nearly 50, I wanted a business relationship and not one where I always felt as if I were having to pass a test. But when I did leave, I immediately felt my dependency on her and, consequently, it was a great loss to me. I was then a non-person.' Even the subsequent West End success of *Pack of Lies*, represented by another agent, could not entirely relieve the pain. When Peggy was given an award by the British Film Institute a few years later, Whitemore sent her his congratulations and suggested that it would be nice to meet. She thanked him but said there was no point.

This was symptomatic of Peggy's fearsomely strong code of behaviour, which she maintained for her new family of writers. She ruled her roost with a redoubtable sense of honour that derived from her own childlike moral directness. Like a child, she felt the world had to be ordered to suit her. Both she and her clients were free to make mistakes within the family code as long as she was the arbiter.

*

'He'd be a fine writer, dear, if only he weren't married to that woman.'

Peggy related to this new family as an extended series of one-to-one relationships, with each moment in the particular relationship being singular, intense and exclusive.

Mostly the relationships were conducted from the office, either on the telephone or in meetings there. She did visit clients, though only occasionally. One of the drawbacks of visiting a playwright's home was the possibility, if not the probability, of having literally and physically to share her author with the author's partner. As well as disliking family and domestic life, Peggy could show signs of jealousy and anxiety when confronted by another claimant to her client's attentions. She was not jealous in the conventional sense; overwhelmingly her clients were men and Peggy believed that she and no one else had to be the woman in the writer's life when it came to his talent. She became whatever woman she thought each male writer needed at a particular time – strict governess, protective mother, colourful coquette, formidable businesswoman. She was the professional expert in ripening the fruits of the writer's talent; any other liaisons might obstruct the writer's obligation, which was to write.

Stability and security, which for many writers were essential prerequisites for the freedom to create, were for Peggy the harbingers of complacency and conventionality, blunting the writer's edge. Peggy's focus on work, in the absence of a family of her own, meant that clients' partners were judged entirely by whether or not they allowed the talent to blossom. Peggy used the same yardstick whether the partners in question were the opposite or the same sex as the clients, although the majority were mostly wives. To Peggy, they posed a serious threat until proved otherwise.

Partners were deemed acceptable if they provided necessary services, like sex and support at home. When Alan Plater came to live in London, Peggy would not speak to his partner Shirley until Peggy had visited their home to check that Shirley had created the right environment for Alan. She waited until they were settled and then came to dinner with them. Two days later, the phone went at their flat. It was Goodwin's Court. An assistant announced that Peggy would now speak to Shirley. Peggy did not see this as a personal matter, either in terms of the writer or the partner. The writer's gift was made manifest in the plays and not in the playwright. It existed over and above the individual, whom it outlasted in the plays that survived after the writer had died. The job of the partner was to help the writer be prepared to write. 'I think it must be harder for the wives than for the writers,' she said, but she stuck to her view that a writer's talent was a gift that was not to be squandered.

Peggy told Charles Wood that there were two professions within which one should not get married – soldiering (memories of her father?) and writing. By definition, therefore, all writers were married to the wrong person. As a consequence many anecdotes about Peggy and her clients' wives adorn her legend, the best known probably being the one Peter Nichols used in his play *A Piece of My Mind*.

Nichols draws on the moment when he was preparing to travel to New York for the Broadway opening of *A Day in the Death of Joe Egg*. He told Peggy he was going to take his wife Thelma. 'You authors are such funny men,' came the reply. 'It's like taking a ham sandwich to a banquet.'

Thelma, the ham, was often confused by Peggy with Charles Wood's wife, Val – Thelma and Val had attended the same school. When Nichols and Wood joined Peggy, both families lived in Bristol, thus giving Peggy greater grounds for mixing them up. 'Poor Charles,' Peggy would complain to Nichols, 'he's got that awful Thelma to put up with.' Nichols would correct her. 'No, Peggy, Thelma is *my* wife.' Peggy would carry on undeterred, confirming the view it was all part of her game plan.

She thought Christopher Hampton's wife, Laura, was 'nice but straight – it's so good for him not to have someone too bright and lively.' She once described Howard Brenton's happiness at home as 'disgusting, like a beached hippopotamus wallowing in the mud'. Yet, when he was hard up, she had offered him a car because he had a family to look after. The car, however, was not intended for him but for his wife so that she could be taxi driver to the children and leave him free to get on with his writing.

Peggy became particularly incensed with Sandra Rudkin, at one point shouting down the phone, 'Shut up Mrs Rudkin and get me David.' Sandra Rudkin, whom Peggy admired and of whom she was generally very supportive, had decided to take a full-time job, which Peggy thought a selfish move. She told David Rudkin that she thought Sandra should work only part-time in order to have more time available to care for the children. Peggy wrote to him: 'I am appalled by Sandra. What work can she be doing which is comparable to your own work . . . ? As soon as your children can stand on their own feet you must get away. PS. I think Strindberg would be able to understand your marriage!' Sandra Rudkin opened the letter and was understandably upset. Peggy apologised by saying that she thought David and Sandra shared everything. In a subsequent letter she wrote: 'Naturally my feeling is that only the author really matters and in any household should be given total preference.'

Jo Riddett, Robert Bolt's first wife, recalls Peggy as being courteous and considerate. She remembers Peggy's kindness to her after her marriage to Bolt had broken down. She and Peggy were not close, but Peggy took the trouble to write to her a letter that offered great emotional sustenance. In contrast to Bolt's 'greed' in the film world, Peggy said, 'You have done nothing vulgar.'

Although Peggy valued loyalty highly, stable relationships implied a permanence of emotions, which was anathema to her. Stability denied the role of passion, which was the supreme authority she respected. Passion, for Peggy, was an extreme form of love, as was appetite and power. None of these was to be found in mutuality, in relationships of sustained responsibility. By her definition, passion had to be spontaneous as well as transient.

She encouraged her writers to be promiscuous; she liked David Hare for it, but criticised him for making a virtue out of sexual libertarianism without allowing its beneficial effects on him to show through strongly enough in his writing. Peggy knew that promiscuity could cause pain, yet pain was an essential, unavoidable part of living. An openness to life, and therefore to pain, was unavoidable if one was to be creative. Providing one had integrity and courage, pain and unhappiness in love could only make one stronger.

Trying to fight this by an effort of the will was doomed. Peggy would animatedly cite the case of Dickens to make her point. 'He pursued a woman for eight years, he captured her, and,' she would conclude in a flourish of delight, 'she *still* didn't love him!' Yet Peggy only survived by suppressing her own feelings of love, and that carried a price. It destroyed something in her while renewing her too. She lived life as best she could in accordance with her own existential view and displayed ruthlessness both offensively and defensively in order to prove that she could and would live her own way.

It seems as if she had tried to love and found it wanting. The story of the pilot lover who died in the Second World War suggested that life had robbed her, but another story that she told with similar metaphorical weight, of going to Paris to love a famous writer only to find that he was in love with, and was loved by, others, suggested that love was an illusion anyway.

Without naming the writer concerned, Peggy referred to this episode in a letter to John Holmstrom:

> There is nothing so rousing in a woman as the knowledge that someone cannot be possessed, that someone is really incapable of feelings which are essential to one's happiness. This arouses a kind of delirium, and a kind of masochism too. The fact that the person who is everything to you isn't really worth having has an added effect upon one's emotions, so that all the possible permutations of loving, hatred, repulsion, disgust and all the rest of it, extend one's feelings in all directions.
>
> But when you try and cure this kind of thing yourself, and you know that you only have to pick up a telephone to start the whole ecstasy and nightmare all over again, it becomes more confusing still, and really it is extraordinary that one ever recovers at all. (Not that it is possible to 'recover' in the way one does when a thing is *played out*.) Who remembers the happy love affairs in their lives? One only remembers the people one did not actually complete one's relationship with, the people who have stirred one's imagination. There is *nothing* deader and less evocative than a completed (and happy) love affair.

Her sense of the finality of the finished past is captured in the same letter in her account of a recent meeting with a former lover:

> The other day I banged into a man who had actually tried to commit suicide in my flat – I can't even remember why. He seemed a nice sort of chap, but for the life of me I couldn't remember *at all* what it was we had together, or why on earth he had tried to kill himself. We talked politely, like distant acquaintances. I think I was the more friendly, because I hoped he wasn't thinking that I remembered what he had done in a fit of madness. I only hoped that he benefited by the feelings which had driven him to that absurd gesture – as far as I was concerned it meant nothing at all, and both then and now it has been no service to me in understanding somebody else.

Yet when Peggy recounted to the director Anthony Page her farewell to sexual passion she described an affair with a young unmarried man at the end of which she was not able to visit a certain part of London where he lived or even look at a certain make of car which he owned. Knowing this to be ridiculous, she seemingly decided to abandon all future prospect of such relationships. 'It seems on the whole better to live entirely within yourself than this absurd attempt to establish a physical connection with another person in order to feel something "spiritual".' Only time, she said, was irrevocable.

Peggy herself was seeking something 'sturdier than passion'. She observed, 'God knows, I'm the most fickle woman in the world, but I've never stuck to anyone I've felt a mere *passion* for.' Her ideal was an 'affection mixed with desire', which she distinguished from love and decided was almost impossible to realise.

Not surprisingly she once advised one of her assistants: 'If you must mix work and love, put work first because it lasts and men don't. If men aren't life-enhancing, ditch them.'

Her strong views on the nature of love, relationships and friendship were underpinned by a great deal of random and eclectic reading about the nature of identity and personality. She delved into psychoanalysis and gene theory, and was particularly fascinated by the notion of archetypes – e.g. the female-slave, the colonial-builder – and of biological repression in the determination of who one loves.

In exploring the idea of similar phenotypes, she wrote: 'The important thing for any happy (or possible) relationship between two people is that they should be *the same kind* . . . My own unhappiness was due to the fact that one wasn't really sharing anything at all . . . The man I used to sleep with was perfectly satisfactory as a physical animal, but he immediately lapsed into something half-dead. It is as if the other person is drinking still lemonade while one is drinking fizzy.'

She believed there was a dialectic at work between biology and character in which certain paths that were laid down – concerning such matters as one's illnesses, profession, enemies, manner of dying as well as type of friends – had to be negotiated for good or ill.

She would cite Euripides' *Hippolytus* as an exemplary play about love, which illustrates the balance Peggy saw in life between the individual and fate. Phaedra's consuming love for her stepson Hippolytus is visited upon her by the goddess Aphrodite, resentful of the young man who is contemptuous of love. Peggy liked the fact that not only is the story usually told from Phaedra's point of view, and here the focus is on the youth, but that Euripides shows destruction stemming from a passion that is both obsessive and capricious.

Peggy was neither religious nor superstitious, but her own belief in a destiny, which she negotiated with stoical individualism, was imbued with a practical mysticism. She had a keen interest in writings and prophetic figures from the Indian sub-continent. She attended the inaugural meeting of the Gandhi Centenary Working Group in 1968 to learn more about him, and also went to meetings addressed by Krishnamurti, whom she admired as a lone crusader. She was thrilled at one gathering when he said that none of the audience understood what he was talking about and she felt that she alone did. 'The only way to be totally unambitious is to follow Krishnamurti,' she once said. 'I would dearly like to be able to have the strength to do so.'

Peggy was a classic Gemini, airy, mercurial and mutable, dual in nature, restless, inquisitive, elusive, inspirational, brilliant. She enjoyed telling the story of the fortune teller predicting that she would be a singer. She consulted the *I Ching*, which was 'used by serious, odd people, who, for some reason or other, don't trust themselves. This is so much better than people who are entirely sure of themselves.'

She was delighted when Alan Plater sent her a Craven Park greyhound racing card, along with a cutting from the local press reporting the success of a dog called Peggy. Plater had backed it in the fifth race as the 4-5 favourite and it won. Just to get the balance right, however, her own name could be a bad omen too. 'Christopher Hampton dedicated his play *Treats* to me and it was pissed on, so that'll teach him,' she said drily.

Peggy also observed that Joe Orton had sneered at an Egyptian wood-carved bird which she had showed him; it was placed on graves in order to take the souls to heaven. 'One is either superstitious or one is not,' she said. 'I don't think Joe should have laughed at it.' He was dead within two weeks.

She found it a continual struggle to renew her inner resources as she ploughed her lonely furrow. Her contempt was frequently directed at those who, through weakness, sought companionship. Yet she often observed that, because she had no opinion of herself, this deprived her of her own interior emotional support in times of crisis. When she started as an agent she felt emotionally exhausted; she had rejected the chimera of friendship and believed that her truthfulness and honesty had left her bereft. She had to grow in self-confidence, and during her years as an agent she did in fact manage to forge intense relationships, with John Holmstrom in the 1950s, for example, with David Hare in the 1970s and, latterly, with the actor, author and director, Simon Callow, in the 1980s.

Callow had appeared in the 1975 Gay Sweatshop production of *Passing By* written by Martin Sherman, a client of Peggy's, and two years later in Joint Stock's production of *Devil's Island*, written by Tony Bicât and directed by David Hare, both also clients of hers. In 1979, Callow called into

Goodwin's Court on Sherman's behalf, and he and Peggy started talking. They discovered they had shared interests in art, literature and music, and a penchant for writing letters.

Not long after this meeting, a case of vintage wine arrived for Callow at the stage door of the National Theatre where he was playing Mozart in Peter Shaffer's *Amadeus*. There was no accompanying note. The National press office telephoned a list of people whom Callow thought might have been responsible and when they reached Peggy, she said, 'Of course I sent it. I'd have thought you would have realised that.' Callow telephoned Peggy to thank her. She told him she was passing Fortnum and Mason, one of her favourite shops, and remembered it was Molière's birthday. She thought how sad it was that no one in England would be drinking his health. It then struck her that there was one person who might, and so, without a second thought, she dispatched the wine.

When Callow was appearing in J.P. Donleavy's *The Beastly Beatitudes of Balthazar B*, he wrote an article for the *Evening Standard* on his experiences and showed Peggy a draft. 'She took off her glasses,' he recalls, 'read it close to her nose, responding out loud every so often, looked up at me and said, 'why don't you write it the way you write your letters to me?" He did, and thereby began his writing career. Without asking Callow, Peggy sent Nick Hern at Methuen a transcript of a lecture he had given at Goldsmiths' College, which expanded on his Standard article, asking if Hern thought it might make a book. Hern was interested, and Peggy arranged a lunch for the three of them, at which a commission for a tome on Callow's time treading the boards was agreed. This became the much-read *Being an Actor*, published in 1985 and dedicated to Peggy.

She had announced to Callow at the very beginning of their relationship that she knew nothing of friendship – a lack of sentiment which he calls her 'monetarism of the heart.' Nevertheless, she was attracted by the 'otherness' she saw beneath his flamboyance, which came from his complex roots; a mix of German and Danish, he was born and brought up in London, with three childhood years spent in South Africa. Forty years apart in age, they became aesthetic soul mates in companionship, both Gemini, both charismatic. Like literary lovers from a bygone era, they came to enjoy a wonderful and extraordinary liaison, marked by the constant exchange of fervent letters, which, to most observers, would pass very well for the friendship about which Peggy said she knew nothing. It was one of the dominant relationships of her life, and Peggy loved him to the end.

In common with people in most walks of life, Peggy considered that true friendship should be separate and free from professional activity. She felt embarrassed that she had only met her clients because of her professional role. 'I don't want to take advantage, I only want to take 10%,' she quipped. But, with a few exceptions, like Bill Roderick or Oscar Lewenstein, who were both theatre people, who else but her clients were her friends? And what measure of friendship can there be for the energy she invested in many of her clients, for instance, telephoning David Hare almost every day for a year?

The mediation offered by the agent-client relationship seemed to suit her. It was both intimate and distanced, not being constrained by contract yet bound by concern, as it were, for a third party, the play. Being an agent to many made friendship that much more difficult, and fame, on both sides of the relationship, made isolation more likely.

Her driven quality – a directed energy that seemed to consume her as if to cheat death – found a more singular focus when she became an agent; before then, sex might have offered the possibility of the full affirmation of life that she was seeking but did not. With the agency, she put her obsessive energy, including it would seem much of her sexual drive, into the nurturing of talent.

Clients were treated like lovers; there was a period of courtship followed by consummation and then marriage when Peggy lost interest and switched affection to another talent. This cycle was repeated again and again, partly because Peggy was always staving off boredom, partly because she considered that a playwright's creative career could only last a decade, and partly because she believed that her passion, being extreme, was necessarily destructive and 'we destroy the thing we love'; when new talent became successful, it was in a sense destroyed for her and it was time to move on.

There was an inescapable sexual aspect to many of her relationships with clients, although, with the exception of Eugène Ionesco, not in the physical sense. Sexual imagery and vocabulary abounds not only in her own conversation but in the portraits of her which are drawn by those with whom she worked. She courted, flirted, titillated, had crushes, dropped favourites and moved on to new flames with boundless zeal.

Her whole comportment, her speech, her gestures, her behaviour carried a strong sexual buzz. Her throaty, 'actressy' voice was part of her armoury, and she flaunted or dwelled on the sexual implications of conversations, bordering on what one director calls 'hot chat'. She swore without a second thought.

The soaring, swooping voice, the piercing, pealing laughter that mixed delight with derision, the headlamp eyes, the windmill arms, the grand hats, the outlandish dresses, the dangling jewellery and the heavy perfume, all were elements of Peggy's make-up that signalled a determination to be her sensual, sexual self on her own terms.

She took great care over how she was turned out and looked startling when she wanted to, even when behaving eccentrically and displaying no sense of how peculiar she might appear. She had the bird-like bone structure associated with star actresses, and high cheekbones with an aquiline nose too. She wore clothes stylishly with no apparent effort. Often, she would emphasise her make-up and wear a full complement of bijouterie. At the times when she was plainer, she would be elegant still. She could act either very 'feminine' or quite un-ladylike. She could look like a schoolgirl, dressed in a pleated skirt, dotted blouse, pop sox and lace-up shoes, or appear glamorously in flowing chiffon and sequined slippers. She might be found in graceful repose on the chaise longue, her left hand playing with her pearls, her right hand holding high her head, thumb tucked under her chin and her fingers resting on her cheek. Or she might stalk her office in bare feet like a jungle creature.

Peggy was very physical with her body, crossing and uncrossing her legs constantly. She often would put her feet up on the desk, revealing her thighs, or hitch up her skirt to rub her rump over a fire; she would scratch her crotch, push up her breasts, or run her hands up and down her legs, then yank up her stockings to their furthest stretch.

She recognised the animal in herself. She saw that she was savage and ruthless as well as sensitive, and found this last quality much the most deplorable. This attitude was consistent with a certain self-deprecating objectivity that was evident in the way she saw pleasure and sex. She would talk of female genitalia in terms of 'damp, tufted areas' and 'that little flap of flesh'. It did not reflect low self-esteem but was more a matter of pitch.

Despite her liberal views on sexual activity, she disliked the pill because it 'dehumanises us and that is partly what is wrong with the world'. This attitude was related to her belief in the wholeness of the body. She was frightened that her body would let her down in her fight with death. She was careful with her diet and was a disciple of the Nobel prize winner Linus Pauling who studied the chemical basis of hereditary disease and advocated the use of vitamins. Peggy visited a noted acupuncturist, and at the time when she was diagnosed as having contracted cancer, she wanted to try self-healing and alternative medicine rather than the hated chemotherapy.

Such views were in keeping with her philosophy that 'we are all everything' and her concomitant belief concerning sex that 'we should all experience everything'. This was the standpoint from which she opposed censorship in the theatre and supported many of her clients, such as Bond, Orton, Mercer, Rudkin, Saunders, Murdoch, and Wood, who crossed swords with the Lord Chamberlain's office.

Her fascination with sex, especially after she abandoned her own active sex life, led her towards a deep interest in sexual practices considered beyond the norm of the time – sex 'on the wilder, darker edges', as she put it, like bondage or homosexual sex. One of her favourite books was the sado-masochistic novel, *The Story of O*, which she did not see as a tale of female submission. She believed its erotic impact was achieved by a style that transcended the individual, a quality she thought it shared both with Greek drama and with talent. She was not a decadent, because decadence meant a lack of commitment and a displacement of sexual energy; she was drawn more to the obsessive in sex and love, and was intrigued by the power relationships that ensued from it, such as she found, for instance, in the work of the Japanese warrior writer Mishima or in Nabokov's controversial novel, *Lolita*.

Peggy loved to talk about sex, and would sometimes 'talk dirty' with her clients on the phone. She especially enjoyed talking to gay men about sex, free of any latent sexual tension that might exist in conversations with heterosexual men, with whom she was more likely to flirt. She herself was only interested in the male role in sex and thought gay men were lucky because, in contrast to heterosexual couples, it was relatively easy for them to have sex at any time and in any place they chose. Ignoring the obvious social and legal constraints imposed on gay sex, it was a view she debated with several of her gay clients and which she found confirmed in the casual and random sexual adventures detailed in the Orton *Diaries*.

Before 1967, however, sodomy was punishable by a maximum term of life imprisonment and the various laws that aimed to punish homosexuals were applied with severity. For Peggy, this outlaw status of homosexuals added spice to her discussions with gay clients. Yet, while she found the legal repression absurd and unnecessary, she was also able to see a moral advantage in the existence of such pressures because they countered easy self-indulgence and reminded one that actions had consequences.

She did not consider homosexuality to be a sin, which was still the common viewpoint when she started her career as an agent. 'We torture ourselves with this Christian standpoint of "sin",' she wrote to one client, 'but what is sin? Provided you harm no one else, can a relationship be sinful?' When she was warned malevolently that one of her clients was a gay whore who was being kept by another writer, she disarmingly responded: 'So what? I don't mind representing a whore, if he is talented as a writer – or as a whore!'

Peggy empathised with two major aspects of the gay world that mirrored her own life, one private, one public. The private dimension centred on acute loneliness. She understood the yearning her clients would tell her about, the constant search for the 'perfect fuck' that they knew would never happen but which held them in thrall. She was not interested in the settled partnerships and preferred to concentrate on the heartbreak and the suffering, the seeming inevitability that relationships were doomed.

Yet she also understood the other side of gay life, the public elevation of the pleasure principle, with its flouting of convention and its celebration of fashion and style. She herself appeared as a camp creation, but she did not borrow her flamboyance from gay men; it came from within. She did, however, flower in their company, playing up to her audience and putting them at their ease. She was not a cross dresser – she was not interested in being a man – nor was she a 'drag queen' type or merely a 'fag hag', although she could outwardly resemble one. Once accused of exhibitionism, she replied, 'Showing off isn't one of my faults, of which I have many'. Yet, undeniably, she could be an outrageous, extravagant, exotic creature who possessed a magniloquent charisma.

She also liked discussing why women thought they could reform men sexually and was drawn to the weaknesses that were often more apparent in gay men than in their straight counterparts and which in turn could lead to more openness and emotional vulnerability.

Peggy had fewer gay clients than is often supposed, but several of her closest confidants were homosexual, in direct contrast to her lack of female friends. To Peggy, it was a man's world; she found men more interesting than women and enjoyed male company more. She had not only survived on her own in that world but had prospered. She had been forced to define her femininity so decisively so early on in her life that it had blotted out other possibilities that were arising as social change occurred.

She saw herself as very feminine but with a masculine spirit. Her view of femininity was predicated on the belief that the ability to give birth was nature's trap for women, although she believed it gave women the edge over men when it came to the balance of power in sex. She, therefore, defined her own sexuality removed from fertility, child-rearing, motherhood and family; her favourite clients – all men – were not, to her, ideal father material.

The female birth trap also meant to Peggy that women could not have children as well as a career. Once she had made her own choice, however, life did not become simple. As she wrote to John Bowen, a gay client of hers, 'Any woman is a mother, lover or governess, and it depends upon the day of the week, the time of day, the year, the events of the night preceding the morning etc. In the office I tend to be nothing but the governess because of the filthy pressure. However, all three are there all the time.' She was curious about role playing and the nature of the mask in art and in life, asking to what extent we consciously conceal parts of ourselves or give out false signals in order simply to survive.

She left conventional morality behind, as other women of her time had done, yet unlike some who might have been a model – Rebecca West, for example – Peggy did not choose to follow a bohemian life or a feminist path. 'I don't care a fig about Women's Lib for myself because there is nothing that Women's Lib can give me,' she wrote, 'but if I spent my days with my own generation, I would become militant, because the men of my generation have this deep-seated superiority, because up to now – and still, of course – men ruled the world (or they think they do, which is the same thing).'

Peggy used her sexuality to get what she wanted, yet was scornful of the ambition and achievements of feminism in its attempts to make progress for women as a whole. She did not like or understand labels and movements in any case; they smacked of special pleading, an admission of failure or weakness. She despised the weak and, in spite of the evidence of her own character, thought women generally were weaker and less able to cope than men.

Women were potential rivals; her successes – early on, in sexual matters, later, as the chief nurturer of playwriting talent – meant that she must have left various rivals vanquished in her wake. Yet she would put her success down to nothing more than endurance, and she used her strength of temperament as a shield for her despair. Her own self-deprecation may have sprung from a strategy of abnegating herself before anyone else had the chance. Paradoxically, her own professional success allowed her to extend her principle of self-renunciation to cover all of womankind. Although in practice she contradicted her own views on women, they were obstinately stuck in an experience from her far past when she determined not to be like the women she saw around her.

She detached herself from what she saw as her gender; she was not cosy and soft and did not talk incessantly about clothes. She also hated being accused of what she regarded as the worst of women's traits, such as being 'bitchy' or indiscreet, though, in fact, she was famous for both.

One of the reasons she read Schopenhauer was because she felt he knew women's limitations. She was upset, however, when a newspaper quoted her once as not liking women; it was just that she found men more interesting. Men surprised her more than women because she shared a sensibility with women and knew, therefore, how they were going to react. Men were not more admirable just more discoverable; moreover, she thought that they talked more about their private lives – as, indeed, they probably did: to her.

When asked why so many agents were women, Peggy replied, 'Maybe men have something better to do.'

She wrote to Caryl Churchill, her most successful female client, that she would like to have been an assistant to some great male director. She said she had considered becoming a director after the war but did not see it as a woman's job. There was a second reason for holding back: she felt that there were too few plays being written that could offer a director sufficient nourishment. But the main obstacle – reinforced by the lack of role models – was the prevailing view, which she shared, that the director's role was exclusively male. On another occasion, Peggy said that she would like to have been a film director; it was the total authorial control that attracted her.

In her own field, Peggy was dismissive of women as playwrights because men, she said, were spared the daily routine that imprisoned women – doing the shopping, the cooking, the laundry – and this meant that men could keep something special for their writing which women had to put into these other, domestic activities. Men were less sentimental and had more disciplined, sturdier talents while women were more concerned with trivia. To Peggy, her two best known female playwrights, Ann Jellicoe and Caryl Churchill, were honorary men.

Peggy identified positively with aspects of strong female characters in plays written by her clients. Like Peggy, these characters did not conform to stereotype either, such as Violet in Robert Bolt's *Gentle Jack*, Jenny in David Hare's *Knuckle*, Susan in his *Plenty* and, curiously, Mrs Elliot in Ted Whitehead's *Alpha Beta*. Many of her female clients were also strong women too, from Ann Jellicoe to Iris Murdoch. Although Peggy represented far fewer women than men, the number was higher than Peggy gave herself credit for; many wrote just a few plays or adaptations, some were primarily novelists, like Brigid Brophy, and literally only a handful were able to make a name for themselves as playwrights.

Peggy's survival had relied on a definition of her femininity that had guided her through the years of solo struggle and had become her bulwark against dependency on men and the dangers of mortality. Her own strength of character, however, could not destroy her inner demons. Her fear of a physical and psychological decline, and of becoming pathetic and losing control, was never put to rest. When she came face to face with one of her most extraordinary female clients, the novelist Jean Rhys, Peggy's dread came frighteningly to life.

In the mid 1960s Peggy had been called in by Rhys' editor, Diana Athill, to resolve a dispute between Peggy's old acquaintance Selma vaz Dias and Jean Rhys, a writer whose work Peggy already admired. Under the influence of drink, Rhys had signed away to vaz Dias 50 per cent of all proceeds from and sole artistic control over any dramatic adaptations of Rhys' work. Peggy saw her task as setting Rhys free.

Peggy had represented vaz Dias in 1954 when she was commissioned to adapt Rhys' 1939 novel *Good Morning Midnight* for BBC radio as a monologue for the main character Sasha. Vaz Dias was to play Sasha. She needed Rhys' permission to make the broadcast and had tried in vain to find her. It seemed as if she had disappeared at the start of the Second World War and had not been heard of since. The BBC's attempts to locate her whereabouts came up with nothing except a rumour that she had died in Paris. Vaz Dias tried one last throw and placed an advertisement in the *New Statesman*. Rhys, who was living in Beckenham, Kent, read it, made contact and the performance finally went ahead.

The broadcast in 1957 signalled not only the 'resurrection' of Jean Rhys but also a revival in her writing, which resulted in the completion of *Wide Sargasso Sea*, often regarded as her finest achievement. Peggy was approached to mediate between vaz Dias and Rhys as publication of the novel became imminent. Peggy persuaded vaz Dias to change the agreement by reducing her share to a third and waiving her rights over artistic control. An ugly situation, which had led the publishers to take legal advice, had been defused and an acceptable solution, however imperfect, had been found. With much thanks to Peggy, *Wide Sargasso Sea* was published in 1966, and Peggy was asked to handle the film rights.

Peggy had read all of Rhys' books and felt as if they shared a past. Both had come to England as young women having been brought up in what to English tastes were exotic countries with oppressed majority black and coloured populations – in Rhys' case Dominica. Peggy was part Jewish and there was a strong suggestion that Rhys had 'black blood' in her ancestry. They both loved Paris; they had both appeared in touring shows; both were handsome in an unconventional sense, had a keen sense of wickedness and fun, and lived for the moment behind various masks beyond the reach of friends. Peggy even said, enigmatically, that they shared the same lover and the same abortionist.

Rhys' mix of mystery, madness and rage struck a chord with Peggy, who was almost 20 years her junior, but she was not taken with the passive side of Rhys, the romantic victim. When Peggy finally met her in the early 1970s, only a few years before Rhys died, Peggy was shocked by what she saw. Peggy described Rhys, then in her eighties, as a painted doll, dressed in brocade, primped up against cushions and still trying to lure men. She had asked Peggy to take her a couple of bottles of gin, which duty Peggy had gladly fulfilled yet then regretted.

The image Rhys presented of decayed femininity scared Peggy profoundly. Rhys had let her life drift out of control and sat staring back at Peggy like her very own picture of Dorian Gray; this is what Peggy might have become if she had let go, might still become if she did not hold on. Peggy saw mortality mock her. In her fright she became utterly contemptuous of Rhys, the writer whom she so admired, as if disgust might ward off the terrible fate that Rhys' frail figure presaged.

Chapter Seven

At Court

'You can manipulate luck, but not talent.'

PEGGY'S LONGEVITY as an agent was a tribute to her remarkable powers of self-regeneration. Staying in the same job in the same building represented the very stability, which to her, in other contexts, spelled death. She, therefore, had constantly to renew and develop, which was a struggle, and the way she did that was to find and nurture young talent, which was scarce.

What Peggy enjoyed most was being able to mould a writing career from the very start, and in the 1960s at her prime she was able to do this with ever younger talent. The cult of youth was carving its way through staid English society and what was considered young was readjusted downwards with each succeeding wave of juvenile achievement. But unlike the purveyors of the new youth culture, which fed on and was fed by marketing and image-making, she did not see herself as a magician, conjuring fame and fortune out of surface impressions. A playwright had to have talent to begin with, as well as the mettle to apply the talent to the exacting task, not just of writing one stage play, but another and then another. It was hard graft.

With the arrival in February 1966 of a script, entitled *When Did You Last See My Mother?* from a twenty-year-old Oxford University undergraduate called Christopher Hampton, Peggy was able to pursue her cherished grail with renewed vigour as she turned his youthful dream of becoming a writer into a mature reality.

Hampton had been writing since he was eight years old. He had written a novel while still at school, and, when it was rejected by a publisher, he had turned to playwriting. Hampton had done nothing with *When Did You Last See My Mother?* until, in his second year at Oxford, he decided to enter

245

it for a competition. Although Hampton's play did not win, when another play that had been chosen by the judges proved too expensive to stage, he was offered a production in its stead. It was well reviewed and brought him several letters from interested agents.

Not sure how to proceed in the face of these offers, Hampton asked his tutor for advice, who suggested he approach Elizabeth Sweeting, the administrator at the Oxford Playhouse, about choosing an agent. She recommended Peggy, whom she had known since her early days at the Playhouse in the mid-1950s. A script was duly dispatched to Goodwin's Court and a couple of weeks later Hampton was summoned to London. Peggy interrogated him, telling him in strident tones what was wrong with *When Did You Last See My Mother?*, in which two former public schoolboys in bedsit land strive to come to terms with their adolescent sexuality as they wait to go to university; they love each other but find this truth hard to acknowledge. One has an affair with the other's mother, who subsequently commits suicide. Peggy recalled that the play 'was so impertinent. He wasn't at all a good writer and he didn't know about women. It took him years to learn.' Yet she liked what she perceived to be a seriousness about his work and was taken enough with Hampton to offer to represent him.

Peggy wrote to Hampton with incontrovertible sagacity: 'You will find that the work you write at Oxford is unlikely to be the best work you will write, and if you can manage to work slowly and steadily, developing all the time, you will go much further than if you try to run too fast and get labelled as a scrappy immature author.'

She warned him against the pitfall of early praise, and finished with a familiar refrain: 'It is really not just a matter of talent – it is a matter of character as well.' It was both a chastening and an exhilarating response. It cut him down to size and encouraged him at one and the same time, says Hampton. The memory of its profound impact remained with him over the decades as he worked 'slowly and steadily, developing all the time' to become an internationally acclaimed writer of stage and screen plays.

Hampton remembers that Peggy was cautious about his immediate prospects. There were not many outlets for such a play as his, in her view; the Arts Theatre 'is simply an empty shell hired for money', she wrote, but the play could be sent to Michael Codron or to Michael White ('superb taste but hates parting with money and it's almost impossible to get an option out of him'), or it might be suitable for a season the Edinburgh Traverse Theatre was due to run at the Jeanetta Cochrane (where *Loot* was to be produced later in 1966).

Codron was considering taking over a long lease on a West End theatre and was discussing a possible partnership with the Royal Court under William Gaskill, who was exploring such a link because of poor box-office takings at the Sloane Square theatre occasioned by what Peggy considered 'a rather bad choice of plays'. The Royal Court, she said to Hampton, was a good theatre for his kind of play, but she was worried that it might moulder there.

A month passed. No news. Hampton was studying in Oxford unaware of the fate of his play. He was then interrupted one day in his college rooms by a somewhat disgruntled porter, who announced grumpily that there was a telephone call for him. It was rare for a porter to bring such a message to an undergraduate and was a departure from college protocol usually associated only with the gravest of news, such as a death in the family. Hampton followed the porter to the telephone. It was Peggy. 'They're putting your play on at the Royal Court. You'd better get down here,' she bellowed.

Hampton was told later that *When Did You Last See My Mother?* had been rejected by a reader, whose criticisms had been passed on to Peggy. She had exploded and brow-beaten Gaskill into reconsidering. At this point, one of the Royal Court's young assistants, Robert Kidd, asked Gaskill if he could direct it and Gaskill agreed. Kidd was looking for a chance to try his hand at directing and had spotted the script lying in the out-tray. The Court did not tell Hampton that Kidd had never directed before; Hampton did not tell the Court he had never seen any work at their famous address.

Gaskill, who says he found *When Did You Last See My Mother?* one of the most attractive first plays he had ever read, gave it two Sunday night performances in June 1966, directed by Kidd. It was very much a young person's event; Kidd was 22, the main actor, Victor Henry, was 21, and Hampton himself was still only 20. Michael Codron transferred the play the following month to the West End, a journey no first play had made before from the Royal Court. Hampton was hailed as the youngest playwright of modern times to have a play in the West End. Some critics echoed Gaskill's own assessment and regarded *When Did You Last See My Mother?* as the finest first play written since the war. The *Times* critic wrote: 'I do not care whether Mr Hampton is 18 or 80, there are things in his work that would be magnificently moving, beautifully understanding, revealing and compassionate for any age.'

The successful commercial transfer sealed a remarkable initiation into the world of theatre for Hampton, all within six months of Peggy's receiving the script. *When Did You Last See My Mother?* turned out to be a seed bed for three of Hampton's later plays: *Total Eclipse*, *Treats*, and his highly renowned *Les Liaisons Dangereuses*. His partnership with Kidd was to extend to five more plays and was cut short in 1980 by Kidd's death from a long-standing pancreatic illness at the age of 37.

Hampton's next work to appear at the Royal Court, in October 1967, was his adaptation of *Marya* by Isaac Babel, one of Stalin's many victims, which was chosen by the theatre to mark the 50th anniversary of the Russian Revolution. Then, in September 1968, came *Total Eclipse*, a drama centred on the passionate, destructive love affair between the dazzling teenage poet Arthur Rimbaud and the married poet, almost twice his age, Paul Verlaine. The play had already been taking shape in Hampton's mind when he made his début at the Royal Court. He wrote *Total Eclipse* during a year that he spent in mainland Europe as a break in his university studies.

Peggy thoroughly approved of this year abroad, not only because it took Hampton to her beloved France but also because it matched her romantic notion of writers working in kitchens or night clubs in the Henry Miller-George Orwell vein. Although Hampton was born in the Azores and brought up as a child in Aden and Egypt, which made him an outsider like Peggy and gave him an objective eye, she felt he was very inexperienced. He had not even had to undergo national service, which had been abolished in 1962.

She both adored the idea of a play based on Rimbaud and Verlaine's relationship and considered Hampton too young to write it. When the script arrived, she thought he had spent too much time researching it rather than living it. She found it too long and not nearly as substantial as it ought to be. She helped him refine the play and subsequently campaigned hard for it to be produced.

Codron had commissioned it but did not want to take it up. Peggy sent it to the Royal Court, which, after a while, appeared to be prevaricating. Peggy sent *Total Eclipse* to the Hampstead Theatre as a competitive spur to the Royal Court and involuntarily produced a scene reminiscent of an episode in Bulgakov's novel *Black Snow*. Bill Gaskill and Robert Kidd were prompted to visit Hampton unexpectedly in Oxford and made him read them the script out loud. They then scheduled the play, which played for three weeks at the Royal Court.

It was directed by Robert Kidd and designed by Patrick Procktor, whose line drawing of Joe Orton, naked except for his socks, was to adorn both Orton's novel, *Head to Toe*, when it was published posthumously, and John Lahr's biography of Orton, *Prick Up Your Ears*. For *Total Eclipse*, Procktor produced watercolour portraits of the two lead actors, John Grillo as

Verlaine and Victor Henry as Rimbaud, in a special programme that included poems by the two poets translated by Hampton. It was financed by Codron and became a collector's item after 1,000 were bought up in the middle of the run.

The production earned itself an unsought footnote in the history of the Royal Court. The theatre had been in the vanguard of the campaign to end the censorship powers of the Lord Chamberlain, and it was during the run of *Total Eclipse* that the legislation was finally passed.

Hampton had been unhappy while writing *Total Eclipse*, which Peggy said was to be expected and no bad thing. She had also warned him of 'second play syndrome'. After the outstanding success of his first play, which clearly bore the stamp of personal experience, she said the critics would be waiting to see if he was a 'one-off' writer without a wider vision. The critical response suggested that this was indeed what they thought. The play did 60% business and did not transfer. Hampton was brought down to earth.

'As a second play,' Peggy commented, 'it does not live up to the promise of the first in the eyes of the critics and so suffered and was a let down.' While Peggy liked the play, and preferred it to *When Did You Last See My Mother?*, she thought that this deflation was good experience for Hampton and would stand him in good stead later when he had come through the current difficult period.

Total Eclipse always held a special place in Peggy's affections. She even uncharacteristically threw first night parties after both its original and its second London productions.

She went into overdrive to get the second London production mounted, in 1981 at the Lyric, Hammersmith. She was staying with Hampton one weekend, and it came up in conversation that he would love to see the play revived. Peggy immediately telephoned David Hare, Simon Callow and Peter James, who ran the Lyric. Hare, who happened to have been a contemporary of Hampton's at the same school, was to direct. Her friend Callow was to play Verlaine. Within three weeks rehearsals had begun and a month after that the production had opened. 'The revival,' says Hare, 'brought back memories for Peggy of Hampton as a young man and of what theatre was all about.'

The critics were more generous than at the play's first outing yet a fine, elegiac production played to only 40% capacity. Peggy kept Michael Coveney's *Financial Times* review, blown up and framed, displayed on the stairs in Goodwin's Court. An 'exquisite and impeccable revival does full justice to one of the best plays of its generation,' he wrote – and Peggy agreed.

When Peggy had first met Hampton, she had, he remembers, in an action familiar to many clients, 'plunged into her handbag and produced a fistful of notes, asking me if I needed money, *dear*. I declined but didn't know if it was a test or not, or if I had passed it or not.' Peggy interpreted his refusal as a healthy lack of interest in success and linked this to his commitment to work rather than considering the possibility that he might be a reasonably well-supported student.

Hampton had also turned down a commission in order to finish his university studies. Peggy supported the idea of his staying on at college to aim for a first in French and German, which he duly achieved in the summer of 1968, not long before rehearsals began for the Royal Court production of *Total Eclipse*. Peggy said that in order to dissuade him from further study, and to help him continue writing, Gaskill agreed to make Hampton the Royal Court's first resident dramatist.

Gaskill remembers offering him the job on the spur of the moment while the two of them were having a drink in the bar of the Royal Court's Theatre Upstairs. Hampton was installed as literary manager too; 'the first time,' Gaskill recalls, 'we'd had someone on the staff who could read both French and German.'

Not only was Hampton represented by the foremost play agent, he was now a paid employee of the foremost new writing theatre. During his time on the payroll there, the Royal Court presented, as well as *Total Eclipse*, his adaptation of Chekhov's *Uncle Vanya*, directed by Anthony Page, and his self-styled bourgeois comedy *The Philanthropist*, a riposte to Molière's *Le Misanthrope*.

Gaskill accepted *The Philanthropist* almost immediately and was set to direct it, yet, despite Peggy's attempts to galvanise the management into action, it took a year for the play to be produced. It became embroiled in the internal wrangles of the theatre, which, at the time, was being run by a triumvirate of Gaskill, Page and Lindsay Anderson.

Robert Kidd came into the picture again, which Peggy found troubling because he had a drink problem. He had not directed at the Royal Court since *Total Eclipse* and had returned to his native Scotland to work. Kidd was hired nonetheless, Michael Codron co-produced, and Alec McCowen played the eponymous philologist, whose catchphrase from the play became 'My trouble is that I'm a man of no conviction – at least I *think* I am.' *The Philanthropist* was a triumph. It played to nearly 90% capacity and transferred to the Mayfair Theatre in the West End, where it ran for three years.

This success, and its resulting financial rewards, made Peggy anxious that Hampton might follow the path of Robert Bolt; she warned Hampton against indolence and enjoying himself too much. Her fears seemed to be realised when his next three productions were all of adaptations, two Ibsens (*Hedda Gabler* and *A Doll's House*) and a Molière (*Don Juan*), rather than of his own new plays.

'At first Peggy couldn't see the nourishment in translating,' says Hampton. 'I knew I could only do one original play every three years or so. Adapting or translating pays the bills and it also feeds into my original work, for example, *Tales from the Vienna Woods* [adapted from the play by Ödön von Horváth, produced at the National Theatre, 1977] fed into *Tales from Hollywood* [an original play, also produced at the National Theatre, in 1983].

'She was easily exasperated and found it difficult to get used to my own rhythm of creating. *The Philanthropist* was unlike my earlier two plays and that surprised Peggy. When I wrote *Savages* [dealing with European complicity in the genocide of Brazilian Indians, produced at the Royal Court in 1973], it was different again, and she understood that she wouldn't know what to expect from me. Her main frustration was waiting so long for the surprise. She feared I'd drift from theatre, so she lectured me on sticking to the theatre and on writing more.'

Hampton has continued throughout his career alternating new plays with translations or adaptations, but it is a practice with which Peggy was never completely happy. 'We argued fiercely over non-original work,' recalls Hampton. 'Peggy became more relaxed about it as time went on because she was less interested in me when I was more successful, but I think she still thought it a waste.'

In one case, it was Peggy who unknowingly embroiled Hampton in a translation, albeit after she had died. Peggy had sent Hampton an early play by Yasmina Reza, whom she represented, after she had interested the director Howard Davies, who was running the RSC's Warehouse Theatre, in it. Nothing came of this but years later, in the mid-1990s, Hampton was staying in Paris just around the corner from a theatre where Reza's play *Art* was showing. He remembered her name, went to see the production, and decided he would like to translate it, which he did. The English version opened in the West End in 1996 and was an immediate hit.

Much to Hampton's irritation, Peggy claimed that it was she who had inspired his adaptation of the late 18th-century epistolary novel, *Les Liaisons Dangereuses*. It was a favourite book of hers and became Hampton's most successful play to date. Hampton, however, says it was not Peggy who brought it to his attention.

Peggy did encourage Hampton to write an adaptation, but it had been a set text when he was a student and since then had been a favourite book of his as well. Hampton had often thought of adapting this book by Choderlos de Laclos and had offered to do so for the National Theatre, but was turned down. When the RSC asked Hampton if he would like a commission after successfully translating *Tartuffe* for the company in 1983, he put forward a couple of ideas, including the Laclos. He was surprised to learn that the RSC had already staged a version, at the Aldwych Theatre in 1962 adapted as *The Art of Seduction* by John Barton, another client of Peggy's. Hampton's approach was sufficiently different and the time gap sufficiently large for this not to be a problem and *Les Liaisons Dangereuses* was commissioned.

It started its theatrical life in 1985 in The Other Place, the RSC's small theatre in Stratford-upon-Avon, directed by Howard Davies, with Lindsay Duncan, Alan Rickman, Juliet Stevenson and Fiona Shaw in the cast. *Les Liaisons Dangereuses* travelled, via The Pit at the RSC's London base, to the West End, New York, many other capital cities around the world and eventually the cinema, garnering awards on the way for several of its participants. Peggy even negotiated a better deal than Hampton had expected for the film, *Dangerous Liaisons*, which opened in 1988, directed by Stephen Frears. The extraordinary success of the play and particularly the film was a surprise both to Hampton and to Peggy, and changed the careers of many of those involved. Hampton won an Oscar for the screenplay, and, much as Bolt had done before him, switched more of his creative energy thereafter into the world of celluloid, although without deserting the theatre to the extent that Robert Bolt had.

Hampton took on a film agent in Los Angeles in the early 1980s, which greatly upset Peggy. She seemed startled when Hampton quoted back at Peggy her own views on cinema and explained that he had made the move simply because, by her own admission, she was not especially bothered about films yet he needed someone who knew the American film scene well. The agent concerned agreed to share commission equally with Peggy and to consult her on all deals, but Peggy remained ruffled.

'Peggy simply didn't enjoy films,' says Hampton, 'and a lot of her attitudes were bound up with her early experiences with Bolt, who was held up as an example of what not to become. Nevertheless, she gave me a lot of good advice about films, especially on working with David Lean [on the film script of Joseph Conrad's *Nostromo*. The project fell through, but the script was eventually published.].'

Hampton's main relationship with Peggy was conducted on the telephone rather than by correspondence. There were many periods when she would call daily. Hampton found her useful to talk to about his work when he needed advice. 'I got stuck on the ending of *White Chameleon* [a partly autobiographical play produced at the National Theatre in 1991],' says Hampton, 'and what she said helped me think about it in a different way. She didn't give me specific advice, although she would have done if that is what I had asked her for. She helped me to organise the material and that's what I needed.

'I didn't show my plays to her as I went along so I wasn't as much fun for her as other clients. I was wary of her strong pronouncements – they were very seductive because they were so definite, but for that very reason you might get stuck with them. The problem was she could be as dangerously wrong as she could be splendidly right.'

Hampton had achieved his breakthrough at the youngest age of any of the writers she had then nurtured; another Oxford student, David Rudkin, for example, was approaching his 26th birthday when *Afore Night Come* first opened in London. For Peggy, she always remembered Hampton as a young talent. What she enjoyed most was the process of establishing him, which she did at a time when she was secure both in her pre-eminence as an agent and in her own image of herself. There was a difference of nearly 40 years in their ages and as huge a disparity in the social and cultural contexts in which they grew up   Hampton was a student in the fabled era of the late 1960s and symbolised the first generation that had enjoyed the growth of higher education without having to face national service.

For Hampton, Peggy was the single biggest influence on his writing career. He, like many others, tolerated her unique and volatile temperament because of that debt.

*

'For the first ten years when I was an agent, the Court
was the only theatre that mattered to me.'

Hampton's success was built on the back of his first decade in the theatre. It was a time when he was associated most closely with the Royal Court, where seven productions of his plays were staged between 1966 and 1976. In Peggy's view, the Royal Court was, and remained still, the most important outlet for serious new writing, and Peggy had become for the Royal Court the most important and influential of writers' agents.

Peggy

The Royal Court under the banner of the English Stage Company was the standard bearer of the new drama and had grown as Peggy had grown. She had come to know successive artistic directors and their colleagues well, and she was listened to by them in a way that no other agent was. The Royal Court even became her local theatre from 1969 to 1978 when she lived nearby in Culford Mansions, just off the King's Road behind Sloane Square.

While for Peggy, John Osborne was the soul of the Royal Court, she knew that George Devine was its guiding hand, without whom it would burst apart. Peggy and Devine were of similar age – she was two-and-a-half years older – and they had acting in common, as they did with playwrights such as Osborne, Pinter and later Ayckbourn. This produced a certain camaraderie and unspoken mutual respect.

Peggy and Devine shared a love of French culture, and of Beckett in particular, and an antagonism towards whingeing, all forms of self-promotion, moral cowardice and being fashionable. Both could be tough but kind, practical yet romantic. Devine, it appears, took her absolutely seriously and recognised that they were battling on the same side. He was wary of 'Peggy-worship' among either her clients or his colleagues, and he could be rather guarded about her, finding her passion a little over-heated; he did not want to be trapped on the telephone with her for too long. He was more comfortable in the male redoubt that he had created at the Court.

She found him 'a curiously interesting man . . . I always feel a bit bruised after a session with him as he's *rough*, but it's rather nice to be able to be rough back and not be misunderstood.'

She had hoped to place Robert Bolt in Devine's first season in 1956 but was not able to. It then took some time for her to establish a close association with the Court. She was not an important figure in Devine's early years – no agent was – but she made an impact through her representation of Ann Jellicoe and, more vociferously, her championing of Ionesco. As well as those two writers and Ionesco's translator, Donald Watson, the list of her clients whose work was presented under Devine, either in Sunday night productions without décor or in the main auditorium, extended chronologically from the first – another translator Dudley Fitts, in 1957 – through John McGrath, Donald Howarth, Harry Cookson, Christopher Logue, Derek Prouse, Fernando Arrabal, and Barbara Wright to Derek Marlowe, Lindsay Anderson, Keith Johnstone, and Henry Livings.

By the time Devine retired at the end of 1964, Peggy was well established as a force at the Court, even if she had yet to represent a significant number of their major playwrights. If she telephoned, she was put through immediately. Any plays sent by her were read quickly. Peter Gill, an assistant director under Devine, recalls being dispatched by Devine to Stoke-on-Trent to see a Peter Terson play immediately on receipt of a letter from Peggy extolling its merits.

Peggy was both elated and exasperated by the Royal Court. She knew its importance both as bricks and mortar, without which the new drama could not flourish, and as a magnet for creative talent – directors, designers, and actors as well as playwrights. Yet it had a propensity towards self-destruction. It had been riven by factions ever since the founding of the English Stage Company. Devine had had to work to an artistic committee for his first three years and only achieved independence in 1959.

In these early years the Court survived on a miserly public subsidy, until 1963 ranging between £5,000 and £8,000, though not always being increased annually. In 1963, the subsidy took a leap to £20,000 and in 1964 to £32,500. Peggy was worried that without Devine at the helm the economics would not improve and the factions at the Court would tear it apart. She feared a new self-righteous orthodoxy that, after Devine, might turn the Court into a citadel of snobbery, which would be unable to renew itself through new challenges. She recognised the need for group solidarity ('holding hands in the dark', she called it), but did not feel that the Court should erect a sign saying 'Keep out, we've got enough talent.'

The succession to Devine was problematic, as subsequent appointments of artistic directors turned out to be. His heir apparent, William Gaskill, was working at the National Theatre and declined to return to Sloane Square just then. Anthony Page succeeded Devine as artistic director in the autumn of 1964 for a year. He was very close to Peggy, often soliciting her advice. He would invite her to run-throughs of plays and seek her response afterwards even if the plays were not written by her clients. John Osborne's *Inadmissible Evidence* was an example. She did not care for the play much yet thought the performance of Nicol Williamson might 'drive the play over the footlights'. She sent back her first night tickets, partly because she had already seen the production and did not like opening nights, and partly because she had been seated amidst the critics, deliberately, she believed, with a view to her influencing them. She felt the Court and Osborne 'should stand on their own feet – I want to keep all my energies for my clients, who need it even more than Osborne does.'

In the autumn of 1965, Gaskill was ready to become artistic director, a job he held until 1972, during which time Peggy rose to her ascendancy. Peggy helped Gaskill through what was a difficult first period, especially after the appointment in 1966 of his new associate Desmond O'Donovan. Peggy was upset when he rejected Joe Orton as amoral and not, therefore, a Court writer, yet he did allow Peter Gill to stage *The Ruffian on the Stair* and *The Erpingham Camp*.

As an artist, she thought that Gaskill was special, but on the business side she felt he lacked directness, yet she valued the care and money he spent on serving writers. Peggy felt that Gaskill did not understand sufficiently what it meant to manage a theatre, that he had to be a diplomat as well as a director. Nonetheless, she thought he should follow his own instinct and ignore the prompting of the outside world.

She was particularly thrilled by his controversial 1966 production of *Macbeth*, starring Alec Guinness and Simone Signoret, which was played with bright light throughout on an empty sandpaper box set designed by Christopher Morley – a design that was to become the model for the RSC's later 'white box' style. 'I was moved to find the Japanese theatre of my youth before my eyes,' she wrote to the critic Harold Hobson, 'with, for instance the astonishing beauty of the three weird sisters and the porter – these figures came from the Gengi Monogatari, as did the conception of the production as a whole. I don't know whether Bill Gaskill intended this, but the fact is that his imagination is global and not insular.'

In 1966, Gaskill re-introduced the Court's schools scheme, which, a year later, became the Young People's Theatre Scheme under the direction of Jane Howell. Several of Peggy's clients wrote for the YPTS, including Edward Bond in 1979 with *The Worlds*. In its inaugural season, Howell resurrected *The Rising Generation*, a pageant that Ann Jellicoe had been commissioned to write by the Girl Guides for their 50th anniversary. It showed an Amazonian ghoul, which oversees the extirpation of the male population and combusts in a nuclear holocaust that destroys all life as it is known. The Guides had rejected the pageant as unsuitable. Jellicoe reworked it for Howell, reducing the numbers involved from 900 to 150.

From 1969 until 1972, Gaskill ran the Court in various combinations of decision-making with Lindsay Anderson and Anthony Page, joined later by Peter Gill as associate director; Peggy said she would be surprised if more than two of them were ever in the same room together. During this period, Gaskill opened the Theatre Upstairs, which embraced the new wave of radical young artists before the Court fell out with them under Anderson's sway.

Under Gaskill, another dozen or so of Peggy's clients had seen their work presented at the Royal Court. The major beneficiaries were David Cregan, a Hertfordshire schoolteacher and writer home-grown by the Royal Court whose play *A Comedy of the Changing Years* opened the Theatre Upstairs in February 1969; Charles Wood, though he was not originally a

Royal Court playwright; Christopher Hampton; Donald Howarth, whose play *Three Months Gone* featuring Diana Dors transferred to the West End in 1970; E.A. Whitehead, whose play *The Foursome* became the first to transfer from the Theatre Upstairs to the West End, in 1971, and was followed in 1972 by a transfer to the West End of *Alpha Beta* from the downstairs auditorium; and another home-grown Royal Court writer, Edward Bond, with whose early work Gaskill was himself intimately connected as a director. Bond, who had no agent when the Court first staged his work, joined Peggy after *Saved* had sent its reverberations through theatre and society.

Gaskill liked Peggy; they shared a hard and emphatic 'black or white' streak, although his determination was expressed much more quietly. He was also chary of her reputation as 'she who must be obeyed' and as an outsider who might manipulate the Court. He recalls her as generous and affable, though often irritating. 'She had the habit of finishing your sentences for you if you hesitated, and she always got the ending wrong. It was a bit alarming, but I liked her 'contradictoriness'. She *was* a power. She was on the side of the writers. She was responding to what was happening and she *did* care, and how many other agents do *that*?'

Peggy's friend Oscar Lewenstein became artistic director after Gaskill's departure, which marked the end of the George Devine era. Although Lewenstein had been a founder member of the English Stage Company, he represented a different strand, more commercial, more popular. There was a continuity, however, in that Peggy's clients continued to be the single most vital source of the Royal Court's programme. The links between the Court and Peggy were extremely close in this period. Writers who had no agent were advised by the Court to approach Peggy, and she in turn would regularly send her new plays to the Court.

The centre-piece for Peggy of Lewenstein's regime was the 1975 season of three Orton plays, *Entertaining Mr Sloane*, *Loot* and the rehabilitated *What the Butler Saw*. Of particular note also was the début in the Theatre Upstairs in 1974 of David Lan with *Bird Child*, and downstairs, the same year, of Mustapha Matura with *Play Mas*, directed by Donald Howarth, which transferred to the West End, the first such success by a Caribbean playwright. Caryl Churchill made her first appearance at the Court, Upstairs in 1972, with *Owners*, and then downstairs in 1975 with *Objections to Sex and Violence*. With Peggy's help, Howard Brenton had received his first production downstairs in 1972, with *Magnificence*, although he had not yet joined her.

In addition, under Lewenstein, his two literary managers, Ann Jellicoe and Donald Howarth, and two of his resident dramatists, Mustapha

Matura and Caryl Churchill, were all clients of Peggy's too. Both Matura and Churchill were 'firsts' for the Royal Court – the first black resident writer and the first woman resident writer.

Lewenstein says Peggy was 'miles ahead of the other agents. I can't think of another agent in England whose opinion would carry as much weight. If you took away Peggy, where would you go?'

The continuity held firm under Lewenstein's successors, Nicholas Wright and Robert Kidd, who were joint artistic directors from mid 1975 to the end of 1976, and under Stuart Burge, who ran the theatre for the next two years, 1977-79. Of Peggy's clients to be presented under these two regimes, Wallace Shawn made a significant début Upstairs in 1979 and seven were debutants downstairs, Peter Gill in 1976, Tony Bicât, John McGrath (with his company 7:84 Scotland) and Thomas Kilroy (with a production from the Abbey Theatre, Dublin) in 1977, Peter Barnes and Leigh Jackson in 1978, and Martin Sherman in 1979. Burge was succeeded by Max Stafford-Clark, who was the incumbent at the time of Peggy's death.

*

'The trouble with being "with it" is that this is the step before being "without it", i.e. the only place an "in" person can go is "out".'

In the Gaskill period, the outstanding playwriting figure was undoubtedly Edward Bond. Born in north London in 1934 and educated at the local state school, he had undertaken national service and a variety of jobs when, in 1958, he submitted two plays, *Klaxon in Atreus' Place* and *The Fiery Tree*, to the Royal Court. Although they were not performed, he was invited to join the Writers' Group, which included John Arden, David Cregan, Ann Jellicoe, Wole Soyinka, and Arnold Wesker. Bond also became a regular play reader for the theatre. In 1962 his own play, *The Pope's Wedding*, was given a Sunday evening performance, on the strength of which George Devine commissioned a new play from him. This turned out to be *Saved*. It had been scheduled for another Sunday night, when Gaskill read it and decided to stage it as part of his first season as artistic director in late 1965.

Saved had to be presented as a club performance because the Lord Chamberlain had demanded severe cuts, including the complete removal of two scenes, and Bond had refused. The play stirred much controversy, mostly related to the scene in which a baby is stoned to death in its pram by some men in a park. Despite the apparent protection of using the club strategy, the theatre was successfully prosecuted on a technicality several months after *Saved* had finished its run. A token fine of £50 was imposed and the defendants – the Court's licensee, Alfred Esdaile, the company secretary, Greville Poke, and Gaskill – were conditionally discharged for a year and ordered to pay 50 guineas costs. *Saved* was the last play to be prosecuted by the Lord Chamberlain and had to wait until 1969 for its first professional production to be offered openly to the British public.

Peggy first made contact with Bond just before *Saved* was performed. She had been approached by play agents abroad who had heard of Bond and assumed, because of his Royal Court connection, that Peggy was sure to be his agent. Peggy rang the theatre only to discover that he did not have an agent. She wrote to him c/o the theatre and offered to pass on to him any enquiry she received. Or, she wrote, 'we could ask alternatively whether you would allow us to read your play [*Saved*] and then come to you suggesting that we might represent you in areas which you require, provided we honestly feel that we could be of real service to you and offer you sufficient enthusiasm.

'It would be nice to find an author who just doesn't want an agent,' she continued. 'I am personally torn between thinking agents parasites, and thinking the work they do is worth very much more than the 10% they demand. You may have very firm ideas on this subject! Anyway we leave it to you to answer this letter any way you wish, or not answer it at all.'

Bond says that he had read somewhere that Bernard Shaw did not have an agent, and thought, therefore, that he would try to do without one as well. He replied to Peggy that he did not think an agent could be of any use to him professionally and that he would not be able to offer an agent any profitable work, especially one who doubted the justification for her professional existence – an attitude which, however, he found charming.

Peggy, in response, picked up on this theme. 'I have not read your play, so I can't possibly whore after your talent (which is, oddly enough, the one interesting thing in being an agent).' Given her avowed refusal to poach, this reflection reveals another of Peggy's frustrations with the job. She concluded the letter with reference to the rumours that had already begun to circulate about *Saved* and which, in just over a month's time after it had opened, would become the currency of the public debate it aroused.

'I hear the play is very violent. I do hope the audience isn't going to behave as if it is attending a public hanging. I remember at the first night at Stratford East when they played the Behan play [*The Quare Fellow*], I happened to be sitting in the first row of the circle and looked around at the faces hanging over the balustrade and they were all grinning like lunatics

– getting a kick *out of* the hanging. Well, it certainly isn't such a long time since Tyburn, and we certainly haven't changed our natures. I greatly look forward to seeing what *kind* of play you have written and what effect you want it to have, and what effect it actually has. An author has this marvellous power to communicate to people – a sort of secret which isn't in the words of the plot. I do envy you this power.'

The following year, after Bond had revised the Middleton play *A Chaste Maid in Cheapside* for Gaskill at the Royal Court, he wrote the screenplay for *Blow Up*, which was to be filmed by Michelangelo Antonioni. 'I felt that I was ripped off over the film,' says Bond, 'so I went to Peggy, took up her offer and she began to represent me.'

Peggy remained Bond's agent from there on, handling an immense span of work that ranged from his remaining Royal Court premières – *Early Morning, Lear, The Sea, The Fool* – to his plays for the two national companies, such as *The Bundle, The Woman,* and *The War Plays,* and the achievements of his period of 'internal exile', when, while celebrated abroad but not at home as one of the world's major playwrights, he created a body of work, both theoretical and practical, aimed more at posterity than the present.

At the beginning of their relationship, Peggy was immediately thrown into the controversy over *Saved,* which had acted as a focus for the widespread dissatisfaction that was felt at the Lord Chamberlain's powers of censorship. A joint committee of both Houses of Parliament had been set up to investigate, and in June 1967 it recommended the abolition of those powers.

The Royal Court, which had just staged Bond's version of Chekhov's *The Three Sisters,* was about to announce for limited club performance in January 1968 Bond's next new play, *Early Morning.* Gaskill knew the dangers. The play, a critique of the repressive legacy of Victorian values and a dream-like exploration of individual freedom, attacked real historical figures, both royal and political, at a time when it was still impermissible to portray living members of the royal family on stage. It not only combined murder, revolution and cannibalism, it had Florence Nightingale as the lover of Queen Victoria. Gaskill could take heart from the welcome recommendation of the select committee, yet, with the year's conditional discharge only recently completed, the Court faced the prospect of a repeat of the legal experience over *Saved.* The theatre was also on the verge of producing two more plays that had been attacked by the Lord Chamberlain: Jean-Claude van Itallie's *America Hurrah* and Charles Wood's *Dingo.* Neither was prosecuted, although *America Hurrah* was not permitted to transfer to the Vaudeville Theatre in the West End and *Dingo* played there instead.

Gaskill decided to proceed with the production of *Early Morning* and, with *America Hurrah* playing at the Court, made the announcement that August. By November, when *Dingo* opened, the decision looked doomed. The government proposed to drop the Bill to end theatre censorship, because of the volume of other legislation, and the Lord Chamberlain's office returned *Early Morning* with the script unmarked, accompanied by the terse comment: 'His Lordship would not allow it.' The whole play had been banned.

To make matters worse, the Arts Council threatened to withhold its grant to the theatre. Good news came a week later when the MP who had chaired the Select Committee, George Strauss, won a place in the Commons ballot for the right to introduce a Private Member's Bill. Two days later, after talking to the Home Secretary, Strauss, a former general council member of the left-wing Unity Theatre, chose to sponsor a Theatres Bill that would end censorship by the Lord Chamberlain.

The Royal Court still faced a severe crisis, compounded by Gaskill falling ill and Esdaile threatening to prevent the production of *Early Morning*, which had now been postponed to March. Following rehearsal problems – the actors were working on other productions at the time – the scheduled three Sunday performances were cut to two. The first, on March 31, was proclaimed by the theatre as a celebration of the twelfth anniversary of the English Stage Company. The second did not happen. It was cancelled by Esdaile after police had visited the theatre. In its place, the cast performed in the afternoon a private dress rehearsal for critics, while in the evening there was a teach-in on censorship. In May, Bond was awarded the George Devine prize for *Saved* and *Early Morning*.

Peggy supported Bond and the theatre steadfastly. She had little direct role to play other than as cheer leader, although she did become involved in the publication of *Early Morning*. Methuen, which had published *Saved* – the bestselling of its new Playscript series – was worried about legal complications, prosecution for obscenity being just one. Peggy understood Methuen's problem; she was an iconoclast not a rebel. As for obscenity, her own view was disarming: 'I never tend to think anything obscene so I'm absolutely no judge.'

While Methuen took legal counsel, Bond was approached by the independent publisher John Calder, a stalwart of the anti-censorship campaign who published Beckett and, of Peggy's clients, Adamov, Ionesco and Mercer. Methuen offered to publish *Early Morning* with two changes, but

Calder was happy to accept the play intact, so Bond went with him. Peggy, however, believed that, in a situation of extreme frustration, Bond had double-crossed Methuen while Calder had acted ruthlessly. She told Bond that he should return to Methuen with his next play, *Narrow Road to the Deep North*, which he did, and Methuen remained his publishers thereafter.

George Strauss' Theatres Bill was given its third reading in May 1968. In July, Gaskill announced that the Royal Court were going to present a season in the spring of 1969 comprising what he hoped would be the first public performances of *Saved* and *Early Morning* along with Jane Howell's production of *Narrow Road to the Deep North*, which had opened in Coventry the month before. The bill became law in September, thereby allowing the 1969 Bond season to stand as the intended affirmation not only of the Royal Court's solidarity with Bond but of his central importance to the theatrical life of the nation.

Peggy became close to Bond for the next few years, a time of enormous creativity for him. Her role was not to find him work, something she rarely did, but to encourage, stimulate and criticise. During this period they both enjoyed exchanging letters – he lived just outside Cambridge and was not often in London. The letters became long and intense, covering an extraordinary range of subjects, from dreams – she was compiling a book of playwrights' dreams, which never materialised – to her favourite topic, the nature of talent.

'First, there is the essential recognition of talent,' she writes in one letter in 1969, in which she dissects her own profession and the world of those who live by the talent of others:

> This means recognising something which nobody else has yet recognised, not a mere matter of reading a very good author's play and saying it's excellent – a thousand people can do that, and they usually declare a play to be very good because of perhaps its faults – 'fine writing', i.e. literary talent has nothing to do with dramatic talent. (It's a matter of originality, selection and choice . . . the dynamic propulsion forward, etc. etc. etc.) Having spotted original unknown talent there is then the task of assessing the author's character in one or two brief meetings. Not just his potential writing talent, but his character *now*, as an unknown, and his character *as it will be* – under the stress of failure, and the even greater stress of success.
>
> Every author is entirely *different* – you cannot imagine the difference between the talents; all of them almost unique, if they are strong . . . Then there's the whole world of the creatures who inhabit the 'market' – each

one with a different lack of talent, each one an individual who must be a channel for the products of the author or painter or musician. And the 'media' are entirely different. Anyone who thinks that writing for the stage is in any way similar to TV, or that writing for TV has anything to do with films, is mad, and incapable of judgement. In the case of all these media . . . it's not just a matter of what is possible NOW, but what *could* and *might* be possible in the future. Which brings me to the business of constantly renewing yourself, constantly being able to develop, yet stay in the same job, with the same people, in the same building. If one doesn't renew inside one suddenly stops: like Binkie [Beaumont], who MADE the British actors-theatre in the '30s and '40s, but too late began to try and catch up when he found that this theatre no longer existed. (But it is now coming back, not because anyone wants it, but because, for some reason, the people who launched the '60s have taken a sabbatical, without knowing it.)

So, the talent is an infinite and continuous pleasure, the pleasures – one of many – *inside the head*. But what of the rest? An agent needs diabolical powers of negotiating and manipulating and persuading – shady and tricky talents to develop, since all the while they must not become a pleasure or a true talent, but merely something which has to be used, with honour, for a legitimate purpose. As soon as it becomes a pleasure, he is *corrupted*. During struggle most of the temptations are hidden – to work is to live – I mean eat and just pay the rent – so this is a safe primitive drive for survival. But when the rent is paid, when there is a little money in the bank, when the agent has met a lot of people – what then? Pleasure beckons and must be resisted; friendships must be curtailed (since friendship takes up time, dissipates the antennae of recognition), late nights make it impossible to work during the day. As for love – nobody still capable of catching that disease DARE fall potently in love as dozens of lives depend on someone who is reason-ably sane!

She turns to the example of Diaghilev, 'the head of everything in this talent line,' whom she admired to the point of spraying his grave on the Venetian island of San Michèle with his favourite perfume. 'You forget that the impetus and *raison d'être* is for *talent*,' she writes to Bond, 'but the appalling detailed work which goes to get something like a ballet on the stage, or even an author "served", is infinitely, infinitely *boring*. The outsiders think how marvellous it was for Diaghilev to have been surrounded by geniuses, but without all the boring work, which is never considered, known or discussed, these geniuses wouldn't have painted, written or danced . . . In the more humble reaches of agencies, the good ones seldom last, or stick it, because *in itself* it requires the almost impossible from anyone who decides to do this job.'

In contradiction of her own experience, she continues: 'So the first ten years are easy – if anyone survives and still recognises talent for ten years – but then some kind of wisdom accumulates, and the creature who is still struggling to launch talent begins to read people without their saying anything, begins to know what is going to happen before it happens, begins to find that as soon as a play in manuscript arrives, let's say, that they can predict, *while reading*, not just the virtue of the play, but the whole history of the play – the casting, the production, the critics' reactions, its destiny, in fact. All this comes instantaneously, like a creation of a short story. The details vary a little, but the whole picture is hideously accurate. So it takes all the weary steps, and the going through of *what is already known* has to be lived through.'

After dismissing the current crop of impresarios and agents, she concludes: 'It's this dual requirement which is so burdensome. A really good, equipped, business talent, can find its mark in thousands of fields. There are millions of good businessmen, good Managers, good accountants, good assistants, good managing directors. And not a few good, perceptive people who recognise talent – at once I think of [John] Calder and Michael White. But we both know that Calder has none of the business acumen or stability, and that White is forced to make more and more money, and puts on *Oh! Calcutta!* instead of certain things he knows about but can't afford to do.

'I suppose it's like everything else. It's *character* which makes for survival, the capability of struggling towards independence, and THEN the ability to stay as humble as when you started, the resistance to pomposity, and superiority and conventionality and selfishness and resistance to jealousy of the creative, greed, or miserliness, or fear of the future (so that everything is geared to what will happen at 60, whereas nobody at all can ensure the world and its inexorable events, and we are just pawns of these events when they come, and to sacrifice one's life for safety at 70 is the most pathetic thing of all). So – everyone who dares play with talent, without having the actual talent, or developing their own, has these weaknesses.

'All the things I list as weaknesses and failures I have myself. And added to it, a kind of wildness, due, I think, to having been brought up in countries with wide landscapes, cruel colours, brutal draughts, the whole indifference of nature set before my eyes. It's like expecting a wild cat to live in a suburban house and not claw the furniture and tear up the curtains!'

As Bond resolutely followed his own theatrical path he became increasingly embroiled in the late 1970s and 1980s in battles with the theatrical establishment – the RSC, the NT, and even the Royal Court – and Peggy began to lose sympathy with him while continuing to act at his behest. She saw in him an insistent desire to make tough deals, as if he had to prove a point; for him to accept anything less than his demands would be a moral defeat.

In the mid-1970s, he agreed to write a new play, *The Bundle*, for the opening season of the RSC's small London theatre, The Warehouse. The financial and human cost of converting the space in Covent Garden into a theatre that met the licensing regulations was far greater than anticipated. On top of that, Peggy felt the RSC had under-estimated in their budgeting for the presentation of new plays. Bond was only asking for terms that were later to become a standard part of a writer's contract – concerning approval over casting, director, and designer, rehearsal attendance fees, and commission fee paid in advance – but which, at the time, and particularly for an over-stretched repertoire company, were threatening the viability of new play work. To make matters worse, Bond was very late with the delivery of the play and even in providing the RSC with a title it could advertise. Peggy said it would not have surprised her if the RSC had pulled out of the negotiation and dropped the play. She even offered to pay the company her 10% commission – a gracious gesture graciously refused. *The Bundle* was finally delivered, Peggy prevailed upon Bond and agreement was reached on the terms. The play eventually appeared very successfully in January 1978.

Bond's progress as a writer was now to be accompanied by a growing belief that he was the only person who should direct the premières of his plays, a view confirmed in his eyes by his British directorial début in August 1978 with *The Woman*, the first new play to be seen on the National's Olivier stage. It upset Peggy, however; she believed that writers should write, yet did not oppose David Hare's or Alan Ayckbourn's forays into directing. She felt Bond did not understand actors and was not a good director for his work, and this difference between them caused their relationship to deteriorate badly.

The growing distance between them was underlined when in 1981 Bond directed his own *Restoration* at the Royal Court with Simon Callow in the lead. Callow has written about his clashes with Bond; they were speaking in two different tongues and could not find an interpreter. Callow summarises the experience thus: Bond 'understands his own plays perfectly and is always right in what he says about them. But translating what he says about them into acting is almost impossible.' For Bond,

Callow was not to blame; he exemplified the corruption of the theatre, its loss to mere sensation and entertainment at the expense of meaning. Peggy was distressed not only because Callow was a close friend but also because Bond, a truly gifted writer, was, to her mind, going wildly astray.

Her disquiet gathered momentum during the 1980s as she saw him become more and more isolated. She felt Bond was in some idiosyncratic way following her own advice by being independent, but with the opposite effect to the one she intended. He was cutting himself off from friends and from life too completely, and the consequent purification was not a spur to creativity, in her view, but an obstacle. She worried that he had written himself out.

Bond regretted the divergence of their views. He continued to seek her understanding and her truthful reactions, which remained of the greatest importance to him. Yet, he felt he had to do what he had to do. He would not compromise because that was what everyone else did. She could admire this stand but found it hard to accept.

As Bond's reputation in the profession for being a righteous, infallible ogre gained credence, Peggy liked to undermine the fearsome image by recalling the shy man with the elfin smile and flashing eyes whom she had met in the '60s, who used to challenge the world as well as himself. She liked the humorous man who questioned his own identity. She recalled asking him how he was going to learn to be an author and giving him a big empty diary, which she told him to begin keeping in order to practise his writing.

Wickedly, she used to retell an anecdote about Bond that, because of its subject, soon assumed the status of myth. The story goes that, following *Saved*, Peggy wanted Bond to have fun before losing himself in another period of austerity when writing his next play. She either urged him to buy or – depending on the version – bought him a red sports car and told him to drive it fast down the Kings Road in Chelsea, then one of the world's most fashionable streets. She used to say what a wonderful sight it was to see him in a fast car with a blonde at his side. Bond has denied the story in all its variants; he says he had always wanted a sports car since the days when he worked in a car factory and, indeed, he did buy one, but not at Peggy's suggestion. It came from a special range – only five were made, he adds, and one of the others was sold to Prince Charles.

Whatever their later disagreements, Bond acknowledges his debt to Peggy; without her encouragement and criticism he would not have been able to write his plays. He told her that his dedication to her of *The Woman* – a play with a rugged female survivor at its centre – was a small public recognition of this fact. He told another, younger client, David Lan, who was complaining of Peggy's wayward behaviour, that she was a woman of taste, discrimination and rare distinction, much to be admired.

Peggy saw in Bond's best writing something of Beckett, in its spareness, in the moral imperative, and in the shock and beauty of the ugly. Looking back, she said Bond's Royal Court plays were her favourites. She thought it the perfect stage for Bond's work. *Saved* stood out for her as a remarkable play and Gaskill's revival production in 1969 she found 'the best thing he has probably ever done'.

After seeing Gaskill's production of *Lear* at the Royal Court in 1971 she wrote to Bond: 'What can I say? A terrifying, terrible experience, but, as you said, full of healing pity and understanding . . . All the same – if the theatre was always like this – *could one survive*? You are becoming a *great master*, my dear.'

She was particularly fond of *The Sea*, which was also given its première at the Royal Court, in 1973, and was again directed by Gaskill. She thought that Coral Browne playing Mrs Rafi – a role in which Peggy and others have recognised elements of herself – should have been more extreme and dotty, more exceptional in her emotional range. 'Bond isn't Chekhov,' she wrote to Gaskill. 'Chekhov is romantic anguish, but Bond is anguish itself. He's sharper, cruder, harder and a little more grotesque.'

*

'Great art is not perfect.'

The Sea was produced under the aegis of Oscar Lewenstein, whose reign after Gaskill as artistic director saw the first stirring of the Royal Court's opening up to women playwrights.

This movement was spearheaded, though unconsciously, by one of Peggy's clients, Caryl Churchill, whose first major play, *Owners*, was presented at the Theatre Upstairs in Lewenstein's first year in office, 1972, and whose mainstage debut, with *Objections to Sex and Violence* in 1975, came in Lewenstein's final year as artistic director. Lewenstein made Churchill the Royal Court's first female resident dramatist. It was fitting that a tribute to Peggy should appear in a programme note for *Objections to Sex and Violence*, and appropriate moreover that it should be written by Ann Jellicoe, Peggy's first client among the Royal Court's new wave dramatists, its first woman playwright and now Lewenstein's literary manager.

267

Peggy

Like Christopher Hampton, the Court's first resident writer, Churchill came to Peggy's attention while she was an undergraduate at Oxford University. A friend of Churchill's had wanted to direct, so Churchill wrote a short play, *Downstairs*, which was performed in 1958 by Oriel College and was taken to the National Union of Students Drama Festival. A fellow undergraduate John McGrath saw the production and put her in touch with Peggy, who was already his agent. Peggy asked to read some of her work and Churchill sent *Having a Wonderful Time*, which an Oxford group performed at the amateur theatre Questors in west London, and a TV play *A Shout in the Street*, which Churchill had also sent to another agency.

Peggy asked to see Churchill, in February 1961, and, after what Churchill recalls as barely a 20-minute meeting, Peggy agreed to take her on. Peggy remembered Churchill as being rather diffident yet intriguing – Peggy liked the fact that she had been brought up abroad, in Montreal, for seven years before going to Oxford. Peggy recognised the talent but was not at all sure what to make of it, and was strangely uncomfortable representing a young woman.

Churchill had been writing TV plays unsuccessfully for a year or so. Peggy asked her to scrap *A Shout in the Street* and begin afresh. The result was a television adaptation of a 15th-century English ballad, *The Brown Bride*, and the idea of dramatising several more. Peggy found the script 'unusual and fresh' and liked Churchill's notion, particularly because the characters, as in Greek tragedy, would be revealed through action and not psychological dialogue. Peggy tried in vain to sell the idea to various TV companies and her failure bothered her. She decided that she had been looking in the wrong direction and that Churchill's talent was actually more suited to radio. She sent two plays, *Portrait of an Artist* and *The Ants*, to radio producer Michael Bakewell. Both had been intended for television but Peggy thought them slight and far better for 'sound'. Bakewell liked *The Ants*, about a group of people in war time in whom love has become extinct, and his production was eventually broadcast on the Third Programme in November 1962.

In spite of this success in placing Churchill, Peggy became anxious at not being able to help her more. Her only theatre work had come via Churchill's Oxford connections; ironically, even this was a production of a radio play, *You've No Need to be Frightened*, which she had written at university and was given a college performance in 1961.

Churchill, however, who had graduated in 1960, aged 22, and had married the following year, was content not to be caught up in the maelstrom of Peggy's nurturing. Churchill found Peggy's characteristic duality disconcerting. Peggy could be both splendidly encouraging and dishearteningly off-putting. 'I think you are very difficult to sell,' she wrote to Churchill in December 1961, 'because your writing is in some respects very slight and poetic (this isn't meant disparagingly in the least) . . . In an odd kind of way you are getting more fey and more esoteric, instead of blunter and sturdier, which is not what I expected! Have you ever thought of writing a novel, or a children's book? I have the feeling that you would find it much easier.'

This last statement seemed like an enormous put-down to Churchill. It conformed to Peggy's view that men made better playwrights because they were more interesting, and that they were more interesting because they were out in the world more. Women made fine novelists because novel writing, she thought, was like an extension of keeping a diary or writing letters, and women were highly skilled at both precisely because they were *not* out in the world as much as men. Churchill, for whom there were no female playwrights as role models, nevertheless took the opposite view; because of the exposure that men enjoy it is possible to know all about them, and this allows women to know all that men know as well as all that women know, which lies beyond men's grasp.

Churchill's next stage production was again linked to Oxford. *Easy Death* was given two performances in March 1962 at the Oxford Playhouse by the Experimental Theatre Club. The play earned Churchill (or Mrs David Harter, as she was known in the agency's ledgers) her first royalty of nine guineas with one guinea going to the agency as commission. Peggy suggested inviting other agents to see the production.

'I don't want to feel that you are in any way being "tied" to me,' she wrote to Churchill. 'Of course I would love to help you, but as you are still at the moment unlaunched from a London point of view, I think you should ask a few agents to see you and if any of them can really help you, you should take advantage of their interest . . . We are getting more and more tied with our existing "launched" clients and I am awfully worried that I can't spend sufficient time and thought upon you. You are talented and deserve very sympathetic handling.'

After seeing the show, she wrote again. 'In some ways it might be better for you to have a male agent, since women tend to find their own weaknesses in their own sex. For instance, I found the production at Oxford too tenuous and over-lyrical, whereas you need strong, anti-feminine interpretation.' Churchill stayed put with Peggy and began to raise a family.

Churchill's arrival in the professional theatre took a long time to come, partly because her domestic responsibilities absorbed a great deal of her energy and partly because she was experimenting – for example, with stage time, and the use of masks and puppets – in ways that were not yet fully achieved and which Peggy often found hard to fathom.

Peggy pondered on whether she was being dumb, or, perhaps, Churchill was being too obscure. In one letter to Churchill, she wrote: 'I know that Pinter genuinely doesn't have symbols and his plays are mysterious to him too but they have an inexorable action with no tricks or gimmicks, which allows one to accept them as they stand . . . I think one can – almost – write a play in a trance, provided one has the rarest and most extraordinary genius. For the rest, I'm sure that playwriting, unlike Zen, must have a deep inner meaning, if it hasn't a clear surface one.'

She was happy if Churchill knew what she was doing and why, and admitted that her own responses probably meant that she was not able to be as adventurous as she should be. ('I have become tainted by the "West End" attitude towards plays.') Whilst trying to be supportive and never pestering Churchill to change direction or take on work she did not like, Peggy at the same time did not shrink from being candid. She could not, and sometimes would not, place Churchill's stage plays with any London manager. She could not think of any theatre, except possibly the adventurous amateur theatre Questors, that would be a suitable outlet for Churchill. In fact, it took the emergence of the alternative theatre movement in the early 1970s to provide such a platform for her.

Nevertheless, Peggy kept working on Churchill's behalf. She introduced Churchill to John Tydeman at the BBC radio drama department in December 1963 at much the same time as he was sending Peggy Joe Orton. Tydeman directed seven radio plays by Churchill in the late '60s and early '70s before she made her entry into the professional theatre in 1972, eleven years after Peggy had begun to represent her.

This came about because Peggy had thought that two of her radio plays – *Not Not Not Not Not Enough Oxygen* and *Abortive* – were not only remarkable but might be appropriate as stage plays for the Theatre Upstairs, where her client Ted Whitehead was the literary manager. This did not work out, but the idea had been planted and future possibilities were discussed.

Peggy had also managed to interest Michael Codron in Churchill's work; he had offered her a commission, which became *Owners*, a moral tale that investigates the relationship between property, power and sexual violence. Peggy said that Codron was not sure what to do with the play. Already receptive to the suggestion of presenting one of Churchill's plays, the Theatre Upstairs offered Codron what Peggy described as a 'first-class try out', and it opened in November 1972. Jill Bennett appeared in the previews until her husband, John Osborne, drove her into a roundabout – some say deliberately. She suffered an injury to her ankle and had to be replaced.

Peggy liked the play and felt it was a breakthrough for Churchill but was disappointed in the production by Nicholas Wright, artistic director of the Theatre Upstairs. 'Jill Bennett was the only good thing in it,' said Peggy, who considered the production a setback for Churchill because, in her view, it was a mess and made the playwright, not the director, seem incompetent. 'Oddly enough,' she wrote to Churchill after the production, 'directors don't learn nearly enough at the Court whereas writers learn the hard way, like you.'

Owners was a watershed: after it, Churchill worked primarily in theatre. Despite Peggy's foreboding, Churchill's relationship with the Royal Court was not harmed. Peggy agreed with the idea that she should be com- missioned by the Royal Court, and in 1974 she became writer in residence. After the initial contact of *Owners*, Churchill's association with the theatre became self-sustained. It grew into an historic partnership embracing some ten productions that was to gain international significance as Churchill, through this collaboration, became established as Britain's leading female playwright – and one of Britain's leading playwrights of either sex.

Following up the themes of *Owners*, although in a more social context, her commissioned play, *Objections to Sex and Violence*, opened in the downstairs auditorium in January 1975, directed by John Tydeman. It played to 29% capacity. Churchill's energies then were channelled into her collaborations with the touring Joint Stock theatre company and the femi - nist group Monstrous Regiment, both of which groups took her into a theatrical terrain that was alien to Peggy and from which she was excluded; their collective work method challenged the notion of the writer creating alone at the desk and necessarily reduced the influence of individuals such as agents who operated outside of the group.

Given the way these groups worked, Peggy was not seeing Churchill's scripts before they were performed. The first of these collaborations, *Light Shining in Buckinghamshire*, produced in 1976 by Joint Stock, already made Peggy feel uneasy. Its story of the millenarian zeal unleashed by the English Civil War told in a series of interlocking short scenes did not strike Peggy as being substantial enough. Its companion piece, *Vinegar Tom*, produced by Monstrous Regiment also in 1976, combines a finely-wrought play about the persecution of witches in the 17th century with militant songs in a contemporary idiom. This, too, did not appeal to Peggy. The ending – a song called 'Evil Women' – Peggy felt made the women all seem like lesbians.

Despite the frequent disjunction between Peggy's views and Churchill's practice, Churchill did stay with Peggy until her death, a span of 30 years. Churchill pays tribute to her energising and supportive role. 'I had wanted to be a writer since I was a child,' she says, 'but it was Peggy who made me feel that the theatre and writing plays are wonderful and worthwhile and that I could do it, that I should do it from the deepest part of myself, and that what mattered was exactly that and not the career.'

Peggy, for example, preferred *Softcops* to *Cloud Nine*, two plays which Churchill delivered at the same time. Peggy felt the former play about punishment and control touched something in the sub-conscious and was the more profound. She held this view even when it was *Cloud Nine* that proved to be Churchill's most long-lived success. Similarly, another of Churchill's commercial success, *Serious Money*, Peggy found well enough crafted but too superficial.

When Churchill brought *Softcops* and *Cloud Nine* to Goodwin's Court, instead of congratulating her on having finished two full-length plays of some complexity, Peggy told her with great concern that she looked very tired and seemed to be bent over like a hairpin. By way of help, she sent Churchill a book on the Alexander Technique, which Peggy had followed and which Churchill also decided to try, to beneficial effect. Peggy also sent her a book by Krishnamurti, whose ability to see the deepest of hidden meanings in the most commonplace of things appealed to her.

Churchill valued Peggy's encouragement and her forthright views throughout the vicissitudes of their relationship. 'She *cared* so much, even if she said odd things. She had no hesitation in saying she disliked your work. Conversely, if she said she liked it, then she really did. It was her values that were important, and having her behind me, someone who you trust saying it's worth proceeding. It kept me going.'

Churchill's main director became Max Stafford-Clark, who was responsible for *Light Shining in Buckinghamshire*, *Cloud Nine*, *Top Girls*, *Serious Money*, *Ice Cream* and *Hot Fudge*. In the autumn of 1979 he deputised as artistic director for the absent Stuart Burge, who was working in television, and the following year Stafford-Clark was appointed to the job permanently. His tenure marked a change for Peggy in her relationship to the Court.

Thanks to Oscar Lewenstein, her influence had reached its peak in the 1970s, some years after she had achieved her supreme position as a new play agent in the commercial world. Lewenstein was a producer and, as had been the case with Michael Codron at the Arts Theatre, was more in need of an imaginative force like Peggy supplying a stream of new plays than a director would have been. Lewenstein's reign was followed by a precarious period under Nicholas Wright and Robert Kidd before the first outsider to run the Court, Stuart Burge, was called in as a steadying hand. He was never going to launch the Court into a new era, however, but in Max Stafford-Clark, such a person stepped forward. Having been artistic director of the Traverse Theatre in Edinburgh and a co-founder of Joint Stock, his new play credentials were impeccable. He brought with him to the Court his own firm ideas about drama and his own equally strong connections with the playwriting community.

He had first encountered Peggy when he was a greenhorn working at the Traverse and had presumptuously phoned her out of the blue in search of new writers. 'Where are you phoning from?' she asked. 'Edinburgh,' he replied. 'You can't afford that,' she said. 'I'll call you back', and did, spending an hour talking to a young director she did not know about the state of new plays.

During Stafford-Clark's time as artistic director of the Court, he and Peggy enjoyed a most amicable relationship, but she found herself liking fewer and fewer plays and caring less and less about the theatre at large. Furthermore, Peggy's failing health in the latter years of the 1980s meant that the agency was treading water.

The theatrical environment had changed radically since George Devine had presented *Look Back In Anger* at the end of his first season; the national companies, which did not exist then, were now regularly staging new plays; many regional theatres were following suit and several had studio spaces dedicated to new work; and the establishment of a viable and extensive fringe network had led to a general increase both in the number of new plays on offer and of those being performed. To Peggy, the Royal Court had now become just another theatre.

She admired the spareness of Stafford-Clark's productions but was suspicious of him as artistic director because she felt he ran the Court for himself. She acknowledged that he was committed to writers but felt that his choice of artistic team (e.g. director, designer) was more important to him than satisfying the writer's needs.

'I know he means well, but to get him to read a play is like drawing a tooth,' she wrote at the start of his regime. And when he did, she was unhappy at the power he exercised and the way he exercised it. 'Max tends to be a pain in the neck because he is frightened and you cannot run a theatre if you are frightened,' she said. 'He cannot quite bear to turn down a play so he goes in for those ludicrous Sunday readings and then threatens the author with a production Upstairs!' He would persuade writers to show him their plays but then make no commitment as to when he might present them. If the writer decided to show the play to another theatre, he would 'go mad'. Peggy thought he would hold up the progress of a play and make himself the power broker.

She wrote to Churchill about him in 1983: 'As I warned you, any play that is shown to Max is in a trap. This is a pity, because one ought to explore the possibility of the Royal Court and Max, but one shouldn't be like a fly in a trap just by sending a play or talking about a play. If only he would allow an author to give a play *freely* and not make it a kind of blackmail! . . . This letter is not an attack on Max, who really needs a psychiatrist to elimi-nate this flaw.' This last remark was for Peggy oxymoronic because she believed, privately, that Stafford-Clark's problem stemmed from his relation-ship to his father, who was none other than a renowned psychiatrist.

Despite her reservations, Peggy could be very supportive to Stafford-Clark. When her client Paul Kember's play, *Not Quite Jerusalem*, was taken up as a film, a world that was completely foreign to Stafford-Clark, she helped the theatre negotiate a good deal for itself although she did not represent the Court. She also offered succour during a troublesome homage to Edward Bond in 1984 when the Court revived *The Pope's Wedding* and *Saved*, much to the disgruntlement of the author. Stafford-Clark, in turn, was happy to send to Peggy new authors who had not yet found an agent.

As the record shows, the list of Peggy's clients who worked at the Royal Court under Stafford-Clark is as long and impressive as that for any of his predecessors; as well as Caryl Churchill and many writers working Up-stairs, it includes ten clients making their début downstairs: David Lan in 1979, Paul Kember in 1980, Stephen Lowe and Dusty Hughes in 1981, John Byrne in 1982, Robert Holman in 1983, Wallace Shawn in 1985, and, in 1986, Anne Devlin, Jim Cartwright and Larry Kramer.

Peggy's Royal Court roll of honour bridged three decades and com-prised an extraordinary gamut of playwrights. In its variety, quantity and quality, it represents a singular expression of, and testimony to, her unique taste and her extensive influence on the shaping of the contemporary theatre.

Chapter Eight

For the Love of Talent

'You don't sell plays for money – it's too expensive.'

In many important ways, Peggy was a pioneer of the publicly subsidised theatre sector, but without meaning to be one. As well as having to find new talent, she saw it as part of her agent's responsibility to create a modern theatre, a theatre for new writing, a theatre that would encourage and show an author's development. To accompany this new theatre, there had to be developed an audience for new writing – a 'professional' audience, as Peggy put it, and not an 'amateur' one that just wants a casual evening out. The prerequisite for such a theatre was the capacity to subordinate economic considerations to artistic needs, and logically this led to the ensemble ideal, a permanent company with permanent directors and other artists.

Whilst the notion of subsidy for writers was horrendous to her, in the values that she pursued and in the work that she promoted, Peggy fought for a theatre that was only able to flourish through public subsidy.

In the years after the war, there was only sporadic and minimal public funding of theatrical activity. Pioneers like the English Stage Company and Theatre Workshop were granted miserly amounts. The big step forward came in the early 1960s and was symbolised by the creation in 1964 of the first Minister for the Arts, Jennie Lee, appointed by Harold Wilson's Labour government.

There was a moment during Peggy's time as an agent when the commercial sector played its part, stoutly led by associates of Peggy's like Michael Codron. Peggy faced no dilemma in advising Robert Bolt to stick with Binkie Beaumont when Peter Hall offered him a commission to write for the new Royal Shakespeare Company. But the thrust that came from the Royal Court, to be given renewed impetus by the RSC and National

Theatre, could only be sustained by public subsidy, especially as the momentum spread outside London. The subsidised sector became the only theatrical territory in which to innovate in new writing, especially as the cost of mounting new plays in the West End became prohibitive.

In this new theatre, there was a commitment to new writing and a higher value put on the text. When new plays were mounted, the playwright was centre stage, certainly in the rhetoric if not always in the practice. Through the work of Peggy's clients and her championing of values that she shared with others who built the subsidised sector, Peggy helped legitimise the British theatre as an arena for serious debate. She brought theatre into the contemporary world and made it possible for playwrights like Christopher Hampton, David Hare and Caryl Churchill to thrive; they could not only earn a living writing as playwrights, they could have their voice heard.

The expansion of the subsidised theatre coincided with Peggy's ascendancy as an agent. She was a principal conduit between the commercial and subsidised sectors, although for many years she did not make any real distinction between them; it was all showbusiness to her. Peggy came from and belonged in the commercial world; that was where she learned the vocabulary and practice of the trade and made her name. She once said that the only romantic thing in the theatre was the box office because the ticket sales could go up or down and there was no certainty in the outcome.

Talent was tested head on in the market place, yet she had contempt for most of the fare on offer in the commercial theatre throughout her life. Many of the brightest talents that she served, like Edward Bond, for instance, only survived through their earnings from subsidised theatres around the world; in the market place, he starved.

Subsidy, she felt, weakened a management's nerve and blunted its judgement because the money at stake was not its own. She knew, however, that when money was the primary stake, nerve and judgement were not put at the service of the writer.

Nevertheless, Peggy took against the notion of subsidy for writers, although at one time she used to believe that artists were special and were owed a living by the community. Later she said no good had ever come of this, and she no longer believed that certain members of the community should support others just because they happened to be artists. She saw subsidy as being 'for the untalented because talent looks after itself. I know the authors are angry with me for taking this attitude – they all want a free ride.'

Likewise, she was wary of commissions – a cornerstone of the subsidised sector – whereby a management pays a writer a portion of a fee in advance to write a play, with another portion of the fee being payable upon delivery of the play and the remainder on acceptance of the play for production by the management. In return, the management has exclusive rights to that play for an agreed period of time. Peggy's concern was primarily puritanical: writers should write because they have to. They should not be paid before writing because the obligation to deliver is anti-creative and means writing for the wrong reason.

She also had practical objections. The subsidised theatre evolved a system of commissioning that she felt limited the scope of agents and, therefore, their ability to act in the writers' best interest. Commissions, she believed, made it easier for the writer to be treated shabbily or even be neglected. The subsidised system to her mind exacerbated aspects of the commercial world that she did not like, for example, the tendency to tie a play for too long a period to a single management. Peggy saw dangers in this both prior to and following production. Beforehand, a management could, within the limits of the contract, hold up a play's progress without fear of redress. The writer had to wait in line until the management decided there was a vacancy for the play, by which time the commission money had been spent and the author was poor again. And afterwards, the management, rather than the agent, could control the future exploitation of the play for the number of years assigned to it in the deal. She preferred to have the leverage of being able to withdraw a play from a dilatory management or sell a successful play to other bidders with much greater rapidity. Competition, in her eyes, allowed freedom and self-respect. Commissioning removed the vital weapon of competition from her armoury.

Even though it had been one of her own writers – Leo Lehman – who had received the first Arts Council bursary, Peggy had similar objections to bursaries, allied to a lack of trust in the Arts Council's ability either to foster new writing or to be of any help to the theatre. Peggy never forgot, or forgave, the Arts Council drama department for its dismissive response to *Waiting for Godot* and to Robert Bolt's first stage play, *The Critic and the Heart*.

Bursaries, Peggy thought, implied premature praise and unearned financial reward, both of which could stunt a writer's development. New talent, by definition, should have to fight if it is original. If it is easily and immediately acceptable then it is unlikely to be original. She disliked the idea of bureaucrats or a committee sitting in judgement over talent. 'Every new talent is by its nature strange and would be repellent to several on a committee,' she said. 'You need guts not bursaries (or perhaps a house to write in – the Arts Council could provide that).'

Peggy

She did float the idea of setting up a Trust in the late '60s which would provide authors with money in order to be able to write. The eventual producing management would then reimburse the Trust. It came to nothing because, on investigation, she believed it would be impractical, particularly in relation to how the managements would purchase their rights. Peggy was also critical, almost to the point of sneering, of the rise of creative writing projects and especially those connected to universities and colleges.

Peggy stood by her views on writers and commissions when she served from 1975 to 1990 on the board of the Hampstead Theatre, which she described acidly as 'middle aged, middle class, middle sex'. She was brought on to the board by David Aukin, who was the theatre's administrator under Michael Rudman. Aukin took over as artistic director in 1979, a controversial choice because the appointment flew in the face of the current orthodoxy; he was an administrator not a director, but this did not bother Peggy in the slightest.

'I wanted to reposition the theatre,' he says, 'and she was a token of that ambition. She remained adamant that writers should write first, on spec for themselves, without being paid, and then deliver. It was not a reactionary view but how she saw the interests of writers.'

Peggy supported Aukin when he rejected an offer of relocation to a larger auditorium – a brave refusal given that Hampstead seats just over 150. The offer was made by developers who wanted the theatre to vacate its site. The higher capacity would have meant a change in policy to sell more seats at the box office, a shift of emphasis that Aukin and the board found unacceptable. 'Peggy was very professional, a conscientious board member,' says Aukin, 'and never interfered. She always wanted to talk about the productions, which were often the last thing discussed at board meetings. I remember her at one preview when I watched her as much as I watched the show. I was sure she was asleep, yet, at the end, she gave as perceptive an analysis of the production as anyone.'

She resigned under Aukin's successor, Michael Attenborough, because of failing health. She enlivened board meetings by her candid opinions and occasional gaffes. She once confused two board members, the actor Hugh Quarshie and the TV presenter Trevor Phillips, whom she congratulated on a splendid performance, which left the normally loquacious Phillips tongue-tied. Ironically, Attenborough's main memory of Peggy is her complaining at board meetings that the writers were being paid too much.

While Peggy fought fiercely in both commercial and subsidised sectors for the rights of playwrights and set standards against which managements and other agents could measure their own deals, she disliked the notion of a standardised writers' contract, which was introduced in the 1970s following militant action by playwrights' organisations to secure for all playwrights a minimum set of terms. A standardised contract regulated dealings between playwrights and managements, who were grouped together according to status e.g. the RSC, the NT and the Royal Court formed one group, the West End theatres another, the regional theatres another.

Peggy disliked the idea of a standard contract with a fixed fee irrespective of a playwright's talent or reputation – what she called 'a kind of Socialism of the theatre' – because she felt it was disadvantageous to writers, not least in reducing the role of agents in negotiating appropriate terms for their clients. To Peggy, each play and each writer was unique, and therefore each play needed negotiating on its own terms. She did not accept that a young playwright just starting out should have the same contract as an internationally renowned playwright of ten years' standing. Nonetheless, Peggy did negotiate very advantageous terms for her writers within the system.

She was not alone among agents in rejecting the notion of collective bargaining between writers and managements. Most of the agents were against the negotiations, with one or two notable exceptions such as Clive Goodwin, who was involved directly in helping writers to organise and win negotiating rights. Although Peggy played no part in the discussions, some of the protagonists on the writers' side, such as Steve Gooch, were her clients and drew on their experience of her to do battle against the management side.

From the days of Robert Bolt onwards, the writers Peggy represented had gained increasing degrees of control over the production process, in matters such as the appointment of directors, designers and lead actors or the right to attend rehearsal. She opposed contracts which would not allow writers to talk to a director or sought for management an absurd percentage of rights, such as were on offer in the early days at Hampstead Theatre.

Peggy always advised her authors to read contracts and never to let anyone else sign them on their behalf. 'If you're clever enough to write a play, you're clever enough to sign a contract and know what it means,' she said.

Yet, in the market place system, even Peggy could not – and did not – negotiate for all her writers all the advances she had achieved for the few. She believed in maintaining differentials and never regarded the eventual achievement of a standard contract for the buying and commissioning of plays and for the conduct thereafter of managements and playwrights as progress for the playwriting community as a whole, let alone a benefit to any individual writer.

It was typical of Peggy, however, that she could hold contradictory, though, not in her terms, inconsistent views on subsidy, as she did on other matters. Despite thinking the subsidised sector made stars out of directors and paupers out of playwrights – by not paying them enough for what were usually short and limited runs – she was in practice generally sympathetic to subsidised theatres and, in particular, recognised that the two national companies could provide for writers the chance to gain a world-wide reputation. Although she believed that the German theatre had been killed by over-subsidy, she acknowledged that theatres in Germany had been able to stage many more new plays than those in Britain because of vast public funding. She believed in the 1960s that the RSC should have had its subsidy increased in order for it to produce more new plays, whereas she was content for the NT to pursue a more conventional repertoire path.

In her negotiations with the national companies, she did not seek to bleed them on behalf of her clients, a position *vis-à-vis* Peggy the commercial managers would dearly liked to have been in. David Brierley, general manager of the RSC who dealt with Peggy for a quarter of a century, remembers her as being very sensitive to the company's needs and showing great understanding about the way the subsidised theatres worked. 'I enjoyed negotiating with her,' he recalls. 'She was much tougher on the West End managers, I suspect. With us she was brisk, energetic, fair and fun.'

Peggy appreciated the role of the RSC and NT in animating the theatre both in Britain and abroad. '*London Assurance*,' she said, 'sold in the West End and on Broadway because of the RSC and not because of its commercial producers'. She was scornful of the new concrete buildings the two companies moved into and believed that more of the money should have been spent on the stages themselves, because that, she said, is where theatre takes place. She was indignant and uncomprehending when she arrived at the Barbican – or the Barbizan, as she called it – for a preview of *Poppy* by her client Peter Nichols to be told the performance had been cancelled due to a problem with the scenery. 'Pathetic, darling, *pathetic*,' was her verdict.

Through her network of Cambridge contacts and several of her clients who were involved in the first seasons of the RSC, she was as influential in the formative years of the company as any outsider. She had known its artistic director Peter Hall from his days at the Arts Theatre. She felt he was immensely gifted as a cultural entrepreneur rather than as a director and that her prognosis of Hall's career had come true. She had written of Hall in 1962, a year after the RSC's first season at the Aldwych Theatre: 'He began as a doctored tom, but much more dangerous. He wanted all the cream at the Arts but the Aldwych and the Memorial Theatre have given him a taste of red meat, and he'll want human sacrifice soon . . . He likes the fruits of success, silly bugger, not realising that this can't last and will destroy what creative ability he started with, leaving him with *nothing*.'

This, however, was the attitude of someone very fond of 'the silly bugger'. Their paths continually crossed and, just before Hall was appointed artistic director of the NT, he even offered Peggy the job of being his literary manager, the role that Kenneth Tynan had fulfilled for Hall's predecessor, Laurence Olivier. She declined and, recalls Hall, muttered that she was too keen on all her authors and on making money. At the age of 65, she did not relish the prospect of learning new tricks and of servicing an artistic director famous for his skills of manipulation. She had influence enough as it was.

To her the NT was a less individual company than the RSC, which, thanks to Hall's legacy, was now known by its personalities. Nevertheless, when Hall finally opened the NT at the South Bank in 1976, she wished him well and hoped that it would revivify British theatre. 'I'm not quite sure how – but it must,' she said. Peggy did not attend the royal opening ('I can't think of anything I'd less wish to go to') and went instead to Paris to see two shows she was representing. When she was approached by the NT to advertise in a souvenir programme commemorating the NT's first season, she refused indignantly: 'We never advertise. It's awfully vulgar and repulsive to do so.'

Peggy liked Hall the buccaneer and supported him in his early days at the NT. She stuck by him when he was subjected to severe criticism and much abuse. He championed new writing at the NT, as he had done at the RSC, and put on the large stages at his disposal not only plays by the older generation, like Edward Bond, but those written by the next wave, Howard Brenton, David Hare, and Stephen Poliakoff, for example, all of whom were Peggy's clients. Brenton's *Weapons of Happiness*, directed by David Hare, was the first new play to be seen in the NT's Lyttelton Theatre and Edward Bond's *The Woman* was the first to be seen in its Olivier Theatre.

The opening of the NT's Cottesloe Theatre in 1977 meant that, along with the RSC's Warehouse theatre, which had opened earlier that year, and the longer established Royal Court Theatre Upstairs, all three major companies were running studio-type spaces for new writing.

Peggy had helped create the climate of the period, in which new writing had become a litmus test for a subsidised theatre and a network of smaller outlets for new writing had sprung up round Britain. She was anxious, however, that new writing had now become an orthodoxy and consequently had become an exercise in fashion, regardless of merit.

She had ambivalent feelings about this. She was worried at first that the studio theatres of the major companies would serve actors and directors rather than playwrights and that much of their repertoire would sink like a stone, having played a short run to a relatively small total audience. Yet she could draw comfort from her experience of the Arts Theatre, which had served as a prototypical studio theatre for the RSC when David Rudkin's *Afore Night Come* had transferred from there to the Aldwych Theatre.

Peggy recognised that the link these studio spaces had with the mainstream theatrical institutions gave them a leverage denied most of the similar venues. Peggy believed the studio spaces could help build new audiences for new plays in the larger auditoria of the umbrella organisations and in turn have a beneficial effect on the repertoire of those larger stages.

For these reasons, she defended the Theatre Upstairs, the Warehouse, and the Cottesloe against attacks from the alternative theatre movement, which had grown in the 1970s with a political agenda that classified the leading subsidised theatres as the new establishment, precisely because they were not to be found in a ghetto. She also found that she often enjoyed productions in the smaller auditoria more than those in the larger spaces. To a young writer who was sending her his first plays and asking if hoping for the Theatre Upstairs was aiming too high, she replied 'I don't see why . . . I know that it has about 150 steps, but that's the only consideration of height.'

Peggy responded with apparently typically contradictory feelings to the alternative theatre movement and the network of small theatres offering new work that became known collectively as the Fringe. She was delighted by the pioneering spirit, the energy and the excitement, and the youthful dedication to work for its own sake. She approved of the rejection of the money ethos and conventional attitudes to success. Theatres like the Bush in west London reminded her of the Q Theatre and of her time running it in the early 1950s.

She helped several theatres financially, like Arnold Wesker's Centre 42 at the Round House, the Open Space, the Hampstead Theatre Club, and the Hull Arts Centre. She became a patron of Ed Berman's Ambiance Lunch Hour Theatre Club and even at 70 could be found majestically wriggling on the uncomfortable seats at its Almost Free venue near Leicester Square. She joined the campaign to keep the ICA theatre open when it was threatened with closure.

There was inevitably a generation gap that could not be completely closed and which made it hard for Peggy to grasp what some of her clients were trying to achieve. A highly politicised writer like Steve Gooch, for example, unwisely in her view, opted out of mainstream theatre and worked instead through a network of venues run by like-minded people with an interest in community-based drama.

Ironically, Gooch had chosen Peggy in preference to the agent Clive Goodwin, who offered a left-wing alternative to Peggy and supported playwrights' militancy. Gooch, however, saw Goodwin's own political agenda as too prescriptive. Whereas Goodwin sought the radical transformation of society and spent as much time on his politics as on his agency, Peggy's mission was to serve talent.

Gooch remembers Peggy and Michael Codron coming to see his play *Female Transport* at the Half Moon Theatre, a small venue that used to be a synagogue in the East End of London. Codron was dressed in his expensive Crombie coat and Peggy arrived draped in fur and pearls. As if entering an alien land with the traveller's mix of trepidation and curiosity, she gave the dilapidated auditorium a look of utter bemusement, which turned into a smile as she discovered, much to her relief, that the natives were not only friendly but practised captivating, if peculiar, habits. She hated her mother for being a snob, but she had inherited a strain of that too – she was the bourgeois who despised the bourgeoisie. Theatrically speaking, Peggy had blue blood coursing through her veins, and, however much fun she had on the Fringe, it was never quite the real thing.

*

*'Perhaps I should take a single ticket to the moon
and start an agency there.'*

Peggy did not engage much with the radical politics of the time, except when it became focused on a broad campaign which touched her, such as the abolition of censorship or the cultural boycott of South Africa.

For the first decade and a half of the agency's life, Peggy's clients had to write under the constraints of theatre censorship. In the early 1960s, several of her clients – notably Iris Murdoch, Bill Naughton, Frank Marcus, David

Mercer, and Joe Orton – were at the leading edge of changes in taste on sexual matters that preceded the abolition of censorship in 1968.

Many writers she represented had run into trouble with the Lord Chamberlain; Peter Barnes had two plays initially banned, *Clap Hands Here Comes Charlie*, for excessive and continuous bad language, and *The Ruling Class* for blasphemy. David Rudkin in *Afore Night Come* circumvented the censor by using the word 'firk', which, when said in a West Midlands accent, sounded indistinguishable from the prohibited 'fuck'. Robert Bolt in *Gentle Jack* was not allowed to use the phrase 'a lion shitting himself with fear' because, while it was acceptable for humans and other animals to do such a deed, it was deemed unacceptable for the symbol of British supremacy. Naughton, in *Alfie*, had to agree to place an abortion off stage instead of behind a screen on stage. Charles Wood faced multiple objections, both to the language used and the business he asked of the actors in his military plays; his *Meals on Wheels*, which had to be abandoned at the Bristol Old Vic because a text could not be agreed with the censor, was visited at the Royal Court by an officer from the Lord Chamberlain's office and the script was found to contain a number of deviations from the one that had been licensed. No action, however, was taken.

Travelling Light by Leonard Kingston, *The Bed Sitting Room* by Spike Milligan and John Antrobus and *The Italian Girl* by Iris Murdoch and James Saunders all had problems with beds. The Lord Chamberlain wished to make it clear that there should be no implication of sexual intercourse taking place in a bed, especially with a third person present, and that no two people either of the same or the opposite sex should ever be in a bed together. Saunders also met difficulties with *A Scent of Flowers*, which could only proceed if a mock burial service were mimed and not intoned.

Peter Nichols was asked to protect his audiences by keeping the disabled daughter offstage in *A Day in the Death of Joe Egg*. When the censor accepted that this would destroy the whole point of the play, he suggested an imaginative alternative: the daughter was to be played by a life-sized dummy. Nichols overcame that hurdle too, and all that remained was to decide what the now reinstated child actress would be allowed to hear; dad was not to ask mum in front of their daughter to go to bed with him. The censor even proposed a practical solution. The child could be pushed offstage before this exchange and wheeled back on afterwards. To the obvious objection that the child could hear every word from the wings came the reply, 'Yes, but she wouldn't be *seen* to!' And so, in order to obtain a licence, Nichols wrote in the appropriate stage directions.

Three of Peggy's clients were centrally involved in the historic fight to end censorship in the theatre; Benn Levy, who had been engaged in the battle since he introduced a Private Member's Bill in 1949, John Mortimer as a laywer and prominent civil libertarian, and Edward Bond as the author of *Saved* and *Early Morning*, two of the key plays to feature in the struggle.

Peggy was more of a supporter than a campaigner. As an act of solidarity in 1965 she joined, as a founder member, the British Humanist Association's Television and Radio Committee, which was established to counter the influence of illiberal ideas, but she was not active. Four years later she briefly served on the committee of The Defence of Literature and the Arts Society, which approached her for a list of actresses who might be prepared to appear nude in the erotic revue *Oh! Calcutta!*. Her clients David Mercer and Joe Orton were among the writers who contributed to the show.

She also supported a Brighton bookshop owner and publisher, Bill Butler, who was prosecuted in 1968 under the Obscene Publications Act. His shop, the Unicorn, issued its own publications, such as *Why I Want to Fuck Ronald Reagan* by J.G. Ballard, as well as selling plays by Peggy's clients. It was a test case; Butler was convicted and fined.

The anti-apartheid campaign came even closer to home for Peggy, although she never became an activist. She was contemptuous of actors who appeared in South Africa, such as Moira Lister, whose family happened to be Peggy's cousins, and was particularly upset when her companion, Bill Roderick, toured there in Robert Bolt's *A Man for All Seasons*. Peggy took advice on the boycott of South Africa from the veteran campaigner Ethel de Keyser and shared her view that the boycott should be total. Yet, as an agent, Peggy felt she had to act according to her clients' instructions, even when they ran counter to her own beliefs. Writers like Robert Bolt, Donald Howarth, Frank Marcus and David Rudkin, who were opposed to apartheid, wanted their plays to be performed in South Africa in order to have some effect, and she agreed to negotiate deals there for them reluctantly. They frequently tried to insist on playing to non-segregated audiences, but this could not be guaranteed. Some – for example, Frank Marcus – donated their earnings in South Africa to anti-apartheid causes.

To Alan Ayckbourn's great credit, as she saw it, Peggy persuaded him to refuse to allow his work to be presented under apartheid on the grounds that it would be seen as a victory for the South African government and a defeat for the British writers who were standing by the boycott.

An Anti-Apartheid Movement press release issued in 1971 supporting the boycott was signed by several of her clients, including John Arden,

Edward Bond, John McGrath, David Mercer, Alan Plater, and Ted White-head. From her own childhood Peggy recognised the importance of sport to the white supremacists and believed that a boycott of sport would be by far the most potent of political weapons.

Mustapha Matura, a black Trinidadian writer who had come to England in 1961 aged 21, recalls Peggy being staunchly anti-apartheid while not understanding racism or how it operated in England. He had worked here as a hospital porter, a display assistant at a cosmetics factory, and a stock-room assistant at a garment factory. These were experiences he wove into his plays, which he began to write at the end of the 1960s. Matura joined Peggy in 1973 after leaving Clive Goodwin's agency.

In his writing Matura was exploring racism and colonialism as a state of mind as well as a political reality, affecting both the colonialisers and the colonised. 'Peggy couldn't handle the issue of racism in my work,' he says. 'She felt I was angry and that this anger was coming through in the plays and marring them. She could not distinguish between the emotion of the plays and my own anger. She could not see how racism affected us all, black and white, and that it was not just a black person's problem.'

She and Matura were talking a different language; she did not allow the particularities of any one group to interfere with the universal and essentially innocent views she held on art and politics. She wanted Matura to be kind and magnanimous to his white friends because, she wrote, his 'children were going to inherit the earth and they must be given training now and not pick up the disgusting habits of cruelty and indifference of the "host" society.'

Matura felt there was no dialogue with her, whereas Peggy felt under attack by him. But she told Clive Goodwin that if Matura 'puts the boot into me or you then we must allow it in order to pay for our collective guilt'. Matura wanted Peggy's power to be used on his behalf but found instead that she was living off her reputation. After a period in association with the Royal Court, during which time he was furious that Peggy asked him to take a cut in his royalty when *Play Mas* transferred to the West End, Matura began to work more with black groups. He was co-founder of The Factory, a community arts and social centre in the Paddington area of London, and of the Black Theatre Co-operative, which took The Factory as its base. Disillusioned with Peggy, he went to another agent in 1980, who, he says, was more interested in the fine print of the contracts than in artistic matters.

Peggy was unable to appreciate fully the concerns of many of her clients involved in drama outside the mainstream. She was worried that 'special category theatre', whether of the political left, or the women's, black and gay movements, would label, and therefore limit, the writer. She was anxious, too, that it was selling itself short with theatre practice that fell below her professional and business standards and with plays that were sentimental and insufficiently challenging. Issue-based theatre or documentary drama, even when created with consummate theatrical skill, she believed was ducking the issue of writing what she saw as proper plays.

She was concerned, for example, that Martin Sherman was going to get stuck as a 'gay' writer. She enjoyed his *Passing By*, which she sold to Gay Sweatshop for its 1975 inaugural season at the Almost Free Theatre. It was a gentle, amusing play about a love affair between two men, and was seen then as a revelation in the theatre. Peggy, however, was looking for a tougher attitude from the playwright. After reading his next play, *Rio Grande*, she feared the worst and told Sherman to stop wearing his heart on his sleeve. He understood the message – 'toughen up'; the next play he wrote was *Bent*.

The play was triggered by Sherman's involvement in the Gay Sweatshop production of Drew Griffiths' and Noel Greig's exploration of gay history, *As Time Goes By*, which refers to the pink triangles worn by gay prisoners in the Nazi concentration camps. Sherman decided this would be his territory. Having acted upon Peggy's advice, Sherman was now faced with her judgement that the play should be taken away from Gay Sweatshop in order for it to reach a wider audience, a view with which Gay Sweatshop obligingly concurred.

Peggy sent *Bent* to Michael Rudman at the Hampstead Theatre; he had produced a play of Sherman's while he was running the Traverse Theatre in Edinburgh. *Bent* became stalled at Hampstead while a gay director was sought. The play, however, was being shown to the kind of gay director who would rather keep gay politics off the stage. Meanwhile, the play was given a rehearsed reading at the Eugene O'Neill Memorial Centre in the USA, which led to an offer of a production from a Broadway producer. Hampstead had by now gained a new artistic director who suggested that Sherman try another theatre. Peggy advised Sherman to accept the American offer. Sherman hesitated. He was not convinced by the American deal and was reluctant to surrender his idea of Ian McKellen acting one of the two lead parts. Sherman had been told by Peggy, and others, that McKellen would never consider playing the role because of his reputation as a major classical actor and because, at this time, he had not yet come out as a gay man.

Peggy

By chance, the day before Sherman was due to return to America, he met Robert Chetwyn, who had directed the first production of *What the Butler Saw*. Chetwyn said that he had read *Bent*, would like to direct it and, moreover, thought it ideal for McKellen, whom he knew from directing him as *Hamlet*. McKellen was acting on tour with the RSC and took nearly two months to reply but he eventually proved Peggy wrong by agreeing to play the part.

Peggy, nevertheless, worked hard to make the play succeed. The producer Eddie Kulukundis finally made this possible in 1979. In the absence of any West End possibilities, he backed the play at a somewhat reluctant Royal Court. *Bent* played to 95% box office and transferred to the Criterion Theatre, which already had a production booked for December, so it could only play for a limited run; a Broadway production followed, with film star Richard Gere taking the McKellen role. Authentic gay drama on a major scale had arrived.

Peggy, however, was never ideological about sexuality, despite representing writers like Sherman and Larry Kramer, whose play *The Normal Heart* was at the forefront of AIDS awareness campaigning. When she promoted John Holmstrom's play *Quaint Honour* in the mid-1950s, its subject matter of schoolboy homosexuality was extremely provocative. Yet she acted not from campaigning, political motives, but because she thought the play was expressing an important truth about human relationships. Likewise, she found Colin Spencer's *Spitting Image*, a potentially scandalous fantasy about a male couple, one of whom becomes pregnant, charming rather than significant. The fall of censorship in 1968 allowed it to be transferred to the Duke of York's from Hampstead Theatre Club, thereby earning it a place in the footnotes of theatre history as the first West End play to deal openly and sympathetically with a gay partnership without gay sexuality being a portrayed as a source of apprehension. Peggy was more concerned that it was booed on its first night in the West End than with its role in the history of sexual politics.

Peggy believed that the intrusion of ideology was a problem for several of her writers and was anxious that the desire to be acceptable as a political playwright would become a dangerous, if not ruinous, diversion. She was aghast, for example, at the thought that Edward Bond, who collaborated magnificently as a librettist with the composer Hans Werner Henze on the opera *We Come to the River* in 1976, had been told by Henze that as a Communist it was his duty to punish people and humiliate them.

All this was a long way from the real world of political struggle, about which Peggy knew very little. Her politics were moral, axiomatic and instinctive. She supported rebels and outsiders, yet this category could embrace both Nelson Mandela, whom, from the time of his incarceration on Robben Island, she regarded as the greatest African alive, and Margaret Thatcher, whom she admired for saying unfashionable things, for her strength of character, her determination to clear up a mess, and for her desire to prevent people feeling that they were owed a living. Peggy, nevertheless, detested her governments and described her once as a 'dreadful old woman with awful teeth'. She admired Shirley Williams at the outset of the Social Democratic Party and preferred David Owen to Neil Kinnock on foreign policy. Peggy even thought John Major sweet. While Peggy generally hated extreme right-wingers she felt socialism was too easy an option; she did not like nationalisation or any notion of collective life. Nevertheless, when the idea arose of turning William Hinton's book *Fanshen* into a play, she responded positively because its account of a Chinese village transformed by Communism told the story of a revolution that had actually occurred; she dearly wished there would be a revolution in England but believed it would never happen.

Peggy did not try to stop any of her clients who followed an active political path, even though this often rendered her a marginal, and sometimes completely absent, figure. The Fringe was to her an undiscovered country, as was most of the world beyond London, which was why the community and political theatre circuit represented, in her mind's eye, an unrealistic career choice for her clients. Yet John McGrath, who had joined Peggy in 1958 while still at Oxford University, found her stalwart as he made his journey from the theatre of the Royal Court and Hampstead, where he had enjoyed early success with *Events While Guarding the Bofors Gun*, to a new agitational theatre of education and entertainment.

The turning point came in 1968 when he visited Paris to witness the uprising against President de Gaulle. He rewrote the first of his Scottish history plays, *Random Happenings in the Hebrides*, in the light of his trip. The change of emphasis was clear in *Unruly Elements*, a group of short plays examining the state of contemporary Britain, which was performed in Liverpool in 1971. Peggy saw the change, but not in socio-political terms. She responded to the writing: 'Tradition and freedom are at war in the plays. One sits back watching what is virtually a naturalistic type play but you keep breaking the wall and talking to us directly . . . so we don't know what to accept.'

That same year, McGrath founded the socialist touring group 7:84 (based on the tenet that 7% of the population owns 84% of the wealth). It became his life until 1988. Peggy was simply not interested in its work because it belonged to another world. She and McGrath just agreed to differ and to remain good friends.

Peggy, however, came face-to-face with this other world as well as the politics of the alternative theatre movement through her representation of John Arden and Margaretta D'Arcy. They came to Peggy via Ann Jellicoe, whom Arden had known since the early days of the Royal Court. Already established as a major writer, Arden joined Peggy in 1967 along with D'Arcy, his co-author and wife, after their then agent had speculated with and lost his clients' money. Peggy refused to take a commission from their earnings until the debts that had accrued from the former agent's misdemeanours had been paid off.

Arden and D'Arcy were fast losing interest in the conventional theatre at this time; their view of the role of the writer and of theatre took a significant turn during a trip to America in 1967, extending discoveries they had made in earlier work in England. On their return, they continued experimenting with all aspects of theatre-making. They only needed the agency for contractual work and moral support. Peggy obliged on both counts and never pressed them to take on any work that they did not want to do. She facilitated as best she could and helped with money and commissions when they were short of cash. She raised money for the Dublin première in 1975 of their epic saga about James Connolly, *The Non-Stop Connolly Show*, a cycle of six plays which spanned a weekend in Liberty Hall.

She and Arden occasionally discussed politics and art, mostly in the early years of the relationship. They agreed about the corrupted state of the theatre, even if they did not agree about the solution; she was dismissive of the West End, the RSC and the NT, and was angry with the Royal Court, too, for pandering to the star syndrome. (She was caustic, for instance, in 1971 about Ralph Richardson's current performance there in Osborne's *West of Suez*, although it brought the desired West End transfer.) She confessed to Arden on one occasion that she hated herself for not insisting that Mark Dignam repeat his performance as the Father in John Mortimer's *A Voyage Round My Father* when it transferred from the Greenwich Theatre to the West End and he was replaced by Alec Guinness. 'Success has left me with many heart searchings; what kind of theatre are we promoting?' she wrote to Arden. 'We have GOT to stop this insidious tendency for the author now to be less important than the star . . . I am deeply concerned, and feel that I too have been dreamy and careless and indifferent, or lazy or disenchanted with the theatre (and you can say THAT again!).'

In Arden, Peggy saw hope for the future. She believed him to have 'the finest talent writing in England and possibly in the English-speaking world'. Yet she could still retain a sense of proportion when it came to praise. *Serjeant Musgrave's Dance*, which he wrote before joining Peggy, 'could be said to be a minor classic,' she commented. 'I'm not saying it is but it *could* be said.'

Her admiration for his writing helped her to withstand the trauma of a succession of rows that marked Arden and D'Arcy's first years with her, although Peggy did not understand the politics of any of the disputes.

Peggy's standpoint can be summed up in her attitude to a wrangle she had in 1969 with BBC-TV over the terms of a contract for Arden and D'Arcy. Peggy was complaining about the trend toward putting ratings before good plays and cost before talent. 'There are thousands of professional playwrights who are turning out workmanlike budgetable plays, which will go on and be forgotten the next morning,' but, in the case of Arden and D'Arcy, wrote Peggy, 'I don't think the ordinary professional rules of budgeting *can* apply . . . Talent of this order isn't a convenient or comfortable thing, and unfortunately requires an enormous amount of work and understanding from other people.'

Such was the viewpoint that guided her through the series of theatrical skirmishes that began with *The Hero Rises Up* in 1968 and was followed in 1972 by a libel suit against Arden and D'Arcy for their play, *The Ballygombeen Bequest*, and the extraordinary clash with the RSC over *The Island of the Mighty* the same year.

Arden had been involved in a musical called *Trafalgar* before he joined Peggy. He pulled out when he saw the work produced by the composers, Jerry Brock and Sheldon Harnick. Michael Kustow, who was running the Institute of Contemporary Arts, picked up on the idea of a show about Nelson and commissioned Arden and D'Arcy. The ICA was situated in a plush Regency terrace on the Mall, and Kustow saw the commission as part of a strategy to make the Institute a more popular arts centre. In keeping both with this aim and with their own theatrical ambitions, Arden and D'Arcy insisted that their melodrama, *The Hero Rises Up*, be played at the Round House in north London, a venue noted for counter-cultural happenings, rather than at the ICA, just down the road from Buckingham Palace. Arguments broke out with the ICA about the nature of the production and grew to such a pitch that Arden and D'Arcy let the audience in to the Round House for nothing.

There was little for Peggy to do except act as observer, counsellor, and defender of her clients. She was already alarmed at the prospect of Arden becoming unemployable and believed that D'Arcy, whom she saw as the more political of the two, was the main cause.

The Round House clash did, indeed, offer a taste of disputes to come. Peggy was called upon to provide similar support in 1972 when Arden and D'Arcy faced a court case over *The Ballygombeen Bequest*, a play about an English absentee landlord and the family which lives on the estate he has inherited in Ireland. The man who claimed to be the real-life landlord attacked in the play, announced through his lawyers that he was issuing a writ for libel and slander, and said that if the play were not taken off, the producing company, 7:84, would become a party to the suit. Leaflets containing his private telephone number and address had been given out at performances in Edinburgh by members of 7:84, and audiences had been invited to protest in person at an eviction that the authors declared he had instituted and was executing.

The play had begun its run in Belfast before appearing at the Edinburgh festival, but the legal trouble only broke out when the play came to the Bush Theatre in London. The matter was then *sub judice* until the case came to court in 1977. Peggy gave advice during the protracted preparation of the case and enlisted support for Arden and D'Arcy (for example, she asked John Osborne if he would appear as a character witness). The jury in the end were discharged and the matter was settled out of court, with each side having to pay their own costs and Arden and D'Arcy having to agree that the play should not be performed or published as it stood. The play, in a revised form, resurfaced later as *The Little Gray Home in the West*.

On the very day the landlord had communicated his intentions to sue Arden and D'Arcy, Peggy was in the midst of the most public of their disputes, a historic struggle with the RSC concerning the production of *The Island of the Mighty* at the Aldwych Theatre. The news of the impending libel action arrived on the day of their opening.

The Island of the Mighty had begun life in 1953 when Arden wrote a play about King Arthur, which interested nobody but the author. He rewrote it two years later but this version fared no better. A decade later, he transformed it into a trilogy commissioned by BBC-TV, which he completed in 1969 when it was duly dropped. At the behest of the Welsh National Theatre, Arden reworked the script for the stage, making it even longer; the company, however, could not cope with the demands made by the new script. The massive play was sent to several London managements but had not been placed until the RSC decided to take it up. The RSC asked for a shortened version, which Arden and D'Arcy wrote together. By mutual consent with the RSC, Arden was present throughout rehearsals while D'Arcy was only going to attend the first run-through, some ten days before the first preview at the Aldwych Theatre in December.

Arden says he raised doubts with the director David Jones during rehearsals about what he was witnessing and was told by Jones that, given time, the actors would find their way to the desired style. When D'Arcy arrived, she felt that this had not been achieved, and that the meaning of the play was being misrepresented. The music, set and costumes also came in for harsh criticism.

Cuts in the text were needed to bring the running time down to a manageable length but the authors felt that they could not undertake such work without a company meeting being held to sort out where things had gone awry. The actors called a meeting and a vote was taken as to whether or not there should be a formal company meeting to discuss the play-wrights' grievances; the vote went against such a meeting taking place. An open forum was organised instead. The cast was clearly divided and feelings were running very high. Arden and D'Arcy realised that it was too late to change the production significantly and that the gap between them and Jones was too huge to bridge. The two writers agreed that the sensible course of action was to turn their backs on the production and go home to Ireland, but only after attending a company meeting.

David Jones went to see Peggy after the run-through to tell her how badly he thought Arden and D'Arcy had behaved, in particular D'Arcy. He said he could not agree to their demand for a company meeting so near to the first performance; it could be de-stabilising for the actors and ruin the show. Maybe one might be possible later. He said he could get the play ready if everyone were patient. Peggy telephoned Arden and D'Arcy to let them know of her conversation with Jones. They insisted she call back to ensure the meeting was scheduled as soon as possible. She talked to Jones again, who said he would not allow such a meeting. She relayed this message to the playwrights. The result was not what she expected.

Arden and D'Arcy decided to go on strike and to picket the Aldwych Theatre. They declared that clauses in their contract were not being honoured. As members of the Society of Irish Playwrights, they felt that the refusal of the management to negotiate over the clauses in a company meeting left them no alternative but to take the equivalent of industrial action. It was a dispute over their conditions of work, not over inter-pretation. Peggy was instructed by Arden and D'Arcy to take their names off the production.

For Peggy, the situation got quickly out of hand. As a go-between, she had been the unwitting catalyst of Arden and D'Arcy's decision to strike. Then she became stuck as the intermediary between the two writers and the RSC, a role she hated. Peggy's office became the campaign headquarters. She helped with legal advice, took hot soup to the picket line and rallied support. She was sufficiently distressed by the events, however, to keep away from a meeting that was called in support of Arden and D'Arcy, and which the agent Clive Goodwin attended. Not all Peggy's clients backed Arden and D'Arcy, while many who had reservations nevertheless signed a letter taking their side. People like Joan Littlewood came to the picket line, although, as Peggy pointed out, Littlewood had never let writers control anything.

During a preview, sympathisers of Arden and D'Arcy in the audience, some of whom had been on the picket line, interrupted the show to demand that the playwrights be heard. They came on stage to be greeted by a mix of boos and cheers. There was pandemonium. D'Arcy went to rip down the back cloth but was stopped by one of the cast. Arden tried to address the audience. He had to shout. He asked if they wanted him to speak and deemed that the 'Nos' outweighed the shouts in favour. Having been rejected by a rough vote of the audience, he and D'Arcy left the Aldwych. They regarded the opportunity to put their case as an adequate substitute for the company meeting they had been seeking unsuccessfully and were now ready to return to Ireland.

Peggy became embroiled in attempts by the RSC to allow Arden and D'Arcy to appear on stage after the official first night, an offer which they declined because it was made through a newspaper letters column and only named one author, Arden and not D'Arcy, an omission they considered a slur on D'Arcy. In an act of solidarity with 7:84, Arden and D'Arcy attended the first night of *The Ballygombeen Bequest* at the Bush rather than the opening of *The Island of the Mighty*. Peggy avoided the Aldwych opening too and went to see the RSC production later, anonymously.

The dispute threw Peggy into a quandary. She was baffled by it and felt at a very low ebb. She accepted that writers might organise, but her pragmatism prompted her to remain neutral, concerned as she was with her duty to all her other clients. She saw an inevitable conflict between writers as trades unionists and writers as artists but accepted that Arden and D'Arcy should do whatever they thought was right. On the other hand, apart from having doubts about the practicality of their campaign, she understood the position of the management involved; what she wanted was the restoration of a working relationship. Above all, she was worried that Arden would become unemployable.

Whatever Peggy's misgivings were about the *Island of the Mighty* dispute, it did trigger a public debate, at a time of nationwide industrial and political upheaval, about the state of theatre, and in particular the plight of the playwright. This in turn led to the formation of the Theatre Writers' Union and a strengthening of the Writers' Guild, and subsequently to the introduction of the standard writer's contract.

As a play *The Island of the Mighty* belonged to an earlier period in Arden's and D'Arcy's life, while *The Ballygombeen Bequest* looked forward to their future, when most of their theatrical work would be concentrated in their home locality of Galway and would not involve Peggy. After the RSC debacle, Arden said he would never work in the British theatre again, and, with a few exceptions when he worked with Fringe companies, he stayed true to his word.

Peggy found their politics, and in particular their Irish concerns, bewildering. In the light of the Prevention of Terrorism Act and the IRA's bombing campaign in Britain, Peggy preferred not to delve too deeply. She did, however, circulate to all her clients a letter Arden and D'Arcy wrote protesting at the British government's treatment of Irish prisoners, just as she had circulated a petition from James Saunders complaining at the inability of the Czech writer, Pavel Kohout, to leave his country to attend a festival in Brussels. She was not apolitical but Arden and D'Arcy saw that, whilst Peggy herself was opposed to exploiters, she kept her politics generalised and did not involve herself with specifics. She had no understanding of the process of social change nor of the struggle to bring it about.

She considered Arden and D'Arcy to be extraordinary people who had a way of attracting disaster to themselves. She once said of Arden to another client, 'He trained as an architect, dear. I'd hate to live in one of his buildings.' Peggy was confused by Arden's relationship with D'Arcy. She liked strong, independent women but did not like wives of writers, yet in this case D'Arcy was a writer too and a co-author. D'Arcy was not stopping Arden writing, on the contrary they were prolific together. Peggy felt the Aldwych crisis had been precipitated by D'Arcy's arrival after several weeks of calm when only Arden was present at rehearsals, and Peggy did not think D'Arcy's influence in general was beneficial. Peggy was nonetheless very concerned when D'Arcy was sent to jail, in 1978 and 1980, both times following protests at the situation in Northern Ireland; Peggy always admired her fighting spirit.

To Peggy, the fact that they were not commercial writers, and never would be, was a liberation from the routine pressures of her job. She could enjoy their idealism 'righting universal wrongs' and defended their integrity fiercely, even though their practice caused her a great deal of bother and stress.

Peggy

'She had a wild quality,' says Arden, 'and was a genuine radical liberal, not trendy. She despised people who made money yet had to make it herself in order to keep the agency going. She didn't sell out but made necessary compromises. She survived by the rules of the world she hated.'

Arden and D'Arcy were not the only clients of Peggy's to challenge accepted notions of the status and role of the playwright in the theatrical hierarchy. Clients like Edward Bond and Peter Nichols had well-publicised disagreements with, respectively, managements and directors, while some, like John McGrath or Alan Ayckbourn, addressed the problem by forming their own companies.

Peggy concentrated her efforts on securing better deals for writers through the traditional means of negotiating with managements. Peggy kept the establishment theatre on its toes and up to date. She only wanted to change the theatre piecemeal, play by play. She had no strategic sense of the culture in which she operated and used her influence to change things on an individual basis. She confirmed the status quo as she modified it. She knew the mainstream world intimately from many different angles and from many years' theatrical experience; she held most of it in contempt, based on her own principles and her inside detailed knowledge of its personnel and its workings, but she could not see an alternative because that was not in her thinking.

'It's no good railing against the system,' she said. 'It's what we've got and when you ask what are we going to do about it, you must either decide to go on writing or not.'.

*

'Talent isn't enough; work and self-criticism are essential'

One writer, whom she took on in 1974, quite against the grain of the time, did decide to go on writing and, much to Peggy's delight, made the system work for him on his own terms. On the surface, Willy Russell was as unlikely to be a part of her agency as was Alan Ayckbourn, but for Peggy that simply added to the attraction. Russell was a challenge and a breath of fresh air.

Peggy saw life as a balancing of opposites and here was a young man from Liverpool who represented the antithesis of the likes of Christopher Hampton, Stephen Poliakoff, and David Hare; Russell was a working-class northerner who had left his state comprehensive school at 15 and, among other jobs, had worked as a warehouse labourer and ladies' hairdresser as opposed to enjoying a privileged upbringing in the affluent south with a public school and Oxbridge education.

Russell had begun writing while studying as an adult at a higher education college. Three of his plays had been performed locally. When he adapted Alan Plater's Hull-based football play *The Tigers Are Coming – OK?* for the Everyman in Liverpool in 1973, Plater suggested that he contact Peggy. Russell, who was finishing his last term of teaching practice, replied that he was only a part-time writer. He was desperately keen to become full-time, but he could see no prospect of this at the time. Oddly enough, Peggy was the one agent of whom he had heard. His father-in-law had been a librarian in Camden and remembered Peggy using the library where he worked. Russell was unaware, however, that Peggy took on new young playwrights; he thought that she only handled West End dramatists.

Russell kept writing and sold a 30-minute play to BBC-TV, which Barry Hanson produced. Now a schoolteacher, Russell entered a *Radio Times* play competition. His wife Annie was pregnant with their first child and he could see no way of achieving his playwriting ambition. The competition offered a life line. Entrants had to submit a full-length TV play and be sponsored by someone in television. Russell approached Hanson, who said he would not only sponsor him but would buy the play too.

Along with three other hopefuls, Russell was invited to a prize-giving lunch in London. He travelled down, assuming the other finalists had also had their plays bought, and was surprised to discover that he was the only one. His confidence aroused, he listened while one of the other writers was announced as the winner and the other two were awarded an unexpected cash prize. Russell thought the judges must have invented a special prize for him too, but he was the only one to be left empty-handed. Beyond rage, he was determined to remedy the situation in however a minor way and took a bottle of scotch as he made for the exit without bothering to wait for the meal. One of the judges, Hugh Whitemore, saw Russell leave and followed him. Whitemore tried to apologise for the judges and said he thought the result was a travesty. He offered to send Russell's play, *Death of a Young, Young Man*, to his agent, Peggy. Russell was not to be mollified and told Whitemore he could do whatever he liked.

A few weeks later, Russell remembers, while he was teaching at school, his class was interrupted; there was a telephone call for him. He thought the worst because it was unheard of to interrupt a teacher unless it was an emergency. He went to the phone. 'Hello dear,' said the voice at the other end, 'I'm going to represent you.' It was Peggy, whom he had never met.

'Now, dear, where are you?' she asked, and on receiving the reply, Russell could hear her turn to her assistant Tom Erhardt and shout, as in disbelief, 'Tom, he's *teaching!*' They talked on the phone for three-quarters of an hour, by which time his next class had come and gone. She told him to send her all his plays and asked if he wanted any money. It was a nice offer, thought Russell, but he replied that he did not wish to take any money that he had not earned himself. Peggy knew she had chosen well.

Following the call, Russell sent her three plays, including *John, Paul, George, Ringo . . . and Bert*, Russell's play about the Beatles, which was due to open at the Everyman shortly. On the day of its first preview, just as a taxi called to take him to the theatre, the phone went and it was Peggy again. 'We must get your Beatles play on, dear,' she insisted. She did not seem to have grasped that it was already being produced. 'What, *tonight*, dear? With *professional* actors, darling. In a *real* theatre.'

She was impressed but would not stop talking. The taxi was waiting, and Russell had to put the phone down on her.

News of the play spread and Peggy telephoned again, to discuss a possible future for it in London. There had already been some interest and one producer had arrived at the theatre, offering £1,000 in notes there and then to buy the rights. The director, Alan Dossor, showed him off the premises.

Peggy came to see the show with Michael Codron, Helen Montagu, the former Royal Court general manager who had turned to producing, and Robert Stigwood, who had acquired the rights to the Beatles music. Peggy wanted Stigwood to present *John, Paul, George, Ringo and . . . Bert* in London, along with Michael Codron. She had also invited her new client David Hare because she was worried that Russell might be overwhelmed by the posse of producers and thought it would help to have a writer present.

The day Peggy went to Liverpool happened to be the day that Russell's baby boy was born. Russell did not arrive at the theatre until after the interval, when he met an old friend, who had come armed with a cele-bratory bottle of champagne. They toasted the good health of Russell's new son until the curtain came down. Russell knew that he had to meet Peggy and Stigwood, although they had not made any specific arrangements and he did not know what she looked like. Well lubricated, Russell made his way through the crowds to the green room and flung open the door. There was a scream. At his feet he found a sprawling, snarling, smartly-dressed lady of advancing years who had clearly been standing just the other side of the door and had been flattened when he opened it.

Alan Dossor quickly helped Peggy to her feet and effected the introduction between client and agent – the first face to face. Peggy's snarls turned to smiles on learning the identity of her assailant and the reason for his recklessness.

As the discussions concerning the play's transfer to the West End proceeded, she put showbusiness and what she called 'this get-rich-quick-grab-fame-and-trample-everyone-else-down-in-the-process' into perspective for Russell, pronouncing self-respect to be more important than money. During a disagreement that arose between the producers and the actors over their London wages, Peggy intervened at her most bellicose in order to protect Russell's interests, fearing that the row might jeopardise the transfer. It being nothing to do with her, she took aim at the director, who, likewise, was not directly involved. 'To see decent honourable people losing their heads and grabbing for more than their share really shattered me,' she wrote to Dossor. 'How can one accept with indifference the spectacle of decent, good people behaving in a vulgar, grasping and mean-spirited way, simply because a play is transferring to London (the arsehole of Europe).

'After all, it's only a *play*, however well done, well written, well directed and acted – it's a transitory thing which will be forgotten the way every play is forgotten, and every star is forgotten and every player is forgotten. You have only to see old Cicely Courtneidge tottering into a first night, unregarded by all, to remember that once she had London at her feet and her attendance at a first night was greeted with the stalls standing up and applauding her.

'I understand barely 5% of the population of England go to the theatre at all; and a play is merely a mirror on life, and it's not the mirror, but life *itself* which is important. By the same token, the actors are PLAYING the Beatles – they are not the Beatles *themselves*, who struggled for years, earning hardly anything, finally reaching unimaginable heights only to be destroyed or destroy themselves (who knows which?)'

She copied the letter to Russell, whom she had excepted from her complaint, and it set the tone for his future view of the profession that he had just embraced. The dispute was settled, in the favour of the actors, and the show transferred successfully with a formidable cast that included George Costigan, Philip Joseph, Bernard Hill, Trevor Eve, and Antony Sher.

Russell's plays sold themselves; he had his own contacts in Liverpool and did not need Peggy for this aspect of his career. She was happy that he kept on writing. Peggy went into battle on Russell's behalf on other fronts. When a drama editor rejected the Beatles play for publication, she snapped: 'You people! You wouldn't know a good play if it bit you!' When his next play received what Peggy saw as condescending reviews in London, she fought back. The play was *Breezeblock Park*, which is set in the houses of two sisters caught up in the competitive consumer race.

'When are you guilt-ridden middle-class critics going to grasp that the working classes have joined the human race?' she wrote to Irving Wardle, critic of *The Times*. 'They are quite able to laugh at criticism of themselves and their values . . . It doesn't really matter that you don't like the play – fair enough. But why talk of "contempt" simply because an author writes a comedy about foolish *working-class* ladies trying to keep up with the Joneses! It would have got an entirely different response if it had been middle-class ladies!'

When Russell's TV play, *Our Day Out*, was returned by David Rose of the BBC because he did not have the money to make it, Peggy sent it instead to Granada, who agreed to buy it. Meanwhile, a director at the BBC, Pedr James, had read the play, liked it and told Rose that the money must be found. Rose agreed and contacted Peggy. She much preferred Rose to be the producer as originally intended and set about unpicking the play from Granada. Rose offered a fee of £15,000, and Peggy immediately raised the figure to £17,000. Rose was in no position to demur. Peggy confided in Russell, 'I always like to negotiate my own percentage, darling, so you don't have to pay for it.'

Russell did not usually show Peggy his plays until he had finished them. He might then re-write them in the light of her response. He recalls that she was a good critic because she read a script like a writer but did not respond like a writer; she resisted the temptation to say how she would have written the play. She poured scorn at first on *Educating Rita*, Russell's play about a working-class woman who enrols on an Open University course, which he wrote for the RSC's Warehouse Theatre. Peggy's complaint was that the character of Frank, the tutor, was so weakly conceived that he barely existed and that, in a two-handed play, this was especially reprehensible.

'She was right,' says Russell, 'but it was the only way I could have written the play. I had to put all my energy into the character of Rita. I was shattered by Peggy's response but I knew in my heart that she was right.' Russell was exhausted. Writing the play had drained him; he had two small children by now and his wife was expecting their third child. 'I didn't know if I could work on the play again. I had to really dredge up my energy, but I put the paper in the typewriter and 24 hours later I had done it.'

Russell reworked Frank's part, leaving Rita's more or less alone. 'Without that shift the play would never have been heard of again,' says Russell. Instead, it became a hit in 1980 for the RSC, directed by Mike Ockrent with

Julie Walters as Rita, before being made into a successful film three years later, in which Walters was partnered by Michael Caine.

Peggy was abroad when *Educating Rita* opened. She returned to England to read a clutch of rave reviews. Yet she never overcame her first impression of the play and could not understand the enormous popularity of what she insisted on calling 'that *little* play'.

She had some more unpicking to do when, by her oversight, the film rights contained a clause relating to the absence of stage productions at the time the film would open, which was contradicted by the stage rights in America that had been disposed of by the RSC. Peggy became extremely agitated when it seemed as if there would be a clash between the film and a stage production. Legal action loomed. Peggy began calling Russell earlier and earlier, until, at 5am one morning, he told her not to worry because, if the case came to court, her mistake would be seen to have been genuine and made unintentionally. Peggy became apoplectic. 'If ever I have to defend a client in court,' she hissed, 'I will close this agency down.' A raw nerve had been touched. Peggy's phobia about courts had its roots in her father's legal struggle to sell the family farm, which had ruined his health as well as his assets. Fortunately for Peggy, the film company did not consider the stage production to be a threat and a court appearance was averted.

With *Blood Brothers*, Russell contacted Peggy after completing a seventy-minute version in 1981 for a company of five actors to perform in schools. He knew that there was something bigger in it and wanted to know if she thought it was potentially the big musical he thought it could be. Unbeknownst to him, Peggy had been to see the production with Tom Erhardt when it paid a visit to the Theatre Royal, Stratford East. She enthused about *Blood Brothers*, finding in the story elements of Greek tragedy, and encouraged him to develop it. She immediately saw its promise, which, for example, Michael Codron, by his own admission, had missed when he saw it. 'I wouldn't have written *Blood Brothers* the musical if Peggy had not liked the idea, which she did,' says Russell.

He wrestled with a new version of his tale about a working-class woman who bears twin boys but cannot afford to support her already large family and gives one of the boys away. Russell became despondent as he struggled with the material, and it was Peggy's motivation that kept him going. He wrote the lyrics and music himself, as well as the book. *Blood Brothers*, with Barbara Dickson in the lead, became another success in Liverpool and London.

The first London production, however, only ran for eight months. Following a UK tour and several foreign productions, *Blood Brothers* was remounted in the West End in 1988 and was still running nine years later. One of the show's songs, 'Tell Me It's Not True', also became a hit. Peggy liked to pull Russell's leg about being the show's composer. A favourite refrain of hers was to ask him, 'Who wrote the music, darling?' and respond in surprise when the inevitable answer came back, 'I did, Peggy, I did.'

By the time of *Shirley Valentine* in 1986, Peggy was already ill. She did not like the production in Liverpool nor the one in London where Simon Callow directed Pauline Collins as the housewife with the insistent urge to escape the constraints of her own environment. Peggy went to a preview of the film in London three years later; it was the last time she and Russell were together in public.

For Russell, 'Every new play is a test, no matter how experienced a writer you are, because it does not yet exist and has never existed. You still face a blank page with trepidation.' Thinking of Peggy, however, helps him through his recurring creative trial. Peggy approved of his ambition to be a popular writer with integrity, which meant working in the commercial theatre and not in subsidised garrets, although all his plays began in the subsidised sector.

'Peggy protected me, guided me through the commercial set-up, and gave me a crash course in how to behave,' says Russell. 'She always said "behave well".' Alan Ayckbourn's experience was a positive influence because he had managed to secure the conditions he wanted in Scarborough and to use the theatre that he ran there as a base from which to come into London. 'I write for audiences I know,' says Russell, 'and a transfer to the West End is a bonus. I don't write *for* the West End.

'She taught me so much. I assumed all other agents were like Peggy, but they're not. Others may love their clients. Peggy often hated us, but she loved the work, and that's the difference. It's the work that counted for her. Peggy always said to me, "Stay true to what you're doing" and that's what I have tried to do. Her other message was: "never be grateful – don't forget, you wrote the words".'

*

'I have as much right to be wrong as right,
and the only thing authors can do is leave me.'

Russell, like Ayckbourn, was always something of an outsider in the agency, a fully paid up member of the 'northern branch' whose plays were quite different from that of the majority southerners. Plays by the southerners came closer to the old fashioned literary tradition of fine writing, which explored the complex interplay of individual sensibilities. They were less likely to conquer the commercial heartland the way Willy Russell did but were to set to occupy the highground of the publicly subsidised theatre.

Peggy devoted a great deal of her energies to such writers, who, like Stephen Poliakoff, were negotiating their way out of a sheltered establishment upbringing in order to bring their plays to life through the prism of the contemporary world. It was Christopher Hampton who, in 1969, introduced Peggy to Poliakoff, an even younger protégé than he himself had been.

While Hampton was resident dramatist at the Royal Court, he had read a review in *The Times* of *Granny*, written by this schoolboy playwright who had put his own play on in a hall in north London after it had been produced at his public school. The review said the play was better than many that were put on at the Royal Court. Hampton went to see the play for himself and met Poliakoff. He suggested that he contact Peggy, and warned him not to call her Margaret. Poliakoff wrote to her asking for advice about the theatre, and sent her *Granny*. He mentioned that on the strength of the *Times* review, he had been offered a commission by a New York producer and several theatres had asked to read the play.

Peggy replied the same day, before she had read *Granny*, saying that she would help him. Three days later, after reading the play, she summoned him to Goodwin's Court.

His first meeting was similar to that of many other clients; she was awesome, a fierce fireball who pointed to the chaise longue on which he was sitting and said, 'That's where Ionesco fucked me.' She talked furiously and said 'fuck' many times. It was breathtaking for a 16-year-old.

She complained about the state of the play that he had sent in, criticising his poor photocopying and incomprehensible page numbering. Angry at what he was convinced was her mistake, he argued back that she must have mixed up the script. They got on well after that, although Poliakoff believes that she always retained the initial image of him as a writer of muddled plays.

Peggy told him that *Granny* was slighter than Hampton's first effort and that he would write two or three plays before he wrote 'a really professional play with true professional merit'. She was rather put out when Poliakoff countered with the news that Hampstead Theatre Club wanted to stage *Granny* but was mollified by the fact that it was to be directed by

303

Richard Eyre, then a relatively new director whom she liked. She felt it might be too soon for *Granny* to be produced but it would probably be all right at Hampstead, where many first plays were produced and the critics tended to be generous to them. In the event, a new artistic director, Vivian Matalon, arrived at Hampstead and cancelled *Granny*.

After his first meeting with Peggy, Poliakoff was not sure whether or not she had actually taken him on but they kept in touch, and it soon became clear that she was indeed representing him. She was annoyed about the New York commission, seeing it as unwelcome interference, and entered into correspondence with the American producer in order to limit the damage. She warned Poliakoff against being seduced by American money, and eventually the commission was allowed to drop.

He recalls that with his second play, *Bambi Ramm*, which he wrote when he was seventeen about a group of school friends, she wanted him to take charge of his characters more – she felt they talked too much and their charm became tedious, a shortcoming which she blamed on his ignorance of life. She had read the play between 3 am and 5.30 am on one Saturday morning – 'a rather lucid time for me,' she said – and compared the effect of his repetitions to being under the influence of chloroform. Poliakoff arranged for it to be performed at a community centre in London. She staggered out at the end of a long evening and in the middle of the street at 11pm tore into him, attacking the construction and duration of the play. Poliakoff remembers her overacting her part, but it had the desired effect. He asked her there and then, 'Should I go on?' 'Of course,' Peggy replied, 'you're fucking talented.'

James Roose-Evans, the founder, and Matalon's predecessor as artistic director of the Hampstead Theatre Club, came to see the production but left before the third act. She thanked him for coming and took the opportunity to point out he had missed the most important part of the play. 'I found things in Act 3 extremely dramatic and disturbing,' she wrote, 'and the whole panorama of the play seems curiously real as far as I am concerned. Boring, of course, because the young are so bloody boring, because they are so self-ambitious'. She described the play as much more ambitious than *Granny*, which Roose-Evans had scheduled, and, because of that, less well achieved.

'Of course, Stephen needs to learn how to live, but I think he should go on writing because I think he knows this play wasn't properly disciplined and that it was hopelessly over-written and over-long,' she wrote. 'At his age, it is almost impossible to impose discipline over your private world. What I really like about Stephen is his absolute originality. He is not trying to write a well-made play, nor is he trying to write like Coward, Orton,

Pinter or anyone else – he is trying to write like Poliakoff, and I think that in a few years' time when he has learned how to select and heighten, he is going to make a considerable mark. I very much admire his character. I was incredibly tough with him after the first night, and he took it extraordinarily well. He has a lot of guts.'

Peggy maintained her tough attitude. Of his next play, *A Starting Place*, she said: 'I found the first twenty-four pages fresh and interesting, and then I got the oppressive Poliakoff blues, which came down on me like a blanket of boredom, and I had to fight to keep my attention on the play . . . A play can be slight and still hold the attention. For some reason or other, slightness isn't your problem, it's more serious – you just can't stop your characters talking and talking and it seems as if you don't really control them, or know what you want them to do. This ends up by absolutely exhausting your audience, yet at the same time puzzling them, because there is a real delicacy and fascination about the people, only you can't keep our interest in the events. As you don't know anything much about the characters, how can you develop them? I think it's basic ignorance of people and life, except the very young, which is the fault. This will be remedied with each year you live, dear Stephen, so don't *worry* about it.'

She invited him to find another agent if he did not like what she was saying, but, although the relationship was fierce, he knew she believed in him and so he stayed.

Peggy was drawn to Poliakoff's determination and to his otherness; his Russian ancestry was still apparent. She felt he was difficult, 'a quirky boy' but an 'original', 'strange and odd'. He remained something of an outsider and was always his own person. He went to Cambridge University at a time of radical student activity but concentrated on his writing. He set up a theatre group to stage his own plays and dropped out after two years to become a playwright. Peggy likened him, rather fancifully, both to the young Cocteau and to Cocteau's 'pupil', the poet Raymond Radiguet, who she felt was 'forced' by Cocteau like an exotic plant. Radiguet had an early death and tasted the fruits of success and sophistication too soon, she said. She did not want the same to happen to Poliakoff and felt he needed testing by life quite severely because he was as young as he was.

Poliakoff recalls Peggy being particularly destructive about *Pretty Boy*, which he finished in his first week at Cambridge. Unusually for her he heard nothing for two weeks. He was in despair, and when she did reply it was the by now common chorus: the play is too long and she was not sure she could represent it. Poliakoff sent it himself to the Royal Court, and, although she had been keen that his work should be staged there, she was stunned when they accepted it for a Sunday night performance. On seeing the production, which marked Poliakoff's professional London début, she was overjoyed. This complete turnaround made him wonder whether she was utterly open-minded or utterly inconsistent.

Her strong reaction against it on the page may have reflected her desire to test his mettle; she was being harsh and blunt but bracing. 'You can't afford another fucking failure, dear,' she said. He felt so poleaxed by the comment that he nearly gave up writing. In fact he never felt safe giving her a play. 'I was physically frightened, sick in the stomach, when I was young because she was so fearsome. We had a rather passionate relationship for two or three years. She was rather aggressive at first,' he says, 'but we then settled down.'

He remembers his First World War play *Clever Soldiers*, which was produced at Hampstead in 1974, as the breakthrough in their relationship. Apart from the fact that she was amused by his using an anecdote she had told him about how John Barton used to chew razor blades, Poliakoff says she felt that he had arrived with this play. It led to his being offered a residency at the National Theatre, which began a fruitful relationship with Peter Hall on both stage and screen.

Poliakoff feels that he wrote too quickly for her liking, which affected her approach to reading his work. He found, contrary to her reputation for sound judgement on the page, that she responded better to his plays on the stage, although she did not always like those of his plays that were successful, such as *City Sugar*, his story about the world of a disc jockey that transferred from the Bush to the West End. Poliakoff recognised that she might change her opinion to deflate the achievement.

She did have a penchant for films set on trains, which they discussed, yet Poliakoff denies that it was she who suggested the theme for his much-praised 1980 film *Caught on a Train*, starring Peggy Ashcroft and Michael Kitchen. A train also features as the setting for his play *Breaking the Silence*, which she steered toward the RSC rather than the NT ('more discerning, less vulgar,' she observed). She told the NT's literary manager, 'You won't do it, dear, and you can't put it on the Lyttelton; the carriage will look like a fucking caterpillar.' As far as the play was concerned, Peggy thought the audience might not believe the central figure could be an inventor and, therefore, might regard the play as a fantasy. Poliakoff rewrote the play to avoid this problem, and it transferred from the RSC's Pit Theatre in London to the Mermaid for a successful run.

Peggy had a low boredom threshold and had trouble with any of his plays that she thought too long. She used to pretend to weigh his scripts when he brought them to Goodwin's Court. She would say: 'I don't know if it's you or the plays that are boring.' As if reprising their first meeting, he would argue back, 'You don't read them properly,' and then they would get on fine again. When a love affair of his broke up, Peggy was delighted. 'You can write a play out of it,' she opined. 'The affair will mean nothing to you in two years, but the play will live on.'

He would listen to her advice and mostly not follow it. He found her ideas banal, like when she suggested he make a female character a stripper to give her more interest. When he did act on one of her suggestions – to remove specific time and place references in *Heroes* – it ruined the play. On the other hand, he did insert one line at her bidding in *City Sugar*, concerning the disc jockey's private life, which Poliakoff thought a valuable addition. He also recalls 'one profound insight, a brilliant flash; she said, "You write the insides of people without always writing the outer skin." It was neither denigrating nor flattering, just true; and it bore a real warning for me.'

For Poliakoff, almost 45 years her junior, it was like having another mother, and it was as complicated as that, too. Her immediate and vivid response to his work, the returning of telephone calls straightaway, even when he was not well-known, and her unyielding commitment to his talent, meant a lot to him and left their mark on all his writing.

'She had the great quality of treating you at the start of your career as if you were as important as one of her most established clients, like Robert Bolt. Her greatest legacy to me was to make me feel that I haven't achieved anything and to give me the aching urge to always get back to the theatre, to try again, to feel when I'm not writing for the theatre that I should be,' says Poliakoff. 'What she gave me was the desire and will to stay in theatre. The destructive things pale in contrast. Her influence is like something imprinted from birth. I think, because of that, my stage plays will be seen as my most important work.'

The same year, 1969, that Peggy took on Poliakoff she took on only one other writer, despite being bombarded by supplicants; that was another young and then unknown talent, Nigel Williams. He sent her a play while he was studying at Oxford University and was flattered by her reaction and attention. But in this case her enthusiasm proved to be the worst possible response; she thought he was brilliant, and he became overwhelmed by her. It unsettled him, and he wrote nothing worthwhile for the stage for nearly a decade, turning to the novel instead. 'She was too much like my mum,' he says. 'I couldn't stand it.' He became fed up with hearing about the successes of other clients, especially the wunderkind Poliakoff, and decided that he had to leave in order to break the spell. Just as he was about to go, Peggy sold his first play to BBC-TV. She would not take commission on the sale because, she said, she had never earned a penny from him before. Despite this breakthrough, he knew he had to move on, and it was only when he changed agents that his stage writing began to flourish, with plays like *Class Enemy*. Peggy, however, had come to feel that he was multi-talented but not truly a playwright, and, indeed, fiction has proved in the long run to be the greater attraction for him.

One of the younger writers who had approached Peggy without luck in 1969 was Stephen Lowe, or Stephen Wright as he was then known. He had just gained his BA Hons. in English at Birmingham University and had finished an opera. She represented his favourite writers, so, when he was looking for an agent, he contacted her. She wrote back: 'I don't think you'll last very long . . . If you're alive in five years, get in touch.'

Five years passed and, then as an actor with Alan Ayckbourn in Scar-borough, Lowe did get in touch again. He had written a seaside-postcard comedy for Ayckbourn, and, with Ayckbourn's recommendation, this time Peggy relented.

She helped Lowe to gain confidence in his writing and supported him through his first years as a playwright. He wrote *Moving Pictures* in the Hut in Brighton. *Touched*, his most important play, was difficult for her to read for emotional reasons, because it reminded her of a personally painful moment in the Second World War, but she found the central character of Sandra remarkable. It is set in 1945 in the hundred days between Victory in Europe and Victory in Japan and tells the story of a group of working-class women in Lowe's home town of Nottingham. It opened, appropriately, at the Nottingham Playhouse in 1977, directed by the theatre's artistic director, Richard Eyre.

A revised version was seen at the Royal Court in 1981, directed by William Gaskill. He also directed Lowe's adaptation of Robert Tressell's novel *The Ragged Trousered Philanthropists* for the touring Joint Stock com-pany and, at the Royal Court again, *Tibetan Inroads*. Peggy was servicing Lowe on the sidelines by this time and finding that she preferred the earlier play *Touched* to his later work. When an ambitious piece, *Seachange*, went disastrously wrong at the Riverside Studios in London in 1984, Lowe was butchered by the critics and found no succour from Peggy. He decided to leave, feeling that Peggy had not offered, and was no longer going to offer, the guidance that she had in the early days.

Poliakoff stayed with Peggy's agency while Williams and Lowe left; Peggy did not suit every talented writer and not every talented writer suited Peggy. She was *the* agent; she was at the centre of that world; she could be choosy. A writer like Peter Flannery, for example, author of *Our Friends in the North*, was encouraged when he first contacted her in the mid-1970s just after leaving Manchester University. But when he sent her his first important play, *Savage Amusement*, an unsentimental look at five young squatters coping with increasingly harsh world, she was discouraging. Flannery had been told that the RSC was intending to present the play at the Warehouse. He came to London and paid his first – and last – visit to Goodwin's Court.

'I could hear a secretary trying to persuade Peggy to see me because I'd come all the way from Cheshire,' says Flannery. 'She didn't want to see me but finally agreed. She greeted me with the words, "I can't do anything for you, dear. You might get a few college performances." I replied that the RSC was going to do the play. "Oh no, dear, that can't be true," she said. I left and never saw her again.' The RSC did stage the play, in 1978, and it formed part of the Warehouse repertoire that earned the company much kudos for its ambition and critique of contemporary society.

She felt the 1970s fashion for political writing to be deleterious, and it is characteristic that, at a time when socially-oriented plays from the publicly subsidised sector were defining the national debate about the state of Britain, she should be looking in another direction. In 1975, for instance, she read some plays by Wallace Shawn, including *Our Late Night*, which had just been seen in New York off-off-Broadway. Orton's biographer John Lahr had mentioned it to her, having written about the play in the *Village Voice*. *Our Late Night*, set mostly at a cocktail party, trawls scabrously through the minds of a couple going to bed. Rather than being concerned with politics, it is more pre-occupied with sex.

Peggy told Shawn: 'I put off reading your plays for a day or two because I was nervous that either I would be inadequate or that your plays might actually be disappointing. The fears were not necessary – I like your plays very much indeed.' *Our Late Night* was the product of a two-year work-shop, which had left its distinctive mark on the wild and idiosyncratic style of the play. Although Peggy was unable to place *Our Late Night* after the Royal Court and Hampstead had turned it down, she found an outlet for its successor, *A Thought in Three Parts*, and this proved a turning point in Shawn's life as a playwright. Peggy guessed correctly that David Hare would be interested in Shawn's work and sent him both *Our Late Night* and *A Thought in Three Parts*. Hare, who was the founder with Max Stafford-Clark and David Aukin of the Joint Stock theatre group, passed *A Thought in Three Parts* – 'new minted and ready for a première,' as he puts it – to the company. Stafford-Clark responded to its ironic humour and thematic boldness, and became the play's director in a Joint Stock production.

A Thought in Three Parts continues Shawn's obsessive exploration of sexual experience. It is made up of three short plays, all of them grim in their view of the most intimate of human experiences, however humorous; in the first, the fear of violence is ever present in the sexual banter of a couple in a hotel room; in the middle play, desolation haunts a tableau of communal orgasm in a youth hostel – no matter how many times a group of men and women change sexual partners and try new means of fulfilment, the end result is the same, emptiness and loneliness; in the third, a lone man fantasises about different types of sexual gratification. The play caused a furore when it played at the ICA in 1977. Questions were asked in the House of Commons, the ICA's charitable status was investigated, group masturbation and nudity were condemned as obscene, and there was much braying for prosecutions. Shawn even feared deportation. When the hullabaloo died down, nobody had been brought to trial or removed from the country, and English civilisation remained unruffled.

When Max Stafford-Clark took over the Royal Court in 1980, Shawn had found his English home for the next decade; *Marie and Bruce*, *My Dinner with André*, *Aunt Dan and Lemon*, and *The Fever*, which also played at the NT's Cottesloe Theatre, were all seen in Sloane Square. By the time of *Aunt Dan and Lemon*, in 1985, in which Shawn explores his thesis that 'a perfectly decent person can turn into a monster perfectly easily,' Shawn had come to engage with the politics of his time, yet in an individual way, unlike that of any of his contemporaries. His portrait of an intellectual drawn towards the extreme right was booed on its opening night in London by those who took the neo-Nazi ideas being propounded by the characters on stage as Shawn's own views.

Peggy did not exert any direct influence on Shawn, a writer living and working in New York very much within his own singular vision. In one notable case, however, she did help in a quite material way. David Hare tells the story: 'Wal was in London in despair because Louis Malle didn't have the money to make *My Dinner with André* [a film based on Shawn's play of the same name, which Malle had already directed on stage at the Royal Court's Theatre Upstairs]. When Wal saw Peggy, she said, 'Oh, but that's ridiculous. I'll call Michael White.' She picked up the phone, called Michael and said, 'Louis Malle wants to make a film from a script by Wallace Shawn.' Michael said, 'Fine, come round and pick up a cheque. How much do you need?' Wal said £25,000 and Michael said, 'It's waiting.

Who do I make it out to?' And that was it. Wal went round to Jermyn Street and picked up the cheque, and they had the budget for the ten-day shoot.'

In the film Shawn meets his friend, the theatre director André Gregory, for dinner and they discuss their contrasting experiences of the world. It was released in 1981 and won a cult following in America and Europe.

Shawn's work was never anything other than shocking and idiosyncratic, both of which traits Peggy admired. He is thankful to Peggy because he felt that his writing had not been taken seriously in New York until his exposure in London. As David Hare says, 'I think only Peggy would have spotted Wal.'

Hare himself had approached Peggy at the end of 1972, when he was beginning to swim against the tide of the times, although he did not join her until 1973. This was the year that *Brassneck*, which he co-wrote with Howard Brenton, was given its première by Richard Eyre at the Nottingham Playhouse, where Hare was then resident dramatist. The contract for *Brassneck* was the first that Peggy negotiated for Hare and Brenton, although it had been set up before they joined her.

Both had been key figures in the development of the Fringe, Brenton with Brighton Combination and Portable Theatre, and Hare also with Portable, which he founded in 1968 with fellow Cambridge graduate Tony Bicât. Hare and Brenton had worked together with other writers on two Portable shows, *Lay-By* in 1971 and *England's Ireland* in 1972. Portable folded and was turned into Joint Stock, the more politically driven practitioners of the Fringe defined themselves as a distinct alternative theatre movement, and Hare and Brenton joined Peggy as they set their sights on new audiences.

Brenton went to her in early 1974 from Rosica Colin, a splendid Romanian woman who had attracted him as Genet's agent, and who happened to have taken on Ionesco, but who did not talk to Brenton and did not seem to him to know the London theatre scene very well. Peggy was the opposite and took an immediate fancy to Brenton's plays – 'because people died in them,' he says. He was despondent about his future when he joined Peggy but remembered the vigour with which she had helped get his *Magnificence* produced at the Royal Court in 1973 although he was not her client. She breathed new life into his work and encouraged him to write what he wanted. 'If you want to write for the National Theatre,' she said, 'we'll arrange it for you – if you write well enough.'

She did not see his plays as political but she did recognise their passion. She insisted, for example, that *Weapons of Happiness*, which deals with the nature of political action and resistance, must be understandable even without any prior political knowledge. She did not regard *Thirteenth Night* as a warning about autocratic tendencies on the left but as the story of the decay of the central character who has a good death.

Despite the huge canvas upon which Brenton writes many of his sprawling plays, Peggy did not consider him at his best as an epic writer, which was why she had taken him to see Kabuki, part of her Japanese obsession; she thought the culture of Japan offered Brenton a key to honing his epic qualities. She told Peter Hall, for whom Brenton had written *The Romans in Britain*, that, contrary to appearances, it had no epic quality. She was worried that if the focus were not on the human story and the play were presented in an epic manner, then it would be attacked as a poor play about war. This, indeed, is what happened when it was staged in 1980 at the NT's large Olivier Theatre.

The play, however, became infamous because the director, Michael Bogdanov, was privately prosecuted by the anti-libertarian campaigner Mary Whitehouse on the grounds that one scene in the production contained an indecent act, namely the simulated homosexual rape of a Druid by a Roman soldier. The Attorney-General had refused to allow a prosecution under the 1968 Theatres Act, so Whitehouse, who had not seen the play but sent her solicitor to it instead, acted under the 1956 Sexual Offences Act. The case went to the Old Bailey, where the prosecution council withdrew the charge on the third day of the trial. Peggy detested Whitehouse and was very supportive of those under attack throughout the arduous period of the prosecution. She kept phoning Brenton and asking, 'What are the shits up to now?'

Hare came to Peggy from Clive Goodwin and instantly became her new obsession, dominating the 1970s as the favoured son. The play that attracted Peggy so compellingly was *Knuckle*, a wry tale of corrupt values and lost love, told in the style of a Ross Macdonald or Raymond Chandler thriller. An international arms dealer returns to the Home Counties stockbroker belt where he was raised in order to investigate the disappearance of his sister. While sleuthing, he exposes his father's culture of old, paternalist capitalism and falls in love with a friend of his sister's, only to find that she rejects him because he turns out to be an accomplice in the very culture he has been attacking; he is willing to lie because he is fighting for Number One, heralding a brash new capitalist ethos that reached its apotheosis under Thatcher in the next decade.

Hare saw himself as a director who happened to turn to writing, mainly to fill gaps in subject matter that he saw being left by his contemporaries.

Goodwin was encouraging him to play the part of the peppery anti-establishment scourge, and was disappointed when Hare showed him *Knuckle*. Goodwin did not see the play as being satirical or strident enough. His efforts to secure a production were half-hearted, thought Hare. Michael Codron had commissioned the play and wanted to take it into the West End. A nine-month wait for a lead actor to finish filming pushed Hare beyond the point of exasperation. He took the advice of Christopher Hampton, a friend from schooldays who had brought him into the Royal Court in 1969 as literary manager. Hampton suggested he show *Knuckle* to Peggy. She adored it immediately and told Hare that he was not a dissident lampooner but a romantic writer.

Peggy said that she did not steal clients from other agents but she did want to invest in the play. Goodwin felt that he could not represent a client in such circumstances and said that Hare should move to Peggy's agency altogether, which he did. Peggy agreed to share the commission with Goodwin for the representation of *Knuckle*, because Hare had written it while he was with Goodwin's agency.

Knuckle became Peggy's obsession for more than a year, through to its opening in early 1974 and beyond. She was so infatuated with the play that, like the Ancient Mariner, she engaged Hare at their first meeting in continuous one-way conversation about it, even telling him the plot. Peggy loved the fact that the friend sets the arms dealer a test which he fails; Peggy would repeat over and over again, each time with a chuckle, that in the end he 'loses the girl'. Peggy saw in Hare a puritan who was attacking compromise and she liked the moral that the man lost his love because he had behaved badly.

She gave Hare a detailed response to the play, especially on the 'peak' scene between the father and the son, the penultimate scene in the play, which she favoured editing down. She thought it too long and unclear in places, particularly where the father is trying to lure the son on to his side.

'You think it's going to be a great success?' Hare asked her. 'Good lord, no. It's going to be a disaster,' came the reply. 'You'll go through hell.' She mollified him by adding, 'But I like it. It's way ahead of its time. You're a collector's writer.' Success or failure would not matter, she averred. Both had to be faced and Hare 'must say fuck to both . . . Managements will go on wanting your work and in 20 years we will all see who was right.'

Hare, nevertheless, became very scared about the prospect of failure. Peggy had to reassure him. 'If you want to be completely at ease, you must write the William Douglas-Home style of play – well-made shit. Yes, failure is POSSIBLE – so what? Joyce failed, Beckett starved, *Carmen* flopped (too avant-garde), Proust was turned down by Gide and his group,' she wrote. 'Dostoevsky starved; all the early Chekhovs and Ibsens failed ignominiously. But they didn't withdraw their plays, they got performed and ended up immortal . . . Only risks will drive you forward. If they aren't risks, they aren't any good.'

Peggy was determined to get the play on. The economics of the West End looked difficult for a play with several locations that shift from one scene to the next and was written by a little known debutant; and those who had heard of him would have considered him a rebel who did not belong in the plush theatres of the commercial sector. The natural place in the publicly subsidised sector would have been the Royal Court where Michael Codron had backed an earlier Hare play, *Slag*, when Hare had moved on from being its literary manager to resident dramatist. The Royal Court, however, was not interested in *Knuckle*.

Peggy attributed the initial rejection to the influence of Lindsay Anderson, who was an associate director of the theatre and quondam artistic director known for his dislike of the Hare generation. In the end, the best deal Peggy could obtain from the then artistic director Oscar Lewenstein was a two-week run downstairs in a six-week summer season of new plays, all done very cheaply. Peggy rejected this for several reasons; the complexities of the staging would have made a commercial transfer virtually impossible, which would have meant, over only a two-week run, Codron losing his money and Hare not earning even enough to pay back Codron's advance. Hare also wanted Brenton's *Magnificence* to be seen, and, if *Knuckle* were withdrawn, *Magnificence* could take its place. It had been waiting more than a year for a production since Brenton had delivered the script, by which time he had become the Royal Court's resident dramatist. Hare thought it was his due. Peggy backed him in this, and *Magnificence* was seen in the downstairs auditorium. (The six weeks were finally divided into two, with the Brenton play followed by David Williamson's *The Removalists*, both produced for the cost of a single production.)

Codron was having his own problems. He had tried several directors, including Harold Pinter, who had turned the play down, before he lighted on Michael Blakemore, who accepted. Peggy was in constant communication with Codron, badgering him and supporting his efforts to mount *Knuckle* in a straight commercial production. She delighted at the prospect of *Knuckle* causing a stir in the West End rather than being praised but ignored in Sloane Square. Peggy persuaded her original backer Edward Sutro to invest in the production, which eventually opened at the Oxford

Playhouse, before going in to the West End on 4 March 1974. It opened the day the Tory Prime Minister, Edward Heath, resigned in favour of Labour's Harold Wilson, having called a general election for the week before on the theme 'Who Runs Britain?'

Hare's theatrical analysis of an unacceptable face of capitalism chimed with the times but not with the critics. They generally gave it a bumpy ride and it flopped, although Codron kept the production running until the end of June. Hare recalls Sutro as wanting to be remembered as the man who had lost all his money on the first production of *Knuckle*. Some critics had challenged Hare on the grounds that his politics were being compromised by the play appearing in the West End, but Peggy was pleased that Codron had spent 'capitalist money on attacking capitalism'. It was no good preaching to the converted or seeking the protection of places like Hampstead or the Royal Court where, she believed, Hare would probably have received better notices.

Peggy saw *Knuckle* as a watershed play, both for the theatre in general and for Hare himself. It certainly proved to be a turning point for Hare. He had retreated to Peggy's place in Brighton at one point during the rehearsals and then to Nottingham in order to avoid the opening night. He found the failure very difficult to handle, and it put his marriage under severe strain. Tussles he had faced with Portable, whether it was venues refusing to book the group or the plays being booed off stage, had only served to convince him that he was hitting his chosen targets accurately and hard. The reception of *Knuckle* brought him up sharp against a different reality, and it was a reality of difficult passage that he was to endure for most of his stage work until 1985 when *Pravda*, co-written with Howard Brenton, marked a sea change.

Peggy saw the process as necessary and positive but still went into over-drive to comfort Hare, support the actors, such as Edward Fox who played the lead, and challenge critics who she believed had missed the point.

To Irving Wardle of *The Times*, she rebuffed the main thrust of his attack and concluded: 'Well, it will soon be an all-revival West End, and the critics will be re-assessing the judgements of Hazlitt and Agate. With a bit of luck, those of us who actually wish to develop and nurture outstanding new writers will have long turned to a more life-enhancing occupation.' Wardle defended himself and asked, 'Would it help if we stifled objections to all seriously-intended new pieces that happened to get a commercial production? I think that readers are pretty sharp at detecting hollow praise and loyal evasiveness.' Peggy was grateful for the reply but was still worried not only about the effect of the reviews on Hare but also on the future in the West End of other young writers like Howard Brenton who wanted to move on from the Fringe and now would find it that much more daunting.

In her letter to Edward Fox, she thanked him for his performance and defended the right of the play to be seen in the West End. 'Every night during the run some hundreds of people will come, and even if they are quiet (and I myself am an entirely silent audience), you must tell them the secret about life which is implicit in this play; that we are all alone, but all together, and we must stand firm and not sell out, and we must be brave.'

To Hare, whom she addressed as 'Life's Delicate Child (as Thomas Mann called your like)', she wrote: 'Fuck the critics. They've all compromised or sold out. They are failures. Along comes a shining child of 26 and tells them what's wrong with them. They aren't big enough to take the blows. Are you really going to allow these grey, shabby lot to break your spirit and your confidence? . . . All that matters is your work. No, not absolutely all. Because you mustn't treat yourself as a person so harshly. It's all inverted conceit, in an odd sort of way. Look OUTWARD, my dear child. Don't muck about picking at your entrails, and shitting on yourself. Your work is more important than you are because it's what everybody can actually hear and see. You have great talent and are mucking about by trying to destroy your nerve. The only way you will get failure is to deliberately *bring it on yourself.'*

The next day, she wrote again.

This is written from home at 6am, a time of day when truth stares one in the face. Now, you either believe that the theatre is important, or you don't. If you do, then you tell the truth on the stage and you expect *to be listened to.* Your play attacks capitalism, and says that the City is corrupt. You say that England is now a place of dishonour. You say this in the heart of the West End, to people who have all had to compromise or sell-out in order to get where they are – the rich first-nighters and the British press. When you find that these people *don't* want to let other people hear what you are saying, you – and the rest of us – say it's because the play isn't 'commercial' and should have been tucked away in a small out-of-the-way hall. It's like a revolutionary who has the opportunity of blowing up Parliament saying *if only* he'd blown up Dewsbury Town Hall he'd have got away with it.

YOU ARE RESPONSIBLE for what you write and you must take the consequences. You have said things in the West End which have never been said before, and you expect to have the notices which greet a well-made play with French windows . . . David, you have to face the firing squad if you want to change the world. Those Arab and Israeli revolutionaries – and the Irish ones – stand up and say 'We did this because we want to change the world.' . . . The *word* is as powerful as a bomb, but we choose not to allow ourselves to believe it . . . The capitalist system of the theatre paid for your attack. The only person running away *is the author*. But you can't run away, because you have *written the words* which can be heard *eight times a week*. Let's all be calm and try and keep the play going. You have to live through the pain, David, and you'll come out on the other side, so Gide tells one!

And in time she was proved right. The following year Hare's own production at the Royal Court of his play *Teeth 'n' Smiles*, which marked the beginning of the new artistic directorial team of Nicholas Wright and Robert Kidd, played to 87% capacity and transferred to the West End with Michael Codron's backing. *Knuckle* was broadcast on television in the nineties as a modern classic, by which time Hare had become the de facto in-house dramatist of the National Theatre; under Peter Hall's regime, Hare wrote and directed *Plenty*, *A Map of the World*, *Pravda*, which broke box-office records, *The Bay at Nice*, and *Wrecked Eggs*; Hall's successor, Richard Eyre, presented Hare's *The Secret Rapture* (directed by Howard Davies) and four Hare plays all directed by Eyre, *Racing Demon*, *Murmuring Judges*, *The Absence of War* (produced separately and as a trilogy on the Olivier stage) and *Skylight*, with a fifth scheduled for 1997.

After *Knuckle*, Peggy became a guide for Hare through life as well as art. She lived through the vicissitudes of Hare's philandering, the break-up of his marriage and subsequent relationships, as well as through the creation and production of his plays and films. She taught him the common sense rules of theatre, the practical things. He would discuss his plays with her and seek her advice; she knew when a play went off the boil and, for example, if a scene was wrong, would advise Hare to see if it had been prepared for properly. When she read *Plenty* a torrent of anecdote erupted from her own experience as she questioned whether or not the heroine Susan Traherne would behave in a particular way. She liked the free-wheeling aspect of the character, a woman who pays the price of madness for making certain choices in a hostile world, but saw something sterile in her too. Peggy felt Traherne was wasteful because she throws away her life, and that was unforgiveable.

Peggy was both attracted by bright people and wary of intellectuals. She wished clients like Hare had not been to Oxbridge because, she said, 'you need something of the child to remain in order to communicate with a mixed body such as one finds in an average audience.' She worried that he was too smart: 'The best thing in Hare's plays are the quotes at the beginning,' she once said mischievously. 'They make the mind dizzy.' And she found in him a double-headed trait that she saw in many clever people, on one side an ability to be manipulative and on the other a tendency to be gullible and to give loyalty too easily to certain people who did not deserve it.

Peggy also felt that he wrote too much by will and did not allow his subconscious to lead him enough. Hare acknowledges that she taught him to trust his sub-conscious; she considered it to be truer than his writing from the conscious. In reply to a letter he sent her from Brighton, when he was badly stuck on a play and explaining how draining it had been to reach as far as he had, she wrote: 'I'm delighted that you're emotionally exhausted, as a play which doesn't emotionally exhaust an author is useless. I'm a great believer in the sub-conscious and, when all is lost and provided one concentrates on the problem when one lays one's head on the pillow, often a way out appears with the breakfast.'

She urged him to trust his own instinct and not to bottle out, and she could be very savage in the application of these principles. She thought he had emotional and professional constipation in the early '80s and criticised *Wrecked Eggs* as full of cruelty and contempt. Hare was resistant to her criticism but later did rewrite the play before it was seen at the NT. She told him, 'One writes poor plays because one behaves poorly. One cannot write good plays if one cares for nothing but oneself.'

Under Peggy's influence, Hare's writing did become less consciously driven. 'The last line of *The Secret Rapture*,' he says, 'made me cry. I don't know why it's there. I told this to the actress who had to say the line when she asked me about it. She couldn't tell why it was there, either. I said, "Let's just trust it." She did, and it worked.'

Peggy once suggested to him that a play could be like music. A theme would be stated when something happened to a minor character; the protagonist would take no notice, and then – the equivalent of the full orchestra – the same thing would happen to the major figure. 'She loved romantic structural ideas like that,' says Hare.

Writing *The Bay at Nice*, Hare drew on Peggy's philosophy – on art, love, selfishness, sacrifice – and on an episode in her life for the character of Valentina Nrovka, played originally by Irene Worth. *The Bay at Nice* covers many Peggy themes: love as pain, the hardness of talent, the effort of will as a futility and a limitation, and the recognition that, in the end, nothing is guaranteed. The episode he drew on was Peggy's affair with the violinist who could not perform unless he knew she was in the audience. In the play, Nrovka tells her daughter that this happened to a friend. When the man's wife died, he came to the friend and said, 'We're free.' The affair lasted a week; she no longer desired him. Nrovka says: 'It seems to me the worst story I know.'

There was a period in the mid-1970s when Peggy was phoning Hare five or six times a day and sometimes writing two or three times a week. Other clients became upset at her fixation with him. This intensity inevitably did not last. He says it cooled in the mid-1980s at about the time of *Pravda* – 'Oh, very funny, dear' – when she felt Hare was formed and able to look after himself. She believed Hare had handled success well and was pleased that he used his money sensibly, for example, to buy a neighbouring house and become a keen gardener. But she had become bored with his success and her obsessive affections had switched to Simon Callow.

Hare is both fulsome and earnest in his unequivocal praise of Peggy. He recalls how, from the time of *Knuckle* onwards, he grew in the light of her moral authority. She gave him the courage to survive. 'I wasn't equipped emotionally for the theatre, and Peggy taught me how to be. Unlike others in the theatre who look at how a play will be received, she's the only one I know who was interested in its intrinsic value, not the value of the market place. Many pretend to know the difference between excellence and success but in fact confuse the former with the latter. Peggy, however, did know the difference,' he says.

He describes her as the formative influence on his playwriting life. 'Nobody has given me more courage to write than Peggy. She conducted herself as I tried to as a writer – no compromise. You could not buy her good opinion. She was incorruptible.'

Unlike most clients, who only expected to get something *from* Peggy, Hare *gave* to her a great deal. He was not only a social companion and valued as a sounding board – on matters of the agency, on plays she wanted to discuss, on problems with other clients – he also offered Peggy, in her third decade as an agent, inner renewal as a talent to be cared for and shaped. His was the last major playwriting talent to fire her, and after Hare, at a time when her disenchantment with theatre was beginning to take a firm hold, every one of her clients was re-evaluated in the light of her experiences with him and her falling out of love with the world to which she had belonged for half a century.

Hare was with Peggy during her last days, and it was he who, in the face of her own obstinacy, emulated his teacher and finally managed to persuade her to go into hospital to die.

Chapter Nine

Memento Mori

'One doesn't regret the things one does but the things one doesn't do.'

PEGGY became ill with exhaustion in 1970, aged 62, and her health remained a source of anxiety to her thereafter; she had a car accident in 1978 and suffered a bad attack of shingles in that year and the next; in 1984 she had an operation to remove a suspected cancerous lump and 18 radium treatments; her legs began to cause her problems, and she was diagnosed as having Alzheimer's disease. From the mid-1980s onwards, Peggy was not able to function properly, although she made no public reference to this. She refused to suffer, which, for her, was a form of suffering, and her spirit remained vigorous.

By the end of the 1980s, she was becoming more hunched and looking her age; there would now be times when she appeared in the office without having fixed her hair or dressed properly, although mostly she still cut the image of her former sprightly, elegant self. She had always had a vanity; part of her survival strategy had been to 'look good'. Now, as if in exaggeration of her former self, she would at certain times become obsessed with the comb and the lipstick.

She saw the humorous side as well, however. She had all her teeth out in 1985 and had a disarming habit of losing her false set, much as she was prone to leaving her handbag in a taxi. One day, she left her false teeth in an Indian restaurant and found it was locked when she went back to retrieve them. (The restaurant returned them later.) On another occasion, in the theatre, she was holding her teeth in her hand, having taken them out to be more comfortable. Making conversation during the interval, and still clutching the teeth, she flung her arms wide to emphasise a point, lost her grip on the dentures and sent them flying across the auditorium. She spent the rest of the interval on all fours, seeking to retrieve them before the curtain went up again.

Peggy

Despite her condition, Peggy did not cease to travel back and forth by tube each weekday from her flat to Goodwin's Court, putting in a full day at the office. She could have retired in 1968 when she reached 60, or in 1973 when she was 65, or any time she chose, but she refused to retire. She became fascinated by other people who, likewise, kept working throughout their old age, and she devoured books on the subject.

However much Peggy castigated her own profession and the theatre world in general, this is what she had come to live for, and her waning desire for it brought her sharp up against her own mortality. Although she accepted the inevitable, she was nevertheless alarmed at the prospect of extinction and the void it would create for Margaret Ramsay Ltd. This was a strong motive for hanging on to the agency; it would seem like doing death's job to give it up. She was not going to submit to death; death had to come and get her.

She maintained certain child-like aspects of her character as a way of cheating death, but it was evident that Peggy was beginning to lose the physical battle. Her memory lapses could no longer be brushed off as delightful eccentricity and her often hazy grasp of detail had become exacerbated to the point where it was a threat to her identity. In common with many who suffer from Alzheimer's, she could recount past episodes with a laser-sharp clarity yet would confuse the present and might repeat a question she had asked only seconds previously.

As she negotiated the years of her decline with as much grace and grandeur as her volatile state allowed, she did at last achieve a minor measure of public recognition when, in 1984, the British Film Institute gave her an award for her contribution to the film and television industry. There was also a mild outbreak of articles and a television programme about her. For years she had told journalists, 'I'm of no interest, dear,' and had refused, as well as scorned, publicity. Peggy would monitor the press cuttings that arrived in the office and destroy any that related to her. The 1987 Joe Orton film *Prick Up Your Ears*, in which she was played by Vanessa Redgrave as the central narrative figure, catapulted her into the limelight. A new willingness to talk in public, although always only following various attempts either to duck or deflate the interview, represented a tacit acknowledgement on Peggy's behalf that she had nothing more to contribute: I will speak because I have nothing to say.

The theatrical landscape had changed beyond recognition – to Peggy's mind, not necessarily for the better. In her more dyspeptic moments, she felt public subsidy had encouraged the growth of a generation of administrators and university graduates who were choking the vitality out of theatre and leading drama into a desert of blandness. Subsidy had also meant an increase in the number of outlets for new plays, and, along with the massive expansion of film and television, this had led to greater mobility of writers between agents. Scripts tended to be sent to several managements, which then competed, rather than a single management being selected in advance as the appropriate one to produce a particular play. Peggy saw old values and courtesies disappearing.

She wanted to keep in touch with the emerging generation of writers but realised that this was becoming increasingly difficult for her. She felt that she was losing touch even in the '70s, and, with certain exceptions and moments of penetrating enthusiasm, she feared that she was losing interest too. Her appetite was blunted. She felt that the theatre's energy – and hers – had begun to dissipate during the '70s. She hoped it might return; by the end of the '80s it had not.

A higher proportion of Peggy's clients than previously were staying with her for only a short while, which was not surprising, considering her enormous client list and her faltering health. Writers such as John Byrne, Jim Cartwright, Nick Darke, Kevin Elyot, Jonathan Gems, and Dusty Hughes, were finding that, even if some of them stayed with Peggy for up to a decade, her initial enthusiasm was not being transformed into a more lasting or fruitful relationship; her increasingly bizarre approach was an obstacle rather than a stimulus to their progress. Many young writers, who in former times would probably have been represented by the agency, were either passing through quickly or going elsewhere. Nevertheless, she was thrilled to be able to take on clients such as Anne Devlin, Stephen Jeffreys and Rona Munro.

Peggy by now had little to do with getting plays placed, although producers and literary managers would still read a script that came from her as a priority. Most of the work was being done by her assistants, led by Tom Erhardt, who for some time had been handling domestic clients whose work did not particularly interest Peggy, like Mike Harding, Bob Carlton (of *Return to the Forbidden Planet* fame) and Ben Elton. Much of this activity had to be carried out using sympathetic subterfuge, because she was not able to play the full part that she continued to insist she would, and Peggy would not – could not – give up the agency or delegate properly. Mostly her clients stayed loyal, though several, especially those who earned their living primarily in TV and film, were approached by other agents; a few did leave. Tom Erhardt was also contacted by several agencies inquiring about amalgamation, either immediately or in the future.

The last years of Peggy's life as an agent were touched with melancholy. The end was finally signalled by two events in April 1991 that came quickly the one upon the other. The first was a fire at 14a Goodwin's Court, and the second, only days later, was the death of Bill Roderick, her companion of 50 years' standing. Both struck deep at the very heart of her being.

Fires broke out on all three floors of the building at around 5 am on Monday, 8 April. The flat at the top and the offices were unoccupied. Peggy and the other staff all turned up to work as normal to find the narrow alleyway beseiged by firefighters. Peggy, already under a lot of stress because Roderick was terminally ill, became very agitated because she had not been informed earlier about the fire and was now not being allowed into the offices, for safety reasons. It was not until the afternoon that she was able to see the damage for herself.

The first floor, where Tom Erhardt had his office, was the worst affected. The middle office on that floor was completely burnt out and Erhardt's office was severely damaged by smoke. The fire did not catch in Peggy's office on the floor above and only singed the leg of the table, but there was smoke damage as well as damage caused by the hoses when the fires were being put out. Most of the records and ledgers were intact, as were the cheques that were in the office. A collection of published plays, many posters and some manuscripts were lost, some of which were irreplaceable. Goodwin's Court had been her life for more than 37 years; it had been more important than any home. Now it – and therefore Peggy – had suffered utter violation.

The police theory was that local vagrants had climbed in to the upstairs flat on the third floor, had drunk as much Drambuie as they could find and had lit fires on each floor on their way out of the building, using books as the incendiaries. Police had fingerprints but no one was ever caught or prosecuted. Goodwin's Court had become a favourite spot for the homeless and the itinerant. Peggy, in the grip of her dementia, talked regularly to the beggars and would give them money, latterly opening her purse for them and pouring coins out. She had recently brought a tramp into the office and had given him coffee as well as cash.

Peggy herself rejected this theory and clung to the belief that a disgruntled writer was to blame. She proclaimed Hanif Kureishi – not a client – to be the culprit, ignoring the frantic efforts of the staff to dissuade her.

Despite the upheaval and with only one working telephone, the agency continued its business. There were many offers of help, as well as calls and letters of commiseration. Robert Holman, one of those who turned up to assist the cleaning up process, recalls a pitiful sight. Peggy, he says, appeared not to have registered the real extent of the damage. 'We'll be OK in a couple of days,' she kept repeating, as if wishing would make it true.

She was reluctant to let anything be thrown away, even if burnt beyond recognition. Staff and helpers had to dispose of things without her knowing. The carpet, charred and soaking from fire brigade foam, had only been laid down for three months. 'You can't throw it out,' she said and, on hands and knees, rubbed at it with a tissue.

Peggy, more diminutive than she had been, took on a slightly macabre look, like Bette Davis on the set of a gothic horror film, a sad figure with the spirit now knocked out of her. When Jack Rosenthal and Caryl Churchill called by, they found her covered in dirt, with ash on her face, surrounded by black plastic bags. On seeing Rosenthal, she asked: 'Why did you come? Your cheques are all safe.' Churchill was amused but Rosenthal was offended; he had only come to give Peggy a comforting hug.

Fortunately, there were flashes of the old Peggy to be found amidst the gloom. When Christopher Hampton called in and said the fire was the work of a failed dramatist, her instant reply was, 'Maybe, darling, but a failed arsonist too.'

Bill Roderick died as they were still putting the office back in order. The loss to Peggy was terrible and traumatic, and the shock triggered an unravelling of Peggy herself. David Hare recalls in retrospect that intimations of this had appeared two years earlier when Bill's twin brother, John, had died and Peggy was disturbed to discover she could not cheer Bill up. Bill clearly felt bereft, as if one half of him had perished. Worse, he told Peggy he felt he no longer had the right to be alive. She administered to him throughout his illness and never wanted him to go into hospital, fearing that once he went in, he would never come out again. When he died, she said to Hare, 'I told him not to go in.'

After his funeral, remembers Hare, Peggy was to be found at the reception 'running around like a demented hostess, forcing more drinks on everyone and behaving as if this were some mad celebration.' About three weeks later she phoned Hare at 6.30 am. 'She never in her whole life had ever complained of anything personal to me,' he says, 'but, that morning, she said in a bewildered voice, "David, I wake up every morning feeling wretched, and I can't work out why." "Peggy", I said, "I think it's what's called grief." "You're right," she said, as if encountering something strange and unfamiliar, "it's grief".'

She had denied death, she had denied love, she had denied grief, but could not any more. She had virtually denied that Bill existed, and it was only on his death that she realised how much she had needed him. Through his death, he was contradicting what Peggy had stood for since she chose to become an agent, a decision that had represented an enormous act of will on her part. She had suppressed powerful emotions, notably to do with friendship, in order to concentrate ruthlessly on serving talent and recasting herself as Peggy the writers' agent. This she had achieved, but those emotions were now welling up out of her control and reasserting themselves. On the face of it, this was supporting an opposite point of view, in which she equally strongly believed; namely, that to live a life of the will – as she in fact had done – was futile. One should rather be guided by one's subconscious. Bill's death was affirming this strand of her philosophy with a vengeance. In the absence of Bill, Peggy the writers' agent was no more; she lost the will to live.

With only her cat, Button, for company, Peggy herself declined rapidly. The staff would visit her in her Redcliffe Square flat in Earl's Court, as would clients and acquaintances. By the end of the summer it was clear that she would not last much longer. Her legs had given out, and she was not able to get in to the office any more. She would not hear of going to hospital, however. The idea appalled her, and memories of her warning to Bill would not go away. David Hare convinced her but only after she had agreed to an interim plan that was never going to happen. The scheme was for Peggy to move into Hare's basement with a nurse. 'The day we transported her,' says Hare, 'it was obvious she was far too ill.' She was taken instead to a private hospital in central London just off Regent's Park. Complications occurred, her health worsened, and Peggy died, aged 83, on 4 September 1991 of bronchopneumonia and carcinoma of the bronchus.

Her funeral service was held at the Golder's Green Crematorium, north London, on 10 September in a non-religious ceremony attended by dozens of celebrated playwrights and theatrical luminaries. It was organised mainly by Simon Callow and David Hare, and it was their generation rather than the older clients who featured in the service; Callow, Hare, Christopher Hampton, Willy Russell and Vanessa Redgrave read extracts from some of Peggy's favourite literature: from a short story by Tom Hopkinson called 'The Third Secretary's Story,' from de Maupassant, Proust, Miyata, Woolf, Gorky, Shakespeare, Cocteau, and Rimbaud. Music by Schubert, Jimmy Durante and Richard Strauss was played.

The spectre of Orton even appeared briefly as the time allowed for the ceremony came to its end and the assembled dignitaries were ushered away to allow the next service to take place. In the office behind the chapel there was a tussle with crematorium officials who were about to follow their normal practice in disposing of the ashes. A witness to the will had to be found to prevent Peggy's ashes, against her express wish, from gracing the grounds of Golder's Green and blowing away in the winds of north

London. Peggy had stipulated a more exotic clime, the cemetery at San Michèle in Venice where Diaghilev is buried.

Peggy had made a will in the 1960s which allowed for the agency's shares to be sold but not for the agency to close. She made another will in the 1970s, leaving her solicitor Laurence Harbottle and her accountant as executors of her estate to run the agency. Laurence Harbottle thought this was madness and prevailed upon her to revise it. At one point she said that she did not want the agency to survive; she was the agency and when she died she wanted it to die too. But in her last will, made in May 1989, in which she named Harbottle, Bill Roderick, and Simon Callow as her executors and trustees, she left her property, most of her effects and £10,000 to Roderick, and she determined the remainder of her estate should be used by her trustees for two purposes.

The first was an immediate and limited objective: 'to secure the continuance sale or disposal of Margaret Ramsay Limited as they think fit'; the second was to divide what was left equally between Bill Roderick and charitable use. This longer term aim was described in the will as to 'benefit writers in need of assistance with particular reference to friends and clients of mine and the encouragement of the art of writing'.

Leaving the fate of the agency to the executors rather than deciding its future herself was an extraordinary act, as if the firm that she had created and led for nearly half her life had nothing to do with her because she had moved on, to death, and the past was therefore of no account. Her unwillingness to make more definite arrangements seemed almost child-like and wilful, and suggested that it was her way of not acknowledging the terminal reality of mortality.

The will's lack of precision over her desire to secure future benefit for writers could, however, be seen as enlightened in so far as Peggy did not know what conditions would prevail after her death whereas trusted survivors could, and she presumed would, react accordingly.

Her will named David Hare, Christopher Hampton, Alan Ayckbourn, Alan Plater and Tom Erhardt to be recipients of mementoes from her possessions, and Simon Callow to have his choice of books, £2,000 and a picture hanging in her sitting room of Venice with a masked figure. Any staff of more than one year standing were to receive £1,000 each. The trustees invited all the other active clients living in Britain to choose keepsakes from her belongings.

On her death, her executors could not find some jewellery of hers, some prints, and the original Orton diaries, the whereabouts of which continued to cause concern long after her death.

By the time she had made her last will, Peggy had finally divorced, in order to protect the agency from potential claims by her husband, should he be alive, or by surviving relatives. She had considered divorce in 1975 in order to remarry for tax reasons. In the end, she decided against this course of action and chose, instead, simply to end her marriage. Proceedings were begun in 1979 and concluded the following year. The petition was served by advertisement as she had no knowledge of her husband's whereabouts, or even if he were alive. The divorce was uncontested, and Peggy never discovered what had happened to him.

Inevitably there was a period of uncertainty at the firm, during which time Tom Erhardt and the staff kept the business alive. Several options were considered for the future of Margaret Ramsay Limited, Play Agent, and it took just over six months to sort out. The executors decided that the agency should continue to exist by merging with another agency which offered complementary strengths. In January 1992, when probate had been granted, the executors and Tom Erhardt decided to concentrate on negotiations with one agency. A letter was sent to Peggy's clients explaining the situation. A few months later, a new company was formed by an amalgamation with the agency owned by Jenne and Giorgio Casarotto, which was chiefly known for its work in television and films. The new firm was called Casarotto Ramsay Limited and was wholly owned by the Casarottos and Erhardt, with an independent chairman approved by Peggy's estate.

It was a measure of the respect in which the clients held both Peggy and Tom Erhardt that more than 90% of her clients joined Erhardt in the new venture. Its commitment to new writing was realised by the appointment to the agency of Mel Kenyon, a former literary manager of the Royal Court.

Peggy's estate turned out to be worth approximately £1.5 million. As Bill Roderick had died before Peggy, leaving her his estate, his share as well as the rest of her money passed into the care of her executors. They set up a trust called the Peggy Ramsay Foundation in response to that part of her will which sought to help playwrights. The trustees were Simon Callow, Michael Codron, Laurence Harbottle, David Hare, John Tydeman and John Welch, a former publisher and managing director of Heffer's Bookshop in Cambridge. The Foundation took into its care the silver salver presented to Peggy by her clients. In its first few years of operation, the Foundation had already made awards to individual playwrights who needed financial help, as well as to the George Devine Award and the Thames Television Writers Scheme (later known by the name of Thames' new owners, Pearson).

The Foundation also instituted its own annual award, of, in its inaugural year, £50,000. It was to be given to a theatre or company selected by the trustees from a list of half a dozen which the trustees would draw up. Each invited organisation would submit a play it wished to produce and the winner would be chosen on the basis of this script. At the launch of the award, David Hare called it 'an act of celestial redistribution' designed with Peggy in mind – quick, without administrative cost, and paid direct to those who were going to produce the play. (What Peggy might have made of a committee deciding on the merits of a play is, however, another matter.) The first recipient was the Hampstead Theatre to stage *The Maiden Stone* by Rona Munro, one of Peggy's clients.

Worth £3 million in 1996, the Foundation benefited from a generous deal that was struck during the agency's merger, whereby it receives on a diminishing scale income generated by existing Margaret Ramsay Ltd. contracts as well as income from new contracts for work undertaken by Peggy's clients who remained with the new company. The sums come from monies due the agent, not from the clients' earnings, and are transferred via Margaret Ramsay Ltd. The old firm, owned by the estate and administered by Casarotto Ramsay under Erhardt's management, continues in name and covenants its profits to the Foundation. Such a financial package, itself a tribute to Peggy's service to playwrights, ensured that her dedication to the cause of new writing was able to endure in practice as well as in legend.

A farewell drinks party was held on 13 April 1992 among the packing cases and empty filing cabinets of 14a Goodwin's Court. Glasses were raised to the nearly 40 years of continuous occupation there by Peggy and her staff. The following morning, the removers arrived. Casarotto Ramsay was duly ensconced in Wardour Street, and Peggy's firm, Margaret Ramsay Limited, Play Agent, was no more.

*

'I'm supposed to be "lucky" for authors, but of course my "luck"
is merely their own talent, which I've been lucky enough
to be allowed to handle.'

Peggy Ramsay had become such a legend within the theatrical profession that it is impossible to detach the person from the myth. It was a myth fashioned out of despair and loneliness, out of zeal and hard labour; it was rooted in a self-denying, almost mystical philosophy of life, which mixed pleasure and puritanism, and embraced an all-consuming belief in something she called talent. Mercurial in spirit, driven by the clash of opposites, she was sharp, canny and deadly accurate. She attacked first before she had to defend and spoke with a child-like directness that unnerved most of her listeners. She had to become somebody different for each of her clients and each of their moods, yet she had to remain always the same Peggy. It was exhausting and exhilarating.

When she found early on in her career that playwrights did need her and did allow her to behave in her mad and maddening way, this unlocked the door to her survival, which depended on shrewdness and taste. She could be wildly wrong, she could change her mind, she could be a terrible agent, but the reality behind her reputation for nurturing so many of Britain's most celebrated writers is nonetheless inscribed incontrovertibly in the history of postwar theatre through the plays her clients have left behind.

Peggy is the grand narrative within which there are many tributary stories, some complex, some simple. She found a role, enjoyed playing the role as well as at the same time despising it, and became the role. She buried herself in the costume, the voice, the gesture, the demeanour. Life was not to be controlled by analysing it – she did not herself, for instance, follow the advice she gave several of her clients and keep a diary; life was to be lived, with the past discarded firmly as she endured, her eyes fixed on the future. Like Orpheus, her motto was 'don't look back.'

Although certain incidents from Peggy's life before she became an agent recur in the stories she told, she was generally vague or evasive about her past. She was bad on detail and dates in any case; uncertainty about who she was made her more intriguing and amused her if others were baffled. She also felt her life was genuinely of no importance, so what value could there be in recounting the facts of it? She used this avoidance as a shield to protect herself, to forget, and to control her own identity. What she chose to remember – and chose to forget – allowed her to define herself.

She began at the beginning by not clearing up what should be incontrovertible, the details of her birth. There was devilment in the issue of the different dates; ironic revenge on her father, who was a doctor; and a joke on life, as well as on anyone who wanted to know the answer, because she was someone noted for being so definite.

Peggy, however, did regard her childhood as the cradle of her adult incarnation, when she cut a distinctly Peter Pan figure in whom innocence was combined with a streak of selfish cruelty. Her extraordinary character had been shaped early on by the Karoo landscape – vast and scorching rather than small and cosy – and by her itinerant, materially secure yet emotionally insecure family. She felt an outsider because of her sterile upbringing and because of her part-Jewishness. She felt rootless, except in the books she had read, and longed to escape the desert of domesticity that beckoned in South Africa.

When she arrived in England, Peggy felt that she had not been equipped with an adequate sense of right or wrong with which to tackle the adventure that lay ahead. Like many displaced people, she felt the need to strive in order to survive. There was enough in common between the two countries, notably the language, for a woman of Peggy's temperament to be able to be astonishing and brilliant whilst also being protective and jealous. She had an aversion to the country that had nurtured her yet was not able to scour it from her soul. She dreamt of its raw nature and was implacably anti-apartheid yet loved the moments when Simon Callow, who went to school there briefly, affected his South African accent for her.

Peggy stayed in England for 60 years but was never fully at home here. While she did not concern herself in any great detail with the state of England, she seems never to have been optimistic on its account. Nevertheless, she did not wish to move anywhere else, and kept the refinements of favourite cultures, such as the French, in the realms of art.

She was unlikely to identify with the English, although that was the nationality she claimed for herself. She always embraced diversity and difference, and her own rootlessness prevented her from taking a narrow view of nationhood. She did, however, idealise the specially gifted because, to Peggy, art was the country to which she belonged and talent was its passport.

She would say England was 'awfully small', touching on both its size and its character. She was not fond of London; she felt it had no sky, trees or grass – 'to see a star is something of an event.' Although she enjoyed walking and would happily pick flowers with great interest with particular friends, she found the English attachment to the countryside despicable and indicative of a complacent narrow-mindedness. In contrast to the stunning South African landscape and climate, England was 'ludicrously wet, with absurd cows . . . There's nothing I like about the English countryside. I long for barbaric views.'

It was not surprising, therefore, that she took her holidays in hot, harsh places like north Africa, which produced a surreal contrast of its own, when, decked out in one of her expansive flowery hats and frothy dresses, she appeared in the African sun as the very image of an Englishness associated with Ascot or Henley.

In many ways she did become English, or at least an English eccentric, in spite of actually being passionate, spontaneous, fun-loving – the opposite of what is usually meant by the description 'English'. She often appeared like a *fin de siècle* grande dame, though not a dandy like Oscar Wilde or Aubrey Beardsley, whom, she once confided, she would like to have represented. She identified more with Madame Bovary; beneath Peggy's iridescent plumage lay a bold and simple heart, which gave voice to bold and simple thoughts. The English often give little quarter to those in whom the heart and the head work inseparably together and who, as a result, lead more courageous, if often rash and hurtful lives than most people will dare venture. But Peggy may well have been tolerated, feared or admired precisely because the English have a felicitous aptitude for accommodating, and even cherishing, outsized behaviour as that of acceptable eccentricity.

She saw her life before she became an agent as a series of reversals through which she grew and renewed. Although she built on two decades of working in the theatre, the early years of being an agent were a struggle, both personally and professionally, as she straddled the fault line in contemporary theatre; the old theatre was fatally wounded but had not yet died and the new was still fighting to be born. She was to be one of its midwives. She came from the old theatre, which she called showbiz, and liked its craft, but she preferred the emotional and dramatic landscape of the new.

Peggy was dedicated to a vanished ideal of the Artist who had special sensibilities and, consequently, special responsibilities but who was, therefore, due special indulgences. At the outset she did not read books about business practice but books about art. She gathered together quotations from many great artists she admired and fashioned from her reading a set of judgements by which she assessed the talent that came her way. There was a time when this romanticism of hers was a liberating force in the face of rampant commercialism. Times changed, however, in some large measure because of her; she became fed up with the theatre and lost touch with a new generation. Yet she blissfully continued to live the contradiction that writers should be holed up in garrets whilst at the same time being properly rewarded for their labours.

It took her nearly a decade to feel that she had properly arrived as an agent, and she then stayed at the zenith of her profession for a quarter of a century. Despite not wielding the power of a top showbiz agent or film producer, Peggy's influence was such that she became a legend. She wielded a different kind of power. Being an agent gave her the form for this power. Her extraordinary ability to encourage writers to write and her massive authority within the theatrical world flowed not from her birth, or from her origins or from her status, but from the force of her personality. Other agents had good judgement; Peggy had star quality.

Being with Peggy was like being in free fall; she saw herself as existing outside of any systems of thought or belief – no moral code, no theology, no ideology – living an unstructured life at the hands of fate. Yet she did have morals, beliefs, ideas, and purpose. Without these, she would not have blazed so gloriously. She lit up places. Being with her lifted the spirit. At her best, she was attractive, vibrant, unpretentious, alluring, charming, winning – and blisteringly rude, which she was allowed to be, like the all-licensed fool, because she did not fear other people's opinion of her and she spoke what everyone else might only think. She was delicate and coarse, sacred and profane. To borrow from Tennessee Williams, she lived life with 'the aristocracy of the passionate soul'.

Her kinetic character – switching without warning from gadfly to nanny, from shepherdess to prophetic sphinx, from temptress to termagant – led to a strenuous form of discourse with her. Her demonstrative, adamantine manner left little room for dialogue or discussion; any change of mind on her part had to be handled with tact and was not to be mentioned directly. Dauntless and dynamic, she was, paradoxically, a madcap too. This was refreshing for her clients because it meant she broke the rules, but it was also terrifying because she might make a mess of things as well. She set her own standards by which to be valued.

Peggy was not for the faint-hearted; everything for her was reduced to the mandatory. Some people found in this assertiveness a bullying, elitist attitude, a short-tempered neurotic overdrive fuelled by narcissism which led to damaging vindictiveness. While all these attributes could be seen in Peggy, the overall picture is out of focus. Complacency, smugness and cant were blasted away by her bracing and alarming directness. She gave the appearance of being the most subjective of people pronouncing the most objective of judgements. She was often deliberately blunt at the outset of a relationship, both as a barrier and as a test, and then would become more relaxed as time went on. Despite her theatrical manner, she had no 'front'; her incessant use of 'darling' and 'dear' carried its own punch. She had a categorical, often curmudgeonly, style spangled by overstatement and over-acting, but her verbal onslaughts and diversions, her circumlocutions and confusions, her Anglo-Saxon vocabulary and truculent veracity were all fired by a determination to serve the talent of a writer. She was forgiven for ritually humiliating her clients in the office because her criticisms were so often accurate and because she exploited her power on the writers' behalf.

Outspoken, loquacious and gossipy, she was infamous for her indiscretions, which were not the genuine gaffes of the John Gielgud variety. They were more meant. Her candour was both a driven power and an emotional openness, behind which lay a volatile temperament and private pain. She struggled with her own wild personality and her emotional vehemence could cut either way; she could be both crack-brained and percipient, or savage and devastating as well as empowering and electrifying. For every tale of Peggy as harridan or harpie, there is a fonder recollection of her being generous, humble and even politely shy, although no less direct for that.

Art was both the most important thing in life and the least, hence her detachment and her passion. To Peggy, art had to be imperative, visceral, compelling, or it was of no use. It either moved her or it did not. Her reactions were instant, powered by a high-octane energy motoring her mind like a hidden computer calculating the permutations in advance, checking the consequences in a split second and delivering a verdict with immense conviction and wit before anyone else had drawn breath. She seemed like a force of nature, infallible, immaculate and unstoppable, yet, as she was the first to insist, in a spirit of typical self-abnegation, she was only an agent; and to Peggy, being an agent was to follow a despicable profession.

The root of the word agent is the Latin meaning 'to do' or 'to act' and is the same as the derivation of the word actor, both appropriate for Peggy. The idea of an agent as a representative comes from the late 16th century and the first professional agents, it seems, were literary agents in the early 19th century. Agents for playwrights appeared later that century but became a fixed part of theatrical life only in the 20th century.

No agent is entirely conventional, but Peggy redefined the role and challenged the notion that agents should be calm, cautious, moderate and well-behaved. Other agents would treat discretion and confidentiality as the cornerstone of their profession, the defining ethical stance, enshrining the notion of the agent as the servant of the client. She turned that on its head by interpreting her 'service' role actively; she was servicing the talent rather than the individual. The individual might need persuading that certain things that were in the interest of the talent might conflict with the apparent individual interest, as when, for example, she turned down work without consulting clients if she thought it necessary. But she would carry out the client's wishes to the best of her considerable abilities if the client so instructed her.

She operated in a market place where plays were a commodity but sustained her writers by throwing the protective cloak of art around them. She guarded her uncommercial clients by keeping enough playwrights on the books who were earning handsomely. Her approach to the market place bore the stamp of instinctive cunning. One could never be quite sure how conscious her negotiating strategy was. She would often fire an early blast, catching the other party off-guard and signalling a warning that she meant business. Matters might even be settled by this method before they came to a head. She was tough, too, even when she was being silky. She was keen to woo the bright managers and knew they would be resistant to the 'hard sell'. Instead, she told them what was wrong with the play which she was sending them, or she might use stealth – 'another manager,' she would say, naming their chief rival, 'is thinking of doing it. Would you be interested in the next play?' She liked to create the impression that the other person was the one wanting to buy rather than Peggy being the one wanting to sell.

She traded on her 'bad mouth' and used it as a weapon in negotiations. In England, the land of compromise and equivocation, it carried shock value, authority, power and purpose. It cut people down to size and that was popular in an insecure and jealous business. Peggy, however, softened the blows of her irredeemable frankness with colourful displays of dottiness. She might seem muddle headed and unthinking but, in the end, she would usually come out on top. She was not a Don Quixote but hard-nosed and practical, even if she might be proved wrong.

Peggy was disgusted by the haggling that she had to undertake yet also found that negotiating a contract could be a sensual pleasure; unlike a relationship, which has to be worked at constantly, a contract involves a period of foreplay followed by the ecstasy and release of consummation.

She used her considerable contacts in the spirit of Diaghilev, a man she greatly admired, to put playwrights in touch with producers, publishers, directors, designers, composers, and actors. She had the knack of knowing everyone without letting anyone know quite how. She was acutely aware of the importance of choosing the right team and placed great store by loyalty and integrity. Her strongest network belonged to what was essentially an Edwardian theatre, in which managers played a key role. The publicly subsidised theatre, which many of her clients dominated, allowed her less individual access to decision-making, although her influence remained mighty.

Most of Peggy's clients wanted her to broker the deals rather than find them work, although some looked to her to get them out of work they did not want. Her outstanding quality as an agent from the writers' point of view, however, apart from the advantages her prestige brought in its train, was not to do with business at all but was the inordinate care she expended on her clients' work and her unflinching dedication to the writers' cause.

On the practical side, she had a noted ability to read a script – 'like a maestro reads a musical score,' said the critic Harold Hobson. She had a knack for visualising a play in her head as she read the text and a strong sense of what would work on stage and what would not. She read plays with both a literary and a dramatic sensibility, thereby avoiding the pitfalls of favouring either the esoteric (literary taste without the dramatic) or the shallow (dramatic taste alone). She was the writer's most loyal mentor and severest critic.

Peggy was probably best in hard times, when she was able to sustain a client because she did not flatter or lie. Failure kept a writer vulnerable while success could lead to over-confidence. Peggy, paradoxically, did crave success for her clients, but despised it, and them too, if they achieved it. Her own success brought her riches, but she had no sense of being wealthy, which was irritating to those of her clients whom she had consigned to a diet of gruel. By ordinary standards, she must have spent a great deal on her clothes, hats, shoes, jewellery, and perfume, as well as on her paintings and *objets d'art*, yet she used public transport until her death and mocked people with chauffeurs. Notwithstanding her occasional gamble with stocks and shares, Peggy did not court wealth but she was more keen on money than she let on. She clutched her handbag as she lay dying, and would come into consciousness, murmur 'Where's my money?' and then fade again.

She was a commercial agent yet did not run a commercial venture, in the sense that its motivation was not to make a profit nor to expand either her list of clients or her premises. She always said she just wanted to earn enough to keep going, though, actually, in the process Peggy accumulated quite a fortune. Talent would pay the bills, she always said. 'In the old days being rich meant terrible people attaching themselves to you. The only pleasure in being rich is to be able to buy what you need.' Her extreme care with money, especially in relation to the office, combined with her outlandish extravagance, buying gifts on the spur of the moment without regard to the cost, can be explained partly by the financial struggle she had endured during the first thirty years she was in England and partly by her philosophy of life – 'one does not buy oneself into ANYTHING', whether it be happiness, good health, friendship or reputation. Her spontaneous generosity was not concerned with price but the value of the present to the recipient.

There was a sense, however, in which success did entrap Peggy. Her accomplishment as an agent demonstrated that she was emancipated from the constraints of her background, her generation and her gender, yet that very success imprisoned her in that role. 'The real trouble is that every career goes on *too long*,' she wrote, 'and that after 30 everything repeats itself – it's just the names that are different. Somehow or other one has to renew oneself daily and not just wait for the seven-year change of cells. Our bloody métier destroys the inner life and one has no retreat from outside attack.'

Unable to retire or delegate properly, she failed in her later life to do what she had always done before; move on to the next phase in her life. She had a yearning to do something else and certainly could have afforded it. She once commented: 'I should much prefer not to work from 10am to 6pm, in order to enlarge upon the latent capacities I have myself . . . There is probably an area of the artist in every human being, and the important thing is to try and see that one gives sufficient of one's life to creativity, so that it is not smothered or withered.' Peggy gave sufficient of her life to creativity, but it was to the creativity of others, and she never succeeded in taking her life beyond that of being an agent.

In the theatrical profession, Peggy's contribution as an agent was regarded as unique and of enormous importance, although she was far from universally liked. In fact, one either loved her 'warts and all' or loathed her. Neutrality was not an option, nor was it expected. Having once been refused membership of the agents' organisation, the Professional Managers' Association, she vowed that she would never join it and stayed true to her word. She hated a portrait of her by the distinguished painter John Bratby, and it was hung out of sight behind the door in Bill Roderick's London bedroom. It was loaned to the Theatre Museum after her death but is now held by the Foundation. She had no interest either in self-promotion or in the more social aspects of the showbusiness world. By her own wish she did not have an entry in *Who's Who* or *Who's Who in the Theatre*. This lack of concern in public recognition was both due to her modesty about her worth and a justified fear of being flooded with unwanted scripts, which is precisely what happened after the BBC-TV Arena programme on her was broadcast. The only publicity she wanted was the agency's name printed in published texts as the place to which people should apply for permission to perform the plays.

She found being an agent an emotionally battering business, having to give her energy on demand to a variety of temperaments, whether of playwrights or producers. Considering how many huge and often aggressive or destructive egos she had to cope with, it is remarkable that she remained so forthright and so vigorous for so long. She developed her domineering style in order to be able to survive, and managed to marry being strident with giving each client what he or she needed. 'It's a heart-breaking job,' she said, 'and almost impossible to do well. One is bound to fail in the end, because one is, after all, living off other people's talents, and this in itself requires the utmost humility and an acceptance of what is sometimes pretty rough behaviour from the talented ones.'

It was *writers*, nevertheless, who moved Peggy's tastes forward and allowed her to blossom into the crucial figure she became. Peggy was responding and nurturing where she could. She had what to her was a sacred covenant with the new and the talented, and an especial interest in the young, because she was older and had the lessons of her life to pass on. 'I'm lucky to have become an agent after lots of emotional experiences,' she said. 'If I'd begun at 18 I might have fallen in love with the authors', which, in her special way, is what she did anyway.

She then fell out of love with them, a pattern that recurred throughout her time as an agent. There was always a plausible reason in each case – this one had become successful, that one was now more interested in films – but, beyond her hunger for the new, it revealed her wilful undermining of stability and the possibility of any lasting attachment.

For Peggy, a writer's current achievement – the play just delivered – was always more important than the writer's past record or the writer's future intentions. Yet she saw a current play both in its own terms and in terms of the long view, of how the writer might develop. She would not take on excellent or even famous writers if she believed that she could not help them develop their talent uniquely with her. She took bad writing personally. She hated the good-but-ordinary – 'not enough time in the world for that' – and preferred the courageous who would struggle to fulfil their potential. A favourite quote of hers came from the South American anthropologist Carlos Castaneda: 'a man is only defeated when he no longer tries.'

She said herself that her only personal interest in the agency business was the actual creating of the plays, and the only real happiness that she found was in working on a script with a writer, which she regarded reverentially. 'This is marvellous and worth all the rest, but it is a secret thing between authors and their agent.'

The nature of this 'secret thing' makes it hard to quantify fully Peggy's legacy, just as it is for any backstage figure. In such a social art form as theatre, which relies on many interlocking relationships and contributions for it to be realised, it is difficult to say exactly who thought of which idea and when; and, in the case of playwrights' work, not surprisingly the authors are reluctant to acknowledge too much input from other sources.

As far as Peggy is concerned, the results are there to be seen in the plays themselves, independent of the various personalities who helped create them, yet also entirely dependent on them too. There is the testimony of Peggy's clients and her many collaborators as well. Together, they pay tribute to Peggy, the unseen hand of so many achievements, as the living embodiment of another of her favourite quotes, from Disraeli: 'You can have anything in the world you want, provided you are prepared not to take the credit for it'

Peggy lives on through her clients' work in other ways too. She was the inspiration, sometimes tangentially, sometimes directly, behind characters in several plays. She appears as herself, although occasionally in disguise, in a crop of texts about Joe Orton, as the head of a ballet school in Martin Sherman's film *Alive and Kicking*, and as Nancy Fraser in *A Piece of My Mind* by Peter Nichols. She found her way into Leo Lehman's *End of the Story*, Charles Wood's TV series *Don't Forget to Write!*, David Mercer's play *The Monster of Karlovy Vary* and Colin Spencer's novel, *The Victims of Love*. Aspects of Peggy can be traced in Marion in Alan Ayckbourn's *Absurd Person Singular*, in Robert Bolt's Violet in *Gentle Jack*, in Elizabeth Bradley in *Today* by Robert Holman, in Valentina Nrovka in *The Bay at Nice* by David Hare and in Edward Bond's Mrs Rafi in *The Sea*.

Peggy said she was lucky to have become an agent when she did because it was the moment when the theatre rediscovered its vigour. The movement was led by playwrights, who, she believed, 'by sheer talent, hard work and originality turned the theatre on its head'. But the spirit of sweeping change that was abroad in the mid-1950s needed people like Peggy. After a period when Britain's leading literary personalities had abandoned the theatre, its postwar revival came from a multitude of non-literary figures. It seems as if she were there for the occasion. She caught the wave and rode it.

She was not a revolutionary but she was a radical who knew that new talent should be unacceptable to the establishment, which is always hungry for new blood. Peggy delivered her clients as they were; she did not make them acceptable, she did not tame them. What happened to them depended on who they were. Her role was to establish the writer; she then lost interest and moved on. Many of her clients flourished through the establishment and changed it as they progressed.

Typically, Peggy did not regard the upsurge in new writing after 1956 as a second Elizabethan age. Nevertheless, however history comes to judge the potency of that fecund period, Peggy's name will be indelibly linked to its core. Her enormous effect on modern drama will not be measured by the discovery of a Samuel Beckett. She knew that she would not find another writer like him because he was, to Peggy, a genius, the like of whom would only appear once in anyone's lifetime. But her impressive list of clients, from Arden, Ayckbourn, Bolt, Brenton, Bond and Churchill at one end of the alphabet, running through Hampton, Hare, Holman, Jellicoe, Mercer, Mortimer, and Nichols, to Orton, Plater, Poliakoff, Rudkin, Russell, White-head, Whitemore and Wood at the other, bears rousing witness to a life lived at the very heart of contemporary British playwriting.

The creation of a new kind of theatre, in which the stage became the natural home of vital ideas and a vastly extended raft of human life, regard-less of class or sexual and moral persuasion, was a major cultural achieve-ment of lasting significance. Peggy was as important an influence in the process as more public figures like the critic Kenneth Tynan. Through her encouragement of the work of non-clients as well as clients, be they actors, directors, designers, producers or writers, she was an inspirer in the same class as George Devine and Joan Littlewood. Peggy had something of the former's professional snobbery and much of the latter's destructive creative energy; all three changed the face of the theatre.

Peggy's character, her talent for stimulating writers, and her ability to read a script and assess its potential, helped provide the theatre with much needed new plays that altered audiences' perception of what theatre could and should offer and changed the theatre's own idea of what it might achieve.

It was clear when Peggy died that there was a profound sense of loss, which has grown with the passing years. As Caryl Churchill says: 'She broke the mould. We will not see her like again. The absence is terrifying.'

Appendix

Notes

This book comes from two main sources: Peggy Ramsay and her clients. Peggy Ramsay allowed me to look through all her papers – the files on her clients, the agency's ledgers, her scrap books, the script logs – and we talked at length about her life and work. These papers are now held by the British Library. I also read the few articles about her that exist (in particular Mel Gussow's extended profile in the *New Yorker* of 23 May 1988) and was able to watch all the film that was shot for the BBC-TV *Arena* programme on her that was broadcast in March 1990. The interview quoted from *Encore* in Chapters 5 and 6 appears in no. 43 May-June 1963.

I also talked to and/or corresponded with more than 200 of Peggy's associates, including some 60 clients; they are listed under the chapters for which the information they gave me was primarily used.

Tom Erhardt and the staff of Margaret Ramsay Ltd. provided information on a range of topics that are covered in several chapters, as did others, such as Robert Bolt, Simon Callow, Michael Codron, David Hare, John Holmstrom, Laurence Harbottle and Oscar Lewenstein. For ease, they are only listed once.

The information provided by these sources was supplemented by further reading, of newspaper articles and reviews, of magazines, and of relevant books. I have not listed the many plays referred to in the book because their identity and authorship is clear from the text.

The Theatre Museum, Covent Garden, London, was very helpful; other reference libraries I used were Brighton, Cambridge, Guildhall, Hounslow (Q Theatre archive), University of Bristol Theatre Collection, and Westminster.

The sources are divided into the people who provided information for the chapter concerned and the main books I consulted.

Chapter 1: Under African Skies

Information about Peggy's family and life in South Africa came from Mary Burnett, Sonia Joseph, Eric Levyno, Michael Morley, Richard A. Venniker, Sue Venniker, and Wendy Venniker as well as from various academic, military and medical establishments.

Chapter 2: If It's Tuesday, It Must Be Macbeth

William Abney, Michael Allinson, Frederick Bartman (and Ch. 5), Peter Cotes, Allan Davis, Charles Fenn, Norman Fenner, Owen Holder, Hugh Hunt, Dermot Lee-Baker, Tanya Moiseiwitch, Joseph O'Conor, Eduardo Paolozzi, Michelene Paton, Richard Pearson, Lars Schmidt, Margaret Shepherd, Joan

Sutro, John Symonds, Bill Turner, Jack Watling, Philip Weathers, Barbara Wright (and Ch. 3), Peter Wyngarde, Peter Zadek.
On Q by Kenneth Barrow (1992)

Chapter 3: Opening Gambit
Frith Banbury, John Barton, Kitty Black, Robert Bolt, Barbara Bray, John Calder, Peter Dunlop (and Ch. 9), Robert Eddison, Nancy Frost, Pam Gems, Peter Hall (and Ch. 8), Jocelyn Herbert, John Holmstrom, Betty Hopkins (Judkins), Ray Jenkins, Eric Kahane, Tom Kilroy (and Ch. 6), Leo Lehman, Laurent Lousson, Sarah Miles, Trevor Nunn, Tim O'Brien, Robert Peake, Jo Riddett (and Ch. 6), Toby Rowland, Paul Scofield, Barrie Stavis, Elizabeth Sweeting (and Ch. 7), Edward Thompson, Adrian Turner, Harvey Unna (and Ch. 6), Donald Watson, Peter Wood.

Upper Circle by Kitty Black (1984)
David Lean by Kevin Brownlow (1996)
The Lost Summer: The Heyday of the West End Theatre by Charles Duff (1995)
Making an Exhibition of Myself by Peter Hall (1993)
Robert Bolt by Ronald Hayman (1969)
Serves Me Right (1994) and *Bolt from the Blue* (1996) by Sarah Miles
The Making of David Lean's 'Lawrence of Arabia' by Adrian Turner (1994)

Chapter 4: Iron In The Soul
Alan Ayckbourn (and Ch. 6), Michael Blakemore, Michael Codron, Carl Davis, Lynn Horsford, Ann Jellicoe, David Jones (and Ch. 8), Henry Livings, Val May, Dafna Mercer-Hadari, Michael Meyer (and Ch. 6), John Mortimer, Iris Murdoch, Peter Nichols (and Ch. 6), John Osborne, Alan Plater (and Ch. 6), Jack Rosenthal (and Chs. 6 and 9), David Rudkin (and Ch. 6), James Saunders (and Ch. 6), Muriel Spark, Stephen Spender, Don Taylor, Peter Terson (and Ch. 6), Nancy Whiting, Clifford Williams, Charles Wood (and Ch. 6), Caspar Wrede.

Alan Ayckbourn by Michael Billington (1990)
J.B. Priestley by Vincent Brome (1988)
Feeling You're Behind by Peter Nichols (1984)
Almost a Gentleman by John Osborne (1991)
Days of Vision: Working with David Mercer by Don Taylor (1990)
The Arts Theatre, London 1927-1981 by Wendy and J.C. Trewin (1986)
Conversations with Ayckbourn by Ian Watson (1981)

Chapter 5: The Ruffian On The Stair
Leonie Barnett, Alan Bennett, Wilfred Harrison, Nick Hern (and Ch. 6), James Kirkup, John Lahr, Frank Marcus, Julian Mitchell, Braham Murray, Pieter Rogers (and Ch. 8), Milton Shulman, Geoffrey Strachan, John Tydeman.
There are very few letters from Peggy to Joe Orton in her Orton file.

Notes

Prick Up Your Ears: The Screenplay by Alan Bennett (1987)
Prick Up Your Ears: The Biography of Joe Orton by John Lahr (1978)
The Orton Diaries edited by John Lahr (1986)
Because We're Queers by Simon Shepherd (1989)

Chapter 6: Queen Bee

Peter Barnes, Howard Brenton (and Ch. 8), John Bowen, Simon Callow, Susanna Capon, Tom Clarke, Richard Cottrell, David Cook, David Cregan, Larry Dalzell, Tom Erhardt, Stanley Eveling, Bill Freedman, Derek Granger, Stuart Griffiths, Robert Holman (and Ch. 9), Donald Howarth, Klaus Juncker, David Lan, Sean Mathias, Sarah Miller, Richard Parsons, Shirley Rubinstein, Antony Sher, Ned Sherrin, David Sherwin, Colin Spencer, Victor Spinetti, Micheline Steinberg, Tom Stoppard, Alan Tagg, Stephanie Tanner, Diana Walkden, Elizabeth Wardle, Irving Wardle, Hugh Whitemore.

Jean Rhys by Carole Angier (1990)
How Plays Are Made by Stuart Griffiths (1982)

Chapter 7: At Court

Lindsay Anderson, Edward Bond, Stuart Burge, Caryl Churchill (and Chs. 6 and 9), William Gaskill, Peter Gill (and Ch. 5), Christopher Hampton (and Ch. 6), Oscar Lewenstein, Anthony Page, Patrick Proctor, Max Stafford-Clark, Nicholas Wright.

Playwrights' Theatre by Terry Browne (1975)
At the Royal Court: 25 Years of the English Stage Company edited by Richard Findlater (1981)
A Sense of Direction: Life at the Royal Court by William Gaskill (1988)
Bond: A Study of his Plays by Malcolm Hay and Philip Roberts (1980)
Kicking Against the Pricks: The Memoirs of Oscar Lewenstein (1994)
The Royal Court Theatre 1965-1972 by Philip Roberts (1968)

Chapter 8: For The Love Of Talent

John Antrobus, John Arden, Michael Attenborough, David Aukin, David Brierley, Margaretta D'Arcy, Howard Davies, Alan Dossor, Richard Eyre, Peter Flannery, Steve Gooch, David Hare, Stephen Lowe, Margaret Matheson (and Ch. 6), Mustapha Matura, John McGrath (and Ch. 4), Stephen Poliakoff, Michael Rudman, Willy Russell, Martin Sherman (and Chs. 6 and 9), Nigel Williams.

Not in Front of the Audience: Homosexuality on Stage by Nicholas de Jongh (1992)
The Lord Chamberlain's Blue Pencil by John Johnston (1990)

Chapter 9: Memento Mori

Nick Darke, Anne Devlin (and Ch. 1), Kevin Elyot, Laurence Harbottle, Dusty Hughes, Stephen Jeffreys, Hanif Kureishi, Doug Lucie, Rona Munro, Timberlake Wertenbaker.

List of Clients

The following names appear in Peggy Ramsay's books. Some clients she represented very briefly – for one or two plays only – and some may have written plays that she made available for production but which were never sold. (Some were Peters and Ramsay clients)

Dannie Abse
Graham Ackroyd
Arthur Adamov
Rhys Adrian
Stanley Alderson
Patrick Alexander
Lindsay Anderson
Jim Andrew
Guy Andrews
John Antrobus
Alexei Arbuzov
John Arden
Michel Arnand
Geraldine Aron
Fernando Arrabal
Tim Aspinall
Louis Auchincloss
Sam Avery (Sam Lock)
Alan Ayckbourn
Marcel Aymé
Isaac Babel
Enid Bagnold
Allan J. Baker
Nigel Balchin
Nigel Baldwin
James Baldwin
Marjorie Barkentin
Peter Barnes
Roderick Barry
Stan Barstow
Basil Bartlett
John Barton
Archibald Batty
Norman Beaton
Hjalman Bergman
Barry Bermange
Nick Bicât
Tony Bicât
James Bierman
Barbara Bingley
Franklyn Black (Frederick
    Bartman)

Vera Blackwell
Ron Blair
Nicholas Blake
Anthony Bloomfield
Myrna Blumberg
Robert Bolt
Guy Bolton
Edward Bond
Elizabeth Bond-Pable
John Bowen
James Brabazon
    (James Seth Smith)
Ray Bradbury
Alfred Bradley
Andrew Bradley
Caryl Brahms
Barbara Bray
Mark Brennan
Howard Brenton
Alan Brien
Jeremy Brooks
Brigid Brophy
Ian Brown
Felicity Browne
David Bulwer-Lutyens
Hugh Burden
Stuart Burge
Alan Burgess
Michael Burrell
Alexander Buzo
John Byrne
Michael Cahill
Harold Callen
Simon Callow
Cyril Campion
Bob Carlton
David Carr
Patrick Carter
Jim Cartwright
Robert Carver
Rosemary Casey
Michael Cashman

Raymond Castans
David Caute
Kenneth Cavander
Michele Celeste
Robin Chapman
Dorothy and Campbell
    Christie
Caryl Churchill
Sandra Clark
Tom Clarke
Irene Coates
Denise Coffey
Tom Coffey
Guy Compton
David Cook
Harry Cookson
Ray Cooney
Angus Cooper
Paul Copley
Eric Corner
Robert Cotton
Richard Cottrell
Richard Crane
David Cregan
Margaretta D'Arcy
Jean Dalrymple
Nick Darke
Jonathan David
Janina David
Madeleine Davidson
Frederick Davies
Windsor Davies
Carl Davis
Christopher Davis
Barry Davis
Denis de Marney
René de Obaldia
Basil Dean
Adam Delaney
Anne Devlin
Arnold Diamond
William Dinner

347

Doherty
Tancred Dorst
Richard Drain
Duffel
Frank Dunlop
Dick Edwards
Eigstill
Kay Eldredge
John Elliott
Chris Ellis
Ben Elton
Kevin Elyot
Shusako Endo
Julian Evans
Colin Haydn Evans
Stanley Eveling
William Fairchild
Eleanor Farjeon
Eleanor Fazan
James Ferman
Jean Jacques Feydeau
Colin Finbow
Tazeena Firth
Dudley Fitts
John Harvey Flint
Foncine
Mik Fondal
Horton Foote
John Fraser
Rosemary Friedman
Rex Frost
Patrick Galvin
David Garfield
Balwant Gargi
Pam Gems
Jonathan Gems
Jane Gerson
Sheridan Gibney
William Gibson
Peter Gill
Stuart Gilman
Alex Glasgow
Michael Glenny
Frederick Gold
Steve Gooch
Goodwin
Ron Grainer
Tom Grainger
David Grant
Günther Grass
Terence Greer
Jonathan Griffin
Stuart Griffiths
Guelma
David Guerdon
Peter Guerney
Christopher Guinee
Wilson John Haire

Jonathan Hales
Doris Hall
William Hall
Christopher Hampton
Terry Hands
Geoffrey Hann
Mike Harding
Michael Hardwick
Manus Hardy
David Hare
Robert Harris
Frank Hauser
Václav Havel
Jacquetta Hawkes
Max Hayward
Robert Henney
Adrian Henri
Bertram Henson
Guy Hibbert
S. Hignett
Marjorie St. Hill
Ronald Hingley
Mary Hocking
Robert Holman
John Holmstrom
    (a.k.a. Roger Gellert)
Ewan Hooper
Tom Hopkinson
Israel Horovitz
Ödön von Horváth
Donald Howarth
Dusty Hughes
Patrick Hughes
David Humphries
Aldous Huxley Estate
Elspeth Huxley
Eugène Ionesco
Leigh Jackson
Lenka Janiurek
Tim Jeal
Stephen Jeffreys
Ann Jellicoe
Peter Jenkins
Ray Jenkins
Arthur Johanssen
Keith Johnstone
Evan Jones
Nicholas de Jongh
Monica Jung
Kenneth Jupp
Eric Kahane
Kahn
Fay and Michael Kanin
Helena Kaut-Howson
James Keller
Paul Kember
Adrienne Kennedy
Jack Kenny

Leo Kerz
Thomas Kilroy
Francis King
Robert King
Leonard Kingston
Heiner Kipphardt
Jack Kirkland
Kitterminster
Adam Kossoff
Larry Kramer
Norman Krasna
Peter Krewies
Gavin Lambert
Dallas Lambert
David Lan
Richard Langridge
Jacques Languirand
Morvan Lebesque
Lee
Leo Lehman
John Lennon
Francis Letton
Benn Levy
Saunders Lewis
Eric Linklater
Edward Lipscombe
Henry Livings
Terence Lodge
Rosie Logan
Christopher Logue
Stephen Lowe
Teresa Lubkiewicz
Margaret Luce
Francis Lynch
David Lytton
Tom MacIntyre
Elizabeth MacLennan
Neil Macmillan
Jimmy Macready
Dmitri Makaroff
Stephen Mallatratt
Kevin Mandry
Ralph Mannheim
William Marchant
Frank Marcus
Derek Marlowe
William Martin
Ernest Marvin
Francis Mathy
Sean Matthias
Mustapha Matura
Mayne
David McGibbon
Neville McGrah
John McGrath
Michael McGrath
Colin McInnes
Alan McMurtie

List of Clients

Michael McNight
Aharon Megged
David Mercer
Michael Meyer
Peter Meyer
Lexie Miccalef
Brian Miller
Chris Miller
Roy Minton
Harry Moore
Nicholas Moore
Aldyth Morris
Edmund Morris
James Morris
John Mortimer
William Morum
David Mowat
Rona Munro
Hope Muntz
Iris Murdoch
Bill Naughton
David Neilson
Georges Neveux
Richard Newnham
Peter Nichols
Ariadne Nicolaeff
John Norman
Tim O'Brien
Joseph O'Conor
Liam O'Flaherty
Richard O'Keeffe
Reggie Oliver
Joe Orton
Tom Osborn
Osgood
Nesta Pain
Clifton Parker
Dorothy Parker
Richard Parsons
John Patrick
A. L. Pattison
Reece Pemberton
Edward and Lilian Percy
Aveline Perkins
James Pettifer
Neville Phillips
Michael Picardie
Robert Pinget
Neville and Stephen Plaice
M. Plant
Alan Plater
James Plunkett
Stephen Poliakoff
Perry Pontac
Alan Pope
Ursula Powys-Lybbe
Tim Preece
Jay Allen Presson

J.B. Priestley
Derek Prouse
Manuel Puig
Jack Pulman
Pol Quentin
Douglas Rae
William Rayner
Peter Redgrove
Henry Reed
Yasmina Reza
Jean Rhys
I.A. Richards
Lexford Richards
Jack Richardson
Andrew Rissik
D. Roberts
Charles Robinson
Matthew Rook
Michael Rosen
Jack Rosenthal
Dina Ross
David Rudkin
Willy Russell
Armand Salacrou
James Saunders
Alan Schneider
Budd Schulberg
Evgeny Schwartz
George Scott-Moncrieff
David Selbourne
Ronald Settle
Margery Sharp
Wallace Shawn
Paul Sheridan
Martin Sherman
Ned Sherrin
David Sherwin
Robert Sherwood
H. Shukman
Barry Simner
George Sklar
Leonard Smith
Norman Smithson
Norman Smythe
William Snyder
Joshua Sobol
Sofronov
Diana Souhami
Muriel Spark
Colin Spencer
Stephen Spender
W.G. Stanton
Barrie Stavis
Michael Stewart
Willard Stoker
Thomas Strangmorn
David Stringer
Caroline Swift

Alan Tagg
Tony Tanner
C.P. Taylor
Christopher Taylor
Don Taylor
Simon Watson Taylor
Peter Terson
Paul Thain
George Theotokos
Richard Thornley
Robert Thornton
Ric Throssell
Tobias
Paul Todd
John Toré
Geoffrey Trease
Rose Tremaine
Raleigh Trevelyan
Henriette Valot
John van Druten
Selma vaz Dias
Adrian Vaux
Philip Vellacot
Boris Vian
Alexander Volodin
Lew Grant Wallace
Cedric Wallis
Basil Warner
David Watson
Donald Watson
Leonard Webb
Fay Weldon
Alwyne Whatsley
Christopher Whelen
E.A. Whitehead
Hugh Whitemore
Tony White
John Whiting
Fred Willetts
Malcolm Williams
Nigel Williams
Tennessee Williams
    Estate
Malcolm Williamson
Noël Willman
C. Wilson
P.G. Wodehouse
Charles Wood
David Wood
Nick Wood
Anthony Woodhall
Dennis Woolf
T.C. Worsley
M. Worth
Barbara Wright
Olwen Wymark
B.A. Young
The Hon. Wayland Young

Index

of proper names and titles of plays, films, and works of literature

Index

Index